THEISTIC FAITH
FOR
OUR TIME:

An Introduction to the Process Philosophies of Royce and Whitehead

George Douglas Straton

University Press of America™

Library of Congress Catalog Card Number: 78-65429

To Three Friends
and
My Family
Whose Abiding Confidence and Love
Have Been Inspiration Indeed:

Robert D. Clark

Wesley G. Nicholson

Charles F. Williams

———

Ruth Riley Straton
and
Kathy, David, Peter, and Jack

Foreword

Josiah Royce and Alfred North Whitehead between them have probably succeeded in clarifying in more penetrating fashion than many who have attempted the task what the idea of God and the problem of belief in God can positively mean as options for philosophic faith in our time. Their systems of thought perform a task of examining and sustaining a theistic perspective on the nature of existence, and the significance of the human being within existence, in unique and powerful modes that it is hoped this study may help to show. In spite of some difference in epistemological stance, and, of course, a good deal of difference in philosophic idiom and style, both men thought in very similar ways on these high themes. We endeavor to point out these relationships in some detail.

My own critical evaluation of the thought of Royce and Whitehead, particularly as it bears on theistic philosophy, arises at intervals in the course of this interpretive essay. In broadest terms, therefore, this essay endeavors to study the idea of theism (and its problems) as philosophy--through the medium of the process interpretation of existence of these two Harvard professors. They lived and wrote at an earlier stage of the idea of God debate in our time. The way they phrased issues, and their conclusions regarding the same have nonetheless remained seminal, and challenging, to the debate as it has continued into the latter portion of this century. Part of my mission is to justify the classification of Royce, with Whitehead, as 'process philosopher.' The former is popularly remembered as 'absolute idealist,' whose thought it might be supposed is in some extremes opposite to process philosophy. Upon looking at them side by side, however, it becomes clear that this is not the case. We bring the two voices together (for the first time we believe) in what amounts to a 'dialogue' on the larger themes: Nature and Being, Human Selfhood, God and Theism, Ethics and Society, Knowledge and the Philosophic Task. This effort therefore constitutes an introduction to the philosophies of these process theologians, and is designed to be an aid to teachers and students in philosophy, religious studies, and related fields.

In pursuing this work, the somewhat earlier vision of Royce is naturally set forth first at each level of the above systematic arrangement. His more felicitous style makes it easier for the interpreter to present initially his ideas, followed by

i

those of Whitehead. This we believe is an aid, often times, to the illumination of the latter's more subtle phraseology and insight.

* * * * * * *

I wish to express my profound appreciation to Professor John B. Cobb, Jr., of the School of Theology at Claremont, for his kindness in reviewing this manuscript in its initial version, and making the suggestion, relative to a revision of form, that has led to publication. His encouragement also as to content has been a major factor in our stimulation to the task.

I wish also to express my gratitude to Mrs. Lloyd L. Armes, of the city of Eugene, for her preparation of the typescript copy requisite to the photo reproduction process. Without her expert attention and many hours devoted to the labor this publication would not have been possible.

* * * * * * *

Note to the Reader: The mechanics of reference in this study are the following: The various editions of primary works by Royce and Whitehead, and edited anthologies of their works, used in this study are fully cited in the Bibliography, pp. 313f. The larger number of our in-text quotations and references give the pages of these editions at the end of the quotation or reference, in parentheses. Where necessary for clarity the page number is preceded by the usual abbreviation of the work, such as PR for Process and Reality, or WI2 for The World and the Individual, Vol. II. Some quotations, including those taken from anthologies, where titles have not appeared in the main text for stylistic reason, have been footnoted in the usual manner at the bottom of the page. Quotations of other authors, or references thereto, and certain extended expository discussion, have likewise been footnoted in the customary manner.

G. Douglas Straton

University of Oregon, 1978.

ii

Acknowledgements

Grateful appreciation is hereby expressed to the following publishers for their kind permission to use certain quotations from the works, cited below, of authors quoted in this study in excess of 250 words. Pages quoted from these works are indicated on our pages where the several quotations appear, identified by reference to the author and either the full title or the customary abbreviation symbol for the title. Publishers and dates are acknowledged again on our pages for appropriate clarity of reference in context.

Greenwood Press, Inc., Westport, reprint publishers of Josiah Royce: The Conception of Immortality, 1971. Symbol: CI. (Originally published 1900 by Houghton, Mifflin, and Co., Boston)

Harvard University Press, Cambridge, Mass., for our use of James Harry Cotton: Royce on the Human Self, 1954.

Princeton University Press, Princeton, for our use of the Beacon Press reprint of Alfred North Whitehead: The Function of Reason, 1959. Symbol: FR. (Copyright 1929 by Princeton University Press)

Charles Scribner's Sons, New York, for use of Josiah Royce: The Sources of Religious Insight, 1912. Symbol: SRI.

Cambridge University Press, New York, for quotations from F.R. Tennant: Philosophical Theology, Vol. II, 1937.

Harper and Row, New York, for use of Josiah Royce: The Religious Aspect of Philosophy, 1958. Symbol: RAP. (Originally published 1885 by Houghton, Mifflin & Co.) And for use of Alfred North Whitehead: Process and Reality, 1960. Symbol: PR. (Copyright 1929 by The Macmillan Co., and Copyright c 1957 by Evelyn Whitehead)

Use of a letter from John Clendenning (ed.): The Letters of Josiah Royce, ⓒ1970 by the University of Chicago Press, Chicago.

The Macmillan Publishing Co., Inc., New York, for use of material from Josiah Royce: The World and the Individual, Vols. I & II, (1899, 1901), 1912, 1913; The Philosophy of Loyalty, 1908; and from J.C. Smuts: Holism and Evolution, 1926. And material from Alfred North Whitehead as abridged with permission of Macmillan: Science and the Modern World, The New American Library, 1948,

Table of Contents

Part I

THE CONCEPTION OF NATURE AND THEORY OF BEING:
The Philosophic Perspectives of Royce and Whitehead

Chapter One:
        ROYCE AND WHITEHEAD ON NATURE, p. 1

Chapter Two:
        THEORY OF BEING, p. 17

Part II

THE IDEA OF MAN OR HUMAN SELFHOOD

Chapter Three:
        ROYCE ON SELFHOOD, p. 59

Chapter Four:
        WHITEHEAD ON SELFHOOD, p. 69

Part III

THE CONCEPTION OF GOD AND THE ISSUES OF THEISM

Chapter Five:
        ROYCE ON THE CONCEPTION AND ARGUMENT AND
        THE PROBLEM OF FREEDOM, p. 79

Chapter Six:
        WHITEHEAD ON THE CONCEPTION AND ARGUMENT
        AND THE PROBLEM OF FREEDOM, p. 125

Chapter Seven:
        THE PROBLEM OF EVIL, p. 161

Chapter Eight:
        THE IDEA OF IMMORTALITY, p. 219

Chapter Nine:
        THE CONCEPTION OF RELIGION, p. 245

Part IV

ETHICS AND SOCIETY

Chapter Ten:
    THE ETHICAL AND SOCIAL THOUGHT OF ROYCE, p. 255

Chapter Eleven:
    THE ETHICAL AND SOCIAL THOUGHT OF WHITEHEAD, p. 285

Part V

ADDENDUM: KNOWLEDGE AND THE PHILOSOPHIC TASK

Chapter Twelve:
    ROYCE ON KNOWLEDGE, p. 299

Chapter Thirteen:
    WHITEHEAD ON KNOWLEDGE, p. 307

Bibliography: p. 313

Part I

THE CONCEPTION OF NATURE AND THEORY OF BEING:

The Philosophic Perspectives of Royce and Whitehead

Chapter One

ROYCE AND WHITEHEAD ON NATURE

Introductory

It might be supposed that Royce, the idealist, with his
rationalist, often intuitive, deductive approach to knowledge,
would have little in common with Whitehead, emergentistic naturalist, who explored primarily the empirical route to knowledge.
Indeed, more or less typical of his life-long view, Royce acknowledged, at an early stage, "We go to seek the Eternal, not in
experience, but in the thought that thinks experience."[1] Whereas
in his massive style and empirical spirit Whitehead asserted, "we
seek the evidence for that conception of the universe which is the
justification for the ideals characterizing the civilized phases
of human society....we are not arguing from well-defined premises.
Philosophy is the search for premises."[2]

Yet both men, mounting an ascent upon the cosmic order from
perhaps somewhat different initial epistemological bases ultimately converge in thought at nearly every important point in
their account of things. This is manifestly true in their organistic description of phenomenal nature, as we shall presently see.
It is true, in more subtle terms, of their depiction of the ultimate metaphysical order of the world, which we may call their
general theory of being, emerging for both men from Plato's doctrine of ideas. It is remarkably evident in their deliniation of
man or human selfhood in dynamic categories as telic process or
telic energy, our concern of Part II. Their ultimate conceptions
of God, enlarged in Part III, as immanental, Cosmic Purposiveness
or Cosmic Personal Reality, for Whom the being of nature is an
intimate and inevitable expression, is a further far-reaching
indication of their parallel perspectives.

As to method itself, the slightest examination of their
writings, of course, discloses that each man is in fact profoundly
an empiricist as well as a speculative rationalist. Part IV of
this study briefly reviews their conception of knowledge and the
philosophic task.

---

1. The Religious Aspect of Philosophy (1885), Harper
   Torchbooks, 1958, p. 289.
2. Modes of Thought (1938), G.P. Putnam's Sons, Capricorn
   Books, 1958, p. 143, emphasis ours.

Furthermore, in this introductory sketch of their resemblances, we may point to several classic theological issues, each worked on in similar ways. Both Royce and Whitehead speak of the "temporality" as well as the "eternity" of the cosmic order at the level of the Divine nature. They struggle with the problem of evil, as against the glow of their theistic faith. Neither does so perfectly successfully but each with great suggestiveness, nonetheless. On one side of his thought, Whitehead appears to embrace the concept of the 'finite God,' as a candid, realistic solution to this perennial problem of theistic philosophy; while on another he seems to announce a doctrine of the 'self-limited' God as the best kind of solution to the problem of evil. Royce also leaves us with ambiguity in this area as he states the issue in terms of "temporality" with the "eternity" of God as somehow the conceptualization which permits light to show upon this problem. As for that other focal difficulty for the logic of theism, the problem of freedom, both men contribute with similar emphases, and with more success, to its solution. How to conceive the relation of the 'wills,' assuming God and man as Personal realities, and preserve the idea of freedom in each, that is, without the absorption of man into God on the one hand, or the binding of God on the other, in necessary structures of determination for all things, as many classic theologies believed true of the Divine? Although Whitehead is less specific than Royce in trying to answer these ultimate questions of freedom, the trend and weight of his thinking on this issue closely resembles Royce's. Royce presents an astonishingly simple, and the only manner of solution possible, we believe, to the problem of freedom. Both philosophers have a vision of immortality. Royce perhaps offers a more positive view of immortality than does Whitehead. However, though Whitehead at first appears more doubtful about immortality and for that reason, as some would say, more appealing to the hard-headed, when read closely he may be interpreted as implying a belief in personal immortality as his own ultimate view in faith.

Granting, then, such similarities and differences between their thought in certain details, perhaps the major distinction between these two theists, and also the larger contribution of each to contemporary theological philosophy, I venture to suggest in the following way. In direct contrast to the positivistic temper of today's world, Royce challenges the twentieth century with a revival of the profounder reasons for believing in God in the first place, by his essentially depth a priori approach to the argument for God. Whereas Whitehead, absorbing the problem of the argument for God up into the empirical description of cosmic order itself as a proclamation of the nature of God, transcends the problem of theistic argument as such, or at least is less concerned with that problem than was Royce. When all is said and done, if Royce bequeaths the more compelling insights as to why

we can from a rational perspective believe in God, Whitehead may
tell us best how to view God, if we do believe in Him, in a
scientific age. If, springing from profoundest interior impulses
of the rational spirit, Royce uncovers a unique ontological argument for God, stemming from Augustine's in ancient times, Whitehead
presents for many modern minds the most adequate conception of
God, in largest empirical and quasi-scientific categories.

Others have noted "common elements" in the perspectives of
Royce and Whitehead;[3] and have pointed to the fact that Royce
"evaluated the validity of his metaphysics in relation to the
claims of science and logic, as much as did Leibniz and Whitehead."[4] A possible tertiary influence of Royce on Whitehead's
belief in cosmic order has been observed, through the noted work
of Harvard professor L.J. Henderson, The Fitness of the Environment 1912, said to be partly stimulated under the influence of
Royce.[5] Hartshorne and Reese have commented that "God, indeed,
in this [Whitehead's] philosophy as in that of Royce, is the home
of all truth...."[6] Hartshorne has also said that Whitehead "was
as truly an idealist as Royce...", but on a firmer kind of ground
(with Charles Peirce), to the effect that "the independence of
things known from particular knowers" was not denied.[7] No one as

---

3. James Harry Cotton: Royce on the Human Self, Harvard
    University Press, 1954, p. viii. Cotton points to "a
    fascinating parallel," in the outlook of Royce regarding
    evolution and the growth of the community, "with White-
    head's philosophy of process in which God is the principle
    of concretion," p. 264. See also brief notations, pp.
    318 and 322 of Cotton's work.
4. John J. McDermott: The Basic Writings of Josiah Royce,
    Vol. 2, University of Chicago Press, 1969, p. 654.
    C.I. Lewis has compared Royce with Whitehead and Russell
    on problems of logic and methodology, Ib. pp. 652-3.
5. Paul Arthur Schilpp (ed.): The Philosophy of Alfred
    North Whitehead, Tudor Publishing Co., 1951, p. 91 n. 168.
6. Charles Hartshorne and William L. Reese: Philosophers
    Speak of God, University of Chicago Press, 1953, p. 274.
7. Charles Hartshorne: "Royce and the Collapse of Iealism,"
    Revue Internationale De Philosophie, 1967, 79-80, p. 50,
    a brief but trenchant 'Whiteheadian' type of critique of
    Royce. At this particular point, I do not think that
    Hartshorne has sufficiently given Royce due credit for
    his practical or qualified 'realism,' so very similar to
    Whitehead's, as we endeavor to show in this study. See
    also Hartshorne: "Royce's Mistake--and Achievement,"
    The Journal of Philosophy, LIII, No. 3, Feb. 2, 1956,
    p. 123f.

far as we know has presented a full comparative essay, as here
attempted. It is puzzling that Whitehead, following at Harvard
upon the renown of Royce within less than a decade of the latter's
death in 1916, and appointed at age sixty-three (1924), to the
same department of philosophy, did not come to realize something
of their affinities in thought, at least in some of the ways here
discussed. Whitehead makes a scant reference to Royce in the
Epilogue of Modes of Thought; but he does not once mention him in
his great work, Process and Reality, though he relates himself to
many other figures, for example among moderns admitting a debt to
Bergson, William James, and John Dewey (p. vii). It is not sur-
prising, however, coming from England originally, that he does
indeed refer to the closeness of F.H. Bradley, the English Hegelian, to himself in certain respects, particularly to Bradley's
philosophy of "feeling" as central paradigm of the way things are
fundamentally related.[8] Speaking in the "Preface" and referring
to the fifth part of Process and Reality, Whitehead makes the
following disclosure, relative to his sympathies toward the
idealist tradition of modern times:

> In this part, the approximation to Bradley is evident.
> Indeed, if this cosmology be deemed successful, it becomes
> natural at this point to ask whether the type of thought
> involved be not a transformation of some main doctrines of
> Absolute Idealism onto a realistic basis. (p. viii)

He observes again on a later page of that work his ties to the
"Hegelian School."[9] In a paper, "Process and Reality" (1932), he
again mentions his relation to English Hegelians like McTaggart
and Bradley, claiming "a very close affiliation" with the latter;
but cites as a main point of difference with the Hegelians "their
feeling of the illusiveness and relative unreality of the temporal
world."[10] It is informative to hear in this same context his
admission that he had "never read a page of Hegel," and to note
his apology for the scant reference to the latter in PR. Perhaps
likewise he had not read Royce! Be that as it may, we undertake
here to draw out the philosophic relationships of Royce and
Whitehead, in the larger aspects of their positions, suggesting
that Whitehead was in major respects nearer to the idealism of
Royce, actually, than to that of Bradley. Not the least of these

---

8.   Adventures of Ideas (1933), The New American Library,
     Mentor Books, 1955, p. 232.
9.   PR, p. 254.
10. "Symposium in Honor of the Seventieth Birthday of Alfred
     North Whitehead" (1932), Science and Philosophy, Philo-
     sophical Library, 1948, p. 124.

agreements was Royce's and Whitehead's acceptance of the Personality of God idea, in contrast to Bradley's denial that the Absolute can be described ultimately as personal being. If we can say that Whitehead was patently an idealist in prominent dimensions of his thought, we can, on the other score, assert that Royce was profoundly a process theologian in many elements of his.[11]

A final word to this brief introductory: Royce's and Whitehead's ethical and social visions follow from their conceptions of Being (intimately involving the notions of human 'selfhood,' 'society,' and 'Deity') as the processive realization of multifarious but harmonizable purposes (Part IV).

We begin our study with the organistic conception of nature. Whitehead, of course, is renowned in our times as 'the philosopher of organism.' It has not usually been observed that Royce, several decades earlier than the time when Whitehead was rising to prominence in the twenties in these terms, was essentially an organicist in his own conception of the natural order. We, therefore, show first this side of Royce's philosophy.

The reference to "life" as the chief paradigm for the description of things is evident in each man. In an essay, in 1895, "Self-Consciousness, Social Consciousness, and Nature," Royce wrote: "there is behind the phenomena of nature a world of finite life, in more or less remote, but socially disposed relations to us human beings." Again in the same place he speaks of "the social relations of the finite beings that together must make up the whole natural world, both human and extra-human"; and farther along he again refers to his "conception of the natural order as a vast social organism of which human society is only a part...."[12] "Life," societies of living beings, the connectedness of things as "social organism," these are some of the foundational ideas of Royce, and later of Whitehead.

---

11. Terminology not usually ascribed to Royce.
John K. Roth has observed that although the methods of process philosophy "are not those of idealism, the broad metaphysical concerns of 'process philosophy' and many of the views it develops put it closer to Royce's thought than...other movements," such as "logical positivism, analytical philosophy, existentialism, phenomenology, and pragmatism" (The Philosophy of Josiah Royce, Thomas Y. Crowell Co., 1971, p. 5, n. 3).
12. McDermott: BWJR, Vol. 1, op. cit., pp. 429-30.

On his side, the latter wrote in his chapter "Nature Alive" (<u>Modes of Thought</u>, 1938), "nature, considered in abstraction from the notion of life...discloses no ground for its own coherence" (p. 202), and continued:

> The doctrine that I am maintaining is that neither nature nor life can be understood unless we fuse them together as essential factors in the composition of 'really real' things whose inter-connections and individual characters constitute the universe. (p. 205)

Continuing with Whitehead for the moment, the latter went on to point out in this same context, that the "absolute" thing about life was its quality of "self-enjoyment." Self-enjoyment is the irreduceable, distinctive quotient of meaning when we refer to "life," or living beings. Life is an entity with a selfhood that <u>feels</u>, however further it may be described. Whitehead here employs his special term "prehension" to indicate this "process of appropriation" or appetition, and elsewhere many times refers to "feeling" as assisting in the definition of prehension. Whitehead includes other absolute characteristics in the meaning of "life," such as "creativity," and "aim" (elsewhere "subjective aim"). Aim is explained in the context just cited as "the entertainment of the purely ideal so as to be directive of the creative process" (p. 208).

Depicting the conception of nature, in what follows we will trace paramount connections between the two philosophers along the route of these ideas: life, process, prehension, aim, creativity and others, to refer to them for the moment in the Whitehead way.

Living things are dynamic, changeful, in constant agitation, anticipation, transition. Therefore along with "life," the concept of "process" itself is present as fundamental to the interpretation of nature. Thus Royce in the same 1895 essay above cited to introduce our subject, continued about the physical world: "in itself, nature, as such, would be neither a world of fixed habits or yet a world of mere novelties, but rather a world of experience with permanence everywhere set off by change." The non-invariable, even "relative" character, of natural laws or "routine" is announced.

> ...the scientifically computable and verifiable routine of rhythmic repetition in inorganic nature is nowhere concretely known to us as phenomenally invariable.... ...the permanence of the phenomenally obvious "habits" of inorganic nature is only relative.[13]

---

13. Ib., pp. 461, 455.

In such passages as this, Royce clearly asserted the fluid or processive qualities of nature. This point, that natural laws themselves are processive and change over the long pull, anticipates that well-known theme in Whitehead. The latter wrote in hid chapter, "Nature Lifeless," (just prior to "Nature Alive" in Modes of Thought): "For the modern view process, activity, and change are the matter of fact. At an instant there is nothing. ...there is no nature at an instant. ...all...matters of fact must involve transition.... All realization involves implication in the creative advance" (p. 200).

Such ideas as the preceding Royce elaborated in his eloquent essay, "The Interpretation of Nature" (Lecture V, Vol. II, The World and the Individual, 1900-1901--peer work in the life of Royce to Whitehead's Process and Reality, 1929). We highlight a few emphases of this essay for our present purposes. Royce calls attention at the outset to the fact that evolution itself constitutes "the largest generalization" or evidence that there can be no "breach of continuity" between mind, as the patent outcome of that process, on the upper hand, and so-called "matter," as the base of it on the lower side of things; and too, that manifestly evolution would be the amplest expression of the flow of things, "a genuine, if hidden inner fluency" (pp. 209, 210, 219, 223):

> ...very possibly material nature is a show of a process that is inwardly fluent." (p. 219)

That there is no nature remaining ever "at an instant" (Whitehead) seems expressed in Royce in the present context were, speaking of both so-called levels, "conscious Nature" and "material Nature," he said:

> In both realms...there are numberless sorts of acts that return not again, so that an irrevocable passing away of states once reached, pervades the stream of experience in both realms alike. (p. 219)

The "prehension" idea of Whitehead is clearly understood by Royce where the latter refers to both regions of nature (the conscious and the material) as "subject to processes which involve in general a tendency of one part of nature to communicate, as it were, with another part, influencing what occurs at one place through what has already occured at another place" (p. 220, emphasis his). This communication is not confined to just that type of conscious awareness of things exemplified in human experience, any more than "prehension" as a technical term in Whitehead was so confined. For Royce, however, our level of conscious communication is an analogy of "more vast and pervasive...natural processes...." The statement appears in the following context:

Ideas in the same consciousness tend to assimilate other
ideas, to communicate their own nature to these other ideas,
to win the latter over to agreement with the first. Minds
tend, in social intercourse, to be influenced by other minds.
Now these vast and pervasive processes of conscious communication possess both a close similarity to, and a continuity
with, certain still more vast and pervasive series of natural
processes which, described indeed as so-called wave-movements,
are amongst the phenomena best known to science. In both
cases the tendency is one towards the mutual assimilation of
the regions of Nature involved in the process. (p. 220
emphasis his)

Idealist proclivities in greater ascendency in the mind of
Royce than in Whitehead, come to fore where the former asserts in
this classic chapter, "That we have no right whatever to speak of
really unconscious Nature, but only of uncommunicative Nature,
or of Nature whose mental processes go on at such different time-
rates from ours that we cannot adjust ourselves to a live appreciation of their inward fluency, although our consciousness does
make us aware of their presence" (pp. 225-6). As cases of such
imagined differences Royce points to the sense of time-span that
individual molecules might experience, in contrast to our own,
for brevity of duration; or to that which rocks, actors in the
wearing away of the Niagara gorge, might have for sense of
longevity--in another dimension of natural experience of time
conceivably passing at a vastly different rate than our own.
We observe that Royce proceeds immediately to say here that he
believes that "Nature in general" reveals itself to be a "vast
conscious process," going on however at different time-spans as
between its various levels of being or streams of process. He
is thus prepared to assert that:

...when you deal with Nature, you deal with a vast realm
of finite consciousness of which your own is at once a
part and an example. (p. 226)

Whitehead, of course, never says anything quite like this;
he never moves this far along the road toward an avowed idealist
point of view. Prehensions for the latter are not always "conscious," as Royce has just proclaimed them to be at least in some
sense, namely conscious but differing as to type of consciousness
of time intervals. For Whitehead the vaster scope of prehensive
"experience" between beings in the cosmic order is declared to be
unconscious or non-conscious (PR, pp. 83, 88, 130, 245-6, 355).[14]

---

14. In Science and the Modern World (1925), he had defined
     "prehension" as an "uncognitive apprehension," and

(Royce, I believe, in all of this is actually more persuasive or coherent as an 'organicist' or 'prehensive-type' philosopher of nature than is Whitehead. The latter's descriptions of prehensive experience that somehow 'knows,' yet is not consciously aware of its neighbor's presence in any way that we would recognize as 'conscious,' appears opaque as description of the cosmic order. Does Royce seize, it may be asked, the prehensive philosophy more forthrightly in his doctrine, just reviewed? Do the possible differing time-spans of different levels or orders of being as described by Royce account better for their modes of experience when said to be non- or trans-conscious in our precise human terms? Whereas Whitehead says that the notion of "experience" cannot be limited to just the idea of conscious experience, Royce implies that the proper meaning of the word experience can never without confusion be disassociated from its central implication of conscious awareness. Be this argument as it may, we return to the more general point of our analysis.)

It is of interest to juxtapose, at this stage, three of the chapters cited thus far in the works of Royce and Whitehead. In the following order they present a progression of thought: Whitehead's chapter VII, "Nature Lifeless" (Modes of Thought), criticizes the Newtonian view of the world as a dead mechanism of discrete, yet somehow connected, but lifeless substances; following this appears chapter VIII, "Nature Alive," which sets forth his general organismic, even vitalistic philosophy. Royce's essay, however, "The Interpretation of Nature" has announced, as we have just seen, 'Nature Conscious." Royce summarizes what he has been endeavoring to say:

> I suppose that the field of Nature's experience is every-where leading slowly or rapidly to the differentiation of new types of conscious unity. I suppose that the process goes on with very vast slowness in inorganic Nature, as for instance in the nebulae, but with great speed in you and me. But, meanwhile, I do not suppose that slowness means a lower type of consciousness. (p. 227)

> Common to all these conscious processes would be their fluency, their inner significance, and their constant inter-communication, whereby more or less novel facts were trans-ferred all the time from one to another region of this conscious world. (p. 228)

---

continued "by this I mean apprehension which may or may not be cognitive" (The New American Library, Mentor Books, 1948, p. 70, emphasis his).

This last quotation suggests again Royce's version of the __prehension__ idea, so termed by Whitehead later, as well as the emphasis on __novelty__ arising out of various modes of such "intercommunication" (again the prominent point at the base of the subsequent thinker's philosophy). In the context, all of this explains in depth how Royce believes evolution transpires (p. 228).

The following Royce paragraphs from the same essay on "Nature" summarize themes we have already mentioned as a striking forecast of Whitehead. The emphases emerging here bear repeating because of their inclusiveness as a list. The Royce terms are nature as "fluent process"; the fullness of "change"; governance by "pursuit of ideal goals"; constant communication; changes as tending toward "novelty"; the "irrevocable passing of...facts"; and description of the apparently constant inorganic processes, like the vibrations of atoms or molecules, in psychological terms as "extreme cases of habits rendered uniform by intercommunication" (p. 230):

> ...the evolutionary changes of the whole conscious world would be based upon processes whose basis would be viewed as threefold. First, they would be fluent processes, full of significant change, more or less obviously governed by the pursuit of ideal goals. Secondly, they would be processes determined, as our own are, by a constant communication with processes going on in other regions. Thirdly, they would be processes that, amidst all the changes, tended, as far as the novelty and the irrevocable passing of life's facts permitted, to the acquisition of definite habits. As these definite habits, so far as acquired at all, would be established under the influence of intercommunication from the whole of the finite world, and as the habits, whenever they appeared, would tend to take the form of repeated rhythms, which, if once more observed from without, would communicate their own nature, we should expect to get, in a summary search through Nature, precisely that superficial impression of an endless repetition of the same types which inorganic Nature, in the uniformity of its Matter, seems to show us. The conceived atoms, all of the same size, the vibrations of the molecules of incandescent hydrogen, all of the same pitch,--these would be appearances of what, in their inner essence, are only extreme cases of habits rendered uniform by intercommunication, like the customs of a nation, or like the sounds of a given language appearing in many men's speech. (p. 230)

The parallel Whitehead ideas and terms would be, once more, fluency, or "process," and constant change; "subjective aims";

"prehension"; "novelty"; impermanence of these novelties as passing facts, etc. Particularly Whiteheadian in scope, and even in language style, is the following Royce passage--ending with the similarity, as a major note in both men, that nature does not have the sole goal (profoundly _teleological_ though both conceive it to be) of "producing a man"--"that atrocious Philistinism of our ...race"!

> It would not be true that Nature sometimes, in an exceptional way, pursues ideal goals. On the contrary, every natural process, if rightly viewed from within, would be the pursuit of an ideal. There would be no dead Nature at all,--nothing really inorganic or unconscious,--only life, striving, onflow, ideality, significance, rationality. Only for us Nature appears to be growing from death to life as the processes grow more like our own, and so more intelligible. But we should have to unlearn that atrocious Philistinism of our whole race which supposes that Nature has no worthier goal than producing a man. Perhaps experiences of longer time-span are far higher in rational type than ours. The evolution of Man would be but the appearance of a type of individuality whose time-span is short, and whose grade of rationality is doubtful, but presumably at least a little lower than that of the angels.... (p. 231)

Perhaps the central word among Whitehead's cosmological terms, until now not mentioned by us, was "actual entity" or "actual occasion." Royce's central expression, "individuality" or "individual"(s) stands close, if not identical, to actual entities in connotation. In this respect, moving along further in the "Interpretation of Nature" chapter we find Royce saying:

> In Nature, as in man, we find individuality linked in the closest fashion with intercommunication, with the mutual interdependence of individuals, and with a genuine identity of meaning and of Being in various individuals. (p. 238)

Presently our examination of Royce's and Whitehead's general 'theory of being' will disclose the primary role that the expressions Individuality and Actual Entity occupy as the focal metaphysical terms in their respective theories. Suffice it now to say, for Whitehead, "actual entities" or "actual occasions" were the basal droplets of "experience," which can be organized in ascending or increasing comprehensiveness of individualization, and into further societies of occasions, along many and various streams of creativity. In Royce's wording above, and in what follows, something very similar is announced. Farther along in this passage Royce mentions the "Absolute Individual," which anticipates Whitehead's definition of God as ultimate "actual entity":

> Our whole theory presupposes that individuals may be included
> within other individuals; that one life, despite its unique
> ethical significance, may form part of a larger life; and
> that the ties which bind various finite individuals together
> are but hints of the unity of all individuals in the Absolute
> Individual. (p. 238)

Anticipating our later, fuller discussion of the theology of these men, the Royce essay just now under scrutiny contains the idea of God's immanence as primary characteristic of the Divine Being; even the expression of nature as the bodily aspect of God appears--a point quintessential in the philosophy of Whitehead.

> We suppose that there is a vast range of extra-human life,
> limited in its nature, like the life of man, and identical
> with the Absolute Life only in that universal sense in which,
> according to our theory, every life, however minute or how-
> ever vast, is in relation to the whole organism of the
> Absolute. (p. 236)

The basal organization of this "Absolute Life" in terms like those of Whitehead's hierarchical 'societies of occasions' is very plain as we continue to peruse this Royce passage:

> To this life, whose presence is hinted to us by our experi-
> ence of Nature, our theory assigns an existence as concrete
> and essentially conscious as that of man himself. And we
> suppose that our human life is a differentiation from this
> larger life of Nature. Our deeper relations with the Nature-
> life we suppose to be, despite all the vast differences,
> essentially similar to the relations upon which our human
> social life is founded. They are relations of communication,
> and of an intimate linkage between the happenings that occur
> in various realms and provinces of the whole life of Nature.
> (p. 236)

In the last three paragraphs, however, of his essay on "Nature" Royce rejects a doctrine of evolution "that regards Nature as in any sense a realm of the genuinely Unconscious, or that supposes the Absolute to come to self-consciousness first in man, or that conceives the process of Evolution as one wherein the life of the natural world, as a whole, grows from the darkness of obscure and unconscious purpose to the daylight of self-possessed Reason. Our general Theory of Being simply forbids every such interpretation of Nature" (p. 240). The paragraph just prior to this states:

> ...our theory differs very deeply from all hypotheses of the
> type of Clifford's "Mind Stuff" doctrine. It is customary,
> in recent thought, for many who appreciate the importance of
> the natural processes summed up in the word Evolution, to
> attempt to conceive that inorganic Nature consists of a vast
> collection of elements of the type of our own sensations, or
> of our simplest feelings. The process of Evolution itself
> is regarded by such views as a gradual coming together and
> organization of such originally atomic elements of feeling
> into complex unities, which, viewed externally, appear as
> more and more organized bodies, while the same masses of
> content, internally viewed, come to take on, more and more,
> the character of conscious and, in the end, of rational
> lives. Our hypothesis, by virtue of its idealistic basis,
> rejects altogether the possibility of any such separate
> elements of Mind Stuff. (p. 239)

And in the last paragraph of the essay on Nature Royce concludes:

> But in rejecting the Mind-Stuff theory of Clifford, our
> grounds are general and positive. That theory implies an
> essentially realistic conception of Being, and falls with
> Realism. The same is true of Leibniz's Monadology. The
> Unconscious we reject, because our Fourth Conception of
> Being forbids all recognition of unconscious realities.
> (p. 241)

Indeed, it here might be pointed out with much validity that
Royce plainly announces, by virtue of his "idealist basis," a
fundamental way he appears to differ from Whitehead. Undoubtedly,
important aspects of Whitehead's views bear close resemblance to
ideas here criticized so sharply by Royce in his reference to
Clifford. To transpose the terms we have been citing directly
into those of Whitehead, Royce denies, in this dialogue with
Clifford, that "prehensions" can be ultimately "unconscious" (a
point mentioned above). Whitehead, however, says that the vaster
order of prehensive experience throughout the cosmic layers and
streams of process is unconscious. Consciousness mounts up only
in man out of the cosmis mass (but, of course, in the latter's
view, apparently it may be preserved in God, and possibly only
in God, "everlastingly").

Granting then, that such differences are to be found between
Royce and Whitehead regarding their concept of nature in a number
of details of whatever larger or lesser importance, the principal
effort of our exegesis thus far (particularly from Royce's chapter
on Nature in The World and the Individual), is to call attention

to basic points of similarity in both philosophes. To illustrate once again, in the midst of his conclusion to the essay on Nature, Royce says that "a simple sensation of feeling, can neither be nor be conceived in isolation" (p. 240). Such a statement, of course, points back to his fundamental challenge of all hard "realisms" and pluralisms, elaborated in the earlier part of Vol. I of The World and the Individual--a challenge which we examine presently in greater detail in Royce's and Whitehead's metaphysical theory of Being. Suffice it here to say, and now from the Whitehead side, that the least examination of his texts (as in "Nature Lifeless") reveals likewise his severe opposition to atomistic materialism, i.e. to a hard or absolutistic realism. As an overall cast to both men's view of things, their joint criticism of hard realism is a chief aspect of the similarities we have been pursuing in them. In sum, what we have endeavored to show thus far is the close resemblance of their 'organistic' philosophy of the natural order.

With profound reverence Royce contemplated the fundamental "orderly cooperation" of nature's "aggregations," and its apparent teleology.[15] Quite the same with Whitehead. This reverent amazement before the order led both men to develop their respective metaphysical systems to account for it--as, to use Royce's words for both, "the process of spirit."[16]

---

15.   "The Mechanical, the Historical, and the Statistical,"
        1914, from McDermott, op. cit., Vol. 2, pp. 732-3.
16.   "Mind," 1916, from McDermott, Ib., p. 761.

Chapter Two

THEORY OF BEING

The statements on phenomenal nature just perused introduce
the reader to each man's theory of Being, that is, his metaphysical world view as a whole. Subsequent parts of this study
present a fuller exposition of further major themes, namely those
of the idea of Man, of God, Freedom, Evil, Immortality, Religion
Ethical Perspective, and finally Knowledge and the Philosophical
Task. Preparatory to these themes the present precis, then, of
Royce's theory of being, followed by a resume of Whitehead's,
will continue to point out connections between the two philosophers and conclude with a summary of the progress our study has
made thus far in drawing out these relationships.

In Volume I of his great work, The World and the Individual,
Royce sets forth four "conceptions of Being." The first three
views, to use his own titles, are "Metaphysical Realism," "Mysticism," and "Critical Rationalism"; his own Fourth Conception of
Being we will designate in our own way, for the moment, as
Integral Personal Idealism. (The second conception, "Mysticism,"
is reserved for later discussion, in Part III, on the idea of
God, where we believe it better fits our expositional purposes.
Also by omitting it at this stage, we simplify, without major
distortion, the development of Royce's perspective in Volume I
of WI).

His essay on realism, "The Independent Beings" (Lecture III,
of the above work), endeavors to show the logical absurdity of
defining the world in any absolutistic "realist" terms, as ultimately a contatenation of so many sundered entities, particularly
the entity of the 'idea' as sundered from the 'object' of its
knowledge--the critical point in the classic idealist-realist
debate. Manifestly, Royce argues, the world is one of actual
links and many common qualities. But, how then, according to a
rigid realist definition of things, is our actual world accounted
for--on the level of the simplest empirical questions that might
be asked? For after all 'apples' do grow on 'twigs,' and are
related to other 'red' colored things, the setting sun, auto-
mobiles, and so on.

Royce's argument against hard Realism suggests the following
logical summary: Take the realistic definition seriously: that

there is absolute sundering between the <u>objects</u> of the world, and
this on two levels of inquiry, thus:

$$0 \text{———————} 0_1 \quad \text{(i.e. any and all 'objects')}$$
$$\text{or}$$
$$0 \text{———————} 0_1 \quad (0_1 \text{ here defined as the 'idea of } 0\text{')}$$

Now such a picture ("Metaphysical Realism") can be described as
inconsistent with our actual world, on broadest empirical grounds,
by a hypothetical syllogism:

> If the world were absolute realism, then there would be
> (by definition) no links or common qualities possible,
> including the 'link' of knowledge--(even the ascription
> of the Realist, that his own idea or theory of the
> world is descriptively correct, could not be known or
> verified).

> But the world has links, relationships, and common quali-
> ties (including sometimes the 'link' of knowledge) or
> the correspondence of the '<u>idea</u> <u>of</u> <u>0</u>' <u>to</u> '<u>0</u>').

Therefore the world is not, or cannot be an aggregate of
absolutely sundered reals, i.e. an absolute pluralism.[1] Surely,
in this lucid and fascinating chapter, Royce does demolish the
possibility of any extreme 'atomism' (ontologically speaking) or
fragmenting 'positivism' (epistemologically speaking). Below he
paraphrases the realist position and concludes:

> ...the many entities of this realistic world have no features
> in common. If they appear to have, this is seeming, is "mere
> name and form"...they are sundered from one another by sbso-
> lutely impassable chasms; they can never come to get either
> ties or community of nature; they are not in the same space,
> nor in the same time, nor in the same natural or spiritual
> order. (pp. 131-2)

> No realist, as he himself now must consistently maintain,
> either knows any independent being, or has ever, in idea,
> found himself related to or expressed an opinion regarding
> one, or, in his own sense of the word "real," really believes
> that there is one. (p. 136)

> That a relative independence, and that both individuality
> and freedom have their concrete meaning in this truer realm,

---

1.   We have denied the consequent, and may therefore deny
     the antecedent of the original proposition.

we shall indeed in due season learn. But what we now learn is
that any definition of absolutely independent beings, beings
what could change or vanish without any results whatever for
their fellows, is, in all regions of the universe, natural or
spiritual, a hopeless contradiction. There are no such
mutually indifferent beings. But this other realm, where no
fact, however slight, transient, fleeting, is absolutely
independent of any of its fellow facts, this is the realm
where when one member suffers others suffer also, where no
sparrow falls to the ground without the insight of One who
knows, and where the vine and the branches eternally flourish
in a sacred unity. That is the city which hath foundations,
and thither our argument already, amidst these very storms of
negation; is carrying us over the waves of doubt. (p. 138)

In such passages, Royce begins his quest for a more unified view
of the world, which, nevertheless, will include and support the
world's manifest "relative" independencies and freedoms.

Of course, at this point, the critic might say that all
Royce has done is to raise an artificial, straw man, in his
description of "realism," and proceed to blow it down; since, of
course, who believes in a radically realistic or pluralistic
world of this kind? To which the reply is, Indeed, who ever
does? But that is just Royce's point. What Royce does, in so
many words, we believe, thus far in his analysis, is to call
attention to a basic rational instinct about our world, an intellectual intuition regarding a requisite 'unity' as lying at the
foundation of things, for there to be any being at all, or any
'order,' and eventually a build-up of things into whatever further
being or complexity there may be. He therefore points here to
what may be called the fundamental rational, or a priori sense of
Deity, to the basic meaning of 'God' for human consciousness,
whatever else 'God' may come to mean for Royce as he pursues his
idealism.

Be this as it may, we will draw attention here, and again
later, to the fact that both Royce and Whitehead together repudiate the radical realism here rejected by Royce. The universe is
a 'continuum,"2 a holy, enduring, though purposively changing
contexture of things, not a single pyrotechnic display, of broken
and gawdy particulars, which quickly sputter out into some eternal
night.

---

2.   A term employed by Whitehead, from Einstein, Part II,
Chapter II, "The Extensive Continuum," PR.

In the next Lecture, No. IV, Royce discussed the Second
Conception of Being, or Mysticism, the philosophy of the absolute
trans-rational unity of the world--opposite extreme to radical
realism, which he has just criticized. (For our previously
announced reasons we will reserve his review of mysticism until
the problem of God is clarified at a later stage of this commentary. In the meanwhile, in Lectures V and VI ("...The World of
Modern Critical Rationalism" and "Validity and Experience") Royce
has moved to a description of the Third Conception of Being.

The Critical Rationalist's position is itself a subtle,
modified type of realism, a Platonic ontology, which describes
being as abstract 'ideas,' 'truth,' or 'validity'; indeed, before
he is done with it, declared by Royce to be "true as far as it
goes." Critical Rationalism will take him far toward his own
conception of Being, and shows how his philosophy, like Whitehead's
later, is primarily and consciously rooted in Platonism. Speaking
of Critical Rationalists, Royce describes their subtle conception
of ultimate things thus:

> ...the one thing to which they remain steadfastly loyal, is
> the Validity of some region of decidedly impersonal Truth.
> As such a realm of impersonal truth they conceive perhaps the
> moral law, perhaps the realm of natural law, revealed to us
> by science, perhaps the lawful structure of that social order
> which is now so favorite a topic of study. Their spiritual
> father is Kant, although they often ignore their parentage.
> Their philosophical creations are a collection of impersonal
> principles in whose independent or realistic Being no one
> altogether believes, but whose value as giving reasonable
> unity to the realm of phenomena, justifies, to the present
> age, their validity. (p. 205)

As further examples that such 'ideal' or idea-objects, however ephemeral, ghostly, and insubstantial they at first may seem,
do nevertheless command our philosophic attention with a persistent claim to a degree of reality and objective validity; such
objects may further be illustrated, he was fond of suggesting, by
"the credit of a commercial house, the debts that a man owes, the
present price of a given stock in the stockmarket...the market
price current of any given commodity...the rank of a given official, the social status of any member of the community, the marks
received by a student at any examination...the British Constitution"--and all other such 'ideas' of a social type (p. 209). To
suggest his meaning further he also pointed to "mathematical
objects" or ideas, e.g. "the value of π, that is, the ratio of
diameter and circumference in a circle," and all other such
mathematical "functions," as examples of "real fact in the

universe" (pp. 212-3); as "stubborn as the rebellious spirits that a magician might have called out of the deep," he says (p. 214). Many times he acknowledges the root of this kind of outlook on being as lying in Plato's doctrine of Ideas.

Because the philosophy of Plato (and the related system of Aristotle) constitutes such a large part of the background of Royce's as well as Whitehead's thought, we will engage here in a brief historical excursus on the Platonic type of philosophy.

Plato's and Aristotle's philosophies were types of 'abstract idealism,' if we may give that term a general definition for the moment as a philosophy, such as Royce is here describing, which believes in an eternal order of truth, value, and form according to which the world of individual beings and all processes are structured.[3] In the thought of these ancient philosophers, Ultimate Reality was conceived to be a system of ideal truths, values, laws and forms of being, regarded as eternal, objective presences beyond man's mind, and above finite process (Plato), or existing as the subsisting patterns for that process immanent in nature (Aristotle). Ultimate Truth, Beauty, and Good, were conceived as objective, metaphysical, spiritual (immaterial) "ideas" or "forms," the eternal laws of being that structure world process. Man in his intellectual and moral life can know, share, or participate in the ideas or forms; as does nature, insofar as her individualities, and processes, reflect or express them.

Plato and Aristotle accepted the objective or idealistic concept of truth. Truth was to them not only the correspondence of thought to things and of thought to its own rules of right reason (truth in its double faceted psychological sense); but also truth meant or had a cosmic reference and dimension, i.e. it was correspondence or conformity of things or natural processes to the laws and forms of thought, or reason, conformity of all things to the mathematical-logical-biological-moral-value order which, they believed, structures being. This point of view Plato and Aristotle inherited from Heraclitus's concept of the universal "logos," the cosmic principle of regulative or formative control of all things according to measure and harmony. Included in this

---

3. Modern critical naturalists share with idealists and theists, of course, the intellectual ancestry of Plato and Aristotle, particularly on the side of the humanism of these ancient philosophers; theists claim them especially on the side of their idealism, and in some respects, no doubt, on that of their avowed, or latent personalism.

structure of truth were all natural and biological forms, or
species (such as 'Man,' 'Horse,' or 'Oak'); artificial species
such as the art objects or artifacts created by man ('vase,'
'house,' etc.); moral, aesthetic, and sentient qualities, ideas,
species, (such as 'justice,' 'beauty,' or 'redness'); abstract,
mathematical, logical qualities, or ideas (e.g. 'number,' 'equality,' 'circularity,' 'greatness,' etc.). The similarities in
appearance or function between the individual members of any given
natural species, e.g. in the biological realm, whether Horse or
Dog or Oak or Man, suggested to these Greek thinkers the existence
of a guiding, spiritual ideal, pattern, or form that such species
embodied and were endeavoring to express. As in man's creation
of artifacts there is an idea or ideal of 'vase' or 'house' in his
mind, the intellectual or spiritual pattern which guides his work,
so there are the many ideas of natural forms objectively presented
to, or resident in the cosmic order that guide its process.

For Plato, subsuming and integrating the entire hierarchy of
'ideas,' over-arching all, is the supreme Idea of Good (Idea
Tagathou)--the Idea of Ideas, because 'good' is found in all the
ideas that structure and harmonize being. 'Good' is their common
denominator, and thus the archetypal Idea. Without ideas organizing being there would be mere disorganized matter or chaos.
When this is realized one may stand in ecstatic awareness of the
Supreme Good (we touch here upon the religious and mystical side
of Plato's thought).

Our footnote below, with diagrams, describes somewhat more
precisely the different cosmological perspectives of Plato and
Aristotle in their ancient setting.[4]

---

4.   These diagrams are based mainly on the Cosmologies
      suggested by Plato's Timaeus and Republic dialogues
      and Aristotle's twelfth book of the Metaphysics.
      Plato presents three coordinate, eternal principles:
      Matter; the realm of Ideas with the Good; and God.
      (In the Parmenides dialogue, Plato speculates that the
      "ideas" may possibly be unitied ultimately within the
      Divine mind itself). Following Plato, Aristotle sug-
      gests two eternal principles: nature or matter-as-
      informed; and God. Accordingly we have:

Impressed by the orderly side of nature, which may be understood in our terms as the physical, biological and psychological
"laws" which science throughout its entire range describes; and

---

<u>Plato's Cosmology</u>: <u>Timaeus</u>, <u>Republic</u>

For Plato, embodied individuals are appearances; abstract
universals (ideas) are the realities. Man's spiritual part
or soul reflects or shares, participates in the Ideas insofar
as he has knowledge. "God," or the <u>Demiourgos</u> (<u>Timaeus</u>),
originally looked to the Ideas and brought order out of the
primeval, material "receptical" or chaos. Thus God is the
principle of creativity, organization, or conformity that
urges matter into ordered form or law, which we call nature.
In the <u>Timaeus</u>, and the Tenth Book of the <u>Laws</u>, where we find
a brilliant version of the cosmological argument, God seemed
to be conceived as fully personal for Plato.

equally impressed with man's need for moral order or law, if he
is to live happily or well in relation to other men socially,
Plato and Aristotle conceived existence as a total intellectual-

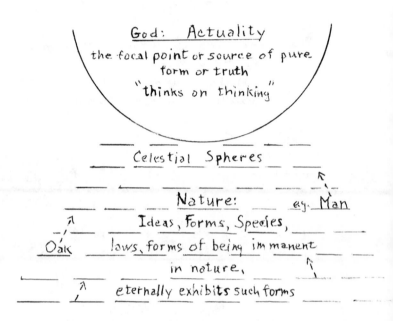

Aristotle's Cosmology: Metaphysics Bk. XII

God: Actuality
the focal point or source of pure form or truth
"thinks on thinking"

Celestial Spheres

Nature: e.g. Man
Ideas, Forms, Species,
Oak   laws, forms of being immanent
in nature,
eternally exhibits such forms

For Aristotle Ideas/forms/universals are embodied in
individual objects, in nature. Reality or nature is
matter-in-formed, growing, developing through various
levels of integration in fulfillment of her highest
potentialities or ideal forms, which have their origin
or are known in the life of God. God is the focal-point
of pure truth or form, the ideal Actuality, or Ultimate
Principle of Formation, toward which all things move, or
conform, as by desire (eros). In Aristotle's Metaphysics
Bk XII, Chap. 7, energeia, "actuality," is a predicate
characterizing Theos, or "God." Also in the Metaphysics
Aristotle uses forms of "eros" (or love) and other terms
for desire, to express the striving of natural formations

value structure, as rationality, reason, or mind(<u>nous</u>).   "...mind
rules the universe," Plato said.[5] Man's capacity for ordered
thought defines his rationality and relates him to or reflects,
the ordered structures and processes of the world outside him.
For Plato and Aristotle, man's rationality of mind, reflecting the
world's rationality of being, equals the full realm of Truth,
which is existence. Existence is therefore, by definition, spiritual for these thinkers. God as the ground or architect of being
is, in quintessential terms, Truth itself. (This insight or
interpretation captured the intellectual imagination of the West
and was for many ages its dominating intellectual theme. Judaeo-
Christian thinkers were quick to adapt it to their expressly
personalistic interpretation of God, from Philo and St. John
through St. Augustine, St. Thomas, and many others subsequently,
including Royce and Whitehead.)

Let us evaluate in broadest terms for the moment this
Platonic-Aristotelian conception of the world. For many minds
it has indeed seemed to be profoundly true. There do seem to
be Ideas, Forms, or Laws, or continuing principles of rational
structure and order, and of orderly evolutionary change,[6] which

---

toward the perfection of forms as God perceives them in
the ideal. (In the <u>Symposium</u>, Plato had discussed the
role of "eros" or desiring love in a similar manner, as
it pertains to the striving of the human soul toward perfection in the Good, the True and Beautiful.) God for
Aristotle is the Unmoved Mover. The question as to
whether Aristotle's God is aware of his world, and accordingly whether He is fully personal, has remained opened.
    To unify and summarize Plato's and Aristotle's
cosmologies and ideas of the Divine, <u>God or the Divine</u>
<u>is the eternal principle of formation, integration, or</u>
<u>actuality ordering creation according to rational law:</u>
-- overarching process as the eternal Ideas (Plato)
-- immanent in process as the eternal Forms (Aristotle),
    though God himself as pure spirit is transcendent to
    the process He influences.

5. <u>Philebus</u> 30.
6. We assume here, of course, such contemporary principles
    or concepts of evolutionary change as genetic mutation,
    replication of kind (with sexual reproduction), natural
    selection, geographic isolation--principles, which in
    their profoundest significance to the mind of faith,
    seem orderly, rational, and filled with form, for the
    reason that without them, living things could not have
    come to be or evolved.

channel, govern, or energize specific streams of process or nature
into similar and recurring types of individuality, and balanced
relationship between individualities throughout all levels of
being, inorganic, organic, psychic, moral, social, and spiritual.
These powers of formation, integration, development and balance
make possible and achieve (actualize) the individualities and
relations of individualities from societies of atoms to societies
of human personalities. Plato was bold to speak of these powers,
in their ultimate terms as "Ideas." (Aristotle's further specific
contribution to the idea of God, and something of its timeless
appeal to many may be suggested in the note below.)[7]

Since the time of Plato and Aristotle, the outlook of some
philosophers, more or less in each case, has resembled the impersonal or abstract idealism, as this essay has referred to it,
which Royce has singled out in his presentation of "Critical
Rationalism." Among these have been--to mention several earlier
and modern representatives--Averroes, Spinoza, Hegel, Bernard
Bosanquet, George Santayana, Nicolai Hartmann, Edmund Husserl,

---

7.   Western theism has had a major root system deep in the
     philosophy of Aristotle. Doubtless, something like the
     following would state in broad terms, the contribution of
     Aristotle to theistic thought in the West. Any common-
     place process of evolution or natural integration would
     illustrate the work of supreme Actuality and its presence
     in the universe: the whole of the evolutionary process
     striving to 'Actualize' itself in the coming to be of
     the countless beings; the growth of an acorn into an oak;
     the expansion and integration of the two cells of the
     zygote into the marvelous complexity of the whole foetus
     and its human brain, filled with the potential personalit
     of a Shakespeare or a Lincoln. The fact and process of
     "Actuality" as the purposive principle of nature's phylo-
     genetic and ontogenetic evolution, transpires under our
     eyes daily in countless expressions, as creative Spirit
     informs and organizes reality according to rational
     "Ideas." Aristotle used the expressions entelecheia,
     "complete reality," and energeia, "actuality," to describ
     that process that seemed to be leading things into their
     final "actual," or completed form (Meta. IX, 1047^a30,
     1050^a23). As he looked out at nature at the evidence of
     this process, it spoke to him of supreme purposiveness
     and intelligence. Whatever else God or the Divine may
     be, he or it is certainly, in the thought of Aristotle,
     the supreme Actualizing principle of process (Meta. XII,
     Chap. 7).

Brand Blanshard.   Philosophers of this type have tended to believe
that impersonal mind, phrased in varied terms, such as, logical
or "immortal essences" (Santayana), "ontic forms" (Husserl),
"specific universals" (Blanshard), best describe, that is to say,
for widest metaphysical generality, what reality is.[8] We return
now to our main line.

   Royce's principal criticism of abstract rationalism (or
abstract idealism) is that it does not adequately account for the
individuality of Being; or, another way to phrase the issue, to
account for the relation of the eternal forms among themselves,
and to real things--indeed problems left unresolved by Plato
himself.[9] In this vein of criticism Royce wrote:

   The partisans of our third notion of the real have, indeed,
   as we have observed, a stately tradition behind them.... Yet
   .... Our critical rationalist lives in a world where nothing
   in the realistic sense is real, but where it is as if there
   were independent realities, which, when more closely examined,
   prove to be merely more or less valid and permanent ideas....
   The truth is, indeed valid, but is it only valid? The forms
   are eternal; but are they only forms? The universal principles are true; but are they only universal? The moral order
   of the world seems genuine; but is it only an order? Is God
   identical with the world of Forms?
      These questions arise in all sorts of ways in our age.
   They remind us that our problem is here once more a problem
   about the meaning and the place of individuality in the system
   of Being, and about the relation of individual and universal
   in our conceptions. (WI 1, pp. 243-4)

   Platonism has been haunted by the dualism that its critics
claim it did not originally overcome--a dualism between a world
of particular realities in their material aspect and a realm of
universal ideas or of abstract 'mind.' (We have seen how Aristotle intended to solve this problem by placing the Forms within
nature from the outset.) Royce's conclusion is that a purely
abstract way of thinking of ultimate reality must be modified;
will must come to be regarded as significant in the cosmic scheme

---

8. In the Gifford Lectures, 1899-1900 Royce had mentioned
    the positions of John Stuart Mill, Wundt, and Avenarius
    as closely resembling his "Critical Rationalist" descrip-
    tion of things, WI Vol. I, p. 239.
9. Parmenides dialogue.

as intellect or ideas.[10] Indeed, can there be intellect or ideas
without will; can there be mind without personality? Some kind
of metaphysics is needed that will actually account for concrete
things, and in a measure describe processes of individuation--from
atoms to personal minds. In the search for an adequate conception
of Being, Royce considered Platonic realism or abstract rationalism, but moved on to a more personalistic concept of reality:

> The world of validity is indeed, in its ultimate constitution,
> the eternal world. It seems to us so far a very impersonal
> world and a very cold and unemotional realm,--the very oppo-
> site of that of the mystic. Before we are done with it we
> shall find it in fact the most personal and living of worlds.
> Just now it appears to us a realm of bodiless universal
> meanings. Erelong we shall discover that it is a realm of
> individuals, whose unity is in One Individual, and that theory
> means, in this eternal world, not theory, but Will and Life.
> (p. 222)

Royce begins to find that will and life as he examines the
very nature or psychological life of ideas themselves, in their
internal meanings. In the case of the knowing mind, for example,
the "external meaning" of any of its ideas would be the extent to
which they do in fact conform or correspond to the object they
purport to describe or represent as ideas, seeking to know or have
'truth' as the goal of their purpose or striving. But it is in
the purposes themselves of ideas, or in their internal meanings,
where the ultimate nature of ideas, and indeed of being itself,
is to be found.

Royce has now moved into his own "Fourth Conception," in
which "being" is defined through the transposition of abstract
ideas into the concrete realizations, or individualities, which
each wishes to become as the outcome of its own telic-striving.
Another way to describe his view is to say he wishes to arrive at
the true definition of being as individuality by clarifying, and

---

10.   It is of interest to note that Aristotle was quite
      conscious of the problem of will, by including the
      desiring principle, (eros) as integral to process at
      large (Metaphysics Bk XII); also that Plato himself had
      considered the problem of will prior to Aristotle in
      the description of the soldiery as the spirited element
      of the State (Republic IV), and again in his discussion
      of eros love (Symposium); but on the whole individuality
      or "particulars" and the impulse of will were a problem
      for Plato, which he tended to cast into the shadow land
      of "appearance," unreality, and even evil.

showing the relation between, the internal and the external
meaning of ideas, as above suggested. To accomplish this task,
and to illuminate its implications in the concept of God--the
Cosmic Individuality of individualities--and to consider God's
relation to these finite individualities, is the central effort
of Vol. I, and much of Vol. II, of The World and the Individual.
As for Whitehead, God in Royce's thought is an integral category
in the conception of Cosmic Order and of "Being." Royce's closer
argumentation for the reality of God as the Cosmic Individuality,
or Personal Spirit of the Whole, we review in our later part,
suffice it here to summarize his general hypothesis of being.

  His essay "The Internal and External Meaning of Ideas" (WI,
Vol. I, Lect. VII), represents the heart of his statement on the
nature of being. This discussion enshrines his central psychological dictum, "An idea seeks its object," (p. 329) and his
stress on "the essentially teleological inner structure of conscious ideas" (p. 310).

  Every idea of judgment about the world intends its truth,
that is, wills to have an adequate correspondence of its 'thought'
to 'things'--to think less of ideas is to defile the deepest
impulse of their very nature, and is absurd.[11] (In asserting that
an idea is "essentially teleological," the reader will no doubt
draw the parallel to Whitehead's central announcement that actual
entities have "subjective aim"). But an idea seeks its aim on two
levels or, perhaps better to say, along two vectors. Not only in
seeking and possessing true judgment in the enquiry into truth
along the vector of intellectual quest does it seek its "object";
but it also seeks its "object" in the sense of pressing toward
self-realization, in the creative impulse. For example, I have
an 'idea' of our proposed Franklin Fireplace installation at home.
How best to get it installed in terms of smoke-free efficiency,
and beauty? The internal meaning of the idea of our stove installation is to get it embodied in the actuality, effectively and
artistically. This is one meaning of the 'correspondence' of the
idea to reality, namely, on the side of its impulse to creativity,
parallel to its impulse to seek 'true' judgment in the truth
enquiry itself, the other meaning of 'correspondence.' In sum,
the psychology of an idea is to seek its own purpose, i.e. the
realization of its internal hope (or 'meaning') that it become
adequately representative. This quest can proceed, on the one

---

11. WI, Vol. I, p. 300f. A central endeavor of this essay
     is to show what the "time-honored definition of Truth"
     as "the Correspondence between any Idea and its Object"
     means, or how such correspondence is achieved (emphasis
     his).

hand, either toward some already existing object or example, that
is to say, toward having and experiencing 'truth' about its world;
or toward some imagined examplar not yet in being, on the other,
which stands to it as ideal or plan, but which indeed may be
brought into being by the very internal striving or purposing, or
will of the idea itself, along the creative vector. Thus far
(early in Lecture VIII, "The Fourth Conception of Being") Royce
draws his point together in the following words:

> ...for our present conception of Being, an individual being
> is not a fact independent of any experience, nor yet a merely
> valid truth, nor yet a merely immediate datum that quenches
> ideas. For all these alternatives we have already faced and
> rejected. On the contrary an individual being is a life of
> Experience fulfilling Ideas, in an absolutely final form. And
> this we said is the essential nature of Being. The essence of
> the Real is to be Individual, or to permit no other of its own
> kind, and this character it possesses only as the unique ful-
> fillment of purpose. (pp. 347-8)

With this theory of being now stated, Royce is prepared to
examine the further empirical question in the largest sense, What
are the "existent realities" that do in fact correspond to this
conception of Being? (p. 393). One such reality is, manifestly,
our own beings. Presumably the other extra-human finite individualities of the world of nature, have an internal life of purposive
striving and fulling of ideas as they pursue 'purposes' analogous
to our own, at various levels of the time-sense, as we heard him
say previously in his organismic conception of nature. Above, and
beyond, and including our own finite individualities, which are
pursuing the fulfillment of their several finite ideas (as just
described), is the larger cosmic order, or Individuality of the
Whole, pursuing or striving to fulfill its larger, inclusive Idea.
God's larger Idea of Ideas--for now we will call the whole, "God,"
with Royce--is to constitute the possibility and the ground for
our own, and all other, finite strivings for individual being.
This is the nature of God's larger 'Individuality,' and we will
hear Royce say, essentially God's 'Personhood,' analogous to our
own. His argument, through several levels of insight, for the
reality or existence of such Cosmic Personal Whole, and how God's
larger Life may be understood to be 'inclusive' of our finite
lives in their freedom, the third part of this study will present;
suffice it just now to say that we have endeavored to outline his
general conception of Being, and have proved it out at least to
the extent of illustrating it in the case of our own personal
finite levels of experience. The second part of this work, on
the idea of man or human selfhood in Royce and Whitehead, will

enlarge upon this teleological conception of Being particularly
as it is expressed in human personality.

Pages 15-16 of this study pointed to Royce's and Whitehead's
criticism of hard "realism" as a general, basic aspect of their
similar philosophic perspectives. We should, however, clarify
this broad point somewhat further, in light of the fact that
Whitehead himself claimed to be a realist rather than an idealist.

Among Whitehead's statements on the Einstein theory his 1922
essay, "The Philosophic Aspects of the Principle of Relativity,"
discloses the wide historic setting in which he frames his thought
relative to the realist-idealist debate, in ascendency at that
time. Whitehead argues on the realist side of the issue. However,
he singles out expressly Berkeleyan idealism for criticism, i.e.
that form in Berkeley which tended toward a radical subjectivist
view of things. Although sympathetic in this discussion with
philosophic realism, indeed a pronounced champion of it in several
statements, Whitehead nevertheless believes, in light of the modern
Relativity conception in physics brought to the fore by Einstein,
that a dogmatic, absolutistic, or hard realism (as we have called
it) is not possible, and acknowledges as his last statement that
the controversy "between realism and idealism" remains unsettled.[12]

Indeed, the whole of his subsequent emphasis as philosopher
of organism and prehension, which we have already previewed, was
to show the basic relatedness of things, and thereby to rebut
essentially the realist position when taken in some rigid sense.
We have just reviewed how Royce accomplished this in his lecture on "The Independent Beings." On his side, though very
critical of the subjectivist and mentalistic idealism which he
believes Berkeley represented, Whitehead's interpretation of
Einstein's contribution to philosophy stresses the "net of the
relationship" in which all things are caught; so that all events,
even that of Berkeley's "crimson cloud" in relation to the rest
of nature, has some degree of "uniform significance," as well,
of course, as "contingency" or unique qualities that give realistic philosophy its credentials.[13] Though indeed at this early
stage in Whitehead's philosophical writing the following lines
make it clear that he is not going to yield the debate to a too
facile or subjective idealism:

12. From John Macquarrie (ed): _Contemporary Religious
     Thinkers_, Harper & Row, 1968, p. 166.
13. Ib., pp. 162-3.

There is a process of nature which is obstinately indifferent
to mind. This is why I feel difficulty in assigning to mind,
or knowledge, or consciousness any essential role in the flux
of fact--[14]

--he concludes by saying:

The general character of its [relativity's] importance arises
from the emphasis which it throws upon relatedness. It helps
resolutely to turn its back upon the false lights of the
Aristotelian logic. Ultimate fact is not a mere aggregate
of independent entities which are the subjects for qualities.
We can never get away from an essential relatedness involving
a multiplicity of relata.[15]

This, of course, was Royce's main point in his lecture on "The
Independent Beings." Likewise, therefore, we have here in Whitehead's essay on Relativity a critical dialogue parallel in theme,
and in much of its spirit, to the dispute with "realism" with
which this study introduced Royce's discussion of being. This
same point, of course, was again later stressed in Process and
Reality where the major thrust of this work, on its critical side,
was to challenge those views which hold to a conception of "individual substances not present in other individual substances, of
the externality of relations..." (pp. 88-9).

To proceed now to Whitehead's smaller classic, Religion in
the Making, 1926, we find a summary statement of his theory of
being, later to be elaborated in Process and Reality. In less
than a page of the former work, Whitehead employs the term
"emergent" three times (pp. 93-4). He also uses this term a
number of times in Process and Reality.[16] Farther on in the same

---

14.   Ib. p. 164. Whitehead certainly comes eventually to
      assign "consciousness" a very essential role in his
      later announcements concerning Deity (e.g. RM, The
      Macmillan Co., 1926, pp. 153, 158); especially in the
      "consequent" aspect of "God," in PR.
15.   Ib. p. 165. Whitehead is here critical of the dyadic
      nature of "Aristotelian logic," which defined judgment
      in the subject-predicate, or subject-object dichotomy.
16.   E.g. pp. 64, 136, 349. The verbal form "emerges" also
      appears in description of the process that produces the
      "originality" that an achieved actual occasion or actual
      entity enjoys in Science and the Modern World, New
      American Library, 1948, p. 176. Again in SMW he spoke
      similarly of "the individual emergent occasion," p. 170;

chapter in Religion in the Making he uses the expression "new instance" and "novelty" several times and defines a "new instance" of things, or "novelty" as "the formation of the actual world with a new set of ideal forms" (pp. 113-14). He is here describing "emergent" quality, or the process of emergence, as fundamental paradigm or description of what takes place in evolutionary build-up or integration. New beings, or things, consequent entities, appear or emerge with new qualities, not present in, and from the standpoint of external observation, not foreseen by, the original elements or entities out of which they spring, or by the combination of which they come into such "new instance" or "novelty." Process and Reality defines "emergent evolution" expressly in this fashion as "the doctrine of real unities being more than a mere collective disjunction of component elements" (p. 349). Earlier, in PR in the discussion on "creativity" as the "ultimate" category, he had made the same point, where he said: "The ultimate metaphysical principle is the advance from disjunction to conjunction, creating a novel entity other than the entities given in disjunction.... In their natures, entities are disjunctively 'many' in process of passage into conjunctive unity" (p. 32). Our opening statement referred to Whitehead as essentially an "emergentistic" philosopher; and we believe it of assistance to the new reader to introduce his more technical thought at this stage under this broad designation. Accordingly, the better to understand Whitehead's conception of things, the following digression discusses the philosophy of "emergence" or "emergent evolution" as a cosmological paradigm widely characterizing the outlook of many philosophers and philosophic scientists of our times.[17]

Among these was C. Lloyd Morgan, British biologist and philosopher, whose distinguished publications Emergent Evolution, 1923, and Life, Mind, and Spirit, 1925, focused upon this concept.[18] The idea of emergence was also given a forceful description at that same period, under the virtually synonymous term,

---

and again of how the "shaped togetherness of things emerges," Ib. p. 174. Further in the same source appear the expressions "emergent value," "the emergent actual occasion," Ib. p. 165, and "the individual emergent occasion," Ib. p. 170.

17. Such figures, to name a few in addition to Morgan and Smuts, were Samuel Alexander, from whom Whitehead says a number of times he derives much inspiration, John Elof Boodin, Henry Nelson Wieman, Pierre Teilhard de Chardin, J.S. Haldane.

18. The Gifford Lectures for 1922, 1923.

"holism,"[19] by Jan Christian Smuts, late South African premier
and cosmological philosopher, in his influential volume, Holism
and Evolution, 1926. To refer to these authors will aid in the
exposition of these concepts that also constitute Whitehead's
primary vision of Being as a process of creative synthesis.
Whitehead's term "concretion" or "concrescence" is the phraseology he preferred, for the emergence or holism ideas. A portion of Lloyd Morgan's classic statement on the philosophy of
emergence follows:

> We live in a world in which there seems to be an orderly
> sequence of events.... Evolution, in the broad sense of
> the word, is the name we give to the comprehensive plan of
> sequence in all natural events.
>
> But the orderly sequence, historically viewed, appears
> to present, from time to time, something genuinely new. Under
> what I here call emergent evolution stress is laid on this
> incoming of the new. Salient examples are afforded in the
> advent of life, in the advent of mind, and in the advent of
> reflective thought. But in the physical world emergence is
> no less exemplified in the advent of each new kind of atom,
> and of each new kind of molecule. It is beyond the wit of man
> to number the instances of emergence. But if nothing new
> emerges--if there be only regrouping of pre-existing events
> and nothing more--then there is no emergent evolution....
>
> One starts, let us say, with electrons and the like; one
> sees in the atom a higher complex; one sees in the molecule
> a yet higher complex; one sees in a quartz-crystal, along its
> line of advance, a still more complex entity; and one sees in
> an organism, along its line of advance, an entity with the
> different kind of complexity spoken of as vital integration.[20]

In his alternate term, General Smuts emphasized the achievement of the emergentistic process of nature in producing new and
higher, or more complicated functioning wholes of being. The
cardinal fact which Smuts cites is "the synthetic tendency of the
universe," the tendency of the world process throughout its various levels to come, and to stay together for enduring periods of
time. With this observation as the empirical basis of his thought
Smuts postulates a metaphysical principle, Holism, which underlies

---

19. From the standpoint of a non-theistic naturalist and
     logician see Ernest Nagel's open discussion of "emer-
     gence" and "holism" in The Structure of Science,
     Harcourt, Brace, & World, 1961, pp. 366-97. Holism:
     from the Greek holos, whole, entire.
20. Emergent Evolution, Henry Holt and Co., 1926, pp. 1-2,
     12, emphasis his.

this tendency. He wrote:

> ...Holism...underlies the synthetic tendency in the universe,
> and is the principle which makes for the origin and progress
> of wholes in the universe.... This whole-making or holistic
> tendency is fundamental in nature...it has a well-marked
> ascertainable character, and.... Evolution is nothing but
> the gradual development and stratification of progressive
> series of wholes, stretching from the inorganic beginnings
> to the highest levels of spiritual creation.[21]

---

21. Holism and Evolution, The Macmillan Co., 1926, p. v.
     Smuts continued with the following illustrations of the
     holistic principle operative in nature:
         "The newt forms a new leg in the place of the
     severed limb. The plant supplies the place of the
     severed branch with another. The regeneration may be
     effected from different organs. Thus if the crystalline
     lens is removed from the eye of a Triton, the iris will
     regenerate a new lens, although the lens and the iris
     in this case have been evolved from quite different
     parts. Numerous similar curious facts of restoration
     could be mentioned. The broken whole in organic nature
     restores itself or is restored by the undamaged parts.
     The cells of the remaining parts set themselves the
     novel task of restoring the missing parts. The power
     to do this varies with various plants or animals, and
     varies also with the different parts in the same plant
     or animal. Generally one may say that the more highly
     differentiated and specialized an organism or a cell is,
     the smaller is its plasticity, or the power of the
     remaining cells to restore the whole in case of injury
     or mutilation. But the fact that the power exists in
     numerous cases is a proof that not only can the cells
     through reproduction build up the original organism
     according to its specific type, but also that when this
     type is damaged, the remaining cells or some of them
     can restore it, and recomplete the whole.... The very
     nature of the cells is to function as parts of a whole,
     and when the whole is broken down an unusual extra task
     automatically arises for them to restore the breach,
     and their dormant powers are arounsed to action....
         "The aspects of co-ordination or subordination of
     parts to the whole is also most significantly illustrated
     by the phenomena of reproduction.... For in reproduction
     the cell or the organism clearly appears to look beyond
     itself, its functions become transcendent, as far as it
     is itself concerned; its efforts and energies are bent
     on objects and purposes beyond itself. In fact, in

To "emerge" as a common verb has meant "to come into view from obscurity or concealment...to come out of some enfolding medium...to pass from obscure to superior condition."[22] Amplified into the philosophic generality of the philosophers just cited, an emergent is something novel; it is a new, unforeseen quality or value. It is not just a resultant, as for example, might be foreseen or anticipated lying at the end of a mathematical summation. It represents a jump 'up' to a new level of being or energy, a wider or higher synthesis of quality. Hydrogen and oxygen combine to form water. Neither of these original elements has the properties or characteristics of water. Hydrogen burns fiercely and oxygen causes things to burn; whereas water quenches fire. The compound, H_2O, seems a new, "higher whole," or integrated unity, with new and unpredictable (?) properties or "values." (Indeed, the combining of hydrogen and oxygen into water may stand as an analogy of the origin of all qualities and 'values.' Qualities and values have their origin and initial meaning in the properties of the emergent wholes that describe the integrative or evolutionary process of nature.)

Hydrogen, carbon, oxygen, nitrogen, and a few other life elements combine to make the marvelous creative synthesis which is life. Life is an emergent energy with peculiar properties: namely those of growth, reproduction, repair, spontaneity of action and reaction relative to environment, having the capacity of transforming exterior inorganic energies into sensory experiences and values, giving living forms awareness of their environment, and accordingly some command or freedom over it. In the thought of these men, the various forms of sentient awareness would be themselves examples of emergent realities. For example, the animal eye interacts with a certain type of cosmic radiation (a ray of light) to produce color and sight, experiences which are essentially emergent wholes, brought into being by the interaction of various energy forms or forces. Similarly, all other sense values or qualities are created as emergents; they emerge into being, by the interplay of organic and environmental processes.

---

reproduction the cell or the organism bears clear testimony to the fact that it is not itself alone, and that it is part of a larger whole of life towards the fulfillment of which its most fundamental functions are directed.... Here more than anywhere else the importance of the whole as an operative factor appears, not merely the immediate whole or individual organism, but also the transcendent whole or the type which has to be reproduced and maintained at all costs." (HE, pp. 80-82)

22. As phrased at the primary language level by Little and Ives Webster's Dictionary, 1957-58, p. 415.

Finally, life in its highest synthesis of mind or personality constitutes a supreme type of 'emergent whole,' the emergentistic philosophers have characteristically said. It comes to be as a higher synthesis of energies; it emerges from forces interacting within the brain, along the nerve or sensory receptors, stimulated by the brain's interactivity with the outer environment. The peculiar quality of mind as emergent activity in the form of "spiritual energy"[23] is its own life of thought, that is, its capacity for abstract thinking, or reasoning, for having ideas, exercising imagination and forethought; including its sensory and emotional tonicity as an experiencing self. This sense of self is profoundly expressed in the self's capacity for conceiving or being aware of values, having plans and purposes in order to bring the future under a command of realized value, or good for itself, in the form of truth, beauty, material security, and love.

We said above that Smuts focused particularly on the _product_ of the emergence phenomenon, that is, the various levels or new _wholes_ that appear. Smaller energy centers or events (electrons, protons, neutrons, positrons, etc.) integrate into atoms; atoms into more complex units, or molecules, inorganic and organic. Holism, like a superordinate and hierarchic field of force, elicits the emergence of the various ranges of organic or living substances. The cell is an area of holism; germ cells integrate or wholize into the various organs of the body. Major organs, and the body altogether, are each greater functioning wholes at higher planes than separate cells. Thirdly, there are the psychic, mental, spiritual, moral, and aesthetic echelons of holism, as above outlined. The ultimate world of holism, according to Smuts, is expressed in human personality, and the system of human values that human personality creates and looks out upon, including the wider social and institutional wholes where values are preserved. (These modern philosophical expressions, emergence and holism, remind us in part of Aristotle's word "Actuality," which meant essentially the principle of material, cosmic integration toward form, as previously described.)

Unlike Morgan in his works on emergence, or Whitehead in his version of the integrative process, Smuts, in _Holism and Evolution_, did not refer to the term "God" as the ultimate description or explanation of process. For Smuts, although there are wider social and institutional wholes where human values are preserved, there is no all-inclusive Cosmic Whole beyond or prior to human personality and the institutional values it creates. There is no

---

23. See our "The Meaning of Mind Transcendency in a Religious Philosophy of Man," _The International Journal for Philosophy of Religion_, Spring 1973.

primordial Unity or trans-human Whole to the world, to which one
might assign the idea of cosmic Consciousness or Mind. To Smuts
there is finite "holism" as a natural or cosmic process at work
primordially in nature, prior to the arrival of man, and coming to
highest expression in him and his civilization. Smuts does not
explain <u>why</u> there is the principle of holism. Apparently he wishes
to remain strictly an 'empirical observer,' uncommitted to further
metaphysical speculation. He simply sees holism as the principle
immanent in the facts and describes it. He does not ask why the
universe is directed toward wholizing itself in its various ways,
and supremely in personality--except vaguely to say that the
coming of finite minds like the human answers the general appetite
of cosmic process for greater wholistic organization.

As left with Smuts, Holism is itself an abstract, impersonal
term or force, perhaps in a class with Bergson's <u>élan</u> <u>vital</u> (in the
latter's <u>Creative Evolution</u>) or Schopenhauer's unconscious Will,
the driving force within nature, manifest in her upheaval into
form. Using the term as a clue for a more theistic point of view,
however, Holism may be viewed (though not for <u>Holism and Evolution</u>)
as part of the evidence of Cosmic Purpose, and Cosmic Mind that
such purpose implies, as indeed evolutionary theists such as
Morgan, Whitehead, Teilhard, and many others, have so conceived
reality.

The concepts of 'holism' and 'emergence,' whether expressly
used as terms, or substituted by some synonymous idiom, is by no
means a dated point of view, confined to the twenties or the
thirties of this century. It is sometimes found for example, as
a conceptualization of scientific workers themselves (entirely
apart from any religious or theistic emphasis). For example, we
refer in our note below to the description of things by John
Keosian, biologist, in his <u>The Origin of Life</u>, 1968. This book
presents the recent history of the artificial synthesis of "all
kinds of organic compounds...abiotically under a variety of
conditions" in the scientific laboratory.[24] It outlines an

---

24.   Second Edition, Chapman-Reinhold, 1968, p. 39. Beside
       its descriptive purpose, the major effort of this study
       is to show how modern biological science, working in the
       above field of experimentation, has effectively demon-
       strated that there is no demarcation line between the
       so-called 'living' realm and the so-called level of the
       non living, or of dead 'matter.' In light of the suc-
       cess of numerous contemporary experiments, outlined in
       this book, the presumption of many biologists is that
       organic molecules and compounds arose 'naturally' from

emergentistic rationale of the evolution of life, in order to
explain evolution, and the import of these modern experiments.

more primitive levels, or out of less organized or less
integrated, earlier situations chemically on the earth's
surface. Proceeding in this vein, and rising to the
level of philosophic perspective a number of times in
this work, under the heading "A Materialistic Outlook,"
Keosian continues to describe the natural process of
the integration of organic compounds from less complex
structures in the following emergentistic terms:
"The materialistic hypothesis took a different approach in applying natural laws to the explanation of the
origin of life... Instead of a chance getting-together of
the elements to form a living thing all at once, materialism viewed the origin of life as the result of a series
of probable steps of increasing complexity, inevitably
leading up to the living state. According to this hypothesis, each successive step resulted in a higher level of
organization of matter possessing properties, activities,
and principles that did not exist at the lower levels.
With the advent of organisms, biological principles came
into being which did not exist at a lower level of organization. From the materialist view, the origin of life
was no remote accident; it was the result of matter
evolving to higher and higher levels through the inexorable working out at each level of the inherent potentialities to arrive at the next level." (pp. 10-11)
"This apparent confusion reflects the necessity of
recognizing the gradual transition of matter into higher
and higher levels of organization embodying newer and more
complex properties. One's definition of life may then
lead to the acceptance of a particular level of organization of matter as a 'living' state but not any level below
it, whereas another's definition may accept a different
level, either higher or lower, as the starting point.
What is important is not an exact definition of life at
the borderline, but rather the recognition, of the existence of increasing levels of organization of matter, and
the understanding of the mechanisms which operate to
bring each of these about. In other words, it would
appear more sensible to approach the problem of the origin
of life not as an attempt to discover the precise point
at which lifeless matter gave rise to the 'first living
things,' but rather as an examination of the mechanisms
oprating in the transition of matter on this earth to
higher and higher levels of organization." (p. 15)
"In the present era many abiotic, organic chemical
events, preliminary to the appearance of living things,
have already been elucidated. Still, life is often

In their <u>American Philosophies of Religion,</u> Henry Nelson
Wieman and Bernard Eugene Meland wrote of the importance of the
concept of emergence to contemporary cosmological philosophy:

looked upon as something more than the chemical systems
that manifest the properties characterized by that term.
This is the result of our holding tenaciously to old ways
of thinking through which we continue to interpret new
findings. These findings confirm earlier inklings that
matter has self-organizing properties,..." (p. 88).

"The thing to bear in mind most urgently is that each
level of organization has its own properties by which
alone it can best be recognized. Also, each higher level,
although incorporating 'structures and processes evolved
at the lower levels,' has new properties not predictable
from the properties of the lower level. This is true of
the whole progression from fundamental particles, atoms,
and molecules to man. Each stage in that progression
incorporates structures and properties of the lower level
but emerges as a new stage with new properties <u>and a pro-
pensity of arriving at a higher level of organization.</u>
Where does life fit in this progression? Nowhere. It
makes little sense to attempt to squeeze anywhere into
this gradual sequence of atages of matter a nebulous unde-
finable something called 'life,' which presumably breaks
this gradual sequence abruptly into two groups--inanimate
and living. That would be the essence of vitalism
clothed in mechanistic terms....

"We recognize a vast variety of forms of life at
various levels of structural complexity reflecting a
corresponding functional and biochemical complexity.
Yet we strive paradoxically to find a single meaningful
scientific definition of all life. If matter, driven by
energy, does go inexorably to higher and higher levels
of organization in an unbroken chain, it would be impossible to draw a line so that those systems on one side
are all 'inanimate' and those on the other side 'living.'
Any serious attempt to do so will drive the line more
on the 'inanimate' side. One could even reach a point
where K.M. Madison's concept of 'living' would hold:
'things as simple as two inorganic reactions meet the
definition.'

"The terms of life and living were at first lay
terms and in that context had the vaguest of boundaries.
For centuries science has been attempting to sharpen the
boundaries; to this day attempts continue unsuccessfully.
This marked lack of success is a measure of proof that

Almost coincidentally with the development of operational concepts in modern physics, and the emphasis upon pattern in Gestalt psychology, modern biology has been formulating a new conception of environment, representing man and life, not in environment, but as environment. Out of this convergence of organismic thinking has developed a concept that has become the key-word of the new idealism, emergence. In this concept, contemporary philosophers of religion who continue the tradition of natural theology have a suggestive insight that may forever break the spell of the mechanistic outlook. The concept of emergence is an important insight, and it is destined to have an influence upon modern thought, comparable to the influence that the concept of orderliness and natural law had upon the thinking of the period when the scientific movement first made itself felt, and that the concept of evolution had upon the thought of the late nineteenth century. Modern philosophy has already appropriated its insight with impressive vigor.[25]

With this recent history in mind, then, of an important descriptive model of evolutionary thought, we may now return to the Whitehead expression of it, and, within the scope of our introductory purpose, look doubtless with somewhat more certain light on his special idiom.

Take almost any extended passage, from Whitehead's philosophical works, examine it closely and the expositor can perceive the outline of his thinking. For this purpose we here refer to his essay "Forms of Process" (Lecture V from Modes of Thought), a microcosm of his process philosophy, and a good base from which to mount a further assent upon his thought.

Whitehead's predominating purpose as philosopher is, on the one hand, "to explain the trend towards order" as "the overwhelming deliverance of experience," and on the other, "to explain ...the frustration of order" (p. 120); the manifest coming together into "modes of unity," "organization" (p. 117), "experiences...of association" (p. 141), and oppositely, the evident separation of things. Therefore, in the descriptive vocabulary regarding being, "process" is "fundamental" (p. 121): "...each ultimate individual fact must be describable as process," because

---

matter goes through a continuous hierarchy of increasingly complex stages, and that there is indeed one evolution, the evolution of matter, even to the level of reasoning power." (pp. 89-90, emphases his)

25. 1936, Willett, Clark, pp. 50-51, emphases theirs.

we cannot think of matter or reality in the "abstract" (with its coming into order and its passing out of order) apart from "time" (pp. 120-21). Being is not static: "...no actuality is a static fact.... The universe is not a museum with its specimens in glass cases. Nor is the universe a perfectly drilled regiment with its ranks in step, marching forward with undisturbed poise" (p. 123). Consequently, the verb "to be" means "historic" transitions, from past, to now, to future (p. 121).

> The essence of existence lies in the transition from datum to issue. ... 'existence' (in any of its senses) cannot be abstracted from 'process.' The notions of 'process' and 'existence' presuppose each other. (p. 131)

Be it noted also that the process and transition take place with a certain openness and indeterminacy--and more on this later.

Further, you cannot have "process" in the abstract--bare process--rather something has to flow, or be in process, for there to be meaning to being as process. To use our own figure, for the moment, a river cannot flow without its water, that is, the individual droplets or elements and qualities of the water as a particular substance. Hence the concept of "individuality," having already appeared above, is integral to the meaning of being, and must be emphasized always with process, inseparable from it and vice versa (p. 133).

> Process and individuality require each other. In separation all meaning evaporates...every individual thing infects any process in which it is involved, and thus any process cannot be considered in abstraction from particular things involved. (p. 133).

To join now the basic awareness of "order" with the basic awareness of "process," to think order--or process as orderly-- is to perceive "forms harboured in the nature of things" (p. 121). "Form" and "order" are synonymous. Forms of order constitute the "existence" of individuals (p. 135), for we perceive "stability of character amidst the succession of facts" (p. 135). At this point a further principle, "potentiality" emerges. For, if "the notion of process is admitted," then "the notion of potentiality is fundamental for the understanding of existence..." (p. 136). Whitehead continues to explain in a beautifully illuminating paragraph:

> The notion of potentiality is fundamental for the understanding of existence, as soon as the notion of process is admitted. If the universe be interpreted in terms of static

actuality, then potentiality vanishes. Everything is just
what it is. Succession is mere appearance, rising from the
limitation of perception. But if we start with process as
fundamental, then the actualities of the present are deriving
their characters from the process, and are bestowing their
characters upon the future. Immediacy is the realization of
the potentialities of the past, and is the storehouse of the
potentialities of the future. Hope and fear, joy and dis-
illusion, obtain their meaning from the potentialities
essential in the nature of things. We are following a trail
in hope, or are fleeing from the pursuit in fear. The potentialities in immediate fact constitute the driving force of
process. (pp. 136-7)

The foregoing developing system of ideas now takes a major
turn to acknowledge the "alternative metaphysical doctrine,"
already hinted. It is that there is a side "of reality devoid of
process," "the obviousness...of factors in the universe to which
the notion of process does not apply" (p. 137); there is present
"timeless fact."

It is precisely with this double faceted assertion, at this
stage made, emphasizing (1) individualities flowing into formed
or ordered character, thus disclosing the potentialities of
things, and (2) the announcement that there is, after all, a fixed
or more permanent side of being; in these two points we begin to
arrive at Whitehead's understanding of "God" or the Divine--as the
eternal ground that harbors all possible form or potentiality,
which natural individualities in their fluency may assume for a
time in vividness of "experience." God is expressly discussed in
the chapter as "The reservoir of potentiality and the coordination
of achievement" (p. 128). Accordingly, citing his debt to Samuel
Alexander's view of Deity, and relating the processive, temporal
side and the static spacial side of things, Whitehead continues
with this perception--

Time refers to the transitions of process, Space refers to the
static necessity of each form of interwoven existence, and
Deity expresses the lure of the ideal which is the potentiality beyond immediate fact.
Apart from Time there is no meaning for purpose, hope,
fear, energy. If there be no historic process, then everything is what it is, namely a mere fact. Life and motion are
lost. Apart from Space, there is no consummation. Life
expresses the halt for attainment. It symbolizes the complexity of immediate realization. It is the fact of accomplishment. Time and Space express the universe as including
the essence of transition and the success of achievement.

The transition is real, and the achievement is real. The
difficulty is for language to express one of them without
explaining away the other. (pp. 139-40)

Finally, there is Deity, which is the factor in the
universe whereby there is importance, value, and ideal beyond
the actual.... There must be value beyond ourselves.... We
owe to the sense of Deity the obviousness of the many acuali-
ties of the world, and the obviousness of the unity of the
world for the preservation of the values realized and for the
transition to ideals beyond realized fact. (p. 140)

From this microcosm of his philosophy leading terms have
emerged, basic to his conception of being. Two of these have been
"individuality" and "form." Individuality has, in more technical
expression, appeared in Whitehead's works as "entity," "actual
entities," "actual occasions," and form, has appeared as "eternal
object." For our own exposition, then, we may now transmute the
terms individuality and form into these further expressions,
reflecting Whitehead's own purpose of attempting to describe
things with greater philosophic precision. Accordingly, we read
in the earlier work, <u>Process and Reality</u>, that "actual entities
and eternal objects stand out" with particular importance among
the "categories" or metaphysical descriptions of things (p. 33).
(The term "God" will recur again later with similar importance.)

It now will be instructive to look at certain of his definitions concerning such terms as "actual entities" and "eternal
objects," as we continue to pursue his idea of being through the
medium of these expressions. From PR:--

'Actual entities'--also termed 'actual occasions'--are
the final real things of which the world is made up. There
is no going behind actual entities to find anything.... The
final facts are, all alike, actual entities; and these actual
entities are drops of experience, complex and interdependent.
(pp. 27-8)

Among these eight categories of existence [which he has
just listed], actual entities and eternal objects stand out
with a certain extreme finality. (p. 33)

...<u>how</u> an actual entity <u>becomes</u> constitutes <u>what</u> that entity
<u>is</u>.... Its 'being' is constituted by its 'becoming.' This
is the 'principle of process'. (pp. 34-5)

An entity is actual, when it has significance for itself.
By this it is meant that an actual entity functions in respect

to its own determination.   Thus an actual entity combines
self-identity with self-diversity.   (p. 38)

Each actual entity is conceived as an act of experience
arising out of data.   It is a process of 'feeling' the many
data, so as to absorb them into the unity of the one individual 'satisfaction.'   (p. 65)

...the process of becoming...is constituted by the influx of
eternal objects into a novel determinateness of feeling which
absorbs the actual world into a novel actuality.   (p. 72)

An actual entity is a process in the course of which
many operations with incomplete subjective unity terminate in
a completed unity of operation, termed the 'satisfaction.'
(p. 335)

The term 'subject' has been retained because in this
sense it is familiar in philosophy. But it is misleading.
The term 'superject' would be better. The subject-superject
is the purpose of the process originating the feelings. The
feelings are inseparable from the end at which they aim; and
this end is the feeler. (p. 339)

...an actual entity satisfies Spinoza's notion of substance;
it is <u>causa sui</u>.... All actual entities share with God this
characteristic of self-causation. (p. 339)

Self-realization is the ultimate fact of facts. An
actuality is self-realizing, and whatever is self-realizing
is an actuality. An actual entity is at once the subject of
self-realization, and superject which is self-realized.
(p. 340)

A feeling is the appropriation of some elements in the
universe to be components in the real internal constitution
of its subject. The elements are the initial data; they are
what the feeling feels.   (p. 353)

The world is self-creative; and the actual entity as
self-creating creature passes into its immortal function of
part-creator of the transcendent world. In its self-creation
the actual entity is guided by its ideal of itself as individual satisfaction and as transcendent creator. The enjoyment of this ideal is the 'subjective aim,' by reason of which
the actual entity is a determinate process.
This subjective aim is not primarily intellectual; it is
the lure for feeling. (p. 130)

In the above quotations describing how an "actual entity" (or individuality) comes to be, the word "feeling" appears as prominent in the process, along with "eternal objects," or forms; or in still more general terms, 'ideas' (the latter term not preferred by Whitehead, because, he says, of its too "subjective suggestion in modern philosophy" (PR, p. 70). We have already pointed out that Whitehead's more technical term for feeling is "prehension" and discussed that expression briefly on pages 9f of this commentary, in reviewing Royce's and Whitehead's conception of phenomenal nature. There, it will be recalled, we indicated that Whitehead did not regard prehensive experience, or "feeling" as always of the conscious or intellectual type--rather he implies that indeed the majority of prehensive experiences are less than conscious. This point is stressed in his dictum "that consciousness presupposes experience, and not experience consciousness" (PR p. 83, see also pp. 130, 355).

Accordingly, while we see a remarkable parallel in the above sequence of Whitehead texts to the Royce view of how individuality comes to be, or how essentially we must define being--namely, as the process of the purpose within "ideas" (Royce), or 'prehensive feelings' (Whitehead), precipitating themselves or building themselves up into concrete actuality or individualities, termed now by Whitehead actual entities or actual occasions; we here stress that this process of the formation of being is thought out in Whitehead more cautiously. He accepts the idea of less-than-conscious prehension or less-than-conscious teleological aims as characterizing the primal impulses of the many "entities," which Royce thought not to be the case. (Recall our previous reflection upon this difference in their outlook, pages 9f of this commentary). In form, however--while acknowledging this relatively important difference of viewpoint on this issue--Royce and Whitehead have both wrought along very similar, and in many salient respects, identical lines about the origin and nature of being. As in Royce, so in Whitehead, we hear that "In its self-creation the actual entity is guided by its ideal of itself as individual satisfaction..." (emphasis ours), and "All actual entities share with God this characteristic of self-causation" (PR p. 339). In other words, for both men, "Being" on both levels (the finite and the Divine) is characterized by the same type of teleological self formation.[26]

---

26.   Seminal phraseology along the same lines referring to the theory of 'being' is used again in his chapter on Feelings, where describing the doctrine of 'feeling' as "the central doctrine respecting the becoming of an actual entity," Whitehead concludes that "the term

(The discussion at this place anticipates our further exposition of Royce and Whitehead on human "selfhood" along these lines, taken up in Part II. Here we leave these further details for the time being to return to several other general points concerning Whitehead's world view which as yet have remained obscure.)

So far we have been looking at Whitehead's general theory of being. This theory describes world process as "creativity." That is to say, there is the possibility of many actual entities of lesser or fragmentary character emerging, or coming into ever more complete groupings of "occasions," and "societies" of occasions, as spurred by "subjective aim." Subjective aims are the purposes, the teleological feelings or appetites (not necessarily conscious) for fellow entities. From these associations each gains, at its new emergent level, a new novel "satisfaction." Where we read (using terms from various passages) that the lure for the ongoing of this process of "concretion" or "concrescence" into higher complexities of actual entities is the "ingression of eternal objects" (PR p. 131), we are at one of the more abstract heights of Whitehead's vocabulary. His 1925 essays, "Abstraction" and "God," (in Science and the Modern World, written prior to Religion in the Making and Process and Reality), help to clarify his meaning at this elevation. He wrote:

...the metaphysical status of an eternal object is that of a possibility for an actuality. Every actual occasion is defined as to its character by how these possibilities are actualized for that occasion. (p. 159)

...actual occasions are selections from the realm of possibilities. (p. 164)

It is clear by this context that "a possibility for an actuality" is any conceivable quality (or "emergent value") such as colors, a shade of "red" or "green" (to imploy his own illustrations), a shape of "sphericity," and so on, that an object may have or assume. Obviously actual entities, or actual occasions-- that is, the objects or individualities of the real world--express complex hierarchies of such qualities, designated "eternal objects." In the chapter entitled "God," of the forementioned work, Whitehead summarizes his conception of the way "eternal objects" get expressed in "actual entities," or in the world's individualities. It incapsulates his whole conception of being. The passage reads:

'in being' is...equivalent to the term 'in realization.'"
(PR p. 356).

We conceive actuality as in essential relations to an unfathomable possibility. Eternal objects inform actual occasions with hierarchic patterns, included and excluded in every variety of discrimination. Another view of the same truth is that every actual occasion is a limitation imposed on possibility, and that by virtue of this limitation the particular value of the shaped togetherness of things emerges.... Actuality is through and through togetherness--togetherness of otherwise isolated eternal objects, and togetherness of all actual occasions....

Every actual occasion exhibits itself as a process: it is a becomingness.... It also defines itself as a particular individual achievement, focussing in its limited way an unbounded realm of eternal objects.

Any one occasion α issues from other occasions which collectively form its past.... It is in respect to its associated hierarchy, as displayed in this immediate present, that an occasion finds its own originality...its display in the present under those conditions is what directly emerges from its prehensive activity. The occasion α also holds within itself an indetermination in the form of a future....

This future is a synthesis in α of eternal objects as non-being and as requiring the passage from α to other individualizations...in which not-being becomes being. (SMW pp. 174-6, emphasis his)

So much, then, for the outline of his general theory of Being. But what beings now actually exist that illustrate this metaphysical description of things? We have already referred to the world's actual objects and individualities as exemplifying "being." But precisely to name several levels of such realities we move again to the Process and Reality text, where Whitehead refers to "electronic" and "protonic actual entities"; and "more ultimate actual entities" lower and dimmer even than these, "discerned in the quanta of energy" (p. 139). He speaks of "each electron" as "a society of electronic occasions" (p. 139), and so on for any such elemental particles, or energy occasions at atomic levels. Whitehead next refers to "living" societies or "life" as examples of actual occasions on the higher levels. Cells and organs and whole animal bodies are such hierarchies; and on to beings of "self-consciousness" or "persons," the "presiding personality" of a body (pp. 164-6). Modes of Thought presents a similar description of how "the different modes of natural existence shade off into each other"--in terms of superordinate or hierarchic patterns of control from "the animal life" down through its "society of cells," the cell's "republic of molecules," to the "infra-molecular," etc. (p. 215). A little later in this chapter, "Nature Alive," he refers to "our immediate occasion" as a "society of occasions forming the soul, and our soul is in our present occasion" (p. 227). These superordinate levels of hierarchically inhering entities or occasions follow from his major pronouncement (against Aristotle) that a 'substance' can be present in another 'subject,' or in Whitehead's own phraseology that an "actual entity is present in other actual entities" (PR pp. 79, 32, emphasis his).

(Whitehead frequently employs the terms "society" and "societies" apparently to describe particularly the more complex orders of actual occasions. He is by no means always clear as to where the term "actual occasion" might be more properly superseded by the expression "society," to designate the more complex organizations.)[27]

At any rate, and a point not yet touched upon in his theme of being as essentially a process of becoming, when actual entities are prehended by other actual entities; and particularly when entities are discussed as immanent or part of larger occasions and societies, they are conceived as having issued "from other occasions which collectively form" their "past." They have given up their independency, which has now perished. Their original aim is now completed, satisfied, or objectified in the life of the larger prehending occasions, and said to be immortalized there as a permanent value character of the more comprehensive unity. (This theme of "objective immortality" is discussed at some length on pages 226f., Part III, of this study, in connection with the general interpretation of immortality in Whitehead's philosophy.)

God is the ultimate and eternal actual entity whose "primordial" nature, or side, harbors the boundless variety of "eternal objects" or possible forms of being, which actual entities or individualities may express or embody, or more carefully described perhaps, for which actual entities provide the actual expression or embodiment.[28] The nature and position of the Divine in the cosmic order is to be subsequently examined at greater length in this study. In the meanwhile, keeping in mind the primacy of his

---

27. Not as clear, I believe, as William A. Christian implies on page 114 of his comprehensive commentary, An Interpretation of Whitehead's Metaphysics, Yale University Press, 1959. A quotation from Whitehead is there given which distinguishes between "societies" and "actual occasions" as between things which endure and things which perish (AI, The Macmillan Co., 1933, p. 262).
28. Cf. Christian, op. cit., Chap 10: "Objects and Events."

notion of <u>actual</u> entities and <u>prehension</u>, let us summarize for the moment Whitehead's philosophy of being.

A brief account of his theory of being, subsequent to that quoted on page 48 from <u>Science and the Modern World</u>, is found in <u>Religion in the Making</u> in a section entitled "A Metaphysical Description," where he discusses the human mind's basic awareness of things "passing in time" (i.e. as process) and the temporal process as taking on "formation," or having form (pp. 88-91). The three-fold, basically Platonic view of his cosmology now appears (recall our earlier exposition of Plato's <u>Timaeus</u> dialogue). The three aspects of things are, according to Whitehead, 1) "The Creativity"; 2) "The realm of ideal entities, or forms," with which we are now also familiar as "eternal objects"; and 3) "God" (p. 90). Beginning with these, a listing here follows with brief descriptions of Whitehead's further half dozen major terms, in addition to <u>actual</u> entities and <u>prehension</u>.

"<u>Creativity</u>": his highest metaphysical generality, "the universal of universals," "the ultimate metaphysical principle" (PR pp. 31-2); the principle of the possibility of the world's emergence into the many novelties or individualities. Creativity is the ultimate character which says the universe can and will have character or characters (i.e. formed beings). It is the highest logical premise with which to start the description of the world. To point to it reflects the rational instinct that only out of something can something come, that only out of eternal being can being come, (a type of insight which lies at the foundation of casual or cosmological arguments for God). Whitehead says that it is like Aristotle's notion of the basal, pure, or abstract "matter," or "υλη," out of which things come (PR pp. 46-7 and see SMW pp. 165-6). It is a dynamic category, however, rather than a passive receptivity," as it may have been in the original thought of Plato and Aristotle (PR pp. 46-7).[29]

"<u>Eternal Objects</u>": "the realm of ideal entities, or forms," above described. Recall Plato's doctrine of "ideas." For Whitehead, eternal objects are the limitless characters or qualities, emergent values, or feeling tones that finite individualities or actual entities or occasions may express or experience.

"<u>God</u>": "God is the principle of concretion; namely, he is that actual entity from which each temporal concrescence receives that initial aim from which its self-causation starts" (PR p. 374). Recall Plato's active <u>Demiourgos</u>, the creative God, who looked to

---

29. See our further discussion of the term "creativity,"
        pp. 144f.

the Ideas as patterns to form the material world. In so many
words Whitehead, as did Royce, is saying that God is the principle
of freedom itself in the universe (a topic to be expanded later
in our consideration of the idea of freedom in the light of theistic belief).

   "Concretion/concrescence": the converging upward of various
factors (subordinate, more fragmented or tenuous actual occasions)
into the emergent wholes of the world's many vectors or avenues
of individualizations, societies of individualizations and epochal
occasions, which is the concrete process of its growth.

   Each instance of concrescence is itself the novel individual
   'thing' in question.... An instance of concrescence is
   termed an 'actual entity' or, equivalently, an 'actual occasion'... ...an actual occasion is a concrescence effected by
   a process of feelings.... An actual occasion is nothing but
   the unity to be ascribed to a particular instance of concrescence... ...the process of integration...lies at the very
   heart of...concrescence.... (PR pp. 321-3, 347)

   "Subjective Aim": all ranges of the impulse to feel, or
prehend in all actual entities, from the highest or most organized
(as in the case of God himself) to the least, most attenuated
"puff of existence" in empty space--endowed by God in each such
instance. That ultimate quality of things which is striving,
teleological, or purposive (PR p. 130). In Process and Reality
where he was defining God as the principle of concretion,
Whitehead immediately continued:

   That aim, determines the initial gradations of relevance of
   eternal objects for conceptual feeling; and constitutes the
   autonomous subject in its primary phase of feelings with its
   initial conceptual valuations, and with its initial physical
   purposes. (PR p. 374)

   In sum thus far, this study has endeavored to point to a
parallel between the cosmological philosophies of Josiah Royce and
Alfred North Whitehead in several salient respects. First of all,
we have noticed their organismic conception of phenomenal nature.
Nature as a whole is to be described by the central paradigm of
"life." Things living, with basic categories of subjectivity, such
as "feeling," "experience," and "knowing," i.e. those internal
relations which experience that things are connected, are the best
clue to what reality in itself is. These organismic modes of
description serve the understanding better than do atomic, substan-
tive, or macroscopic masses and inertias, which the earlier modern

view, under the pragmatically successful inspiration of Newtonian
mechanism, asserted reality to be. Starting with <u>life</u> as model,
we may discover for understanding all the deeper ramifications of
nature (as symbolized in the involuted, complex probing itself of
Whitehead's <u>Process and Reality</u>)[30] in such a way as to include all
things, from atoms, to living beings, and on to stars, and even
God, in an ultimate philosophic perspective, and leave nothing out.
Whereas if we commence with gross and massive 'substances,' themselves ultimately stony and inert, in mechanical, that is, exter-
nally related motion only, as the basal paradigm for realities, we
will surely leave "life," and the whole of internal experience,
from feeling to consciousness, out of the ultimate descriptions;
with our philosophic attempt less than coherent, and empty of faith
in any transcending meaningfulness or purposefulness of existence.
The way of both Royce and Whitehead is to conceive things in the
alternative approach of <u>organism</u>.

Their major difference at this level appeared in the reluctance of Whitehead to go beyond the idea of "prehension" as a less-
than-conscious mode of "experience" for the vast majority of the
world's entities or individualities, in their various streams of
interflow and mutual sensitivity. Royce, however, was willing to
declare that no spark of individuality in howsoever microscopic or
tenuous form, at one extreme, or materially integrated, or macroscopic in form at another, was genuinely without "conscious"
awareness of its neighbor. He explained other types of consciousness than our own, each on their respective planes of perceptivity,
in terms of diverse time-senses of swiftness or slowness, as for
example the instantaneous beat of the atom or the geological age-
lessness of the pulse of the rock.

Secondly, as we peer a little more deeply into their theory
of being in this summing up glance, a corollary point to that of
the organismic and processive interpretation of nature is the
similarity of both philosophers in rejection of what Royce termed
"metaphysical realism," and we have called hard realism. Patently,
however, Whitehead stands nearer than Royce to the "realistic"

---

30. Whitehead's <u>Process and Reality</u> is as comprehensive as
     a galactic system. It contains swirls within swirls of
     brilliance, and opacity; and, pursuing the figure, its
     globular clusters naturally radiate from his own com-
     pression of thought and expression, around which the
     larger mass gravitates. For many for our time, scien-
     tific and religious people alike, this book has seemed
     to be, if not the system for the ages, at least for our
     epoch a true account of the cosmos, dynamically per-
     perceived, yielding a basis for faith in its purposive-
     ness and spirituality.

account of things, in his doctrine that some entities or individualities may have less-than-conscious "perceptions" or prehensions,
that is, "experiences" that are below the threshold of conscious
experience. (I put it this way, because if there are supposed
"feelings" among sub-human and sub-animal entities or individualities of a type below the <u>conscious</u> <u>feelings</u> with which human beings
and animals are acquainted, those extra human and animal entities--
by virtue of a vast, near absolute difference in degree from us in
this respect--would be in their most intimate and subjective
characteristics of "being" essentially unknown or alien to us, and
probably to themselves.[31] They would be "reals," in fundamental
quality standing out and apart, and other from us, which Royce
believed he could not allow in his own description of things.
Accordingly, I am fairly sure at this point that Royce himself
would have probably called Whitehead a "realist" and subjected him
to the criticism of his "Independent Beings" essay--at least at the
point where Whitehead allowed unconscious "experience"). Be that
possibility as it may, we continue.

Thirdly, moving now into their advanced theory of being as
such, we find that both men, rejecting hard or atomistic realism,
utilize the classic Platonic philosophy of "ideas" in similar, but
also in distinctive, fashion. The similarity between them is evident in the growth of both of their philosophic outlooks (relative
to their central definitions of being) from Plato's doctrine of
ideas. Both want to get away from <u>abstractionism</u>, and assert that
the description of the world order is not ultimately best done by
pointing to bare "laws," logical abstractions, forms, universals,
or, in short, abstract ideas or essences, of whatever range,
mathematical, logical, biological, or social. The universe is not
just an interlocking system of circles and geometric abstractions,
or other bodiless forms, species, and genera. It may be these
things but in addition, it is, at least centers of being, that is,
"individualities," or "actual entities" (the core, parallel terms
for both Royce and Whitehead). Indeed for Whitehead, enunciated
in his "ontological principle," there is nothing beyond or higher
in being than actual entities or individualities themselves; and
Royce himself in his critique of the Third Conception of Being, or
Platonic abstractionism, clearly embraced the same "ontological
principle." The common denominator of their thought is their
identical accounting of being as individuality in terms of the
striving of the various individualized streams of process toward

---

31.   I would say that trees and plant life, and unicellular
organisms, must be viewed as having a degree of "conscious" feeling, however dim we may imagine that to be
at those levels.

the fulfillment of "purpose," that is, of interior, internal <u>aims</u>
(Whitehead) or acts of <u>will</u> (Royce). Royce phrased it as the
"internal meaning of ideas," seeking to fulfill or actualize themselves. Whitehead depicts actual entities, aiming to inform themselves with the eternal objects or the primordial ideas. For the
latter these possibilities of formation and order may be raised
up out of the abstract "creativity," that is, the cosmic potentialities of things (ultimately associated with the "unconscious,"
primordial 'mind' of God) by the various aims of actual entities.
When Whitehead, as his basic view of the individuation process,
asserts that:

> In its self-creation the actual entity is guided by its
> ideal of itself as individual satisfaction... (PR p. 130),

I find a nearly identical proclamation in Royce, at an earlier
point in time, in such a statement (compounded from two) as:

> ...an individual being is a Life of Experience fulfilling
> Ideas***an idea or will fulfilled by a wholly adequate
> empirical content...of...satisfied idea....[32]

A divergence of attitude from the Platonic base of their
philosophy may be noticed, when we realize that Whitehead ultimately gives to the "realm of eternal objects" (viz, the possibilities of all forms of existence) a status of impersonal mind
in the eternal, primordial, and unconscious side of God's nature;
whereas Royce wished to shatter forever this kind of outlook.
Royce sought to disperse the abstract radiance of a Platonic
eternity, or heaven of ideas of this kind, into the actual fact
of the eternity of the cosmic order conceived as an integral
system of concrete individualities, to wit, our own, along with
nature's many forms of individuality, within a Divine Individuality. Ideas have no ultimate status apart from the minds and
wills of personal beings themselves, says Royce. The Platonic
ideas, as bare ideas, that is to say, as mere abstract "universals" or "validities," are only a provisional myth of philosophic
language, through which philosophy must finally work its way.
It must leave behind (however suggestive and inspiring the moment
of the passage) such outmoded "Third Conception of Being." His
Fourth Conception of Being, as we learned, averred that the cosmic
order has always been <u>individual</u>, or <u>realized</u> <u>truth</u>, rather than

---

32.   Excerpted in the following order from the two central
       chapters on the subject in WI, Vol. I, Lecture VIII,
       "The Fourth Conception of Being," and Lecture VII, "The
       Internal and External Meaning of Ideas," pp. 348, 337.

just abstract or anticipated truth (and he will finally say, on
his side, eternally Personal truth). In his cosmology, Whitehead
remains in major respects essentially Platonic, in the original
sense of that adjective, though he strives valiantly to overcome,
or to meet the problem of individuality inherent in the original
Plato, which Plato himself left unresolved.

To amplify briefly, in retaining "primordial God" where
eternal objects are abstractly 'stored' as the possible, impersonal archetypes of eventual concrete beings or entities, Whitehead sides with the historic Plato, whereas Royce breaks with
Plato more completely in the effort to construct an integrated
Personal idealism. On the other hand, as previously suggested,
in his "ontological principle" announcing that the ultimate
reasons for being are actual entities or individualities themselves, and that in fact nothing lies behind them or anterior to
them, Whitehead approaches Royce's modification of original
Platonism, respecting its doctrine of abstract (and impersonal?)
ideas. Royce implied that such Platonism, or critical rationalism, might be accepted as high myth only--the starting place
for an adequate philosophical conception of things, but by no
means its conclusion. Which man breaks with the Platonic thrall,
or utilizes it more effectively for the philosophic needs of the
modern scientific age, the reader must decide for himself. Certainly Royce and Whitehead are not radically opposed in their
interpretation of Plato. Indeed, if we stress the aspect of
Whitehead's thought which he called the ontological principle,[33]
we can read him as substantially in agreement with Royce, in a
fundamental respect in the manner suggested in this paragraph.

If this be the correct way to interpret Whitehead, then, to
be sure, both men are essentially followers of Aristotle at this
place, stressing the conception, as the Scholastics phrased it,
of universals in things, rather than universals as prior to
things.

Up to this point the study has anticipated further dimensions
of the parallel between Royce and Whitehead, such as their dynamic
processive, non-substantive view of human selfhood or personal
being, or as telic energy (to apply our own idiom); their common
view of God as Personal, or at least, of the personal as being
part of the meaning of the Divine; the problems of freedom and
evil; their similar methods as empirical rationalists, or

---

33. Discussed in PR, pp. 27-8, 36-7, etc.

rationalistic empiricists, and so on. We now venture to turn to these special topics, which this review of their general interpretation of nature and theory of being has touched from time to time.

Part II

THE IDEA OF MAN OR HUMAN SELFHOOD

Chapter Three

ROYCE ON SELFHOOD

In this part we discuss the similarities of Royce's and
Whitehead's philosophical psychologies, viz, their ideas of man,
or the self and human personality.

Both philosophers describe man's selfhood or personality in
what we have called several times in our own terms, telic process,
or alternatively telic energy. Negatively stated first, these
philosophers disavow the older style spiritual substance, tran-
scendentalist and simplistic view of soul-spirit as more or less
passive, immaterial, timeless, by definition immortal interior
unit (e.g. the Vedanta and Sankhya Hindus, Plato, Descartes,
Locke). Positively expressed, in general terms, along with many
other contemporary philosophers and psychologists, Royce and
Whitehead embrace an essentially 'personalistic theory' of mind
and human selfhood, as holistic, functioning process, as unity-
amid-complexity, as telic energy or drive, which comes into its
own fullest or highest sense of "being," self-realization or selfhood, as the outcome of personal goal-seeking, of driving toward
chosen ends--in the classic thought of Royce, as acts of "will"
seeking to realize aims, purposes, ideas, and ideals. Selfhood
is teleological process.[1]

Among many such definitions, throughout Royce's writings, of
the process that constitutes personal being we select the following as typical.

---

1. We are speaking here of a general similarity of person-
    ality theory among many scholars in company with Royce
    and Whitehead (e.g. Bowne, Lewin, Allport, Heidegger).
    They all referred in their varying idiom to man's higher
    conscious awareness as witnessing to the sense of Self-
    hood as telic striving and dynamic unity-in-process, or
    process coming into an ultimate sense of unity and per-
    sonhood. In his Gifford Lectures, even C.A. Campbell,
    while using traditional language in describing man as
    "spiritual substance" (suggesting a Cartesian dualism),

"Being," or "individuality," he wrote--and we are here pointing first to the "being" involved in our own sense of self, selfhood, and personality--"is...the expression of Selective Interest" (WI 1 p. 455). And again, "Individuality is a category of the satisfied Will" (WI 2 p. 432). Personal being in our own cases (as also in the larger life of God, he believed) is "idea" focusing or precipitating itself into concrete actuality through will or purposive activity. Or in slightly different terms, personal being comes to be as ideas (that is, plans, purposes, ideals) will their individuality or concrete realization in actualized life.

Here is a definition, it seems to us, which describes with exact insight what in fact human beings are, are doing, and hope to be, from the standpoint of their own interior (or existential) awareness of themselves as persons: we as 'selves' are a teleological process coming into focus or 'reality' only through growth toward realization of some one, or a few, supreme life plan(s). We have seen how Royce elaborated this point in his more technical terms of the "internal meaning of ideas" (the element of will or purposiveness in ideas) becoming actualized or realized in their "external meaning"--that is, in their truth judgments, and in their creative achievements (pp. 28-30 of this commentary).

Any life has to limit, narrow, focus, let fall away extraneous, or supernumerous, ideas, plans, ambitions, hopes, expectations, into some one or a few viable options, which we may then strive to realize or achieve. At the end of this development and while in the progress, we 'find ourselves,' as we say, the actual person that we gradually become--the teacher, lawyer, politician,

---

betrays his essential modernity in this regard in the following processive account of selfhood, admirable for its lucidity:
"The person _is_ the self, _qua_ functioning in terms of its definitive and normal character. Indeed the person, so far from being an entity different from the self, may be said to be something which the self tends gradually to become. The self starts upon its career with a variety of native instincts, impulses and capacities closely dependent upon its association with a particular animal body. Through the self's actions upon and reactions to its physical and social environment on the basis of these given propensities and powers, the relatively stable system of dispositions we call its 'character' is gradually built up, and the self grows into what we call a 'person.'" (On Selfhood and Godhood, George Allen & Unwin, 1957, pp. 88-89)

mountain climber, model railroad enthusiast, husband, wife, League of Women Voters member, and so on. To employ some of Royce's express terms again, in the realization of our "exclusive affections" or "loyalties" we become the personal being that we hope to be in all of its many-faceted, but naturally delimited variety. Selfhood is the construction of our "causes." Royce phrases this philosophy of selfhood in the following further ways:

> By an individual being, whatever one's metaphysical doctrine, one means an unique being, that is, a being which is alone of its own type, or is such that no other of its class exists.

> ...if you look closely at that region of our consciousness where first we come nearest to facing what we take to be an experience of individuality, you find, I think, that it is our selective attention especially as embodied in what one may call our exclusive affections which first brings home to us what we mortals require an individual being to be. (WI 1 pp. 455, 457)

> ...an individual...is no abstract conception, but...is a conception expressible only in terms of a satisfied will. An individual is a being that adequately expresses a purpose. Or again, an individual so expresses a purpose that no other being can take the place of this individual as an expression of this purpose. And the sole test of this sort of uniqueness lies in the fact that in this individual being, just in so far as its type gets expression at all, the will or purpose which it expresses rests content with it, desires no other, will have no other.
> I conclude then, so far, that if this world contains real individuals at all, it is a teleological world... (CI pp. 47-8)

Neither in the Divine example nor in the human, does selfhood have a thing-like reality. Royce is against any doctrine of the self viewed as mere static "substance" of either material or spiritual quality. The self is not some hard core of inexplicable fact. As Royce phrased it in The World and the Individual, "For us a soul is no Monad, but a life individuated solely by its purpose" (WI2 p. 238).[2] As he later phrased it in The Problem of

---

2. In his Unpublished papers Royce wrote:
    "...the Self is never an object of anybody's feeling or observation. The Self, considered merely as the Subject of knowledge is known only as the 'Knower.' Viewed abstractly, in this its character as subject of knowledge, the Self is no thing, no Substance, no Soul, no 'collection

<u>Christianity</u>, it is "no mere present datum" (p. 245). On the
Cosmic (i.e. God's) as on the finite side (man's), "the Self is
not a Thing, but a Meaning embodied in a conscious life" (WI2
p. 269).[3] Selfhood is a 'being' of function, a precipitate of
"meaning," a deposit of purposes in their actual achievements.
Selfhood is a teleological, that is, a <u>moral</u> <u>process</u>. Royce said,
"The life of our consciousness is...a life of watching our deeds"
(WI1 p. 39). It is "in its higher forms, in large measure an
essentially Ethical Conception" (WI2 p. 269).

If, however, selfhood be initially no spiritual thing, soul-
substance, or realistic entity of any kind, what, in the human
case, is the original 'given' of its condition for Royce? Practi-
cally phrased what Royce initially assumes as the originally given
is an unformed capacity or potentiality of the human being, in its
psychophysical powers, to acquire perceptual, conceptual, and
interpretational or evaluative experience of its world. More

---

of feelings,' no so called 'active principle'"(quoted by
James Harry Cotton: <u>Royce on the Human Self</u>, op. cit.
p. 18, Royce, Unpublished papers, folio 65, no. 7, p. 57).
   "Whatever the Self as Subject is, it is nothing
immediate, like a pain, or like a stone, that you stumble
upon" (Cotton, op. cit. p. 18, from Royce, Unpublished
papers, folio 62, p. 39).
   The Self's identity through successive experiences
may be "profoundly true but is not immediately evident"
(Cotton, op. cit., p. 18, from Royce, Unpublished papers,
folio 62, p. 16).

3. In this same context Royce continued to draw the parallel idea of selfhood on the finite plane with selfhood
on the Cosmic plane by the following: "Our general
idealistic theory asserts that the universe in its wholeness is the expression of a meaning in a life.... Our
idealism has depended, from the first, upon the thesis
that the Internal and the External meaning of any finite
process of experience are dependent each upon the other,
so that if the whole meaning and intent of any finite
instant of life is fully developed, and perfectly embodied, this Whole Meaning of the instant becomes identical with the Universe, with the Absolute, with the life
of God. Even now, whatever you are or seek, the implied
whole meaning of even your blindest striving is identical
with the entire expression of the divine Will" (WI2 pp.
270-1). And later in the same volume again, among many
such statements: "The human Self...is not a Thing, nor
yet a Substance, but a Life with a Meaning" (WI2 pp.
425-6).

particularly, we find a resemblance, and express reference to, Hume's discussion of the problem of personality, or personal identity. Hume had said that there is no foundational experience of self as spiritual entity, underlying particular perceptions or conceptions. The passage in question, however, clarifies that Royce is no Humian in this regard--a subtle and all-important difference from Hume appears. I quote in full:

"I enter" then, that is, I observe, I watch, I find, I know. But, adds Hume, what I know is always some content of consciousness, some impression or idea. Yes indeed; but to say this is explicitly to say that, when I know this content as immediate, my knowing itself is not the content known, but is just precisely the knowing thereof. That I know, this truth is itself more than the content known. And so Hume, in the very act of asserting that the known is, as such, merely content, and never other than content, mere ideas, and never a peculiar thing called a Self...explicitly asserts that the Knower is, and is more than the content known. I as Subject of knowledge, am indeed never the known content; but that is the very proof that the Self is not, and cannot be reduced to the series of states that it knows.[4]

Royce expressly criticizes Hume in this paragraph: "...the Self is not, and cannot be reduced to the series of states that it knows" (where Hume--and also James in an unguarded moment--left it). It becomes plain that Royce adopts Kant's position. The self is, initially, a "unity of apperception" of some kind--but, to be sure, without our being self aware of ourselves as substance in a Cartesian sense. Indeed, in his early "Thought Diary" Royce pointed to this Kantian orientation in the following terse line: "The Ich denke = Unity of Apperception = Activity of present moment," and continued a colloquy with Kant about the subtleties

---

4.   A point which Cotton's perceptive commentary seems to overlook in the immediate context of this quotation. Royce on the Human Self, op. cit., p. 19. The quotation was made by Cotton from Royce's Unpublished papers, folio 62, pp. 24, 26-27.
        The self is not just "the Ego of the passing moment" (WI2 p. 269), i.e. a flux of states of consciousness; note also The Problem of Christianity (1913), The University of Chicago Press, 1968, p. 253, where appears another criticism of the Humian theory of the self as "a mere flight of ideas, or a meaningless flow of feelings."

of this position.[5] We also have further allusions that Royce thought along the line of Kant in this problem. The Spirit of Modern Philosophy (1892) contains an extended appendix, in which Royce wrote:

> I have pointed out how he [Kant] appealed to the transcendentale Einheit der Apperception; I have pointed out how this Einheit is, for each of us, our true self, and how the appeal is constantly made to it by every one of us, in so far as he is rational. This notion is so far unquestionably Kantian.[6]

Again a 1906 essay, "The Modification of Kant's Conception of the Self," contains the following:

> Kant makes...efforts to set his epistemology upon an independent basis. The efforts grouped about the central idea of the Transcendental Unity of Apperception are the deepest.[7]

In his comprehensive discussion of these matters J.H. Cotton --to whom we are much indebted for a number of these insights-- pointed out that Royce's view of the self, indeed his entire philosophic position, begins with a "doctrine of the present," as the factual and irreduceable epistemological given. In a passage which highlights Royce's fundamental empiricism, Cotton says:

> He...preferred to start with the experience of the present moment, which included given facts, fragmentary purposes, relations, inferences, and what else?[8]

---

5.   Cotton, op. cit. p. 25, from Royce, "Thought Diary," August 30, 1880. See also Josiah Royce: Fugitive Essays, ed. by J. Loewenberg, Harvard University Press, 1920, p. 33, for "Thought Diary" entry of August 30, 1880.
6.   W.W. Norton & Company edition, 1967, p. 490.
7.   Lectures on Modern Idealism, ed. J. Loewenberg, Yale University Press, 1919, p. 61.
8.   Cotton, op. cit. p. 22. The full paragraph reads: "It should be clear that the simple ideas of Locke, the Impressions of Hume and the 'hard data' of Bertrand Russell are abstractions. They are products of logical analysis. They are never given in empirical isolation. Royce never identified any given in experience because he did not believe that the given could be identified. He therefore preferred to start with the experience of the present moment, which included given facts, fragmentary purposes, relations, inferences, and what else? That was the problem of his philosophy. He proposed to

Of course, this initial epistemological standpoint of Royce in the 'fact' of the 'present moment' does not solve all epistemological questions that may be raised. For example, Cotton asks, "The problem of the self is...how can selfhood be achieved out of momentary flashes of experience."[9] Royce himself worried with this initially fundamental insight of the 'Now,' which he believed was the beginning of selfhood and all experience. How to get beyond this solipsism, so to speak, of the present moment? We hear his efforts to do so in his essay "The Implications of Self-Consciousness," in Studies of Good and Evil (1898). He there says that the self-of-the-moment never abides as such but is forever passing away in one time-direction and yet reaching in the other toward the self of the future, thus implying its own ultimate freedom from captivity to just the passing moment, its transcendence to any abstract 'moment' of static time. It thus anticipates its final nature as time-inclusive.[10] This, at least, seems to be the direction in which Royce's thought is pressing in the above mentioned essay.

One of the major philosophic efforts of Royce, of course, was to assign to the self--however Humian, ephemeral and unsubstantial its empirical beginnings may be--an ultimate unity and coherence, reality, and being of spiritual personhood (associated permanently with God) as the outcome of its telic striving; and this precisely the imagination of Hume was unable to achieve.

Indeed, in his essay on personality formation, "The Human Self" (WI2 pp. 245f) Royce himself further underscores what we have been pointing out relative to his positions vis-a-vis Hume and Descartes. He accepts certain aspects of both of these earlier philosophers of selfhood, but also indicates how he wishes to go beyond them to a more adequate conception. I present a resume of his discussion in this lecture:

First, true to his characteristic idealist approach to philosophical issues, he states that insight into the deeper "mysteries of Nature" may best begin with a study of "the self" and "self-consciousness" (p. 246). He next reviews two prominent theories

---

begin with the present experience, to study it and to analyze its elements and to discover what was implied in it. This was his early formulation of the problem of knowledge and he never changed it. In this, I submit, he was more empirical than the empiricists who start with artificial logical constructs. Royce took less for granted than they."

9. Ibid. p. 25.
10. D. Appleton & Co. 1906, p. 59.

of the self in modern times. One is that of the "empirical and phenomenal Self," which holds that the self is first known to itself as "the series of states of consciousness," i.e. of our passing "feelings, thoughts, desires, memories, emotions, moods," and so on (p. 257). This description at once reminds us of Hume's radically empirical, phenomenalistic, or associationist view of selfhood, as no more than the "bundle of impressions," which Hume made so famous. Also brought to mind is the ancient Buddhistic theory of self. The early Buddhists announced the 'self' to be only a radical aggregate (skandhas) of bodily functions and states of consciousness, without inherent unity. Is Royce going the way of such radical empiricisms? He himself certainly accepts this "theory of the empirical Ego" (p. 261) as the place to commence the study of human personality. Congruent with this theory, he believes that the interaction of the human organism mass with its social fellows is what awakens us first to a sense of self-consciousness or self-awareness. Royce declares that "the distinction between the Self and the not-Self has a predominantly Social origin..." (p. 260, emphasis his).[11]

The second theory of selfhood presented in his discourse is the radically realistic, or Soul-Substance view of Descartes, which he here again opposes (pp. 266-8, 276). The self is no metaphysical "entity" or initially self-certifying transcendent unity, totally independent of, and known a priori, apart from experience or intercourse with the world.

He next discusses a third theory of selfhood, his own "idealistic type," in the way we have already shown. The self is a teleological process coming into fulfillment or final self-realization as it pursues its purposes and ideals, attempting to make their "internal meanings" actualized in "external meanings" or achievements -- this process recapitulated in his own words:

> ...the self is not a Thing, but a Meaning embodied in a conscious life. Its individuality...its unity.... ...no individual self is or can be isolated, or...sundered from other selves, or from the whole realm of the inner Life of Nature itself. (p. 269)

However, Royce expressly says he wishes to retain the classic Cartesian affirmation of, and respect "for human individuality" or

---

11. We have here quoted WI2. The social origin of the sense of self is elaborated further in the later contexts of The Philosophy of Loyalty (1908) and The Problem of Christianity (1913). See our subsequent discussion of this theme relative to those contexts (pp. 261f., 268f).

personality, but he accomplishes this in his own way. A sense of self-unity and self-integrity develops, or comes into reality as result of the teleological process we have been describing (p. 267). On the other score, he wishes to avoid the danger into which bare empirical theories of the Ego often fall, namely the danger of "the Ego of the passing moment" (p. 269)--that is, the self conceived as mere flux of inner states of feeling, like the Buddha's skandhas, or Hume's radical associationist view.

Along with Kant, however, Royce was weak in not acknowledging more explicitly, as other idealists have done (e.g. B.P. Bowne; C.A. Campbell), that the sense of the metaphysical 'unity' of the self as 'power' or energy (two basic signs of 'reality') arises, if not initially, then inevitably with selfhood's genesis or transit, until in mature philosophic self-reflection there is the awareness, over and above and surrounding the Buddhistic or Humian "states of consciousness," a "consciousness of States."[12] Such a realization contemporary idealism may well interpret as knowledge, a priori, of essential spirit or 'soul' in process of coming to be. In other words, that side of Descartes which implies selfhood's a priori sense of its unity and reality may be vindicated, but in the process terms here stressed, rather than in Descartes' original simplistic substance and dualistic categories. Royce almost, but did not quite break the barrier into this level of possibly true insight about the self. Perhaps the nearest he comes to doing so I find in a brief, metaphysically unelaborated statement in his Outlines of Psychology: "But the unity of consciousness is a fact constantly forced upon us whatever our point of view. For no one can observe a mental variety of inner states without finding these states together in his one inclusive condition of mind."[13] We pass now to our second figure.

---

12.   The terms in which Borden Parker Bowne challenged Hume in this debate, Theory of Thought and Knowledge, Harper & Bros., 1897, p. 21. See also a decisive version of essentially Bowne's point, C.A. Campbell: On Selfhood and Godhood, op. cit. p. 73; Also, Peter A. Bertocci, "A Temporalistic View of Personal Mind" in Jordan M. Scher (ed.): Theories of Mind, The Macmillan Co. (Glencoe Press), 1962, pp. 393-420.
13.   The Macmillan Co. (1903), 1916, pp. 87-88 (emphasis his).

Chapter Four

WHITEHEAD ON SELFHOOD

The following brief discussion of Whitehead's process
philosophy as it bears upon the idea of man and self may be opened
with several statements from Modes of Thought similar to those of
Royce on the particular issues just reviewed.

The essence of existence lies in the transition from datum to
issue. This is the process of self-determination....
One main doctrine, developed in these lectures, is that
'existence' (in any of its senses) can not be abstracted from
'process.' The notions of 'process' and 'existence' presuppose
each other. (p. 131)

Descartes' 'Cogito, ergo sum' is wrongly translated. 'I think,
therefore I am.' It is never bare thought or bare existence
that we are aware of. I find myself as essentially a unity
of emotions, enjoying hopes, fears, regrets, valuations of
alternatives, decisions--all of them subjective reactions to
the environment as active in my nature. My unity--which is
Descartes' 'I am'--is my process of shaping this welter of
material into a consistent pattern of feelings. The individual
enjoyment is what I am in my role of a natural activity, as
I shape the activities of the environment into a new creation,
which is myself at this moment; and yet, as being myself, it
is a continuation of the antecedent world. If we stress the
role of the environment, this process is causation. If we
stress the fole of my immediate pattern of active enjoyment,
this process is self-creation. If we stress the role of the
conceptual anticipation of the future whose existence is a
necessity in the nature of the present, this process is the
teleological aim at some ideal in the future. This aim,
however, is not really beyond the present process. For the
aim at the future is an enjoyment in the present. It thus
effectively conditions the immediate self-creation of the new
creature. (pp. 228)

And now a line of central importance:

The key notion from which such construction [i.e. a metaphysical cosmology] should start is that the energetic activity

considered in physics is the emotional intensity entertained
in life. (pp. 231-2)

Earlier than Modes of Thought, Whitehead had said something very
much along the same line in Adventures of Ideas:

> ...any doctrine which refuses to place human experience out-
> side nature, must find in descriptions of human experience
> factors which also enter into the descriptions of less special
> ized natural occurrences....
> The science of physics conceives a natural occasion as a
> focus of energy. Whatever else that occasion may be, it is an
> individual fact harboring that energy. The words electron,
> proton, photon, wave-motion, velocity, hard and soft radiation
> chemical elements, matter, empty space, temperature, degrada-
> tion of energy, all point to the fact that physical science
> recognized qualitative differences between occasions in respec
> to the way in which each occasion entertains its energy....
> The notion of physical energy which is at the base of
> physics, must then be conceived as an abstraction from the
> complex energy, emotional and purposeful, inherent in the sub-
> jective form of the final synthesis in which each occasion
> completes itself. (pp. 186-7)

The two points we wish to elicit from the above quotations
are: (1) the statement that the self is teleological process
rather than Cartesian substance; and (2) that our inner mental
life is analogous, at least, to the "energy" concept of physics.

In the first place, a general observation about these two
points: To call attention to an important comparative detail
relative to the first one, in the quotations above from Modes of
Thought we hear Whitehead discuss the empirical Ego as obvious
starting point for a philosophy of selfhood in terms tantamount
to those in Royce's "The Human Self" essay. Whitehead refers to
finding himself first "a unity of emotions, enjoyments, hopes,
fears, regrets, valuations of alternatives, decisions"--i.e. the
multiplex, empirical states of consciousness of which Royce spoke
as constituting the initial factors. In the very same sentence,
and continuing in the next, Whitehead concludes his point by
stating that these factors are aroused or stimulated to initial
unified awareness, or in his own words, "into a constant pattern
of feelings," as "subjective reactions to the environment." Here
we have Whitehead's way of referring to what Royce had called the
"social origin" of the "empirical Ego."

In the second place, however, a new emphasis emerges in
Whitehead, it seems to us. It is his extended discussion of the

"energy" concept of Physics as analogous to, or another anterior form of, the energy which is known immediately in the processes of the self's mentality. In Process and Reality, Whitehead mentions that there are various "forms under which energy clothes itself" (p. 177). He calls some of these "quantitative," by which he apparently means those forms described by physics; and others "qualitative," by which he seems to mean, on the other hand, "emotional" and "feeling" forms, and gives "consciousness" and "intellectual mentality" as examples (pp. 365, 387-9). These selections conclude by a reference again to the "alternative forms of energy" and their "transformation from one form to another form." Thus he implies that mental experience is a transformed type of energy, though of course, intimately or organically related to subordinate, purely 'physical' types, an emergent from them in the thought of Whitehead.

Though possibly implied in his own discussion of nature, Royce nowhere that we have found, says quite so much (for a spiritual philosophy of man in this regard) as Whitehead does in the statement that "the energetic activity considered in physics is the emotional intensity entertained in life." Be this as it may, however, this latter point is expanded in a passage (again from Modes of Thought) somewhat more abstruse than the several foregoing, but in typical Whiteheadian fashion nonetheless insightfully eloquent:

It is to be noticed that our exposition is nothing else than the expansion of the insight that 'power' is the basis of our notions of 'substance.' This notion of 'power' is to be found in Locke and in Plato, flittingly expressed and never developed. Our experience starts with a sense of power, and proceeds to the discrimination of individualities and their qualities....
The essence of power is the drive towards aesthetic worth for its own sake. All power is a derivative from this fact of composition attaining worth for itself. There is no other fact. Power and Importance are aspects of this fact. It constitutes the drive of the universe. It is efficient cause, maintaining its power of survival. It is final cause, maintaining in the creature its appetition for creation. (pp. 162-3)

These same things—personality formation as telic process, and self reality as emerging or concrescing energy mode—were said in further, more elaborate (or careful) ways in Process and Reality. A few examples:

It is fundamental to the metaphysical doctrine of the philosophy of organism, that the notion of an actual entity as the unchanging subject of change is completely abandoned. An actual entity is at once the subject experiencing and the superject of its experiences. It is subject-superject, and neither half of this description can for a moment be lost sight of. The term 'subject' will be mostly employed when the actual entity is considered in respect to his own real internal constitution. But 'subject' is always to be construed as an abbreviation of 'subject-superject.' (p. 43)

An actual entity is at once the product of the efficient past, and is also, in Spinoza's phrase, causa sui. Every philosophy recognizes, in some form or other, this factor of self-causation, in what it takes to be ultimate actual fact. Descartes in his own philosophy conceives the thinker as creating the occasional thought. The philosophy of organism inverts the order and conceives the thought as a constituent operation in the creation of the occasional thinker. The thinker is the final end whereby there is the thought. In this inversion we have the final contrast between a philosophy of substance and a philosophy of organism. The operations of an organism are directed towards the organism as a 'superject,' and are not directed from the organism as a 'subject.' The operations are directed from antecedent organisms and to the immediate organism. They are 'vectors,' in that they convey the many things into the constitution of the single superject. (pp. 228-9)

The philosophies of substance presuppose a subject which then encounters a datum, and then reacts to the datum. The philosophy of organism presupposes a datum which is met with feelings, and progressively attains the unity of a subject. But with this doctrine, 'superject' would be a better term than 'subject.' (p. 234)

A feeling cannot be abstracted from the actual entity entertaining it. This actual entity is termed the 'subject' of the feeling. (p. 338)

The term 'subject' has been retained because in this sense it is familiar in philosophy. But it is misleading. The term 'superject' would be better. The subject-superject is the purpose of the process originating the feelings. (p. 339)

The subject, thus constituted, is the autonomous master of its own concrescence into subject-superject. It passes from a subjective aim in concrescence into a superject with objective immortality. At any stage it is subject-superject. (p. 374)

The world is self-creative; and the actual entity as self-creating creature passes into its immortal function of part-creator of the transcendent world. In its self-creation the actual entity is guided by its ideal of itself as individual satisfaction and as transcendent creator. (p. 130)

Or as Whitehead more succinctly phrased the main point just now under consideration, we are in "process of self-construction for the achievement of unified experience..." (PR p. 271). In another line of poetic cast he summarizes, "life in its essence is the gain of intensity through freedom" (PR p. 164).[1]

This process of self-creation of the finite self is intimately associated with, or reflective of, the progressive self-creation of God (recall the essentially similar conception of Royce):

An enduring personality in the temporal world is a route of occasions in which the successors with some peculiar completeness sum up their predecessors. The correlate fact in God's nature is an even more complete unity of life in a chain of elements for which succession does not mean loss of immediate unison. This element in God's nature inherits from the temporal counterpart according to the same principle as in the temporal world the future inherits from the past. Thus in the sense in which the present occasion is the person now, and yet with his own past, so the counterpart in God is that person in God. (PR p. 531)

In a section of Adventures of Ideas, beginning with the title, "Personality," Whitehead addresses himself to the finer, and perhaps critical point, asked of Royce earlier: What is the irreduceable, original 'given' in selfhood? To reply Whitehead uses an analogy drawn from Plato's cosmic "Receptacle" (of the Timaeus dialogue), applying it to the original self. I here paraphrase Whitehead's transmutation of Plato for this usage.

---

1. In his study, A Christian Natural Theology, based on Whitehead, John B. Cobb, Jr. has well summarized the points we have endeavored to draw together here thus far from various Whitehead texts: "In Whitehead's view, therefore, the soul is not at all like substance undergoing accidental adventures in time. It is constituted by its adventures. It can attain richness and depth only through this variety and quality of the entities it encounters and its own willingness and ability to be open to what they can contribute." Westminister Press, 1965, p. 56. See especially chapter II, "The Human Soul."

(The Platonic terms as translated are in single quotes.) The self
in its original datum is a 'receptacle,' 'bare of all forms,' a
'natural matrix'--an empty (?) but expectant 'unity,' or a capacity
for such unity; progressively filled or enriched by the 'transitions...of the things that enter into it' (pp. 188-9).[2] The doctrine of "subjective aim," it seems to me, in <u>Process and Reality</u>,
refines this effort at answering a difficult question:

> This doctrine of the inherence of the subject in the
> process of its production requires that in the primary phase
> of the subjective process there be a conceptual feeling of
> the subjective aim. (p. 342)

> Each temporal entity...derives from God its basic conceptual
> aim, relevant to its actual world, yet with indeterminations
> awaiting its own decisions. (p. 343)

> ...the initial stage of its aim is an endowment which the sub-
> ject inherits from the inevitable ordering of things, concep-
> tually realized in the nature of God. The immediacy of the
> concrescent subject is constituted by its living aim at its
> own self-constitution. Thus the initial stage of the aim is
> rooted in the nature of God, and its completion depends on
> the self-causation of the subject-superject. (p. 373)

To summarize, we have here a philosophy like Royce's telic-
energy view of selfhood. In our human case, selfhood starts with
an initial something, an "initial stage" (our psycho-physical being
or powers, naturally), that can (is endowed by God to) project a
"subjective aim" toward which it may move in self-realization and

---

2.   In this context Whitehead continued, under a heading,
      "Immanence": "This is at once the doctrine of the unity
      of nature, and of the unity of each human life. The
      conclusion follows that our consciousness of the self-
      identity pervading our life-thread of occasions, is
      nothing other than knowledge of a special strand of unity
      within the general unity of nature. It is a locus within
      the whole, marked out by its own peculiarities, but
      otherwise exhibiting the general principle which guides
      the constitution of the whole. This general principle is
      the object-to-subject structure of experience. It can be
      otherwise stated as the vector-structure of nature. Or
      otherwise, it can be conceived as the doctrine of the
      immanence of the past energizing in the present." (p.
      190)

completion. (Here it seems to me Whitehead identifies, as did Royce earlier, part of the very meaning of "God" with "freedom" itself, an ultimate premise which theism must adopt in its effort to solve the problem of the relation of the "wills," and an issue to which we shall later return.) Apparently, Whitehead's abstruse coinage, "superject," is meant primarily to connote the manner in which selfhood in our individual cases manifestly does project its aims and ideas, or ideals, its plans and purposes, out before its questing vision, and then endeavors to move toward accomplishing those ends; and in the process, experiences its "satisfactions" and self-completion, coming at last into what Royce had called "individuality" and "personality." Because of its Cartesian substance connotations in the language, we have seen how Whitehead was reluctant to use the term "subject." Fortunately, however, for the reader he permitted himself to do so, though subordinated and compounded with "superject."

What have Royce and Whitehead achieved in behalf of a spiritual philosophy of man? To conclude with our own synthesis and highlight: A religious and spiritual philosophy of man may indeed view the human type of reality, in our individualized examples, as unified spiritual mind or 'soul'; an energy level in its own right that comes into being and reality as a result of the process of "intensification,"[3] when nerve energy is raised to sufficient pitch so that it becomes a conscious type, or mind energy, with the new qualitative powers of the psyche, known in our selfhood and personhood.[4] We thus continue an important aspect of the traditional religious view of man as transcending spiritual 'being,' or spiritual 'reality'; but in contemporary scientific, energistic, or process terms, often phrased as the philosophy of emergence. We have already seen that "emergence" has been the basic paradigm of many evolutionary thinkers of our times: Bergson, Alexander, Lloyd Morgan, Smuts, Wieman, Whitehead, Teilhard, to recall again a few among the naturalists. Idealists also like Royce have expressed or assumed this principle in their acceptance of evolutionary thinking. This kind of philosophizing relative to what selfhood is as telic energy or telic process was

---

3. J. Arthur Hadfield in B.H. Streeter et al., Immortality, The Macmillan Co., 1922, p. 65.

4. In debate with mechanistic views of mind, I have recently explored this form of philosophical psychology in some detail, "The Meaning of Mind Transcendency in a Religious Philosophy of Man," International Journal for Philosophy of Religion, Spring 1973, pp. 39-52.

powerfully expressed in the philosophic psychologies of both
Royce and Whitehead.[5]

Their thinking, expressly repudiated the original Platonic-
Cartesian "substance" philosophy about the initial soul. They put
in its place the concept of a process or energy mode which develop
into a sense of unity. What constitutes the original, irreduceabl
'given' in selfhood? We saw that both men assumed in their separate ways, that of course, an organic thing, with psychological
potentialities is originally present, but that full selfhood or
personhood is not present until effort begins to create it, or
precipitate it at a more advanced stage. The human foetus at the
early stage is not a soul or person. It is an organism mass,
capable of becoming spiritual mind, personality, and soul as the
eventual result of the interaction of this mass with a world,
yielding the emerging experience of growth, consciousness, and
self-realization, as the concrescent product of its telic striving.

---

5. See John E. Smith's greatly perceptive article: "The
    Contemporary Significance of Royce's Theory of the Self,"
    Revue Internationale De Philosophie, 1967, Nos. 79-80, p.
    77f, in which is stressed two points concerning Royce's
    contribution: First, as Royce's view was avowedly a
    correction of the Cartesian conception of an original
    soul-substance intuition, it may be cited as a needed
    advance on modern radical individualism's and existen-
    tialism's idea of the self as sheer freedom. Second, and
    relatedly, the telic energy view (as we have phrased it)
    of the self in terms of purposive willing seeking reali-
    zation of ideas or ideals retains the significance of
    iealism's philosophy of "essence" as well as existential-
    ism's emphasis on "existence" for a fully adequate con-
    ception of the self as morally self-creative process.
    See especially pp. 87-9. These same things, of course,
    could well be said of Whitehead's similar conception of
    the genesis of selfhood.

Part III

THE CONCEPTION OF GOD AND THE ISSUES OF THEISM

Chapter Five

ROYCE ON THE CONCEPTION AND ARGUMENT
AND THE PROBLEM OF FREEDOM

'Theism' customarily denotes the conception of God as
'Personal' Reality or Mind. In highest manner or way, God is
conceived to be <u>self-conscious</u> life. This distinguishing characteristic or act of being self-aware is analogous at least to
our own sense of being a 'person.' As two of the most noted
theists of 20th century times, we are due to hear from Royce and
Whitehead regarding the main <u>issues</u> of theism. Given this conception of God, philosophic debate frequently perceives these
issues in terms of:

    the problem of argument or 'proof' -
    the problem of human 'freedom' -
    the problem of 'evil' -
    the idea or problem of 'immortality,' and
    the conception of 'religion.'

Royce and Whitehead discuss their theistic conceptions of God,
and these attendant issues, in this part. Furthermore, our role
as in the preceding exposition will be to introduce observations
from time to time on these matters regarding theism as philosophy. Before beginning this task, however, it will no doubt be
helpful to outline the program ahead somewhat further.

In the case of Royce, after disavowing classic dualistic
theism, we will hear his general argument for God, along with
the developing idea of God as immanent Cosmic Mind. Next, we
will listen to his classic refutation of impersonal absolutism;
and move thence to his treatment of the Divine Reality and human
freedom. Included as an aspect of freedom is the last important
theological problem with which he dealt, namely, the conception
of God's reality in relation to human community.

On his side, Whitehead will call our attention first to the
wonder of the cosmic order, next outlining what to him are the
intimations of God in the midst of this order. Climactically,
we will come to his characterizations of the Primordial-Uncon-
scious and the Consequent-Conscious aspects of God, along with
his conception of the way the Divine Reality and other entities
(among them the human entity in its freedom) are related. Like

those just mentioned for Royce, these steps point in their brief way to the intellectual biography of Whitehead as theist.

What we have listed above as the "issues" of theism are primarily to guide our own discussion. Though Royce and Whitehead themselves have spoken to each of these issues, they do so more directly or fully to some of them than to others. In any case, this interpretive essay endeavors to trace the thought of each philosopher-theologian along these perspectives. Turning first to Royce and thence to Whitehead, we will treat as more or less a natural unity the first two issues together, namely, those of argument and freedom, within the framework of their personalistic conception of Deity; and then proceed to examine the last three topics--evil, immortality, and religion--as classic concerns arising within theism. In the course of our 'dialogue' on these high themes, related terms and problems, like those of 'time' and 'eternity,' will naturally arise. Such we will endeavor to treat at appropriate places.

A recent study by Professor Peter Fuss[1] raises the question whether Josiah Royce abandoned his metaphysical "absolutism" expressed in such earlier writings as The Religious Aspect of Philosophy (1885) and The World and the Individual (1899, 1900), for an entirely new concept in The Problem of Christianity (1913), where the theory of the "Community of Interpretation" is presented? In his searching work, Professor Fuss argues that Royce apparently relinquished his early absolutistic idealism for the sake of maintaining human freedom and the realities of moral consciousness.

We mention this issue raised in contemporary Royce scholarship because of its intrinsic interest to this part of our own investigation. We assume that Royce did not essentially abandon his idealistic theism. Rather he deepened it by indeed making it less abstract, or more open, truly 'personalistic' and vital. This movement of his thought, away from an earlier more absolutistic frame, perhaps, and toward a process type of theism, is evident even in the middle period of The World and the Individual, the Gifford Lectures.

Be the outcome as it may, however, this question involves

---

1.   The Moral Philosophy of Josiah Royce, Harvard University Press, 1965. See author's review of this work, The Journal of Bible and Religion, July 1966, pp. 287-290.

the several phases of Royce's philosophy, sometimes cited as the
larger milestones of his intellectual pilgrimage, such as his
early metaphysical idealism and absolutism (RAP); his psychological theory of the self (both Divine and human) as a dynamic
teleological process (perspectives which we have already to
considerable extent analyzed - WI); and his ethical and social
thought, subsumed by his Philosophy of Loyalty and Community of
Interpretation themes (PL and PC).

Our present task will be to review these major phases of
Royce's philosophy in the endeavor to answer the very critical
question Professor Fuss raises. In so doing, we hope to show
how Royce's insight helps to solve the first two crucial problems of theism, namely, the question of argument or proof, and
next the relation of the Divine Being or Reality (once assumed)
to our human finitude and freedom. This endeavor will point to
Royce's description of the essential nature of Christianity,
under his immanental, spiritual theism, as the socially recre-
ative force, and to this extent will encroach upon the subject
of our following part concerned with the ethical outlook of
Royce--and of Whitehead.

Royce's rejection of Classic Dualistic Theism of the
ecclesiastical tradition in the west[2] should first be pointed
out. This appears in his early work, The Religious Aspect of
Philosophy. If one takes the notion of something being 'outside'
another literally, then it seemed to Royce that "Dualistic
Theism" was in error. He arrived at this conclusion on the
score that God, conceived as creator of a world outside or other
than himself in some radical realistic sense, would have to
appeal to, or utilize "a Law, above both producer and product,
which determines the conditions under which there can be a
product at all" (p. 274, emphasis his). Such a situation, Royce
believed, would render God "finite." More of this context, on
such a central theological problem, should be repeated to give
Royce's point a more adequate hearing:

> Dualistic Theism here confronts us, the doctrine in
> which the wise of so many ages have found so much support,
> the doctrine of a Father, separate from the world of created
> finite beings, who directs all things, pities and loves his
> children, and judges with supreme truthfulness all human
> acts.

---

2. E.g. as in Thomas Aquinas, Summa Theologica, Part I
   Q.3, a.8; Q.13, a.7, Anton C. Pegis: Basic Writings of
   Thomas Aquinas, Random House, 1945, Vol. One.

But now the idea of an infinite creative Power outside of
his products involves...serious difficulty.... Let us
exemplify.
    'Let there be light,' shall represent a creative act.
If the light that results is simply a fact in God, then our
difficulty is avoided, but the very conception of a power
creating anything external to itself is abandoned....

Hence either God creates nothing external to himself, or
else, in creating, he works under the laws that presuppose
a power higher than himself, and external to himself. In
the briefest form: Acts that produce external changes imply
adjustment of means to ends. The creation of external
things is such an act. Unless an actor is identical with
the product itself, he must therefore be subject to the
external conditions of adjustment, i.e. he must be finite....

Now even so, an absurd and self-contradictory account of the
act of creation must not be allowed to escape us by pleading
that creation is a mystery, and that nobody can see how God
makes things. For, mysterious as creation may be, we can be
sure that if creation is of such a nature as to involve an
external power and an external law, outside of God's creative
power itself, then God is himself not infinite....

A single Infinite Power is, properly speaking, a misnomer.
If a power produces something that is external to itself,
then the very idea of such an occurrence implies another
power, separate from the first, and therefore limiting it.
If however the power is identical with its own products,
then the name power no longer properly belongs to it. For,
as we shall see when we come to speak of the world in its
other aspect, namely, as eternal, the conceptions of power
and product, of cause and effect, and of all like existences,
are found to be only subordinate to the highest conception
of the world as Thought. (pp. 271, 274-5, 278-9, 287)

    Such a view of God's intimate or immanent relation to the
world--that is of it 'in' Him--would be quite consonant Royce
believed with an evolutionary conception of natural process, and
eloquently so stated in a chapter devoted to the subject in The
Spirit of Modern Philosophy (1892), where he concluded one
section of the essay on Evolution with the words: "...the
outer order of nature will embody...the life of a divine Self"
(1967: p. 291).

    In the above discussion one primary conception of the
Divine stands out thus far for Royce: God is immanent, 'creative' Thought. What argument does he now adduce to intimate the

reality of such cosmic "Thought" and "Self"?

Royce and the Ontological Argument

Royce's early reputation as an Absolute Idealist was established by his essay, "The Possibility of Error."[3] This discourse was a kind of inverse form of Augustine's impressive version of the ontological argument in ancient times, in which he had rendered the theme positively in terms of the possibility of truth to human experience--a theme profoundly rooted in the idealism of Plato.

The burning insight of the classic ontological argument announced that the human mind or intellect has an innate, a priori sense of "absolute truth" which "points to an Absolute Mind as its source and foundation."[4] Book II of St. Augustine's essay On the Free Will, where the first systematic presentation of the argument appears in western thought, defined God in fundamental way as whatever is greater, or higher than man's reason or mind, and then endeavored to show that "truth" itself-- Veritas--fills this definition and, accordingly, must be "God." What Augustine argued was that in the truth experience, human beings psychologically seem to perceive an objective reality, and a power, that could only be described by the highest philosophic category, "God." The main point of his reasoning was that truth is commonly known; or, as it were, "seen" with the "eye" of the mind or intellect, by all and sundry who will pay attention to right reasoning. That truth is commonly known, he believed, suggests its objective source, its metaphysical objectivity and reality. Augustine argued that we can all see and know the ranges, for example, of mathematical truth (and we might add today 'scientific' truths) commonly; and when we think deeply about it the ranges of moral truth commonly. Truth, accordingly, seemed to him to be that which is 'higher' or 'greater than' man's mind; that is, more inclusive than any one, finite human mind. For example in the mathematical dimension, human beings perceive the solution(s) to the Pythagorean theorem commonly. In science all alike can work the experiment in a chemical laboratory that reveals the composition of water to be two parts hydrogen and one part oxygen. These elements appear

---

3. Chapter XI, The Religious Aspect of Philosophy.
4. As phrased by Georgia Harkness in a context discussing the "coherence criterion" of truth, Conflicts in Religious Thought, Harper & Bros., 1949, p. 72.

as the objective 'law' of 'water's' being. In the moral sphere,
many have believed that human experience, as illuminated ultimately by profoundest rational insight, can come to know foundational 'moral truths' with something of an absolute certainty.
In order to live harmoniously and well with one another as personal beings, all high cultures have come to perceive that human
beings have to abide by five primary moral rules: respect for
life, for truth, for possessions, for other's spouse, and for
the ideal of living generously, benevolently, and forgivingly
toward others. Thus, truth in its ultimate ranges seems inclusive of all finite minds, and our experience of coming into
knowledge seems like a discovery to us, an exploration of the
intellectual realm that is the cosmos. The early Greek expressions for this realm were <u>Nous</u> and <u>Logos</u>--cosmic mind and reason
always present, prior to our individual knowledge of it. From
this Greek and particularly Platonic idealism St. Augustine
elaborated a systematic argument for God as the mind of "Truth,"
the personal source of all being. His efforts stated in ultimate
fashion the possibilities of the rational argument. Royce
acknowledges this Augustinian source of his own inspiration
(RAP p. 437; WI 1 pp. 228-30).[5]

5.   The main history of the ontological argument between
      Augustine and Royce continued with the classic discus-
      sions of Anselm, Descartes, and Kant, a sweep of time
      from the 4th through the 18th centuries.
          Following one aspect of Augustine's original version,
      St. Anselm (11th cent) stressed the <u>logical implications</u>
      of the 'God idea.' Augustine had said "...grant that
      that is God than which nothing is known to be superior"
      (Bk II, <u>On the Free Will</u>, Richard McKeon ed.: <u>Selections
      from Medieval Philosophers</u>, Vol. I, Charles Scribner's
      Sons, 1929, p. 29). Anselm started with the same point:
      that God must be defined as "a being than which nothing
      greater can be conceived"; and concluded, therefore,
      that His <u>existence</u> is implied in the very <u>idea</u>, since an
      <u>existing</u> being would be 'greater than' a non-existing
      being--i.e. that the 'idea' itself is self validating as
      reflecting ultimate 'existence' or reality ("Proslogium,"
      <u>St. Anselm</u>, The Open Court Publishing Co., 1944, p. 7f).
      Beyond just the <u>logical</u> sense of the argument in which
      Anselm had been mainly caught up, Descartes, in the 17th
      century returned the argument to the more inclusive
      <u>psychological</u> sense in which Augustine had discussed it.
      Descartes senses the meaning of the 'God idea' as in-
      cluding three orders of 'Perfection' or Absoluteness:
      Absolute Truth, Absolute Good (that is, Perfection of
      Character), and Absolute, Originating or Sustaining

He effectively recreated Augustine's version of the ontological argument, but in terms of the question, "How is intellectual error possible?" (RAP p. 384f). How do I know that I err

---

Power (tying the ontological into the cosmological
theme). In sum, the Perfection of Thought, Character,
and Power is what Descartes means when he says he has a
most certain and self-validating idea of God or the Perfect Being, arrived at in the following existential
steps (Meditations III & IV):
   a) Aware of his own finitude or imperfection of
      thought, character, and power, he is
   b) Therefore aware of Perfect Being as the Ultimate
      Standard by which he tests or knows his own
      imperfections in these respects.
   c) The idea refers to objective reality, beyond his
      own mind as its cause, for the idea of 'perfec-
      tion' could not arise in him, a finite or 'imper-
      fect being.'
The monk, Gaunilo, in Anselm's time, and Kant in the
late 18th century, mounted a criticism of the ontological
argument to the effect that it is a vast fallacy to attempt to leap from a subjective notion, or mere 'idea,'
within our own heads (such as that presented in the ontological argument about God), to an alleged objective
counterpart or reality outside us; and many critics since
Kant have followed him in this kind of refutation. The
more technical discussions of the Gaunilo-Kantian type
of criticism center around a point that Kant raised.
Although, he said, there may be "synthetical" a priori
judgments in certain limited cases, as in some forms of
mathematical reasoning, you cannot have valid synthetical judgments a priori about high matters of metaphysical speculation, such as the reality of God, of
freedom, or of immortality (to cite his own classic
examples). Contemporary criticism also takes the form
of whether "existence" can be a logical "predicate" or
not. (Such issues as these are discussed in the following symposia: John Hick ed.: The Existence of God,
The Macmillan Co, 1964; Alvin Plantinga, ed.: The Ontological Argument, Doubleday & Co., 1965; John H. Hick &
Arthur C. McGill, eds.: The Many Faced Argument, The
Macmillan Co., 1967). Perhaps an even more ultimate
question of logical theory, which would bear upon the
ontological argument, would be whether logical inference
or reasoning is essentially linear and horizontal, or
whether it is in nature integral, organic, or wholistic?
(Daniel Sommer Robinson: The Principles of Reasoning,

sometimes in judgment, as a common fact of intellectual life?
Like Augustine's and Descartes's versions, Royce's contribution
to the ontological argument moves at a psychological depth. The

------

D. Appleton-Century, 1947, pp. 107-15). The type of
reasoning found in the ontological argument would certainly be integral or wholistic.
    Upholders of the ontological argument (who at this
point manifestly stand within the Platonic and idealist
tradition) have pointed out in so many words that
Gaunilo and Kant have missed the point of the argument
in saying that the idea of God is suspect simply because
it is an idea. These defenders have challenged this
nominalist assumption of Gaunilo, Kant, and their followers, by saying that it overlooks the real insight or
spirit of the argument. The argument really says that
"The presence of the Ideal is the reality of God within
us" (A. Seth Pringle-Pattison, The Idea of God, Oxford
Univ. Press, 1920, p. 246). In a wider context, speaking
of 'The Possibility of Truth,' but which we here may
expressly apply to the Gaunilo-Kantian type of criticism,
D.E. Trueblood has said: "The fact that we know with
the mind does not mean that we cannot know what is outside the mind" (Philosophy of Religion, Harper & Bros.,
1957, p. 37). Even more to the point, Aimé Forest has
suggested that the argument is not a "passage," from the
inward to the outward, as the classic criticisms have
alleged; rather the argument is a true "perception,"
inward and upward, to an all-encompassing reality (Hick
& McGill, op. cit., p. 285f. Along these lines, Edward
Caird, the British idealist and contemporary of Royce,
spoke eloquently for the argument in the following terms:
He said,
"The thought of God ceases to be regarded as simply one
among many other thoughts we may have, and becomes the
idea of the unity which is presupposed in all our consciousness of the particular existence either of ourselves or of anything else, an idea which in some form
or other we must have. The argument, therefore, according to this interpretation of it, is not from an idea
viewed as a subjective state of the individual mind to
an object corresponding to it; but rather the idea of
God, by its priority to all distinction of objectivity
and subjectivity, is to be regarded as at once the principle of being and of knowledge, and therefore at once
objective and subjective.... This, no doubt alters the
form of the argument--as an argument from an idea in our
minds to something out of our minds.... Rather, we are

psychology of error is that, when I am aware of error, there is awareness (a priori) of a larger, more comprehensive source, standard, or ground of judgment or truth against which I plot or

---

now bound to say, the division of subject and object, as a division in our consciousness, is possible only on the presupposition of a unity which is beyond the division and which manifests itself in it" ("Anselm's Argument for the Being of God," The Journal of Theological Studies, I, October 1899, quoted by Hick and McGill in the above cited symposium, pp. 215-16).

The essence of the Ontological argument, at least in the "Hegelian Use" of it, is, as Caird said "the general truth, that the consciousness of God is not separable from but presupposed in the consciousness of self" (quoted by John Hick in his section on "The Hegelian Use of the Argument," Hick & McGill, op. cit., p. 215).

In any case, the general soundness of such an argument would indeed ultimately rest on the acceptance of the idea that synthetic judgments a priori are valid or possible, at least in many instances, and therefore presumably also in this highest experience or form; and, which is probably to assert the same thing, upon acceptance of the view that judgment must essentially be regarded as integral, organic, or wholistic, rather than merely horizontal or linear.

It is noteworthy, of course, that eventually Kant himself believed he discovered the profoundest intimations of God in human moral experience. His views on God's reality as argumentatively discussed at various levels in his moral essays, The Critique of Practical Reason, The Metaphysics of Morals, and the Posthumous Fragments, were certainly "synthetic" and "a priori" in judgmental tone (an inconsistency, we believe, with his previous negative dictum in the Critique of Pure Reason, regarding such modes of judgment as they applied to arguments for God). Discussion of the problem of synthetic judgment a priori may be found in C.H. Langford: "A Proof that Synthetic A Priori Propositions Exist," Journal of Philosophy, Jan. 6th, 1949; A.C. Ewing: The Fundamental Questions of Philosophy, The Macmillan Co., 1951, chap. 2; Brand Blanshard: The Nature of Thought, 1939, 1955, The Macmillan Co., Vol. II, p. 407; Blanshard: Reason and Analysis, George Allen & Unwin, 1962, p. 288f; a bibliography on the subject "Is There Synthetic A Priori Knowledge?" William P. Alston & Richard B. Brandt, Eds., The Problems of Philosophy, Introductory Readings, Allyn & Bacon, 1967, p. 620. See our brief account of Royce's defense of synthetic judgment, Part V of this study, pp. 302f.

test my error. Error implies a full body of rational coherence
or relationship, "an organism of thought," he believed (p. 393),
in which the thinker becomes aware of his error. The psychology
of all our judging, or truth searching, is fragmentary, incomplete. Thus the partial and incomplete nature of our present
knowledge suggests the more perfect "Absolute Truth." Our
present knowledge of the world is partial; for example, our partial knowledge of the cause and cure of cancer, or of the nature
of quasars. There is the ultimate truth about cancer, and quasars, that awaits our discovery, and so with all other aspects
of our present incomplete or fragmentary knowledge of things.
The incompletion of our knowledge, and our imperfect awareness
of the 'truth' of things, intimates completed knowledge and
absolute truth. Our human experience of seeking truth is often
one of the progressive refinement of judgments. We decide today
that a certain thing must be the case or the 'truth'; but by
tomorrow we have perceived it, either through logical clarification or through experience, in a new or larger light. Today's
more perfect insight either radically cancels out or denies our
yesterday's judgment as totally inconsistent with our new,
fuller understanding of things; or it perhaps perceives it as
incomplete, as partially true--by degree true, as if measured
against some larger background.

How high up from the ground are you unless you see 'the
ground' in order to make the judgment? How can a curve be
plotted unless in reference to the coordinate system which defines it? How can you tell black, or shades of gray, unless you
know something about white against which you make the judgment?
An ultimate "Truth" then is the ground of judgment and the primal
idea of "God" present to the mind--so the argument believes.
Viewing the processes of thought this way, a former student aptly
paraphrased Royce's argument: "A more intelligent judgment on
our thoughts is only relative to the fact that there is a higher
or better view of this thought, therefore all this...presupposes
that through the echelon of judgments there is a supreme Infinite Thought or All-inclusive Mind."[6] We quote a few of the
memorable lines closing Royce's essay (and the main argument
leading up to them in the notation below):

---

6.   Carl Boyer, Colorado College, Spring, 1959. The core
     of the Possibility of Error argument proceeded thus:
     "The conditions that determine the logical possibility
     of error must themselves be absolute truth..." (RAP
     p. 385, emphases here and following are Royce's).
     "We have not the shadow of doubt ourselves about the
     possibility of error. That is the steadfast rock on
     which we build.... How is...error possible.... What

...there is no stopping-place short of an Infinite Thought.
The possibilities of error are infinite. Infinite then must
be the inclusive thought....

All reality must be present to the Unity of the Infinite
Thought....

...here we have found something that abides, and waxes not
old, something in which there is no variableness, neither

---

is an error?... ...common sense will readily admit
that if a statement is erroneous, it must appear erro-
oneous to every 'right mind' that is in possession of
the facts.... (pp. 390-1, emphasis his)
"A judgment cannot have an object and fail to agree
therewith, unless this judgment is part of an organism
of thought.... Either then there is no error, or else
judgments are true or false only in reference to a
higher inclusive thought, which they presuppose, and
which must, in the last analysis, be assumed as Infinite and all inclusive. This result we shall reach by
no mystical insight, by no revelation, nor yet by a
mere postulate such as we used in former discussions,
but by a simple dry analysis of the meaning of our own
thought..." (p. 393).
"And to sum up, let us overcome all our difficulties
by declaring that all the many Beyonds, which single
significant judgments seem vaguely and separately to
postulate, are present as fully realized intended
objects to the unity of an all-inclusive, absolutely
clear, universal, and conscious thought, of which all
judgments, true or false, are but fragments, the whole
being at once Absolute Truth and Absolute Knowledge.
Then all our puzzles will disappear at the stroke, and
error will be possible, because any one finite thought,
viewed in relation to its own intent, may or may not
be seen by this higher thought as successful and adequate in this intent..." (p. 423).
"In short, error becomes possible as one moment or
element in a higher truth, that is, in a consciousness
that makes error a part of itself, while recognizing
it as error....
"Either there is no such thing as error, which statement is a flat self-contradiction, or else there is an
infinite unity of conscious thought to which is present
all possible truth..." (p. 424).
"You cannot in fact make a truth or a falsehood by your
thought. You only find one" (p. 431).

shadow nor turning. No power it is to be resisted, no plan-
maker to be foiled by fallen angels, nothing finite, nothing
striving, seeking, losing, altering, growing weary; the All-
Enfolder it is, and we know its name. Not Heart, nor Love,
though these also are in it and of it; Thought it is, and
all things are from thought, and in it we live and move.
(RAP, pp. 431, 433, emphasis his, 434-5)

Two premises of this Roycean argument are apparent: that
"error" is to be defined as 'incomplete thought'; and that logical 'judgment' or 'true judgment' is a part of an "organism of
thought." Royce apparently accepted that theory of judgment
which claims it to be integral, organic, or wholistic, rather
than horizontal or linear. The acceptance of this view of judgment makes synthetic a priori reasoning possible, and accordingly the acceptance of ontological arguments for God as valid.
On the other hand, the limiting of judgment to the one plane, or
linear view probably rules out a priori synthesis, and arguments
for God based on it. (See our Notation 5 above presenting a
brief history of the ontological argument.) The force of
Royce's 'proof' will rest on whether the premises above acknowledged seem to one to be valid or not. (See 93f. for further
evaluation of Royce's argument.)

Royce left us several subsequent versions of his idealistic
argument for the Conscious Unity of the World, or Personal
Cosmic Mind.[7] His second effort followed in the "Conception of

---

7.   We call the reader's attention to a perceptive study by
     Father Edward A. Jarvis, S.J.: The Conception of God
     in the Later Royce, Martinus Nijhoff, The Hague, 1975,
     in which the author examines at length the various "con-
     ceptions" as he perceives them through Royce's major
     works, from RAP to PC, with an excellent resume on pp.
     169f. Fr. Jarvis points out a number of subtle differ-
     ences in various levels of the Roycean argument for
     God, but attests to a common basic character in each of
     them in the following lucid terms:
         "All of Royce's arguments for the existence of God
     proceed from his idealism whereby he concludes to the
     nature of reality from the nature of thought. Whatever
     form each argument takes, it always involves the need
     to explain the possibility of error or the possibility
     of attaining truth. This always requires the trans-
     cending of present momentary consciousness for what is
     objective, normative and whole in reality. This, in
     turn, always occurs through some triadic structure
     whereby individual judgment corresponds to its object

God" address (1895) expounding the theory of an "Absolute Experience" underlying or surrounding our human experiences, as
reflected by their fragmentary, finite nature. This was an
emphasis implied in his original Possibility of Error essay, but
which does not, in the subsequent Conception of God address,
take the point of the discussion on error much farther, in our
view.

The third approach to the problem of argument or proof,
pointing to the existence of Absolute Mind, concerns the question
of the world's ultimate unity or non-unity (WI1, pp. 398-400)?
At this place in his Gifford Lectures, Royce invites us to study
the issue in terms of a negative proposition (to show the absurdity of the opposite proposition is sometimes a helpful way to
clarify an argument). Let us assume, he suggests, contrary to
'unity,' that there is diversity, sundering, and non-relation-
ship, either absolute or partial, among the elements, objects,
and phenomena of our world. But in the attempt to assume diversity and non-unity is implied all along the knowledge as to why
the universe is alleged to be non-unified, either totally or in
part. Such knowledge is precisely the intimation, he believes,
of the wider Absolute Knowledge or Truth that embraces the
whole, and renders ultimate diversity impossible, and the philosophical pluralisms and radical realisms based on such an hypothesis self-contradictory. This a priori exercise, Royce implies,
in addition to ruling out the supposition that the world is non-
unified, establishes the fact that it is unified in a certain
way, namely, in terms of the idealist's concept of an ultimate
spiritual or mental unity. Not only formal unity is found, but
the quality of such unity in Absolute or Cosmic Mind.

If the sundered finite forms of consciousness are by
hypothesis not mutually inclusive, their very sundering,
according to our conception of Being, implies their common
presence as facts to a knower who consciously observes
their sundering as the fulfillment of his own single meaning. (p. 399)

A fourth type of argument, related to what has just preceded, appears as his refutation of F.H. Bradley's Impersonal
Absolute[8] in support of the idea of the Personality of the

_____

through the medium of some higher insight" (pp.
169-70).
      See our further comment on Fr. Jarvis's study,
notation 26, p. 112, bearing upon his interpretation
of Royce's conception of God.
8.   F.H. Bradley: Appearance and Reality, 1893.

Absolute as self-conscious Unity. Recall in Part I that we had
deferred Royce's discussion of the Second Conception of Being,
opposite to Realism, namely, Mysticism, the metaphysical implications of which he asserted pointed to the conception of Being
as the Impersonal One (WI1, Lects. IV-V). For this brief reference to his criticism of mysticism we may employ his challenge
of Bradley's impersonalistic monism as exactly pertinent to the
problem of classic mysticism as Royce interpreted it.[9] He
argues on Bradley's grounds that the 'trans-personal' or 'impersonal' Absolute would have to know (that is, be ultimately and
constantly conscious of) the examples of selfhood or personality
on the finite plane in its attempt to rise above them in this
regard; for they are, after all, contained within itself.
Accordingly, the Absolute in and of itself cannot be conceived
to 'rise above' the category of self-consciousness, the quintessential sign of the personal (WI1 pp. 551-2). He concluded:

> "And thus...we are free, upon the basis of the general
> argument of these lectures, to assert that the Absolute is
> no absorber and transmitter, but an explicit possessor and
> knower of an infinite wealth of organized individual facts,
> --the facts, namely, of the Absolute Life and Selfhood."
> (WI1, p. 587)[10]

---

9. Royce cited Hinduism as the classic form of mysticism
    of which he was critical. Apparently he was unaware
    of the great Indian medieval theologian, Ramanuja
    (11th century), who developed a highly personalistic
    conception of Brahman and the world that bears a
    striking resemblance to his own Integral Personal
    Idealism.

10. In the dialogue with Bradley preceding this conclusion
    Royce had argued:
    "The Absolute therefore must not merely be A, but
    experience itself, as possessing the character of A.
    It is, for instance, 'above relations' (according to
    Mr. Bradley). If this is a fact, and if this statement
    is true of the Absolute, then the Absolute must experi-
    ence that it is above relations. For Mr. Bradley's
    definition of Reality must not, like the mystical Abso-
    lute, merely ignore the relations as illusion. It must
    experience their 'transformations' as a fact,--and as
    its own fact. Or, again, the Absolute is that in which
    thought has been 'taken up' and 'transformed', so that
    is is no longer 'mere thought'. Well, this too is to
    be a fact.... The Absolute, then, experiences itself
    as the absorber and transmuter of thought. Or, yet
    again,...'personality'.... Well, this transcendence

Attending, then, these various forms of his argument for God, is Royce's view of such Cosmic Unity as Active Personal causation or world "meaning,"[11] based on the problem of what it means "to be," which we have previously described as constituting his principal exposition in The World and the Individual, Vol. I. Finally, The Problem of Christianity presents the thesis that the Personal causal "meaning" or Divine Spirit in the World has its social expression in the Christian community. At this depth God is known not only in the abstractions of a rational perception of things, but felt in the warmth of the 'Spirit.' Presently we will return to this level of Royce's insight.

Further Criticisms of Royce's Argument
for God and Replies

Beyond our brief evaluation on page 90, we can suppose several further types of criticism of his principal argument

---

of personality is a fact that the Absolute itself experiences as its own fact....
"...The Absolute...is above the Self, and above any form of mere selfhood [according to Bradley]. The fact that it is thus above selfhood is something 'not other than experience'; but is wholly experience, and is the Absolute Experience itself. In fine, then, the Absolute, in Mr. Bradley's view, knows itself so well-- experiences so fully its own nature--that it sees itself to be no Self, but to be a self-absorber... aware of itself in the end, as something in which there is no real Self to be aware of.... But if the Absolute is all these things, it can be so only in case it experiences itself as the possessor of these characters. Yet all the concrete self-possession of the Absolute remains something above Self; and appar- ently the Absolute thus knows itself to be, as a Self, quite out of its own sight!
"Now...We know, at all events, that...Mr. Bradley's Absolute is a self-representative system.... And we know, therefore, that the Absolute despite all Mr. Bradley's objections to the Self, escapes from selfhood and from all that selfhood implies, or even transcends selfhood, only by remaining to the end a Self. In other words, it really escapes from selfhood...only by experiencing as its own, this its own escape. This consequence is clear" (WI1, pp. 551-2).
11. See pp. 113f. for further discussion of Royce on the idea of causation.

from the experience of Truth and Error.

The first of these, suggesting Gaunilo's and Kant's classic rebuttal of the ontological argument (often followed by modern critics--see notation 5), Royce himself answered in his essay on truth and error. We may phrase the question as follows: How does Royce answer the possible objection that his Higher Infinite Thought is only a possible or hypothetical, critical thought, rather than necessarily an objectively real, Cosmic Thought? I.e. Why does the 'Absolute Thought' have to be a Reality, more than, or something lying beyond, a mere subjective imagining in human heads? How does one pass from the thought or idea within our finite minds to the reality or existence beyond us of Infinite Mind? Royce replied, there must be an objective, or more inclusive standard of truth in an Infinite Mind, else our truth judgments, fearing that they are only subjective, would be rendered uncertain on all sides; we could, and would be, in no wise sure that they ever or anywhere apply to objective conditions. Psychologically we would be powerless beings, at the very center of our life and existence--namely, in our effort to know our world in which we must make our way. The reader may judge for himself the force of Royce's own reply to the perennial Gaunilo and Kant type of criticism of the ontological argument:

> Without it there is for our view no truth or error
> conceivable. The words, This is true, or This is false, mean
> nothing, we declare, unless there is the inclusive thought
> for which the truth is true, the falsehood false. No barely
> possible judge, who would see the error if he were there,
> will do for us. He must be there, this judge, to consti-
> tute the error. Without him nothing but total subjectivity
> would be possible; and thought would then become purely a
> pathological phenomenon, an occurrence without truthfulness
> or falsity, an occurrence that would interest anybody if
> it could be observed; but that, unfortunately, being only a
> momentary phantom, could not be observed at all from without,
> but must be dimly felt from within. Our thought needs the
> Infinite Thought in order that it may get, through this
> Infinite judge, the privilege of being so much as even an
> error. (RAP p. 427)

As indicated above in the brief notation on its history, contemporary upholders of the ontological type of theistic argument point out that its real genius may be to show that the intellectual awareness of the Divine is not a 'passage' anywhere, as if from a here to a there (which the nominalist criticism just reviewed implies). Rather the 'ontological sense' is a 'perception' in depth, or in height, a sensing of Mind, surrounding, permeating, upholding, judging, and authenticating our

own, albeit partial insights or experiences of 'truth.' As with
Plato originally, its force for its proponents bespeaks immediate
experience; and it is undoubtedly somewhat 'mystical.' Though
Royce himself roundly criticizes classic, Monistic Mysticism, his
own effort at constructing a proof for God based on the immediacy
of ontological awareness, is to that extent, mystical. Ontological arguments and theistic mysticians purport to get at the
very "being" of God by a kind of certainty or immediacy analogous
to sensory experience.

A second major question about the argument from truth, particularly at the level expounded by Augustine or Royce, might
be raised concerning the implication that truth judgments have a
standard, or point to a standard beyond material relationships?
From the simplest empirical standpoint, critics might say that
objective material relationships themselves, rather than Augustine's or Royce's All-inclusive Absolute Truth or Mind, are the
standard of our truth judgments. How might Royce endeavor to
reply to this kind of fundamental criticism, possibly more far-
reaching and perhaps more devastating than the preceding form of
criticism?[12]

---

12. A type of criticism Royce himself acknowledged in
    similar terms in his 1912 work, The Sources of Reli-
    gious Insight, Scribner's, pp. 139-50. In the middle
    portion of that late study of religion, after repeating
    the substance of his early Possibility of Error essay
    for the particular purposes of the later book, he re-
    plied to this "pragmetic criticism" in the following
    words:
       "If a man says that the workings of his ideas are
    to be tested by 'scientific experience,' then again he
    appeals not to the verdict of any human observer, but
    to the integrated and universalized and relatively
    impersonal and superpersonal synthesis of the results
    of countless observers.
       "And so, whatever you regard as a genuine test
    of the workings of your ideas is some living whole of
    experience above the level of any one of our indi-
    vidual human lives" (p. 150).
       In our opinion, however, this effort at reply
    was not as effective as his own earlier discussion of
    the larger implications of idealism as such, as set
    forth in the essay, "Reality and Idealism," from The
    Spirit of Modern Philosophy, which we here utilize in
    our own manner for Royce.

His reply, of course, would embrace a whole watershed of
thinking philosophically, to the effect that the very question
itself is mounted upon a 'materialist' (or a simplistic 'realist') bias about the cosmic order; whereas we more accurately
interpret the cosmic order idealistically, that is, from the
standpoint of the Platonic tradition, rather than from the perspective and assumptions of Lucretian materialism. In the first
place, it should be kept in mind that Royce himself is no narrow
'a priorist,' aperch his ivory tower, gazing only at heaven; he
would wish to be called an 'empirical' philosopher in the very
deepest meaning of 'experience,' as meaning inclusion of many
dimensions of perceptivity (or prehension), logical as well as
sensory, poetic or aesthetic as well as prosaic. (Part V of this
commentary has discussed at greater length the epistemological
outlook of Royce.) The slightest acquaintance with his writings
makes plain that his philosophic method attempts to be a fully
'coherent' or synoptic one, and thereby strives to be adequately
'empirical' or sensory, scientific, or inductive, as well as
'rational' and deductive. He is no enemy of empiricism, and
accordingly his argument for God is not in opposition to science
or the empirical spirit, but rather inclusive of it. To return,
however, to the point we began a moment ago.

His essay "Reality and Idealism," Chapter XI in The Spirit
of Modern Philosophy (1892), while mainly expository in intent
of the particular type of idealism that Berkeley espoused, certainly discloses Royce's own position regarding the general
viability of idealism as a philosophy, and indeed the ultimate
necessity, he believed, of looking at the world from the platonic
standpoint. That outlook stressed the ultimacy of spiritual
'ideas,' rather than the primacy of dead or inert 'masses'; of
reason and the spirit rather than opaque and spiritless 'material'
quantities. Thus, while not a direct reply to our second question about his theistic argument, it is a relevant passage and
would disclose the mode in which he would himself have probably
replied to it. What follows here is our own effort, reflecting
his "Reality and Idealism" discourse, to speak to such a question as raised above. In terms of the issue now before us, as
idealist Royce upholds in this passage Berkeley's (and Plato's)
main point as to why 'material' objects and relations cannot be
the ultimate standard for knowledge or truth. It would represent
his way of replying to the positivist and radical analytical
views of knowledge, centered in the simplistic 'verificationist
principle' that knowledge comes only by, and is delimited to,
sense-experience.

First, Royce would charge the critic to define what he
means by 'material relationships,' alleged to be apart from, or

other than, relationship in idea--he would call attention to the dogmatic dualism (or realism) lying covert in the criticism. The argument for God from truth does not accept a radical dualism between truth judgments or truly connected ideas, on the one hand, and 'material relationships' ·on the other, as the criticism implies. According to the argument from knowledge, truth judgments or true ideas are reflected in material relationships; 'material objects and relationships' are not one kind of thing, and 'rational explication of them another. But rather the explication and the beings and their relationships are in some sense mutually implicated or reflective. How can we be aware of any objects and relationships unless we are rationally aware of them? Unless we are rationally aware, that is, in some sense in terms of 'secondary' and 'primary qualities' (or ideas) we are not aware at all, and would know of no objects in relationship. Ultimate Mind or Truth does not entirely (or perhaps not at all) transcend nature, but has expression in nature. At this point we might hear Plato or Berkeley ask: What are objects and their 'relations' anyway but 'ideas' basically? Objects and material relations are so clothed with ideas that we never get to some kind of naked substance or formless reality beneath them. Reality is ideas, or at least on the side of material relationships, she seems to be materially embodied ideas. Do we ever know of any raw reality apart from form? Plato posited a primal, formless matter (or 'receptacle'), but he admitted the very great difficulty of conceiving it apart from form,[13] and hesitated to say that this was possible.[14]

With greater certainty Aristotle believed that elemental or "prime matter" never existed apart from form.[15] There is no stark matter or absolutely inchoate being, crouching and hiding somewhere beneath the luminous structure of rational form or idea. Radical dualism may be true, but the burden of proof rests on those who assume that there is such disassociated matter existing somewhere in a formless (i.e. unknowable) corner of the universe. Royce simply believed, and, of course, quite with Whitehead, that Plato and Aristotle long since won this intellectual battle with the materialists at an early time in the history of western thought.

Secondly, a further point clarifying the argument in the light of the present criticism takes us to the very heart of the

13. Timaeus, Plato, Selections ed. Raphael Demos, Charles Scribner's Sons, 1927, pp. 410-14.
14. Parmenides, Ib. p. 362.
15. W.D. Ross, Aristotle, pp. 73-4, Methuen & Co., 5th Ed. 1949.

problem that Royce was discussing in his Possibility of Error
essay. Royce there endeavored to say that truth is judgmental
or conceptual correspondence of thought to things, or right
awareness of relationships. But how is this rightness or correctness or this truth of judgmental or conceptual awareness
established--i.e. how is the frame and picture of thought within
us known to be in agreement with, or correspondent to, the order
and structure of things around us? How do we move from the
simple definition intellectually of truth as the correspondence
of thought to things (probably 'true' itself as far as it goes)
to the full experience of truth as 'being,' ontologically, which
overcomes the separation of 'thought' and 'things' in the certainty of knowledge? Only by the sense of the total Mind, we
have heard him say, that embraces us and things. Not by the
material or empirical relationships themselves initially or
alone; for, on a radical empirical or sensory basis, we are
never perfectly certain that we have perfectly conceptualized
the relation of A to B in logical or descriptive judgment; there
is a limit to empirical experience as simplistically understood;
there is always "the possibility of error." Only by the standard of the Infinite Perceiver, Conceiver, Thought or Mind, which
objectively holds all things in their proper relationships, and
on their courses in process, and subjectively discloses itself
to the human mind in true judgment, particularly in logical, and
ultimately in moral judgment, do we find a standard for judgment.

To support Royce at this level of his insight, if we divine
his thought correctly, many truth judgments, even in the field
of natural science, are made prior to empirical verification of
the fact.[16] Indeed, much logical truth seems a priori and the
categorical form in which the empirical investigation of nature
must proceed. Accordingly, it seems that some truth judgments--
many of them of paramount importance--are not solely dependent
on an initial observation of material relationships. Particularly does this seem true in the realm of elemental moral truth-
judging, to which we pointed in the previous brief discussion
of Augustine's version of the ontological argument (p. 84).

A third conceivable problem is to meet the possible criticism of the Possibility of Error essay that one could arrive at
the conception (and the being!) of 'Infinite Error' as easily as
'Infinite Truth,' on Royce's own terms--at some Ahriman of Error,
who might destroy the Mazda of Truth and thus cancel the force

---

16.   As often illustrated in Einstein's mathematical deduction that light would be bent in a gravitational field
announced prior to the discovery of this fact empirically by Eddington; and other such examples announced
by Relativity physics.

of the argument. Royce has not spoken to such an issue, but we will try to do so in his behalf.

In reply then we would suggest that the higher Inclusive Judgment would cancel the error of the error (or the ignorance of the error), since it would replace the ignorance with knowledge, or "truth." That is to say, it would know the why of the error--it would have, or know, the truth above the error. Accordingly, you could not conceive of "Absolute Truth" as containing, or cancelled by, or replaced by, or vitiated by an "Absolute Error." An error is only an "error" so long as ignorance about this error continues. Once that ignorance is dispelled, it is no longer "error," but truth; and this is precisely what the Absolute is, according to Royce, in its ultimate life. It is full, comprehensive, coherent Truth. It might be said that it contains or has "error," in itself only in the sense that it would, or can, anticipate the errors that finite judgers might make, but at the same time it would know why they were errors; it would know or be the fuller truth about the ignorance. From its final standpoint, it would dispel the ignorance.

Such would be the way Royce might attempt to meet the criticism.

We continue with our own addendum. Error is disconnection or lack of clear relationship of ideas. To imply an "Infinite Error,' or even a wider more inclusive error, an erroneous judgment would have to "know" its error; i.e. why it is in error. This would at once break the hypothetical compounding or build-up of errors. 'Greater error' could only mean a wider more radical disjunction or dispersion of ideas and judgments about our world. A 'progress' of thought toward a 'unity' of thought in error is, as a possibility, self-contradictory. A movement of thought in error is toward ever greater disjunction and dispersion of ideas in judgment; a direction of ever more fragmentation, separation, and plurality of judgments. If one erroneous judgment be seen or understood to be connected with another erroneous judgment, a network of true relationships is thereby born--given the erroneous premises of our false judgments, from which we have started out toward our 'infinite error.' ('True' conclusions may always be derived validly even from premises which are false materially.) But truth is then beheld at work in the crevices and interstices of erroneous judgments. By the time we have supposed we have arrived at our infinite, all-inclusive error, this leaven of truth would have swelled to the point where we would realize why we have in hand an infinite error. Such circumstances could only imply that we are aware

of the infinite background or totality of truth, by which we
could ever judge that we had, or had arrived at, 'infinite
error.' The process of error itself, its evolution and destiny
tends to swallow up its own progeny and give them rebirth, or
redemption anew in truth. The Mazda of Life and Truth, as in
Zoroastrian eschatology, would eventually most certainly defeat
the Ahriman of Error and Evil.

A fourth level of criticism is perhaps the most fundamental,
though it relates to the second type above discussed and may
simply be another form of that same problem. In any case, it is
the radical criticism that the whole argument from knowledge, or
from "truth and error," is premised on an inconclusive and question begging supposition about our world; namely, that the world
is, objectively speaking, a 'rational order'; or that our thought
processes within find 'correspondence' with a 'rational order'
outside observing 'minds.' The sceptic, the positivist, the
radical analyst, would deny that there is any ultimate meaning
to the statement that 'the world is rational order.' "The discovery of a Mind in the universe through the intelligibleness of
the universe to us..." (the precise way William Newton Clarke
phrased the sense of the argument)[17] is denied as a question
begging position.

We can best reply by referring first to a context in Royce
himself, namely, his refutation of radical realism, presented in
Part I of this study. The point of Royce's discussion there was
that the world cannot be conceived as a radical <u>disjunction</u> of
particulars--that such conception breaks down, is contradictory,
and as we pointed out leads inevitably into what is another side
of the primal idea of 'God,' namely, as ultimate and necessary
'Order.'
Expanding this point we ask: How far can such a proposition
regarding the discovery of 'order' be sustained when nature's
so-called 'laws' and 'orderly' processes are empirically and
closely examined? Does the world conform to 'law'? Are there
not, rather, many incoherences, disconnections, ineptness in
process, abortive events, conflicts and 'evils' that belie the
thesis that nature is throughout an 'orderly' or 'rational'
process? Another way to state the criticism is to ask, is it
not possible that man's 'rational mind' imposes its own 'order'
or system upon the helter-skelter of nature's motions; and as
he studies her, implies order out there for his practical purposes, when actually there may not be such--or at least the
degree or extent of order he alleges? Are not the 'order' that

---

17. <u>An Outline of Christian Theology</u>, Charles Scribner's
Sons, 1898, p. 105.

man perceives in science (and especially the 'order' he expresses
in his morality) arbitrary kinds of human legislation? The contemporary of Royce, above cited, Wm. Newton Clarke, stated such
a criticism forcefully (and in a moment we will allow him to
reply to it):

> It is sometimes said...that this finding of a Mind in
> the universe means simply that man projects his own mental
> processes into things around him, and reads in the universe
> the likeness of himself.... It has sometimes been suggested
> that there is nothing strange in man's understanding the
> universe, since he belongs to it and is part and parcel of
> its method. There is no need of a mind in the universe to
> render it intelligible to man, since man, who is a product
> of the system, has the same qualities with it, and might
> naturally be expected to understand it.[18]

In reply it may be said that the crucial point of this
level of the discussion is the balance of seeming 'order' to
'disorder,' or lack of order in nature. Do not the critics over-
state the case for nature's disorder? If nature were fundamentally 'disorderly,' or 'irrational,' how, as Clarke asks, could

---

18. Ibid. p. 108. Another statement of such radical posi-
     tivist view was given by Karl Pearson in his Grammar
     of Science (3rd edition), pp. 82, 86 (quoted by Daniel
     Sommer Robinson: The Principles of Reasoning, op. cit.
     p. 294): "A scientific law is the resume or brief
     expression of the relationships and sequences of cer-
     tain groups of perceptions and conceptions, and exists
     only when formulated by man.... The law of gravita-
     tion is not so much the discovery by Newton of a rule
     guiding the motion of the planets as his invention of
     a method of briefly describing the sequence of sense
     impressions which we term planetary motion.... The
     statement of this fomula was not so much the discovery
     as the creation of the law of gravitation. A natural
     law is thus seen to be a resume in mental shorthand,
     which replaces for us a lengthy description of the
     sequences among our sense impressions. Law, in the
     scientific sense, is thus essentially a product of the
     human mind, and has no meaning apart from man. It
     owes its existence to the creative power of his intel-
     lect. There is more meaning in the statement that man
     gives laws to Nature than in its converse that Nature
     gives laws to man."

man ever know her at all? Or if man merely imposes order, how
is he ever sure that this imposition or attribution is a correct,
i.e. a pragmatically useful one, or even an approximately correct one? His idea of nature would not work or be of use, and
he could not depend upon it, unless nature were in some sense
like it. How is he ever certain of any of his scientific judgments? The possibility of knowledge assumes an objective order
which comes to be known. Further the empirical test is that
there is much order, indeed vast reaches of order and seeming
'rational' connectedness objectively in the universe. Further,
to say that man knows the system simply because he is a product
of the system is to assume rationality at the outset within the
system. The world brought forth man as its product; one of
man's highest attributes is his questing rationality or desire
for rational experience; man's main desire is 'to know,' that is
to say, rationally to understand the system. Replying to his
question above, and answering the positivist philosophical
descendents of Hume, Wm. Newton Clarke points out the difficulty
of a philosophy that would, in some extreme way, deny objective
order or rationality to the universe.

> ...this explanation does not account for the facts. Man
> studies out the nature of an ellipse, and then discovers
> that the planets move in ellipses. For the fact that the
> planets stand the tests that prove their orbits to be
> elliptical, man certainly is not responsible. This is not
> a mere finding of himself in the universe. He could not
> mathematically demonstrate elliptical orbits from the move-
> ments of the heavenly bodies if they were not there. Man
> is discoverer, not creator, and the universe bears witness
> to another Mind than his....
>
>   Why should there be any such thing as understanding
> the universe? Who proposed that the universe should be
> understood? If the order from which man came forth is mind-
> less, what is there in it to give any guaranty or suggestion
> of understanding? What is there in such an order to bring
> forth a being who can think of that which has produced him?
> If there is no understanding mind in the premises, whence
> comes understanding mind in the conclusion?... If there was
> no mind in the universe before man, two wonderful things
> happened. Man, a part and product of the system, grew up
> greater than that which had produced him, with a power of
> understanding that had never been put into the world by any
> mind or power whatever, and had never been thought at all
> until he discovered them.[19]

19. Clarke, op. cit., pp. 108-9.

Admitting, of course, many gaps in the human knowledge of
the world and much seeming incoherency and disorder or 'evil' in
natural process, a cautious but constructive conclusion to this
stage of our problem would be to say that on the whole nature
exhibits <u>reasonableness</u>, a manifest <u>degree</u> of knowable form and
order. Indeed, nature exhibits such an extensive degree of
knowable connectedness that the argument from knowledge in its
empirical mood has surely a general validity. The general facts
are that nature presents us with regularity of succession throughout much of her observable field; sufficient to allow men to
formulate descriptive symbols and concepts of her processes.
Many of these seem, at least, tentatively right, as our best
approximations to what she really is, or may be, within her own
depth of being. Scientific approximations, which we call
'natural laws,' are not entirely wrong or irrelevant (though
sometimes they are found to be so and must be reformulated);
rather many of them are proximate certainties, are nearly and
virtually adequate correspondences. And science may advance
confidently in its discovery of 'nature's laws,' believing that
its progressing understanding of them approximates more and more
to her own inner workings. Error is possible to a degree, in
which the scientific symbol does not exactly correspond to the
event. This of course necessitates science's constant re-exam-
ination of her hypotheses; and the reformulation implies an
ultimate inherent rationality, or human knowability of the
world, on the basis of which an understanding of the need for
reformulation arises, and a successful reformulation may proceed.

What present-day science means by 'laws of nature' and her
'rationality,' is her general reasonableness and general knowability or 'conformity' to 'law.' This does not imply that the
universe is a rigidly fixed, mathematical-like structure throughout, as a narrow or frozen type rationalism might conceive her,
as, for example, Spinoza seemed to do. Living beings, growth,
evolution, natural experiments with novel form, striving, conflict of forces, and some defeats along the way; maleability,
a degree of yet unformed structuredness, real freedom and indeterminacy are as rationally necessary to our kind of world,
devoted to the coming to be of creatures of finite freedom with
real alternative destinies or histories, as any factors could
possibly be. The rationality of the universe does not mean that
she is an immobile mathematical grid-work, but that she is
process and history with all the finer possibilities, as well
as the dangers and frustrations, of a real history. Is it not
something like this that a circumspect science, and philosophy,
would mean by the total 'rationality' of the world? Nothing in
this broader concept of her rationality--which gives reign to
certain looseness and freeplay of parts--is contradictory to the
argument for God from knowledge or truth, in the spirit of

Augustine or Royce, or to the general law of sufficient reason
which an open rationalism assumes in its exploration of reality.
The universe's very _plasticity_ and _looseness_ of process, her
dynamic coherency, is her ultimate 'rationality.' For because
of this, change of form, development toward forms of greater
complexity and thereby inherent greater capacity, are possible,
and have proved to be (at least on the surface of one planet
that we know about, and can statistically conjecture concerning
at least 100,000 other life support planets in our galaxy)[20]
the actual fact requisite to the coming to be of finite forms of
spiritual personhood, which defines the creative work of God.
Today, as the Greeks could not fully realize, the world order
may be described as dynamic, evolutionary _Nous_ or _Logos_.[21]

---

20. Astronomer Louis Berman, University of San Francisco,
     statistically estimates the "numbers of communicative
     civilizations" in our Galaxy as 100,000. _Exploring_
     the Cosmos, Little, Brown & Co., 1973, pp. 403-6.
21. F.R. Tennant, repudiating the absolutistic notion of
     the meaning of nature's conformity to law or ration-
     ality(such as espoused, e.g. by Spinoza), and himself
     adopting an open or dynamic conception of the meaning
     of "conformity," concludes his chapter on this subject
     in the following memorable words (_Philosophical The-_
     ology, Vol. II, chap. I, pp. 21-3, Cambridge Univer-
     sity Press, 1937):
     "The logically and scientifically unwarrantable asser-
     tion of immutable and all-pervading law, dictated by
     things whose very nature constitutes them a closed
     system within which every change is fated...becomes
     absurd when taken for adequate description of a whole,
     to but a part of which it is known to have but approx-
     imate application.
         "When the travesties of such reign of law...are
     set aside, there remains the fact that laws have ob-
     tained and do obtain, whatever the future may bring
     forth. And this fact must have a sufficient reason....
     Unvarying concomitance or sequence is, indeed, logi-
     cally distinct from necessary connexion, but it points
     to Actual connextion and necessitation.... If we rule
     out the _prius_ of necessary law we must also rule out
     ungrounded coincidence, as no satisfactory explanation
     of Nature's conformity to law....
         "...On the other hand, it is upon such conformity
     to law, more correctly called regularity evocative of
     law, as the world evinces--and must intrinsically
     possess in order phenomenally to manifest it--that
     theistic argument is ultimately based. In the

The traditional term we have just used--Logos--to conclude
our statement in amplification of Royce's concept of the world
as order may remind the reader of his eloquent paragraph ending
the "Reality and Idealism" Lecture. We cite it at this place as
capturing the full sweep of his conception of God, or "this
divine Logos," as Personal Cosmic Mind (SMP p. 380):

> The world, then, is such stuff as ideas are made of.
> Thought possesses all things. But the world isn't unreal.
> It extends infinitely beyond our private consciousness,
> because it is the world of an universal mind. What facts
> it is to contain only experience can inform us. There is
> no magic that can anticipate the work of science. Absolutely
> the only thing sure from the first about this world, however,
> is that it is intelligent, rational, orderly, essentially
> comprehensible, so that all its problems are somewhere
> solved, all its darkest mysteries are known to the supreme
> Self. This Self infinitely and reflectively transcends our
> consciousness, and therefore, since it includes us, it is
> at the very least a person, and more definitely conscious
> than we are; for what it possesses is self-reflecting knowl-
> edge, and what is knowledge aware of itself, but conscious-
> ness? Beyond the seeming wreck and chaos of our finite
> problems, its eternal insight dwells, therefore, in absolute
> and supreme majesty. Yet it is not far from every one of
> us. There is no least or most transient thought that flits
> through a child's mind, or that troubles with the faintest
> line of care a maiden's face, and that still does not con-
> tain and embody something of this divine Logos.

And to like effect two paragraphs, one from <u>The Conception of</u>
God (1895) and another from <u>The World and the Individual</u>:

> In brief then the foregoing conception of God undertakes
> to be distinctly theistic, and not pantheistic. It is not
> the conception of any Unconscious Reality, into which
> finite beings are absorbed; nor of a Universal Substance,
> in whose law ethical independence is lost; nor of an Inef-
> fable Mystery, which we can only silently adore...I am cer-
> tainly disposed to insist that what the faith of our fathers

---

relatively settled order of Nature we may see the
first link of the chain of facts which, while they do
not logically demand, nevertheless cumulatively suggest
as reasonable, the teleological interpretation in which
theism essentially consists, in so far as its intellectual aspect is concerned."

has genuinely meant by God, is...identical with the inevitable outcome of a reflective philosophy.   (CG pp. 49-50)

...what our...conception asserts is that God's life, for
God's life we must now call this absolute fulfillment which
our...Conception defines, sees the one plan fulfilled through
all the manifold lives, the single consciousness winning its
purpose by virtue of all the ideas of all the individual
selves, and of all the lives.   No finite view is wholly
illusory.   Every finite intent taken precisely in its wholeness is fulfilled in the Absolute.   The least life is not
neglected, the most fleeting act is a recognized part of the
world's meaning.   You are for the divine view all that you
know yourself at this instant to be.   (WI1 pp. 426-7)

This last statement, of course, anticipates the problem of
freedom within the compass of Royce's Integral Idealism.   To
that problem we will turn, after the following brief digression.

        *   *   *   *   *   *   *   *   *   *

A house-keeping point, but an important one, may well be
considered briefly at this transition, where Royce and his type
of idealist philosophy has often been misunderstood by its
opponents.   It is a clarifying item regarding terminology, which
may also serve as introductory to our discussion of Royce's
solution to the problem of freedom, next taken up.   Royce's verbalization, "Absolute Truth," central concept in his form of
idealism, has many times been attacked as connoting a conception
of the universe as ultimately some kind of monolithic rigidity,
the "block universe" (James' critical expression)--which by
definition simply freezes out any possible finite differences
and freedoms, dynamic aspects, evolutionary and developmental
particulars, etc.   He himself, of course, does not believe this
to be a just criticism, as his great labors to refute monistic
"mysticism," and to clarify his philosophy in behalf of real
freedom in the finite case (as in God's too) attest.

But idealists may grant the point of critics regarding the
verbalization "Absolute Truth," as possibly leading to the misconception just described.   Royce himself, of course, would at
once reply that it is not the only term he has used to describe
the Ultimate or 'God.'   It is only one, among several that may
be employed.   From the standpoint of his full perception of
things some of these other expressions probably better yield
his meaning.

Whereas Royce does employ the expression "the Absolute,"
many times, and "Absolute Truth," "Absolute Experience,"

"--Knowledge," etc., he also many times refers to the "all-including thought" (RAP p. 425), "the Infinite Thought" (RAP p. 433), "the All-Enfolder" (RAP p. 435). We may take these latter phrases as more open-ended, less fraught, perhaps, with the dangers above described. If 'truth' has the connotation of something 'decided,' 'fixed,' 'settled,' or 'absolute,' the thought that thinks the truth is ever moving, searching, and open to the new and unexpected vista. In any case, these last terms, and those that immediately follow here, may be emphasized to correct the impression of the 'block universe'; indeed, they may well be substituted for the phrase "Absolute Truth." For us, then, Royce better refers to the ultimate in such terms as

"all-including thought"

"...fulness of the life of God" (RAP p. 441, 1885)

"...the divine World-Self as a Thinker, and...this his fullness of Being" (SGE p. 166, 1898)

"What is, is for us no longer a mere Form, but a Life ..." (WI1, 1899, p. 342)

"...God is the Absolute Being, and the perfect fullness of Life" (Ib, 394)

"...the self-conscious organism of the Absolute..." (WI2, 1900, p. 442)

We are here suggesting that the expression "Absolute Truth" means in Royce's complete outlook the Fullness of Truth in Being. We would recommend for idealistic philosophy a correction of fundamental expression along this line. Royce himself suggests the 'Fullness of Truth in Being' in his references to "fullness of life," "fullness of Being," etc. a number of times in the lines just quoted. In any case, this language "fullness of being" is a clue to his largest thought, and prompts the following brief commentary on it, anticipating our study of how he dealt with the problem of freedom.

We take as the true, coherent definition of truth the time-honored one of the correspondence of thought to things, of ideas to the way the world is; truth is a psychological judgment that tells what reality is. It therefore refers to and includes being itself as well as the judgments about being.[22]

We may avoid the sentiment of frozen rigidity in the traditional terminology, "Absolute Truth." Human beings do not know or have Absolute Truth--only God would have or know what

---

22.   Addendum on the Definition of Truth: Can we define "truth" only in the terms "that which is"?, (Thus "error": "that which is not"?). "That which is" would be a partial, incomplete definition of truth. "That which is" implies knowledge of what is, or of being--how can I say "what is" unless I mean I know what is? If I say "X is," I mean I know that X is. Thus our "correspondence" definition of truth is implied--truth is the correspondence of our thought to what is, or to things. Truth is our awareness of what is (and of what can, and perhaps ought to be or become). (Likewise, "error" is not what is not, but error is an erroneous process of judgment, and this indeed is many times a psychological fact.)
In any case, "that which is" is not solely material facts and their relationships; accordingly truth even under this definition includes psychological process, judgmental thought, value thought, and the whole realm of what we call "spirit."
To be sure, I can refer to nuts in the forest as examples of what is, that I do not directly (or empirically) know, or am aware of; or I can refer to objects and "laws" or orderly processes and relationships of nature, that, as a scientist I do not yet know, or have discovered, or have acquaintance with directly-- such things we must declare "must be" apart from our present or immediate knowledge. But when I venture to talk about nuts, or as yet undiscovered scientific objects and laws, like 'quasars' and 'black holes,'-- beyond the point of their raw existence--I am at once involved in quality perceptions (primary and secondary), in judgments as to their properties and relations, qualitatively and logically, and am involved in the experience of a subject, i.e. myself, as "knowing," or as endeavoring to get his forms, and processes of thought into correspondence with these things. We are thus back in the realization that truth is an implicative system, meaning a subject-thinking-or-endeavoring-to-conceive-reality; we cannot in over simple sense say merely that truth is "what is." In the realm of "what is" I cannot leave my own subjectivity out, with its basic drive to know what is.

that is. It may indeed mean a totality of knowledge and of
being transcending our own, which in part the concept of God has
traditionally meant. We can rest assured that "Absolute Truth"
would not be an all-devouring, undifferentiated Absolute or a
"block universe"--which would deny finite orders of being, difference, distinctions, and freedoms. Instead of the expression
then, "Absolute Truth" (if it be an unacceptable one), the
better description of things is "the fullness of Truth in Being"
--based, as we have just seen, on expressions Royce himself used.

What does "the fullness of Truth in Being" (and in Process)
mean?

Whatever other world facts it may mean the "fullness of
Truth in Being" would include in its meaning our own reality as
personal lives in their finitude, freedom, and experience of
growth, interaction and dependence.

The "absoluteness," then, or fullness of God's Truth would
best be understood in, or as, his steadfast moral purposes in
bringing forth the worlds and establishing the conditions for
finite process and freedom; and his beckoning of life toward the
moral ideal, i.e. toward the harmony of life with life in love
and justice. Royce said as much as this, but now perhaps we go
beyond his express, utterance, and draw from a parallel idealist
tradition in American philosophical letters--that of the 'personalist' school of Boston University--which stressed above all
the Personal quality of the Divine life.

If we employ the term "absolute" in reference to God, we
keep in mind that the expression carries meaning only under that
of the Divine "personality." God may be called the Absolute
because He is fundamentally a Person, the Personal ground of
the world. His Personality defines His absoluteness. We quote
Albert C. Knudson on the absoluteness of God in terms of the
'Personal,' as highest qualification of the Divine Nature, the
ground at once of the world and of our ultimate freedoms. The
only correction that we would presume to make of the following
large perspective would be to refer to the Absolute, not as "the
independent ground" (this to avoid the implications of classic
dualistic theism), but to refer to the Absolute as the self-
dependent ground of the universe. In any case Knudson said,

If the idea of a metaphysical Absolute is to be retained,
it should be in a causal sense of the term; and in this
sense there is not inconsistency between it and the idea of
personality. From the causal point of view the Absolute is
the independent ground or cause of the universe.... Everything is dependent upon it for its existence; and it is this

that constitutes its absoluteness. But absoluteness thus
understood does not exclude the power to know and the power
of self-control. These powers, which are the essential constituents of personality are also essential to the Absolute,
if he be regarded as absolute in power.... The common judgment must, then, be reversed. Instead of saying that personality is inconsistent with absoluteness, we must say,
rather, that perfect personality is possible only in the
Absolute. The contrary view rests upon a mistaken conception of what metaphysical absoluteness is.[23]

The Divine Reality and Human Freedom

One of the larger purposes of his Gifford Lectures, The
World and the Individual, was to show that there is no mutual,
logical contradiction between the idea of the freedom of God as
Personal Absolute and that of men in their finite freedom.
Royce endeavored to solve the problem of the relation of the
Divine to the human "will" in terms reminiscent of Kant. Whether
he himself was consciously following a Kantian inspiration in
the effort to solve this problem remains undetermined. But we
draw the two together, by citing a seminal line in Kant's philosophy, in order the better to explain Royce's effort regarding
this matter.

In contexts expounding the principle of the freedom of the
will, the third facet of the Categorical or moral imperative,
Kant had written, "every being that cannot act except under the
idea of freedom is just for that in a practical point of view
really free" (emphasis his).[24]

In the history of Idealism, in a later context, of course,
than Kant, Royce attempted to solve the problem of the relation
of the Divine to the Human will in terms of a similar emphasis
on the idea of freedom. At the end of the 18th century, Kant
spoke in the context of a more traditional dualistic theism, or
personalism, with God understood as something other or transcendent to his world, as in the classic Hebrew-Christian tradition, with the world and man as the created product of the
Divine Will. However, for Kant, God and man join in legislating

---

23.   Albert C. Knudson, The Doctrine of God, Abingdon
       Press, 1930, pp. 304-5.
24.   Kant, Selections, ed. Theodore Meyer Green, Charles
       Scribner's Sons, 1929, p. 335.

the "moral law"[25] similarly by virtue of the creative fecundity
of the idea of freedom itself, the central idea in the sense of
'personality' and its sacred reverence, which Kant had announced
in his second statement of the moral imperative. In a similar
perspective of inspiration, at the close of the 19th century,
Royce spoke in the context of his Absolute or Integral Idealism,
with God or the Divine Mind understood as being in some sense
the total life of the world itself raised to the concept of an
Absolute Consciousness. Both Kant's and Royce's thought, however, converge in the idea of freedom. In it they divine a
solution to the problem of freedom for a theistic philosophy,
Kant implicitly, and Royce explicitly. Like much great thought,
that solution is astonishingly simple.

It is that we are all free, yet we all have the idea of
freedom commonly. Moral or responsible freedom is the Idea that
connects all men, and constitutes the Life of God Himself on the
side of the Divine individuation or concretion of things into a
world of finite individualities and persons. We are 'in' the
'being' of God, in the sense that we are a part of this, the
Divine Meaning or Idea for the world. But this meaning or idea
is precisely that we should be free. We hear Royce say that "we
are full of the presence and the freedom of God" (WI2 p. 417).
In terms now already familiar to the reader, from our discussion
in Parts I and II, we endeavor to clarify further Royce's insight
relative to this issue by the following analysis.

The clue to Royce's thinking about freedom was his teleological understanding or definition of personal selfhood, in
both the finite case and the Divine or Cosmic case. Royce considered the "self," on both the Divine and human planes, as a
teleological process that comes into 'reality' in man's case, or
achieves its cosmic destiny in God's example, only through growth
toward realization of a supreme life plan, or purposive 'ideal.'
God's 'life plan' would be the totality of meaning of the cosmic
process as a whole, as the process of personalization itself.
God's purposive act, from His inclusive height, provides for the
coming to be of finite persons, implying all the systems of
material energies requisite for their ultimate appearance as
derived beings of the spirit. They are His children, like Him
because sharing with Him in the quintessential Idea of Freedom,
the ultimate spiritual energy or force. Recall that the telic
drive toward fulfilling the internal meaning of ideas defines
ultimately the meaning of 'personhood' on both planes of reality,

_____

25. Summarized in the first facet of the moral imperative:
'so act that the maximum of thy action may become, or
be seen to be, a universal law.'

that is, on the Divine or Absolute dimension, as well as on the human.[26]

---

26.   Edward A. Jarvis in The Conception of God in the Later
      Royce, op. cit., Note 7, p. 90 calls attention to a
      larger problem of exegesis, relative to the conception
      of God, from a perspective that is in considerable
      difference to the one we have been pursuing here on
      Royce as a type of 'process' philosopher. On page 31
      Fr. Jarvis asserts that Royce's conception of God in
      RAP is distinguished "from all process philosophies
      which view God as evolving or as somehow contained
      within the process of time and change." And again on
      page 85 he says, relative to the middle period, "Royce
      also continues to reject any theory of evolution of
      God's consciousness. His position on the nature of
      God's consciousness as eternal, unchanging and trans-
      cendent precludes this in The World and the Individual
      as it did in the early work."
          We would agree with Fr. Jarvis that the early
      work, The Religious Aspect of Philosophy, does not
      specifically reveal the dynamic conception of the
      Divine selfhood as the larger case of telic-energy
      which is somehow inclusive of our own finite cases of
      such processive personhood. We believe, however, that
      the latter description of God is particularly charac-
      teristic of the WI, and is present throughout Royce's
      subsequent works. The WI conceives finite purposes
      as growing, and achieving fulfillment in God's ulti-
      mate perspective, under the impulse of their own free-
      dom--to be defined as identical to God's own freedom,
      (acknowledged by Jarvis, p. 67, in terms very similar
      to our own pp. 110f. above). But this expansive quality
      of the Divine perception of things, would suggest
      that for Royce there is present a conception of a
      continuing enlargement, enrichment, or 'growth' of the
      Divine consciousness itself by its very knowledge of
      our own finite achievements and satisfactions, much as
      Whitehead understands the cosmic situation. The point
      is succinctly made in William James and Other Essays
      where Royce said, "...the whole universe needs your
      spiritual triumph for the sake of its completion..." And
      "...God wins perfection through expressing himself in
      a finite life and triumphing over and through its very
      finitude" (The Macmillan Co., 1911, pp. 182-3). Father
      Jarvis's interpretation of this particular issue, how-
      ever, though somewhat too limited, in our view, does
      remind us, to be sure, of the fundamental ambiguity

The essence of Royce's position is that there is no conflict if we properly define reality or cosmic process as a whole
in this way. That process must be described as Infinite Personality in the act of releasing or realizing its 'purpose' or
'idea,' namely, the creation of the grounds of possibility for
the coming to be of finite lives, with their release, in turn,
of finite purposes and ideas in progressive enrichment of the
whole. God is the willer of the conditions (of whatever sort
necessary, both material or otherwise) of finite freedom. This
is the distinctive nature of the Absolute Life and Activity. In
Part II we learned that for Royce, individuality, in both man
and God, is defined by its fulfillment of a single purpose, in
constant realization of some over-all or commanding 'idea.' To
summarize thus far, the single or all-commanding purpose on a
cosmic scale, which would define its greater Individuality, is
its aim to will into being, as the supreme Idea, or Idea of
ideas, the conditions for finite individuality to appear in its
freedom (WI1 pp. 424-7, 433-70),[27] with opportunity thence to
move in its own telic life toward its own personalization under
the common idea of freedom, as responsible to the moral good.
This means, in substance for Royce, that God is defined as the
ground or condition that makes personal being possible, and
summons that being toward its own ultimate self-realization in
its loyalty to loyalty, Royce's theme in our next section.

At a later time, Paul Tillich's trenchant phrase, God as
"the Ground of Being," or "the Power of Being," describes, I
believe what Royce said earlier in our century concerning a
fundamental definitional notion of God. The particular value
of Royce's way of saying it was that he analyzed this notion
from profoundest introspective standpoint in freedom itself.

Now to carry the argument a step farther into the idea of
causation, Royce went on to say that the difficulty of understanding the relationship between the wills is cleared up when
we realize that the 'power of will' cannot be conceived mechani-
cally or quantitatively in terms of efficient causality--that
is, in terms of billiard balls or forces hitting each other.
(Indeed, in spite of some statement which appears to the con-
trary--WI1 pp. 467-70--it is assumed by Royce that God may have

---

discussed in our subsequent criticism relative to the
problem of 'time' and 'eternity' in Royce, (see pp.
173f.
27. See also CG pp. 201-3, and many further passages of
like import: WI2 pp. 415-27; SRI pp. 159-61.

an aspect as <u>efficient causality</u> in being the origin of, or
ultimate ground or maintainer of the world, reflected in the
productive forces or energies of nature.)[28]   But God's relation
to finite freedom, once it appears, must be thought out in terms
of final causality and teleological paradigms--quite as Whitehead did at a later time in his "subjective aim" principle.   In
mechanical terms the problem of the wills is indeed insoluble.
Rather than the idea of "causation" with its connotation of
material efficiency or compulsion, we must use the teleological
conception of "meaning."   I can <u>mean</u> or <u>propose</u> something.
Another self can enter literally into <u>my</u> <u>meaning</u> or <u>proposition</u>
through the sharing of spiritual ideas.   So can we with God in
the supreme Idea that is our freedom, and His supreme "meaning"
(WI1 p. 466).   Thus God does not <u>cause</u> us at the highest reach
of our persons; He <u>means</u> us.   This spiritualizing of the conception of causality--indeed its substitution by a different dimension of thinking altogether--is a necessary step toward the
solution of the problem of the wills.   Royce has told us that
being is deeper than causation understood in any mechanical
sense:

> ...we have said that all causation, whatever it is, is but
> a special instance of Being, and never can explain any of
> the ultimate problems about Being.   (WI1 p. 467)

> Being is everywhere deeper than causation....   (WI1 p. 469)

> Therefore are you in action Free and Individual, just
> because the unity of the divine life...implies in every
> finite being just such essential originality of meaning as
> that of which you are conscious.   (WI1 p. 470)

We are, then, 'in' the 'being' of God, in the sense that
we are a part of the Divine meaning, implication, or <u>intent</u>.
But this meaning or Idea of ideas is precisely that we should
be free (WI1 pp. 466-70; WI2 p. 276).

It should be kept in mind that for Royce selfhood does not
have a thing-like reality, of either material or spiritual
quality.   Royce is against any 'realistic' doctrine of the self.
It is not a hard core of inexplicable fact; we heard him say,
it is "no mere datum."   On the Cosmic as on the finite scale it
is essentially "a <u>Meaning</u> embodied in a conscious life" (WI2

---

28.   "...our experiences of Nature...hint of a vaster realm
of life and of meaning of which we men form a part,
and of which the final unity is in God's life" (WI2
p. 204).

p. 269). Thus God on his side is not conceived as a kind of
divine Substance which 'wills' as a secondary and derivative
function of its 'being.' He does not possess a solid kind of
being, or fixed, realistic entity, which later bestirs itself
and sends forth its power. Rather for Royce it would seem that
the Cosmic Being and the Cosmic Willing and Individuation are
one and the same process. God as Person has a 'being' of
'process,' 'function,' and 'meaning' identical with his purposes,
just as finite individuals have. For Royce, the cosmic process
of individualization and personalization is possible only because
in its ultimate reaches of meaning it itself is Conscious and
Personal. Royce would answer Bosanquet's dictum that "to will
a will is to will its content" by saying that such a way of
putting the problem is too materialistic or quantitative, too
mechanical. Both God and men are purposing spirits; and the
purposes of two personal beings can, in a manner of speaking,
become identical, as spiritual ideas, as suggested above,
without implying the mutual destruction or cancellation of their
respective selfhoods.

To summarize and conclude concerning Royce's solution to
the problem of the wills: In The World and the Individual he
wrestled most strenuously with the problem of his alleged "absolutism," or as his critics have put it, his "block universe"
theory of reality, in behalf of both human freedom and the
Divine freedom. He endeavored to solve the problem by ruling
out any notions of mechanical causality for describing the relationship of the Divine to the human "will." He substituted
rather the concept of a spiritual or moral relationship, centered in the idea of freedom itself, the Idea of ideas (reflecting, we believe, an emphasis in Kant), where the divine and the
human realities, or orders of being, may, without logical or
metaphysical confusion, be conceived to meet. God and man are
mutually self-expressed in the world's ultimate "meaning" as the
meaning-for-freedom, which is the central spirit of the world
process. We believe, that a solution to the problem of the
wills must follow Royce in this thinking.[29]

---

29. To state it in a slightly different way, God's "will"
     must ultimately be defined in terms of what the cosmic
     process is manifestly doing in providing for the
     coming to be, the freedom, and the moral growth of
     finite spirits--not in terms of Mohammed's or Calvin's
     idea of God's will as inexorable force, analogous to
     the gross gravities and compulsions of physical nature.
     In Mohammed's or Calvin's form of theism there was no
     solution to the problem of freedom. The diagram in
     Note 30 may assist the reader in understanding Royce's

A few excerpts from the mansions of his eloquence on this
subject follow here from the essays "Individuality and Freedom,"
"Universality and Unity," "The Human Self," and "The Union of
God and Man":

> No accusation is more frequent than that Idealism
> which has once learned to view the world as a rational whole,
> present in its actuality to the unity of a single conscious-
> ness, has then no room either for finite individuality, or
> for freedom of ethical action... (WI1 p. 433)

> In sum, then, as to the most general form of the abso-
> lute unity, our guide is inevitably the type of empirical
> unity present in our own passing consciousness, precisely in
> so far as it has relative wholeness, and is rational. If
> one asks, "How should the many be one, and how should the
> whole take on the form of variety?" I answer, "Look within.
> You may grasp many facts at once; and when you have even the
> most fragmentary idea, your one purpose is here and now par-
> tially embodied in a presented succession of empirical facts."
> If you ask, "But how can many different ideal processes be
> united in the unity of a single idea?" I answer, "That is
> precisely what in your own way you can observe whenever you
> think, however fragmentarily, of the various, and often
> highly contrasting, ideas that occur to your mind when you
> grasp the meaning of any hypothetical or complex proposition,
> --such as the present one." ...But if for the divine mind,
> some still more inclusive form takes up our time-stream into
> a yet larger unity of experience, all the more is what we
> mean by temporal succession present together for the Absolute
> Experience....
> And now what our Fourth Conception [of Being] asserts
> is that God's life, for God's life we must now call this
> absolute fulfillment which our Fourth Conception defines,
> sees the one plan fulfilled through all the manifold lives,
> the single consciousness winning its purpose by virtue of
> all the ideas, of all the individual selves, and of all the
> lives. No finite view is wholly illusory. Every finite
> intent taken precisely in its wholeness is fulfilled in the
> Absolute.... You are for the divine view all that you now
> know yourself at this instant to be....

We have no other dwelling-place but the single unity of the
divine consciousness. In the light of the eternal we are

---

conception of the relation of the Divine Mind to the
Human mind and freedom as we have interpreted him in
the text above. (We have referred to the orthodox
Sunnis interpretation of Mohammed.)

manifest, and even this very passing instant pulsates with
a life that all the worlds are needed to express. In vain
would we wander in the darkness; we are eternally at home in
God.   (WI1 pp. 424-7)

What we see, however, is that every distinguishable portion
of the divine life, in addition to all the universal ties
which link it to the whole, expresses its own meaning. We
see, too, that this meaning is unique, and that this meaning
is precisely identical with what each one of us means by
his own individual will, so far as that will is at any time
determinate, uniquely selected, and empirically expressed.
So much then for the general relations of Absolute and
Finite will.   (WI1 p. 466)

By this meaning of my life-plan, by this possession of an
ideal, by this intent always to remain another than my
fellows despite my divinely planned unity with them,--by
this, and not by the possession of any Soul-Substance, I am
defined and created a Self.   (WI2 p. 276, Royce's emphasis
omitted here)

Remember...that you are in your inner life, in the way that
psychological analysis has now rendered familiar,--an insubstantial series of psychical conditions, physically and
socially determined.... And then, when you have done all
this, ask afresh this one question: How can I know all
these things? And how can all these facts themselves possess
any Being? You will find that the only possible answer to
your questions will take the form of asserting, in the end,
that you can know all this, and that all this can be real,
only by reason of an ontological relation that, when rightly
viewed, is seen to link yourself, even in all your weakness,
to the very life of God, and the whole universe to the meaning of every Individual. In God you possess your individuality. Your very dependence is the condition of your freedom, and of your unique significance.... ...we are full of
the presence and the freedom of God....
    ...as to our whole definition of the nature of the
Divine Life. If our foregoing argument has been sound, our
Idealism especially undertakes to give a theory of the
general place and of the significance of Personality in the
Universe. Personality, to our view, is an essentially
ethical category. A Person is a conscious being, whose
life, temporally viewed, seeks its completion through deeds,
while this same life, eternally viewed, consciously attains
its perfection by means of the present knowledge of the
whole of its temporal strivings. Now from our point of
view, God is a Person.... ...his life...is the infinite

whole that includes this endless temporal process, and that
consciously surveys it as one life, God's own life. God is
thus a Person, because, for our view, he is self-conscious,
and because the Self of which it is conscious is a Self
whose eternal perfection is attained through the totality
of these ethically significant temporal strivings, these
processes of evolution, these linked activities of finite
Selves. (WI2 pp. 417-19)[30]

---

30. Royce's conception of the nature and relation of the
     Divine Mind to the Human--a suggestion:

Finite Mind and Experience

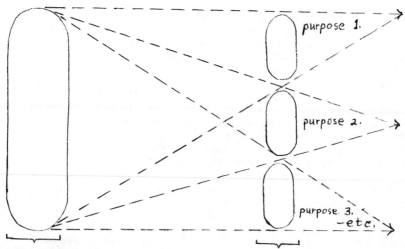

Total idea of our own human
freedom, willing its concrete
realization in particular
finite ideas and their
purposes, 1, 2, 3, etc.

Separate free ideas and
their purposes, i.e. of
freedom in any particular
direction of interest.

Human experience: we are complexes of ideas and purposes in
an ultimate unity of 'freedom,' 'selfhood,' 'individuality'--
finite mind. Each finite purpose is more or less independent,
of its associates, but not totally so; this is the analogy
of our freedom to God's.

The Divine Reality and Human Community

Royce considered the self a teleological process coming into focus or reality only through growth toward realization of a supreme life plan, or purposive ideal, a process consummated by the ethic of Loyalty within the "Community of Interpretation."

God's Infinite Experience in Relation
to Finite Experience

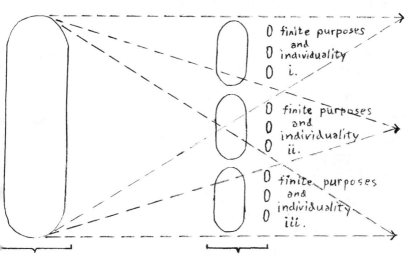

God's Idea of Freedom
'willing' (or 'meaning') its
concrete realization in
f.i, f.ii, f.iii: the Idea
of ideas that connects all
individuality or personhood
and constitutes the Life
of God.

Our ideas of our freedom
constituting our personhood
or individuality.

What did he mean by the concept finally attained in his
most mature philosophic years, the "Community of Interpretation"? Royce believed that his achievement solved the tension
between the natural élan of the self, pushing toward the fulfillment of its own life plan or purpose, and the realization
that fulfillment and true satisfaction in one's personal existence cannot be attained apart from love, self-giving, and
service in a communal cause. Service is, for Royce, the interpretive process. Individual men must become committed to the
community of interpretation. That is, and we cite Fuss's able
summary at this place:

> The goal of this community is thought to be that final
> interpretation in which each truth would be known in rela-
> tion to every other truth, and each value or interest that
> has survived the critical scrutiny of the community as a
> whole would be harmonized with every other similarly
> established value of interest.[31]

Professor Fuss himself acknowledges that his conception of
the later Royce (cited in our opening comments on Royce's view
of God, p. 80) is a guess. An alternative view may now be
offered. We suggest that Royce finally developed his metaphysical idealism in the direction of a much more open theism
than allowed by his early "Possibility of Error" essay in The
Religious Aspects of Philosophy. We have just reviewed how
Royce in The World and the Individual argued with his critics
over his alleged absolutism, against the block universe theory
of reality, indeed in behalf of freedom as the very central
emphasis of his system. Royce would never have allowed that
his philosophy led to the view that "we are emanations of an
Absolute Will whose cosmic designs we cannot do otherwise than
fulfill"--Fuss's description of his subject's earlier philosophy.[32]

Royce may indeed have abandoned the "absolutism" of the
essay, "Possibility of Error," in the sense that he was constantly aware of the problems his version of the ontological
argument and the idea of God it endeavored to sustain presented.
He strove to meet these problems in his later works. Surely,
however, he did not abandon his theism, that is, his belief in
God as Personal Cosmic Spiritual Energy. Rather he opened up
his earlier idealism and made it more truly personalistic in the
development of his ethical theory, which Fuss so well describes.

---

31. The Moral Philosophy of Josiah Royce, op. cit., p.
     252.
32. Ib. p. 262.

At the same time, through his "Philosophy of Loyalty" theme, and
finally his "Community of Interpretation" idea, Royce endeavored
to make his philosophy more explicitly Christian. The Problem
of Christianity is a 20th-century idealist interpretation of the
kingdom of heaven. His deeply moving expositions of Christian
love in that work, uttered against the background of his manifest
faith in a Personal God, make very plain that he had not abandoned his theism.[33]

   In the light of Royce's persistent theism, then, what
became of his idealism when it reached its clearest ethical
focus in the "Community of Interpretation"? For The Problem of
Christianity, "community" is not a new and entirely original
factor, contrary to will or to love, those agents of individuality previously acknowledged in The Conception of God and The
World and the Individual. Rather it comprises an enlargement of
their implications, an application of "the spirit of my absolute
voluntarism to the new problems which our empirical study of the
Christian ideas, and our metaphysical theory of interpretation
have presented..." (PC p. 350). We cannot possibly avoid community, if we have love, just as there is no lasting community
without love. In Royce's own words, "Metaphysically considered,
the world of interpretation is the world in which, if indeed we
are able to interpret at all, we learn to acknowledge the being
and the inner life of our fellowmen..." (p. 294).[34]

---

33. E.g. PC, op. cit., pp. 87-9.
34. I find that I am in essential agreement with Royce's
    noted interpreter, Gabriel Marcel, on this large ques-
    tion concerning the continuity rather than the discon-
    tinuity in the conception of the Absolute between the
    earlier and the later works, La Metaphysique de Royce,
    Aubier, Editions Montaigne, 1945, pp. 212-4: "...il
    paraît bien certain...que la théorie de l'interpréta-
    tion ne se substitue pas à la quatrième conception
    de l'être, mais la requiert au contraire comme son
    fondement" (p. 212). "...la théorie de l'interpréta-
    tion peut être regardée comme l'expression authentique
    et approfondie de cette quatrième conception de l'être
    qui se formulait dans les ouvrages antérieurs en un
    langage encore inadeqat" (p. 214).
       See also Andrew J. Reck" "Royce's Metaphysics,"
    Revue Internationale de Philosophie, 1967, 79-80, p.
    8f., who likewise accepts the thesis of the coherency
    between Royce's earlier and later thought concerning
    this issue.

The Problem of Christianity has transformed Royce's earlier
term, "meaning," into "interpretation." The social process in
its profoundest meaning or achievement is one where persons
mutually understand each other in the dimensions of empathy and
love so that a common on-going life may be secured (pp. 314-9).
"Interpretation" or "the will to interpret" goes beyond just
the will to 'perceive' and to 'conceive,' to the will to 'love';
it stands as the divine impulse because its end is "complete
mutual understanding" (p. 319). Finally, Royce joins this
"Community of Interpretation" to his former conception of the
Absolute.

If in one body of Royce's writings we find the conception
of the differentiation or dispersion of the divine "meaning"
into finite freedom as a kind of supreme cosmological principle,
we cannot overlook his final and complementary conception of the
Absolute as "community" (pp. 317-19). He says that "this essentially social universe, this community" must be declared to be
"the sole supreme reality, the Absolute..." (p. 350). As the
principle of togetherness, of community, without which neither
the community nor the individuals whom the community nourishes
could exist, Interpretation is indeed "absolute." It is the
very principle or power of ethical existence, the moral bond or
relationship itself.

The Absolute has here been thoroughly warmed up and moral-
ized. It is spiritual process: It is love--Royce's modern
counterpart to the New Testament's 'Holy Spirit.' It is not the
passionless, cosmic Thought of the essay, "Possibility of Error."
In The Problem of Christianity Royce may sound sometimes as
though he is saying that God, or the Absolute, is but a verbal
hypostasis of his principle of Interpretation. Yet on the whole
I think he meant to retain his belief in the Divine Spirit as
Cosmic Reality, now viewed, however, less abstractly or less
merely logically, but rather more in psychological-moral dimensions as immanent Spirit, called in his own words, "God the
Interpreter":[35]

> And, if, in ideal, we aim to conceive the divine
> nature, how better can we conceive it than in the form of
> the Community of Interpretation, and above all in the form
> of the Interpreter, who interprets all to all, and each
> individual to the world and the world of spirits to each
> individual.
> In such an interpreter, and in his community, the
> problem of the One and the Many would find its ideally

---

35.   Pages 268f. of this commentary enlarges on this theme.

complete expression and solution. The abstract conceptions and the mystical intuitions would be at once transcended, and illumined, and yet retained and kept clear and distinct, in and through the life of one who, as interpreter, was at once servant to all and chief among all, expressing his will through all, yet, in his interpretations, regarding and loving the will of the least of these his brethren. In him the Community, the Individual, and the Absolute would be completely expressed, reconciled, and distinguished....
...if love for this community is awakened,--then indeed this love is able to grasp, in ideal, the meaning of the Church Universal, of the Communion of Saints, and of God the Interpreter. (pp. 318-19)

Royce is not just the academic philosopher; he obviously became the Christian theologian, who attempted--along with others, such as Borden Parker Bowne, who worked from slightly different perspectives--a grand union of Judeo-Christian personalistic sentiment and categories with those of 19th and 20th century philosophical idealism.

(Here we refer the reader to our further discussion of Royce's ethical and social views in Part IV.)

Chapter Six

WHITEHEAD ON THE CONCEPTION AND ARGUMENT
AND THE PROBLEM OF FREEDOM

Whitehead can be discussed somewhat more briefly than Royce on the issues of theism thus far treated, namely, the idea of God, argument or proof, and freedom.[1] Whitehead has no consciously elaborated formal argument. Indeed, what argument we find is of the cosmological-teleological type. As we stated in the introduction to this part of our commentary, Whitehead simply begins with an acknowledgement or affirmation that nature exhibits order, and expresses his own reverential wonder at it. In so many words, this order is itself a direct expression or manifestation of an organizing principle, conceived as ultimate Cosmic Mind or Telic, Proposing Spirit. This supreme Reality is "Personal" at least on the temporal, developmental side of its being ("Consequent God"); but remains "unconscious," or impersonal on the eternal, and abstract side of its being ("Primordial God"). In his words again, the Consequent side of the divine nature is the supreme "principle of limitation" (a term appearing early in the development of his theological thought, SMW). Consequent God is postulated as the principle of limitation to account for the specific types of individuality or entities that the world actually exhibits, out of the limitless wealth of possibility of quality that the eternal objects represent in the mind of Primordial God.

The first part of this essay suggested that Whitehead's description of the Divine Nature, was more truly or literally Platonist than was Royce's view. He was, however, very much less a Platonist than Royce in his omission of any thing like

---

1. *Whitehead's Philosophy, Selected Essays, 1935-1970*, by Charles Hartshorne, University of Nebraska Press, 1972, is the insightful commentary on Whitehead's conception of God by his most noted living interpreter. A sketch of Whitehead's philosophy as a whole is presented, but these distinguished essays are centered on elaborating the theistic theme in Whitehead. Hartshorne labors to reveal the rational and religious superiority of Whitehead's immanental, processive, Cosmic Theism to the classic, dualistic views of Deity. He succeeds with many subtle nuances of exposition that suffuse these originally independently written essays.

the latter's semi-mystical ontological argument, based on the
human truth experience, which was adumbrated in Plato's dialogues, particularly in the Republic. Whitehead's argument for
God, in so far as we find one, is reminiscent, however, of
another side of Plato. The latter's Book X of the Laws enshrines
a profound version of the cosmological argument. Like the Laws
dialogue, Whitehead relies on the empirical side of reason for
his own vision of the presence of God in, and to the world.

Classifying Whitehead as among the "Cosmic theists" of our
time, Wieman and Meland captured his thoroughly empirical approach to the problem of belief in God when they wrote:

The cosmic theists...do not start with a belief in God
which they try to defend by using the findings of science
to support the concept of a divine ground and goal of the
process of nature. Rather they seek to find something in
the process itself which they can hail as the reality
demanding our supreme devotion.[2]

Belief may follow; it does not precede scientific investigation.
And empirical investigation is the best guide to what shape
belief or idea shall ultimately take.

Royce's noted idealist pupil and fellow teacher with White-
head in the department of philosophy at Harvard, William Ernest
Hocking, paraphrased his colleague in the following record. It
points out Whitehead's essentially different initial stance from
Royce. As remembered discussion, Hocking quotes the following
Whitehead sentiments:[3]

"Becoming is its own explanation...I am very near to
absolute idealism.... But where I differ is, your Absolute
is a super-reality. My point is, when you try to get a
ground of reality more real than the given, you get an
abstraction: your super-reality is an under-reality.
Reality is always emergence into a finite modal entity."

Though there is no ontological argument in Whitehead, there
is "the ontological principle," which, indeed is probably why
such an argument cannot arise in Whitehead's empiricism! The

---

2.   Henry Nelson Wieman and Bernard Eugene Meland: Amer-
      ican Philosophies of Religion, op. cit. p. 229.
3.   Not to be considered ipsissima verba Hocking indicates
      in a note in his chapter, "Whitehead on Mind and Nature,"
      Paul Arthur Schilpp, ed., The Philosophy of Alfred North
      Whitehead, op. cit., pp. 385 & 386.

ontological principle was that there are no <u>reasons</u> more inclu-
sively ultimate than all the actual entities, or individualities,
themselves (among which God is one) as explanatory of being.
They are themselves, with their powers of prehension and integration, their "creativity," the ultimate given facts. In Whitehead's words:

> This ontological principle means that actual entities are
> the only <u>reasons</u>; so that to search for a <u>reason</u> is to
> search for one or more actual entities. (<u>PR</u> p. 37)

Thus, if we are to search for God, we must search empirically; or doubtless more true to the priorities in Whitehead's
empiricism, we should say that our empirical searching of things
<u>may</u> <u>lead</u> us in fact to a supreme principle of order in "God."
"...the sheer statement, of what things are, may contain elements
explanatory of why things are" (SMW p. 94).

Let us focus for the time-being on such argument as we find
in Whitehead for God as World Orderer.

First, from his <u>Science and the Modern World</u> (1925) and
<u>Religion in the Making</u> (1926) several sayings are selected to
illustrate his characteristic approach to the problem of argument
or proof as centering in the manifestation of order:[4]

> According to this argument the fact that there is a
> process of actual occasions, and the fact that the occasions
> are the emergence of values which require...limitation, both
> require that the course of events should have developed amid
> an antecedent limitation composed of conditions, particular-
> ization, and standards of value.
> Thus as a further element in the metaphysical situation,
> there is required a principle of limitation. (SMW p. 178)

---

4. The point that the main argument for God in Whitehead
is woven around, the problem of "order," bespeaking the
necessity of a "principle of limitation," is penetra-
tingly discussed in a book by Kenneth F. Thompson Jr.,
<u>Whitehead's Philosophy of Religion</u>, Mouton, The Hague,
Chapter I: "Why the World Requires God." Thompson
singles out four levels of manifest cosmic order in the
Whitehead discussion which point to such cosmic limitation, or God as the principle of order: logical
order, the spacio-temporal continuum, the evidence of
particularity in process, the fact of the realization
and preservation of value.

The definite determination which imposes ordered balance
on the world requires an actual entity imposing its own
unchanged consistency of character on every phase. (RM
p. 94)

There is an actual world because there is an order in nature.
If there were no order, there would be no world. Also since
there is a world, we know that there is an order. The
ordering entity is a necessary element in the metaphysical
situation presented by the actual world.
    This line of thought extends Kant's argument. He saw
the necessity for God in the moral order. But with his
metaphysics he rejected the argument from the cosmos. The
metaphysical doctrine, here expounded, finds the foundations
of the world in the aesthetic experience, rather than--as
with Kant--in the cognitive and conceptive experience. All
order is therefore aesthetic order, and the moral order is
merely certain aspects of aesthetic order. The actual world
is the outcome of the aesthetic order, and the aesthetic
order is derived from the immanence of God. (RM pp. 104-5)

    This account of what is meant by the enduring existence
of matter and of mind explains such endurance as exemplifying
the order immanent in the world. The solid earth survives
because there is an order laid upon the creativity in virtue
of which second after second, minute after minute, hour after
hour, day after day, year after year, century after century,
age after age, the creative energy finds in the maintenance
of that complex form a centre of experienced perceptivity
focusing the universe into one unity. (RM pp. 111-12)

    The order of the world is no accident. There is nothing
actual which could be actual without some measure of order.
The religious insight is the grasp of this truth: That the
order of the world, the depth of reality of the world, the
value of the world in its whole and in its parts, the beauty
of the world, the zest of life, the peace of life, and the
mastery of evil, are all bound together--not accidentally,
but by reason of this truth: that the universe exhibits a
creativity with infinite freedom, and a realm of forms with
infinite possibilities; but that this creativity and these
forms are together impotent to achieve actuality apart from
the completed ideal harmony, which is God. (RM pp. 119-20)

    Second, in the Function of Reason essay (1929) Whitehead
argues that the ordering tendency must be interpreted as the
quality or force of "Reason" in the universe, in order to account
for the upward tendency of evolution, including the manifest
telic striving of individualities of all kinds toward ideal or

future goals, counter to the downward tendency of material organization toward disorder (or entropy).   The Function of Reason
essay contains no full teleological argument.   It does, however,
avow that the purely physiological or materialistic cosmologies
do not account for the many expressions or levels of "final
causation" that are perceived at work in the natural order.   The
clue to this telic or purposive work is "Reason."   Thus Whitehead
presents us in this essay tantalizing patches of a teleological
argument, of the following kind.   Their suggestiveness, however,
leads the thought of the reader doubtless a significant way
beyond where the acclamations of order, and thus an Orderer, left
us in Religion in the Making.   The Function of Reason points to
the intimations in nature of a "final causation" with the characteristic empirical caution, and the typical philosophic construction of Whitehead:

Why has the trend of evolution been upwards?   (FR p. 7)

The universe, as construed solely in terms of the
efficient causation of purely physical interconnections,
presents a sheer, insoluble contradiction.   (p. 25)

In the animal body, we can observe the appetition towards
the upward trend, with Reason as the selective agency.
(p. 24)

...Reason...directs and criticizes the urge towards the
attainment of an end realized in imagination but not in
fact.   (p. 8)

In the animal body there is, as we have already seen,
clear evidence of activities directed by purpose.   It's
therefore natural...to argue that some lowly, diffused form
of the operations of Reason constitute the vast diffused
counter-agency by which the material cosmos comes into
being.   This conclusion amounts to the repudiation of the
radical extrusion of final causation from our cosmological
theory... [by] Francis Bacon at the beginning of the seven-
teenth century....

...the primary function of Reason.   ...is to constitute,
emphasize, and criticize the final causes and strength of
aims directed towards them.   (p. 26)

A satisfactory cosmology must explain the interweaving of
efficient and of final causation....

...Reason is the practical embodiment of the urge to transform mere existence into the good existence, and to transform

the good existence into the better existence. (p. 28)

The two tendencies upward and downward cannot be torn
apart....
      We shall never elaborate an explanatory metaphsics
unless we abolish this notion of valueless vacuous existence.
...each actuality....   ...is the presentation of its many
components to itself, for the sake of its own ends. ...each
actuality is an occasion of experience, the outcome of its
own purposes. (pp. 30-1)

...every occasion of experience is dipolar. It is mental
experience integrated with physical experience. Mental
experience....   ...is the experience of forms of definiteness
in respect to their disconnection from valuation of what they
can contribute to such experience. Consciousness is no
necessary element in mental experience. The lowest form of
mental experience is blind urge towards a form of experience,
that is to say, an urge towards a form for realization.
These forms of definiteness are the Platonic forms, the
Platonic ideas, the medieval universals.... (p. 32, emphasis his

Mentality....   ...brings the sheer vacuity of the form into
realization of experience....
      The higher forms of intellectual experience only arise
when there are complex integrations, and reintegrations, of
mental and physical experience. Reason then appears as a
criticism of appetitions. It is a second order type of
mentality. It is the appetition of appetitions.
      Mental experience is the organ of novelty, the urge
beyond. It seeks to verify the massive physical fact, which
is repetitive, with the novelties which beckon. (p. 33)

Reason is the special embodiment in us of the disciplined
counter-agency which saves the world. (p. 34)

      It may be observed that "reason" in these passages (espe-
cially in our fifth quoted paragraph) sounds like a kind of
ultimate, lower case cosmic "nous," equivalent, or perhaps
pointing, to what Whitehead later terms unconscious "Primordial
God."

      Thirdly, an argument with the "Positivist" definition of
cosmic "Law" as "merely Description" appears in Adventures of
Ideas (1933) (pp. 119-33). Recall our own discussion on this
subject in the previous chapter. We dealt with it as a fourth
level of criticism that may be raised against Royce's argument
for God as Cosmic Truth, Orderliness, or Law (pp. 100f.).
Whitehead's discussion adds its measure of strength to our

support of Royce in this respect. He refers to the discovery of the planet Pluto, as an example of human investigative intelligence finding objective 'order' or 'law,' and concludes:

At last it is discovered by human reason, penetrating into the nature of things and laying bare the necessities of their interconnection. The speculative extensions of laws, baseless on the Positivist theory, are the obvious issue of speculative metaphysical trust in the material permanences, such as telescopes, observatories, mountains, planets, which are behaving towards each other according to the necessities of the universe, including theories of their own natures. The point is, that speculative extension beyond direct observation spells some trust in metaphysics.... (AI p. 132)

As was pointed out in our earlier discussion of Royce, however, it should be borne clearly in mind that Whitehead also meant an open-ended, dynamic 'order' (pp. 103-4 of this commentary). This conception of the orderly progressiveness of the cosmic order was eloquently summarized in a paragraph in Process and Reality:

...if there is to be progress beyond limited ideals, the course of history by way of escape must venture along the borders of chaos in its substitution of higher for lower types of order.
      The immanence of God gives reason for the belief that pure chaos is intrinsically impossible. At the other end of the scale, the immensity of the world negatives the belief that any state of order can be so established that beyond it there can be no progress. This belief in a final order, popular in religious and philosophic thought, seems to be due to the prevalent fallacy that all types of seriality necessarily involve terminal instances. It follows that Tennyson's phrase,
          "...that far-off divine event
          To which the whole creation moves,"
presents a fallacious conception of the universe. (PR p. 169)

*   *   *   *   *   *   *

To summarize thus far, Whitehead has not presented a comprehensive empirical argument for God, of either a cosmological or teleological sort, comparable in fullness to the efforts of Royce in giving a broad, classic version of the ontological argument in the 'truth experience.' Whitehead's reverence, however, for the 'order' of nature points to one of the main aspects of the cosmological or causal idea, as it bears upon the issue of 'proof.'

The following brief commentary is our own effort to carry a
little farther forward the Whiteheadian vision of the cosmic
order.

The cosmological argument yields four fundamental categories
or ideas of God or the Divine. The unfolding, integrating, or
evolution of things suggests "Absolute Origination,"[5] Creative
Energy, or <u>Ultimate Power</u>. Existence itself suggests uncondi-
tioned, or <u>Eternal Being</u>.[6] The organization, and by-and-large
orderly processes of what exists and evolves, suggests ultimate
Coordination, or <u>Original Order</u>. And awareness of myself as
existing suggests the absolute or <u>Primal Love</u> that makes my
existence possible.[7] Whitehead's discussion bears upon stage

---

5. Wm. Newton Clark, op. cit., p. 110. In Clarke's context
    such phraseology need not imply a dualistic theology or
    creation <u>ex nihilo</u>, but, optionally, "an underlying and
    determining cause" (p. 111).
6. As argued, for example, in Thomas Aquinas's 'Third Way.'
7. I use Walt Whitman's following lines to suggest the
    point intended here; and the philosophic phraseology of
    George Holmes Howison perhaps to somewhat similar
    effect:
    Immense have been the preparations for me,
    Faithful and friendly the arms that have help'd me.

    Cycles ferried my cradle, rowing and rowing like
        cheerful boatmen,
    For room to me stars kept aside in their own rings,
    They sent influences to look after what was to hold me.

    Before I was born out of my mother generations
        guided me.
    My embryo has never been torpid, nothing could
        overlay it.
    For it the nebula cohered to an orb,
    The long strata piled to rest it on,
    Vast vegetables gave it sustenance,
    Monstrous sauroids transported it in their mouths
        and deposited it with care.

    All forces have been steadily employ'd to complete
        and delight me;
    Now on this spot I stand with my robust soul.
            (<u>Oxford Book of American Verse</u>, 1952, pp. 343-4)
            *   *   *   *   *   *
    "The true love wherewith God loves other spirits is
    not the outpouring upon them of graces which are the

three of the cosmological argument: that giving the category of Original Order.   May the human sense of Original Order, as one of the basal meanings of God or Deity given to intelligence, be derived thus?[8] (The following brief excursus also extends the comments made on page 19 of this commentary, in reference to the significance of Royce's argument against absolute or radical "realism"):

The derivation of the concept of Eternal Order, or that the world could not possibly come by chance, begins with the question of chance itself? First, what do we mean when we say that the world might possibly have come "by chance"? Do we mean by chance the random motions and the random contact of some kind of elemental units or particles?[9] We have to begin an argument with

---

unearned gift of his miraculous power; it is the love, on the contrary, which holds the individuality, the personal initiative, of its object sacred....
"Love...now has its adequate definition: it is the all-directing intelligence which includes in its recognition a world of being accorded free and seen as sacred,--the primary and supreme act of intelligence, which is the source of all other intelligence, and whose object is that universal circle of spirits...The City of God" (The Limits of Evolution, The Macmillan Co., 1904, pp. 257, 361).

8.   This discussion appeared in slightly different form in the author's essay, "The Personal Significance of Time, Space, and Causality,"Andover Newton Quarterly, November 1960, pp. 22f.

9.   Among several meanings that the word chance might have, such as:--
--that relative to the fall of dice, or other examples where something unexpected happens, like meeting a friend 'by chance' or finding an object 'by change,' etc.
--the 'indeterminate' or 'random' occurrences of certain natural phenomena like Heisenberg's principle of the 'indeterminacy' of the electron's 'position' relative to its 'velocity'; or the 'mutation' of the 'genes,' within the DNA molecule structure, as partial explanation of evolutionary variation,--
chance, in some ultimate philosophical sense (or radial positivism or tychism, after the Greek goddess Tyche), would mean the total, absolute randmness of a given motion or process--utter incalculability, unlimited indeterminateness, complete or endless unpredictability, with no scintilla or possibility of character continuity:

some concept; let us start with this one: the root idea in the concept of nature as 'mechanical' or mindless.   To assume that the primordial particles or units or energy quanta could, in finite or infinite time, arrange themselves by chance contact into this present order of nature presupposes that the particles have the capacity or potentiality for order already.   And this order is implied at three necessary places or stages.

(I).   Each particle must be determinate, that is possess a character, or be a law or an order within and of itself.   If such hypothetical particle inside itself were in a state of perpetual flux and change, no combination of such particles would at any instant hold; in other words, this present order of the world could never arise.   There must be some constant, a determinate, stable character of the particles themselves.   We must posit regularity, stability of being, that is, law or order in the system at the start.   We see that rational, meaningful constancy must stand at the very beginning.

(II).   Further, there must not only be rational constancy or order within the particles, but also rational (i.e. 'perceivable') connection or order between the particles.   If they are to

---

the motion or change of a body or process from one state, position, characteristic, phase, or operation to another without possibility of ever tracing any connection, or 'causality,' or of perceiving or understanding the dependency of the second state to the first, or the third to the second, and so on.   Tennant describes such a meaning of chance in widest cosmological sense in the following terms: reality conceived as "...a self-subsistent and determinate 'chaos' in which similar events never occurred, none recurred, universals had no place, relations no fixity, things no nexus of determination, and 'real' categories no foothold" (Philosophical Theology, Vol. II, op. cit., p. 82).

If 'rationality' be defined as seeing connections or relationships, and the tendency of understanding to perceive the whole coherency of a situation or phenomenon, then such 'chance' motion would be totally irrational, without 'sufficient reason,' rationally groundless, an inexplicable brute fact, or surd event.

Is our universe credible as founded on such total absence of principle?   Our argument above attempts to speak to this level of question.

cohere into higher more complex order at some future time, they must be <u>related</u> in some fundamental rational way. Again relationship or <u>rational</u> unity is assumed from the beginning; the basic factor of order is given.

(III). Add to this the third level of 'order' implied in the very power of orderly integration and formation which we do in fact find throughout numerous streams of organization and individuation, building and leading up to highest cosmic integration on the finite plane in man (and no doubt similar beings on other planetary scenes), and the concept of original order, integral to the very meaning of what we perceive, seems to theistic faith, overwhelming.

The result is that you cannot start or continue the world conceived as beginning with an indeterminate mass of particles (or energies) in chaos. The hypothesis breaks down on rational grounds. There is, we believe, but the opposite hypothesis remaining--namely, that order, rational unity, and not chaos is the original factor and the continuing constructive factor. Moreover, this cannot be the barest, ragged, minimal patchwork of order (the plane where John McTaggart, for example, as a critic of theism admitted there may be meaning to the concept of deity)[10] but order sufficient to account for the actual, elaborate, vertical integration that we find as the larger fact of our world, leading, on one finite plane, to man. (A detailed analysis of 'evolution' and the problems of the descriptive terms, 'mechanism' and 'purpose,' in the light of modern evolutionary theory, as lying at the heart of the problem of the teleological argument would arise at this stage as an element of the cosmological argument.)[11]

Further on the Conception

We have already sketched whitehead's conception of Deity at a number of places (pp. 3-5, 50f., 79, 125). His mature discussion of God centers around the two poles of the Divine Nature, characteristically phrased by him, the "primordial" and "consequent"

---

10. <u>Some Dogmas of Religion</u>, Edward Arnold, 1906, p. 186.
11. Presented by this author in a paper "Mechanism and Purpose in the Theological Interpretation of Evolution," North West regional meeting of the American Academy of Religion and the Society of Biblical Literature, Portland, Ore., Spring 1971.

aspects of God. It seems to me that the following passages
summarize this primary, "dipolar" way of talking about God.
These selections also suggest further basic perspectives and
issues, relative to the Whiteheadian God: such as, even prior
to his talk about primordial and consequent God, the fundamental
definition of the Divine as the rational "limitation" itself, or
"the ground of rationality," the cosmic Nous (once again to
employ the classic reference from Greek philosophy), which is
nonetheless described as "the ultimate irrationality." Or there
is the problem of the relation of the "creativity" to "God."
Was the former something more ultimate than the latter in Whitehead's thought? Further, what is the exact meaning of God as
"the principle of concretion" and the relation of God as the
"concretion" to God as "primordial" and as "consequent"?
Endeavoring to clarify the complex and sometimes obscure text
(and trusting that our sequence and abridgment of these sayings
do not distort or oversimplify too greatly the essential points
he had in mind) we have arranged these basic thoughts on God
under leading headings.

As the Ground of Rationality,
or Principle of Limitation

Thus as a further element in the metaphysical situation,
there is required a principle of limitation.... This attribute provides the limitation for which no reason can be
given: for all reason flows from it. God is the ultimate
limitation, and His existence is the ultimate irrationality.
For no reason can be given for just that limitation which it
stands in His nature to impose. God is not concrete, but He
is the ground for concrete actuality. No reason can be given
for the nature of God because that nature is the ground of
rationality....

If He be conceived as the supreme ground for limitation, it
stands in His very nature to divide the Good from the Evil,
and to establish Reason 'within her dominions supreme.'
(SMW pp. 178-80)

...'God' is that actuality in the world in virtue of which
there is physical 'law.' (PR p. 434)

...God...is...the outcome of creativity,...the foundation
of order, and...the goal towards novelty. (PR p. 135)

How Related to Creativity

In all philosophic theory there is an ultimate which is
actual in virtue of its accidents. It is only then capable

of characterization through its accidental embodiments, and
apart from these accidents is devoid of actuality. In the
philosophy of organism this ultimate is termed 'creativity';
and God is its primordial, non-temporal accident. (PR pp.
10-11)

...it is to be noted that every actual entity, including
God, is a creature transcended by the creativity which it
qualifies. (PR p. 135)

...there is no meaning to 'creativity' apart from its
'creatures,' and no meaning to 'God' apart from the creativity and the 'temporal creatures,' and no meaning to the
temporal creatures apart from 'creativity' and 'God.'
(PR p. 344)

...God and the actual world jointly constitute the character
of the creativity for the initial phase of the novel concrescence. (PR p. 374)

As Primordial

[God is] an underlying eternal energy in whose nature there
stands an envisagement of the realm of all eternal objects.
(SMW p. 107)

...God.... Viewed as primordial...is the unlimited conceptual
realization of the absolute wealth of potentiality. In this
aspect, he is not before all creation, but with all creation.
...when we...consider God in the abstraction of a primordial
actuality, we must ascribe to him neither fullness of feeling,
nor consciousness. (PR pp. 521-2, emphasis his)[12]

One side of God's nature is constituted by his conceptual experience. This experience is the primordial fact in
the world, limited by no actuality which it presupposes. It
is there infinite, devoid of all negative prehensions. This
side of his nature is free, complete, primordial, eternal,
actually deficient, and unconscious. (PR p. 524)

The primordial appetitions which jointly constitute
God's purpose are seeking intensity, and not preservation.
Because they are primordial, there is nothing to preserve.
He, in his primordial nature, is unmoved by love for this
particular, or that particular; for in this foundational

---

12. Here parts of three adjacent paragraphs are joined.

process of creativity, there are no preconstituted particulars. In the foundations of his being, God is indifferent alike to preservation and to novelty. He cares not whether an immediate occasion be old or new, so far as concerns derivation from its ancestry. His aim for it is depth of satisfaction as an intermediate step towards the fulfillment of his own being. His tenderness is directed towards each actual occasion, as it arises.
     Thus God's purpose in the creative advance is the evocation of intensities. The evocation of societies is purely subsidiary to this absolute end. (PR pp. 160-61)

His unity of conceptual operations.... ...is deflected neither by love, nor by hatred, for what in fact comes to pass. (PR p. 522)

     As to my own views of permanence and transience, I think the universe has a side which is mental and permanent. This side is that prime conceptual drive which I call the primordial nature of God. It is Alexander's <u>nisus</u> conceived as actual. (SP p. 126, emphasis his)

The 'primordial nature' of God is the concrescence of an unity of conceptual feelings, including among their data all eternal objects. The concrescence is directed by the subjective aim, that the subjective forms of the feelings shall be such as to constitute the eternal objects into relevant lures of feeling severally appropriate for all realizable basic conditions. (PR p. 134)

As the Principle of Concretion

In the place of Aristotle's God as Prime Mover, we require God as the Principle of Concreation. (SMW p. 174)

One task of a sound metaphysics is to exhibit final and efficient causes in their proper relation to each other. (PR p. 129)

...efficient causation expresses the transition from actual entity to actual entity; and final causation expresses the internal process whereby the actual entity becomes itself. (PR p. 228)

...there are two kinds of fluency. One kind is the concrescence which, in Locke's language, is 'the real internal constitution of a particular existent.' The other kind is the <u>transition</u> from particular existent to particular existent. This transition, again in Locke's language, is the 'perpetually perishing' which is one aspect of the notion of time; and in another aspect the transition is the origination of the present in conformity with the 'power' of the past....

One kind is the fluency inherent in the constitution of the particular existent. This kind I have called 'concrescence.' The other kind is the fluency whereby the perishing of the process, on the completion of the particular existent, constitutes that existent as an original element in the constitutions of other particular existents elicited by repetitions of process. This kind I have called 'transition.' Concrescence moves towards its final cause, which is its subjective aim; transition is the vehicle of the efficient cause, which is the immortal past....

   'Concrescence' is the name for the process in which the universe of many things acquires an individual unity in a determinate relegation of each item of the 'many' to its subordination in the constitution of the novel 'one.'
   The most general term 'thing'--or, equivalently, 'entity'--means nothing else than to be one of the 'many' which find their niches in each instance of concrescnece. Each instance of concrescence is itself the novel individual 'thing' in question....
   An instance of concrescence is termed an 'actual entity' --or, equivalently, an 'actual occasion'....   (PR pp 320-1, emphasis his)

...the process of integration...lies at the very heart of the concrescence....   (PR p. 347)

What is inexorable in God, is valuation as an aim towards 'order'; and 'order' means 'society' permissive of actualities with patterned intensity of feeling arising from adjusted contrasts. In this sense God is the principle of concretion; namely, he is that actual entity from which each temporal concrescence receives that initial aim from which its self-causation starts. That aim determines the initial gradations of relevance of eternal objects for conceptual feeling; and constitutes the autonomous subject in its primary phase of feelings with its initial conceptual valuations, and with its initial physical purposes.... In this way there is constituted the concrescent subject in its primary phase with its dipolar constitution, physical and mental, indissoluble.
   If we prefer the phraseology, we can say that God and the actual world jointly constitute the character of the creativity for the initial phase of the novel concrescence. The subject, thus constituted, is the autonomous master of

its own concrescence into subject-superject.   ... determin-
istic efficient causation is the inflow of the actual world
in its own proper character of its own feelings, with their
own intensive strength, felt and re-enacted by the novel
concrescent subject.   ...in complex processes of integration
and reintegration, this autonomous conceptual element modi-
fies the subjective forms throughout the whole range of
feeling in the concrescence and thereby guides the integrations. (PR pp. 373-4)

...the dipolar character of concrescent experience provides
in the physical pole for the objective side of experience,
derivative from an external world, and provides in the mental
pole for the subjective side of experience, derivative from
the subjective conceptual valuations correlate to the physical feelings....   In this way the decision derived from the
actual world, which is the efficient cause, is completed by
the decision embodied in the subjective aim which is the
final cause....   Thus the mental pole is the link whereby
the creativity is endowed with the double character of final
causation, and efficient causation. (PR p. 423)

...God....   ...is the principle of concreation--the principle
whereby there is initiated a definite outcome from a situation otherwise riddled with ambiguity. (PR p. 523)

As Consequent

The 'consequent nature' of God is the physical prehension by
God of the actualities of the evolving universe. (PR p. 134)

...God, as well as being primordial, is also consequent. He
is the beginning and the end. He is not the beginning in
the sense of being in the past of all members....   The completion of God's nature into a fulness of physical feeling
is...the world in God. He shares with every new creation
its actual world....   God's conceptual nature is unchanged,
by reason of its final completeness. But his derivative
nature is consequent upon the creative advance of the world.
    Thus, analogously to all actual entities, the nature of
God is dipolar. He has a primordial nature and a consequent
nature. The consequent nature of God is conscious; and it
is the realization of the actual world in the unity of his
nature, and through the transformation of his wisdom. The
primordial nature is conceptual, the consequent nature is
the weaving of God's physical feelings upon his primordial
concepts....

The other [the consequent] side originates with physical

experience derived from the temporal world, and then acquires
integration with the primordial side.   It is determined,
incomplete, consequent, 'everlasting,' fully actual, and
conscious.   His necessary goodness expresses the determination of his consequent nature.   (PR pp. 523-4)

...the problem concerns the completion of God's primordial
nature by the derivation of his consequent nature from the
temporal world....

The consequent nature of God is the fluent world becoming
'everlasting' by its objective immortality in God....

God is completed by the individual, fluent satisfactions of
finite fact, and the temporal occasions are completed by
their everlasting union with their transformed selves, purged
into conformation with the eternal order which is the final
absolute 'wisdom.'   (PR p. 527)

It is as true to say that the World is immanent in God,
as that God is immanent in the World.
It is as true to say that God transcends the World, as
that the World transcends God.
It is as true to say that God creates the World, as
that the World creates God.
God and the World are the contrasted opposites in terms
of which Creativity achieves its supreme task of transforming
disjointed multiplicity, with its diversities in opposition,
into concrescent unity, with its diversities in contrast.   In
each actuality these are two concrescent poles of realization
--'enjoyment' and 'appetition,' that is, the 'physical' and
the 'conceptual.'   For God the conceptual is prior to the
physical, for the world the physical poles are prior to the
conceptual poles.   (PR p. 528)

The image...under which this...growth of God's nature is best
conceived, is that of a tender care that nothing be lost.
The consequent nature of God....   ...saves the world as
it passes into the immediacy of his own life.   It is the
judgment of a tenderness which loses nothing that can be
saved.   (PR p. 525)

...his consequent nature...is his infinite patience.   ...
tenderly saving the turmoil of the intermediate world by the
completion of his own nature.   ...the intermediate physical
process...is the energy of physical production.   God's role
is not the combat of productive force with destructive force;
it lies in the patient operation of the overpowering

rationality of his conceptual harmonization. He does not
create the world, he saves it; or, more accurately, he is
the poet of the world, with tender patience leading it by
his vision of truth, beauty, and goodness. (PR pp. 525-6)

God and the world stand over against each other,
expressing the final metaphysical truth that appetitive
vision and physical enjoyment have equal claim to priority
in creation....

God is the infinite ground of all mentality, the unity of
vision seeking physical multiplicity. The World is the
multiplicity of finites, actualities seeking a perfected
unity. Neither God, nor the world, reaches static completion. Both are in the grip of the ultimate metaphysical
ground, the creative advance into novelty....

This final phase of God's nature is ever
enlarging itself. In it the complete adjustment of the
immediacy of joy and suffering reaches the final end of creation. This end is existence in the perfect unity of adjustment as means, and in the perfect multiplicity of the attainment of individual types of self-existence. (PR pp. 529-31)

As Personal

...every actual entity, including God, is something individual for its own sake....   (PR p. 135)[13]

---

13. God, along with all other individualities is, in
     Whitehead's technical term, an "actual entity." But
     unlike all other actual entities, which are synonym-
     ously called "actual occasions," God is declared to be
     not an actual occasion (PR pp. 135, 168). The main
     distinction apparently is that actual occasions are
     conceived to be those individualities which are of
     finite duration or "perishing," whereas God is the only
     actual entity which is not perishing but of everlasting
     duration. See William A. Christian: An Interpretation
     of Whitehead's Metaphysics, op. cit., pp. 12-13, for
     further discussion of this subtle distinction. Christian
     points out that whereas actual occasions abstract their
     conceptual prehensions from their physical prehensions,
     it is not so with God whose "conceptual prehensions...
     are underived or primordial and constitute his primor-
     dial nature" (Ib. p. 13).

The consequent nature of God is conscious....

It is determined, incomplete, consequent, 'everlasting',
fully actual, and conscious. His necessary goodness expresses
the determination of his consequent nature. (PR 524)

An enduring personality in the temporal world is a route of
occasions in which the successors with some peculiar completeness sum up their predecessors. The correlate fact in God's
nature is an even more complete unity of life in a chain of
elements for which succession does not mean loss of immediate
unison. ...in the sense in which the present occasion is the
person now, and yet with his own past, so the counterpart in
God is that person in God. (PR pp. 531-2, emphasis his)

...the love of God for the world...is the particular providence for particular occasions. ...God is the great com-
panion--the fellow sufferer who understands. (PR p. 532)

The consciousness which is individual in us, is universal in
him; the love which is partial in us is all-embracing in him.
(RM p. 158)

How Related to Plato's and Aristotle's Views

I have envisioned a union of Plato's God with a God of the
Universe. (DANW p. 178)

...Deity expresses the lure of the ideal which is the potentiality beyond immediate fact.

...Deity...is the factor in the universe whereby there is
importance, value, and ideal beyond the actual.... We owe to
the sense of Deity the obviousness of the many actualities of
the world, and the obviousness of the unity of the world for
the preservation of the values realized and for the transition to ideals beyond realized fact. (MT pp. 139-40)[14]

He is the lure for feeling, the eternal urge of desire.
His particular relevance to each creative act...constitutes
him the initial 'object of desire' establishing the initial
phase of each subjective aim. A quotation from Aristotle's
Metaphysics expresses some analogies to, and some differences
from this line of thought: "And since that which is moved
and moves is intermediate, there is a mover which moves

---

14. In a context discussing Plato, Leibnitz, and Samuel
     Alexander.

without being moved, being eternal, substance, and actuality.
And the object of desire and the object of thought are the
same. For the apparent good is the object of appetite, and
the real good is the primary object of rational desire. But
desire is consequent on opinion rather than opinion on
desire; for the thinking is the starting point. And thought
is moved by the object of thought, and one side of the list
of opposites is in itself the object of thought;...."
Aristotle had not made the distinction between conceptual
feelings and the intellectual feelings which alone involve
consciousness. But if 'conceptual feeling,' with its subjective forms of valuation, be substituted for 'thought,'
'thinking' and 'opinion,' in the above quotation, the agreement is exact. (PR pp. 522-3)

It seems to this interpreter that the several basic facets
of the idea of God in the complex Whiteheadian discussion can be
usefully highlighted, as we have done, under the organization and
captions just employed. In Whitehead's thought God is to be
defined as Rational Ground or Limitation, as Creativity, as
Primordial, as the Principle of Concretion, as Consequent and
Personal, and is to be understood as essentially a modern interpolation of aspects of Plato's and Aristotle's conceptions of
Deity. These various perspectives in Whitehead's discussion
might be combined--perhaps without too great oversimplification--
into a summary statement of the conception of God as Primordial
Unconscious Mind of Value and Consequent Conscious Preserver of
Finite Achievement of Value.

In any case, we will now look at several critical problems
of exposition that may be helpful to the reader's understanding
of the just presented 'basic thoughts' on God in Whitehead's text,
leading into an evaluation of his view of God, and pointing out
how his conception relates to the contribution of Royce on the
same subject. Passing over the point of God as the ground of
rationality for the moment, we begin with the issue of the relation of God to the Creativity, mentioned in our introductory
remarks on page 136. The discussion will then take up in order
the further items mentioned on that page, referring to Plato
and Aristotle, as we proceed.

First, although sometimes Whitehead seems to distinguish
between 'God' and 'the Creativity'--as if the Creativity were more
like Plato's original spacio-material Receptacle, distinct from,
but co-equal with God, we do not believe that, on the whole,
Whitehead meant to give the Creativity a separate status in being;
and certainly not anterior to, or more ultimate than God.
Recall the discussion on page 50 of this basic term. In
our interpolative account, it was point out

there that 'creativity' represents the eternity of God, that is, his eternal <u>creative</u> <u>purposiveness</u> as 'eternal being,' of which, or from which, all being is derived. We wrote, and here repeat for our present emphasis, Creativity is the ultimate character which says the universe can and will have character or characters (i.e. formed or ordered beings) of many kinds. It is the highest logical premise with which to start the description of the world's order. It is in fact the ultimate order that our previous argument from order perhaps discovered. To point to it reflects the (rational) instinct that only out of eternal being can being come (the <u>ex</u> <u>nihilo</u> <u>nihil</u> <u>fit</u> insight of the cosmological arguments for God). In Tillich's language, Whitehead's 'Creativity' is Being-itself, or the Power-of-being, identical to the ultimate meaning of 'God.' This exigesis may be interpolated, I believe, from the text:

> ...there is no meaning to 'creativity' apart from its 'creatures,' and no meaning to 'God' apart from the creativity and the 'temporal creatures,' and no meaning to the temporal creatures apart from 'creativity' and 'God.'

And it also seems clear by:

> ...God and the actual world jointly constitute the character of the creativity....

In the third sentence, fourth paragraph quoted under the caption God as Primordial, "his primordial nature" is expressly identified with "this foundational process of creativity." Again, at the end of that selection we read of "God's purpose in the creative advance."

In discussing the Creativity as not implying something egregiously separate from God, Whitehead's interpreter, Charles Hartshorne, writes the following about this difficult conception:

> ...the creativity is not an actual entity or agent which does things; it is the common property or generic name for all the doings.[15]

When Whitehead says that creativity in general is wider than God, he is simply pointing out, as I take it, that not all decisions are God's self-decisions. He is not denying that all decisions are in some manner enjoyed, possessed,

---

15.   "Whitehead's Idea of God" in Paul Arthur Schilpp (ed.): <u>The Philosophy of Alfred North Whitehead</u>, op. cit., 1951, p. 526.

by God.[16]

God appropriates the actions, the decisions, of others, he does not decide just what they are to be.[17]

Finally, in speaking of the Creativity, where Whitehead uses the strange locution that "God is its primordial, non-temporal accident" (PR p. 11), he seems to mean that things can happen to, or within God, by way of new or novel experience, as is the case with all personal being. God himself can and does grow. (See Hartshorne WP, pp. 88-9, where this possibility with God is described as the ever present Divine self-surpassing or self-transcending freedom.) If the foregoing be the correct view in Whitehead of the "creativity," then also where he has said that God is "transcended by the creativity" (e.g. PR p. 135), we may read this as equivalent to the statement that God is the latter's "non-temporal accident." In sum, such phrases seem to point to the openness of Consequent God as Cosmic Person to the possibility of having developmental or self-transcending experiences in Himself--in part defined by the contribution to this Divine life of finite entities' achievements of value.[18]

Second, in discussing Whitehead's conception of God it is probably most useful to proceed next to the idea of the "Primordial" side of the divine nature. Referring to the last two of the original Aristotelian quatrain of causes,[19] there must be that aspect which is the _formal_ and _final_ 'causality' of things; the primordial 'Mind,' where all possible (and doubtless limitless) _form_ and _value_ 'reside.' Such Primordial matrix is revealed in the fact that entities, in the process of material association and integrations by their appetitive striving, do appear with

---

16.   Ib. p. 528. Hartshorne continues at this place with the perceptive comment: "Even we enjoy many decisions that we do not make, particularly the radically sub-human and, in our awareness, not individually distinguishable decisions of the bodily members, such as cells or molecules.

17.   Ib. p. 527. Hartshorne elsewhere, not directly referring to Whitehead, but in a work profoundly Whiteheadian speaks of "creativity...as the principle of existence itself," The Logic of Perfection, Open Court Publishing Co., 1962, p. 209.

18.   See subsequent summary on the issue of freedom in Whitehead, pp. 156-9 , and the discussion of Immortality, pp. 226f.

19.   Material, efficient, formal, and final.

forms, and experience values; that is, novel, emergent qualities
of "feelings" and "satisfactions," in the hierarchical orders and
kinds observed of natural phenomena. Thus God "viewed as primr-
dial...is the unlimited conceptual realization of the absolute
wealth of potentiality...not before...but with all creation...."
This is the "mental and permanent" side of God, the "prime conceptual drive...Alexander's nisus[20] conceived as actual," but
"deficient," and "unconscious," says Whitehead. Where Aristotle
himself was ambiguous on the point, Whitehead clearly joined God
and the World in this respect. We thus come next to the principle of Concretion, which illuminates this union, and which
Whitehead expressly reminds us differs from Aristotle in the way
just mentioned: "In the place of Aristotle's God as Prime Mover,
we require God as the Principle of Concretion" (SMW p. 174).
(What will be regarded as a larger problem in the characterization
of Primordial God as "unconscious" will be considered presently
in the discussion of the Consequent side.)

In the meanwhile therefore, and thirdly, the term concretion/
concrescence refers to the process whereby Primordial God becomes
(or is ever becoming) Consequent God; i.e. it describes in some
detail how (or declares that) the primordial forms or possibilities become the world's and God's realized actualities. It is
clear by the preceding passages, that the coming together of
lesser entities into more complex levels or hierarchies of entities, with their new, emergent possibilities of "enjoyment,"
"satisfactions," or value-"intensities" expresses the very life
and "growth of God" Himself, and what is meant by God as "the
Principle of Concretion" (issuing in the Consequent nature). We
have noticed that Whitehead defines concretion in some contexts,
as "the process of integration" (PR p. 347). (And I believe it
would also be correct to assert that integration exemplifies, or
is even synonymous with, creativity in Whitehead's thought.) In
any case, where Whitehead says in such statements as, God is
"that entity from which each temporal concrescence receives that
initial aim from which its self-causation starts," he is first
referring to what he himself a number of times in the same contexts otherwise calls, more classically, and perhaps simply,
final causality. As Concretion, God is the alluring principle,
the ultimate telos, the final causalities of things.

But the word "concretion" seems itself at first misapplied,
since the very expression calls up the idea of things 'concrete,'
that is, material, obdurate, mechanical powers, the efficient
causalities of things in the world. In some of these contexts
Whitehead distinguishes "efficient causes" as the principle of

---

20. Principle of striving.

"transition," or the external influence of one entity upon
another, the second type of "fluency"; the first type being the
internal fluency of "concrescence," the final, teleological causation just explained. However, he also refers to concrescence as
having a "dipolar" character in a number of places. Accordingly,
we believe that he endeavors (e.g. in the second from the last of
the passages quoted under the caption, p. 140) to include in the
idea of concrescence "the physical pole" and "the objective side
of experience, derived from an external world," i.e. "the efficient causation"--expressions all mentioned together along with
final causation. At any rate, "concretion" is a complex idea,
not totally confined to final causality. In some contexts at
least, it also encompasses efficient causality. If our exposition is correct at this place, Whitehead is suggesting (as we
believe every adequate theism must eventually do) that whatever
else God may also be he is both types of causal principle: the
efficient and the final, the material and the purposive. That
he is efficient power, the material efficiency that founds and
sustains existence on the level of basal nature under the general
rule of law, Whitehead has expressly said: "God is that actuality in the world, in virtue of which there is physical law"
(PR p. 434).

We amplify, therefore, that Space and Time, Gravitational
force and Radiational powers; the integrative Atomic and Molecular Energies; the principle of Mutation which differentiates
living forms in evolution--i.e. the principles of life, its
growth, and evolution on the physical plane (specifically the
mutational, replicative, and natural selective processes--which,
from one standpoint, are perceived as the factors of utmost
necessity, if there is to be free evolutionary experimentation
with varied forms and the possibility of their rising toward
beauty and goodness beyond bare survival); all may be understood
from the ultimate perspective as aspects of God's luminously
rational, efficient power or being. God's sustenance of the
cosmos is a dynamic, purposive sustaining (that is, 'concrescing')
--itself growing, by appropriating and preserving (and here we
move back into Whitehead expressly again) all values with which
lesser entities may emerge in the multifarious dimensions of
their own novel experiences and growth, in fulfillment of their
own telic strivings. At the same time these events define the
fulfillment of God's purpose for them and Himself. The estab-
lishment of a solid or efficient base for things, or the efficient causalities themselves--no doubt with certain 'mechanical'
aspects at some levels--ultimately glow with purposive or rational
meaning; for without them there obviously could be no further and
higher development of process into finite streams of

purposiveness.[21] Accordingly, if in a number of sayings concrescence seems limited to the final causalities themselves, by
implication it must also necessarily include the efficient causalities of things--and this, as we have observed, Whitehead himself suggested in his references to its dipolar or complete
nature.

In the fourth place, then, the final emphasis, and the most
comprehensive thing now said of God in the discussions of the
Consequent nature, are the points that God is the "conscious" or
personal preserver of value. Accordingly, the following might
be cited as central to Whitehead's view of the Consequent nature:

> The completion of God's nature into a fulness of physical
> feeling is...the world in God.... ...his derivative nature
> is consequent upon the creative advance of the world.... The
> consequent nature of God is conscious. ... 'everlasting,'
> fully actual, and conscious. ...the fluent world becoming
> 'everlasting' by its objective immortality in God.... The
> image...under which this...growth of God's nature is best
> conceived, is that of a tender care that nothing be lost.
> The consequent nature of God.... ...saves the world as it
> passes into the immediacy of his own life. ...which loses
> nothing that can be saved. ...his consequent nature...is
> his infinite patience. ...tenderly saving the turmoil of
> the intermediate world by the completion of his own nature....
> He does not create the world, he saves it: or, more accu-
> rately, he is the poet of the world, with tender patience
> leading it by his vision of truth, beauty, and goodness....
> ...the love of God for the world...is the particular provi-
> dence for particular occasions.... ...God is the great com-
> panion -- the fellow-sufferer who understands....

An adequate theism, we suggest, must assert something like
the foregoing about God. The central point being that, if He is
preserver of value, He must be in some real sense discriminator
between values (and disvalues), and therefore "conscious" or
personal as Whitehead depicts Him. Therefore, I believe that
these statements about God as "conscious" and as "love," and by
obvious implication as 'personal' or 'personality,' should be
taken quite literally. The paragraph under the heading As
Personal, page 143 above, appears to state this quite expressly,
where he writes that "in God's nature is an even more

---

21. A perspective on the teleological argument discussed
at some length in the aforementioned paper by the
author, see note 11, p. 135.

comprehensive unity" of "enduring personality"--(if, in the two
sentences I have correctly indicated the grammatical antecedent
to "the correlate fact" expression). Also there were the statements in RM, "The consciousness which is individual in us, is
universal in him; and the love which is partial in us is all-
embracing in him" (p. 158). We allow, of course, as Whitehead
himself did, an ultimate dimension of literary 'image' or metaphorical quality to such human language about Deity.

The problem, however, now arises, if God be personal reality
or Cosmic Personality, by virtue of his conscious discrimination
of values, for whom "it stands in His very nature to divide the
Good from the Evil," why is consciousness and the Personal quality
denied his Primordial pole? Here is the fundamental inconsistency, it seems to us, in an otherwise magnificent and true conception of the Divine. For, it seems to me, you cannot leave
God as abstract form and value, or impersonal truth, on the one
hand, and have Him also the ground and truth of the personal on
the other.

Royce believed that the idea of individuality or personality
is the cosmic leaven. Once introduce it, it will permeate the
whole loaf. Thus Royce himself moved away from the consideration
of Platonism, or the Third Conception of Being, as an adequate
philosophy, described on pages 27f, in our earlier section of
commentary. The heart of Royce's discussion was that "ideas"
have an intrinsic dynamic. They are internally restless or
unstable, as it were, by virtue of their purposes--until by movement outward from their internal meaning toward the accomplishment of these purposes in their external meanings they are
finally fulfilled, in the concrete "individualities" that they
intend to become. We will not here repeat what was there elaborated as the Roycean philosophy of being. Our intent in referring to it at this place is to say that it seems to us to be the
adequate reply to the problem that Whitehead leaves before us at
this stage of our exposition of his Primordial God, namely, as
abstract truth, the unconscious Platonic Mind or Matrix of the
"eternal objects," i.e. the forms and laws of being.

To engage Royce with Whitehead in dialogue at such a critical moment, if in imagination we can presume to risk such a
dramatizing of this point, we might have heard the former say:

'Can the realm of "Truth" or "Ideas," of the "Forms" (your
"eternal objects"), the ultimate realm of the cosmic intelligence
or purposiveness (Primordial God), remain 'abstract,' that is,
without seat and focus in personal will and consciousness? How
would you ever get these dead and lifeless entities ever to
bestir themselves and move in the directions of the many

'concretions" with which you so accurately describe the cosmic
process of being? As we may raise such a question of the original Platonic-Aristotelian idealism we may pose it for its contemporary counterpart in this aspect of Whiteheadianism. How
can "purpose" arise out of the subconscious or unconscious mind-
edness of the ultimate impersonal Cosmic Truth, or Intellect, or
Nous--a Truth and Intellect that would not know of its own existence and powers? Actually, of course, Plato and Aristotle
realized this problem themselves, and attempted to solve it by
introducing some element of Personality in each case--that is,
an element of supreme cosmic forethought or self-conscious
purposiveness into their respective systems. Plato endeavored
to accomplish this in his principle of deity, or the Demiourgos
in the Timaeus; Aristotle tried it by implying that God was at
least conscious of himself as the focal point of all rational
truth and form in his own supreme virtue of "thinking on thinking."
Whitehead has, of course, done likewise in his own Consequent
God conception. But all three come out with but a semi-personal-
ism, with the various cosmographical principles non-unified in an
ultimate rational perspective: What relation does the Demiurge
(God as the 'creativity') have to the Ideas, subsumed in the
Good, Tagathon, in Plato's original system? How does Aristotle's
Energeia, or supreme Actuality-God, who thinks on thinking,
relate to the world of material form, striving by eros or desire
to be like His perfection? How does, or why does, Cosmic Primordial Impersonality initially bestir itself in the direction of
its own fulfillment in Consequent Personality, in Whitehead's
conception of things?

    'Thus, we ask the question of Whitehead's system that we
asked of the original Platonism, from which his outlook has
largely sprung. Can a value system that regards "personality"
as a prominent and doubtless supreme expression of value and
being on the finite plane, long be denied its reality on the
ultimate or Primordial cosmic plane? Consider the 'Idea of Man,'
one of the transcendent ideas that a significant stream of process
or development in the natural world fulfills: If there is the
Idea of Man, that is, if the idea of self-conscious, intelligent
and moral life exists in the realm of Ideas and ultimate Truth
(among the eternal objects, Whitehead's term) as a possibility
for process, would not this personalize that primordial matrix
of being as by definition? Quite like our leaven, already introduced as a figure of speech, it must by its dynamic nature, its
internal meaning and external striving, suffuse with its truth
the entirety of being, issuing in the personalizing process which
is being.'

It is hard to fathom what Whitehead's response to Royce
might be in this connection--and no doubt somewhat idle to
attempt a reply for him! But since the latter has addressed the
former in our reconstruction, we will appeal to Whitehead to
answer, in the spirit of his thought, with the following comment:

'Josiah, your way of criticizing my Primordial God thesis
is perhaps difficult to refute on mere logical grounds; but I
shall still stick to my view, for no doubt somewhat larger empirical reasons. There must be the element of the primordial unconscious in God in order to account for the world facts as I perceive them--their jagged openness oft times, their risks, the
manifest truth that the good does not always prevail, nor the
"personal"--in short, because of the problem of evil, later taken
up; and it may be that I have better spoken to that issue than
you have done. The sheer empirical mass of things, in their
imperfections, manifests a certain limitation to God--if indeed
"unconsciousness" in his primordial depth be that given element
that may assist us in the account of evil at a later stage in
this dialogue. I must acknowledge a certain finitude, that is,
if there be a solution to the problem of evil in our form of
theistic vision? At least, such is one option to my account of
evil.'[22]

Beyond such a hypothetical direct criticism by Royce of
Whitehead's failure to perceive 'Personality' also in God's
Primordial nature, further related problems might be raised.
If there is logical tension within the idea of God's Consequent
and Primordial poles as to the personality-impersonality issue,
certain finer points of that issue come out in statements that
characterize the primordial side (though we grant that it is not
always possible to say exactly which statement fits which side
of God):

-as not having "fullness of feeling,"
-containing "appetitions" which seek "intensity, and not
 preservation," or the "evocation of intensities" prior to
 the "evocation of societies."
-being "unmoved by love" for particulars, nor "deflected
 ...by love" for them.
-as being "indifferent alike to preservation and to novelty."
-as, re any "immediate occasion," aiming at its "depth of
 satisfaction as an intermediate step towards the fulfillment of his own being," etc.

---

22.   See our fuller discussion on these matters pp. 179f.,
       especially pp. 192f, with note 41, p. 195.

God in such statements seems pure Eros, pure striving. Yet there is an 'Agapic' side of God, in Whitehead's thought:

-a "tenderness...directed towards each actual occasion, as it arises."
-"a tender care that nothing be lost" but that "saves the world as it passes into the immediacy of his own life... a tenderness which loses nothing that can be saved."
-an "infinite patience," "the poet of the world, with tender patience leading it by his vision of truth, beauty, and goodness."
-"the love of God...is the particular providence for particular occasions."
-"the great companion" and "fellow sufferer who understands."
-"love...all-embracing," etc.

Whitehead reserves such statements as these latter six apparently for the Consequent side of God. Yet had he included them in the Primordial side, that aspect would have been personal by definition, and the tension within the composite Whiteheadian God would not, we believe, be present; or at least not have been so great. For example, had he said as the foremost point about God, "the love of God...is the particular providence for particular occasions" (undoubtedly an attribution of the Consequent God since it describes the last or "the fourth phase" of cosmic development, PR p. 532), would it have been also possible for him to say (and this expressly of the Primordial God) that he is "unmoved by love" for particulars (PR p. 160)?

We return now to the first level of description previously indicated, that citing God as the Rational Ground of being, and speak to the puzzling statement in the same context that God is "the ultimate irrationality." Was this a confusion at the very foundation of Whitehead's thought? Did it possibly contribute to the subsequent confusion about so large a question as the love vs. the love-indifference respectively in the Consequent and the Primordial faces of God?

Doubtless, as interpreters point out, the principle of limitation in Whitehead meant that there are many (perhaps an infinite number) of logically coherent 'possible worlds' in the Divine conceptualization of possible things, but only this world is the one we have and know--as a result of the divine "limitation." That is, for whatever 'reasons' or 'purposes,' logically unfathomable to us, God has (arbitrarily?) imposed, or limited this world to be the one actually that it now is. Accordingly, the "limitation" is the "ultimate irrationality."[23]

But Whitehead's announcement that God, as the principle of
limitation, is the "ultimate irrationality" appears on the
surface as patently contradictory to other statements of the same
context, such as that "all reason flows from it" and that God "is
the ground of rationality," for whom "it stands in his very
nature...to establish Reason 'within her dominions supreme.'"
That the reference to God's "irrationality" cannot be construed
as just a verbal slippage on Whitehead's part is borne out by the
fact that thrice within this passage he declares that "no reason"
can be given for God's nature.

Could he have been pressing here toward the ultimate point
that any theistic philosophy must make, namely, that you cannot
go behind reason to explain reason? Such indeed would be the
ultimate redundancy, the last irrationality! The posit of "God"
as the ultimate reason for things, with His purposiveness, brings
thought at last to rest. It need not look farther, as if behind
God, to ask why Him? He is the ultimate Sufficient Reason for
things--that is the meaning of the very word "God." But in
several pointed statements Whitehead obviously does not go this
way. He avers that for the limitation "no reason can be given";
and again "no reason can be given for just that limitation which
stands in His nature to impose.... No reason can be given for
the nature of God, because that nature is the ground of rationality...."

Bringing together this problem with the previous one, we
therefore suggest that had Whitehead more clearly conceived of

---

23.   Lewis S. Ford has succinctly described the principle of
      limitation in this sense as meaning "that alternatives
      to the metaphysical principles may well be self-con-
      sistent, though never actualized. Logic and mathematics
      explore the nature of self-consistent systems, while
      metaphysics must look to experience to see which one is
      generically exemplified," from "Whitehead's Differences
      from Hartshorne" in Lewis S. Ford (ed.): Two Process
      Philosophers: Hartshorne's Encounter with Whitehead,
      American Academy of Religion Studies in Religion, No.
      Five, 1973, p. 68.
          See our subsequent discussion of the idea of the
      Divine "limitation" in the context of Whitehead's
      treatment of the problem of evil, pp.   179f, and pp.
      193f.

Primordial God as Personal Love he would have broken through to
the highest level of meaning of the Divine Reason as the ultimate
ground of the world. The ultimate rationality of the Divine
would be its Love that forever proceeds forth to establish its
world--such love is the ultimate explanation of the world, its
possibility and reality, its rational ground, its meaningfulness;
the clear and highest <u>reason</u> for the world's being. Possibly
more simply and directly put, had Whitehead a clearer concept of
Personal Love, in Primordial, as well as in Consequent God, he
would have phrased his conception differently at this basal point
of his thought, and avoided the ambiguity or the difficulties we
have encountered above, without doing the essential structure of
his philosophy damage in other respects. That God may be the
ultimate limitation, but His existence the ultimate <u>Reason</u> was
never in doubt in Royce.

Whatever the outcome of such a controversy as this,[24] the
central conceptions of 'being' in both Royce and Whitehead are
quite the same in the larger perspective, as we earlier tried to
demonstrate. And here again in the discussion of God, at least
on the Consequent side of the Divine nature, something very
similar to Royce's view of the Cosmic personalizing process is
eloquently said by Whitehead. If I can further abridge his words,
without too great misconception, they seem to describe God as the
Agapic pouring out of Himself into those primordial conditions of
the world out of which its individualities or actual entities in
all of their multifarious levels and dimensions, may arise:

> God is the infinite ground of all mentality, the unity of
> vision seeking physical multiplicity. The world is the
> multiplicity of finites, actualities seeking a perfected
> unity. Neither God, nor the world, reaches static comple-
> tion.... This final phase of passage in God's nature is
> ever enlarging itself.... This end is existence in the per-
> fect unity of adjustment as means, and in the perfect multi-
> plicity of the attainment of individual types of'self-
> existence. (PR pp. 529-31)

---

24 See authors' "The Personal Significance of Time, Space,
    and Causality," <u>Andover Newton Quarterly</u>, November 1960,
    pp. 22-34--where it is discussed that the human mind's
    reflection upon such primordial realities or experiences
    as one's sense of 'time,' 'space,' and 'causality' sug-
    gests their ultimate nature and meaning as aspects of
    personal mind in God.

The Issue of Freedom in Whitehead's Theology

We have already pointed to Whitehead's solution to this
problem in a number of places as closely resembling Royce's
effort, especially in Part II, on the idea of man. Here we will
briefly summarize. In many lines Whitehead, as Royce, solves the
problem of freedom by announcing that the spirit of God is reflected in, and identified with, the spirit of freedom itself in
man--particularly in the spirit of responsible moral freedom.
There is, of course, nothing new in all of this. The great
prophets of the Old Testament essentially performed this intellectual service for the west, and many sages in other cultures
have done so in similar manner. What we have been saying, however, in this regard is that Royce solved the problem in highest
philosophical terms in the only way it can be done we believe;
and that Whitehead has done it in the same way in his somewhat
more difficult philosophical idiom. Thus:

...God...issues into the mental creature as moral judgment
according to a perfection of ideals. (RM p. 119)

Each temporal entity...originates from its mental pole,
analogously to God himself. It derives from God its basic
conceptual aim...with indeterminations awaiting its own decisions. This subjective aim...remains the unifying factor
governing the successive phases of interplay between physical
and conceptual feelings. (PR p. 343)

In the lines just quoted, we suggest that "conceptual aim"
can be clarified as to meaning by being translated 'idea of freedom' itself (or the expression certainly implies this in part,
whatever further subtlety it may contain);[25] likewise the

---

25.   For further study of the problem of freedom in White-
       head we recommend William A. Christian's Chapter 18:
       "God and the World: Transcendence and Immanence,"
       esp. pp. 368-9 and 376 (Yale, 1959, op. cit.). His
       commentary on God's relation to the world through
       "conceptual aim" reads in part: "God is immanent in
       the world as the source of initial conceptual aim....
       He presents a possibility and evokes an appetition"
       (p. 376, emphasis his).
            In our view, the awareness of such "possibility"
       and the stirrings of "appetition" toward its realiza-
       tion constitute the point or area where the Divine and
       the finite orders of reality must be conceived to be

expression "conceptual feelings" closing the Whiteheadian statement here can be translated 'ideas,' with the Roycean interpretation of their 'internal' and 'external meanings' added for

---

conjoint in the idea of freedom, as discussed above.
Regarding this point, the view of Whitehead I have
expressed may doubtless be a somewhat free interpolation. His texts, however, remain open to this kind of
development. Whitehead's prevailing announcement that
God is responsible for the initial subjective aims of
individual entities suggests the type of solution that
I have endeavored to offer for the problem of freedom
in Royce and Whitehead. Our exposition of the problem
of freedom (possibly more definitely suggested in Royce
than in Whitehead) is the only way we believe that
theism can go, if the idea of the relation of the Divine
and human 'freedoms' is to be coherently understood.
If Whitehead is saying something similar to Royce, in
our phraseology that the idea of freedom is the solution to the problem of relatedness of freedoms, then
Professor Christian seems in error, in our view, in his
general expositional dictum, a number of times repeated,
that "Between God and an actual occasion there is no
sharing of immediacy" (Ib. p. 406). Whitehead certainly
implies that there is a sharing of immediacy in his
subjective aim principle.
Further, to look at another related issue in the
same context of Christian's concluding chapter, I would
say that Whitehead's many passages announcing a mutually
immanent, organic-like, hierarchic relatedness of actual
occasions to or within God, are not duly accounted for.
On the other hand, however, I believe a main point of
Professor Christian's must be upheld. It is that in
Whitehead, God's relation to the world cannot be conceived as that of a super, Diving "Organism" with
inhering finite cell-like organisms in some precisely
literal biological analogy. By "the philosophy of
organism" Whitehead does not mean that the World is an
"Organism" in a literal way; and Professor Christian
has, of course, thoroughly aired this point in an
exhaustive and illuminating manner (Ib. pp. 158f, 407-
9). On our own side we continue that for Whitehead
"organism" seems a metaphorical expression meaning
"organic-like." The universe exhibits many internal
relations, resembling organisms and their internal
streams of connections with their many organs, more
than it exhibits mechanistic relationships of only

further insight. In drawing the parallel between Royce and
Whitehead about the freedom of God in relation to the freedom of
man, and to all other entities, the key point is that "conceptual"
or "subjective aims" are derived from God. Or perhaps more precisely rendered, the <u>initial</u> <u>stage</u> of such aims are so derived,
or express "the nature of God." Thus we hear Whitehead say:

> ...the initial stage of its aim is an endowment which the
> subject inherits from the inevitable ordering of things,
> conceptually realized in the nature of God. The immediacy
> of the concrescent subject is constituted by its living aim
> at its own self-constitution. Thus the initial stage of the
> aim is rooted in the nature of God, and its completion de-
> pends on the self-causation of the subject-superject....
> ...God is...that actual entity from which each temporal con-
> crescence receives that initial aim from which its self-
> causation starts. That aim...constitutes the autonomous
> subject...with its initial conceptual valuations, and with
> its initial physical purposes....
>   If we prefer the phraseology, we can say that God and
> the actual world jointly constitute the character of the
> creativity for the initial phase of the novel concrescence.
> The subject, thus constituted, is the autonomous master of
> its own concrescence into subject-superject. (PR pp. 373-4)

And it might be added:

> The 'superjective' nature of God is the character of the
> pragmatic value of his specific satisfaction qualifying the
> transcendent creativity in the various temporal instances.
>   This is the conception of God, according to which he is
> considered as the outcome of creativity, as the foundation
> of order, and as the goal towards novelty. 'Order' and

---

external character, after the fashion of classic
Newtonian masses, or classic atomism. The connections
of the cosmic order are not 'mechanical' impacts and
propulsions in their depth character. Whitehead's
paradigms for how things are related and influence
each other are biological in illustration: they are
in terms of sense experience and feelings, or as he
generalizes, "prehensions."
     At any rate, one thing seems certain. Like Holy
Scripture itself, it may be said that Whitehead in his
complexity is open to varied exegesis.

'novelty' are but the instruments of his subjective aim....
It is to be noted that every actual entity, including God,
is something individual for its own sake; and thereby transcends the rest of actuality. And also it is to be noted
that every actual entity, including God, is a creature
transcended by the creativity which it qualifies.... The
Freedom inherent in the universe is constituted by this
element of self-causation. (PR p. 135)

Such depictions, we believe, imply a mutually inherent cosmic
totality, logically speaking, under the idea of freedom, that at
once constitutes the 'freedom' of all entities and makes possible
the progress of all together (God's included) in the cosmic
advance toward value experience. "The freedom inherent in the
universe is constituted by this element of self-causation," we
hear him close the above context, (which had also cited with
approbation Spinoza's definition of substance as causa sui in
illumination of his own view of God and other actual entities,
PR p. 135).

While to be sure it is not perfectly clear in all places
what Whitehead may have had exactly in mind regarding freedom,
the above passages, and others already indicated, are open to
the interpretation that they closely resemble Royce's more
generalized view of the cosmic situation on this subject.

Chapter Seven

THE PROBLEM OF EVIL

In his earlier, doubtless more 'absolutistic' frame of
thought and phraseology, Royce had eloquently stated the problem
of evil in the terms which were, more or less, to challenge him
throughout the development of his Integral Idealism:

> So far we have come in joyful contemplation of the
> Divine Truth. But now is there not a serpent in this Eden
> also? We have been talking of the infinite goodness; but
> after all, what shall we still say of the finite "partial
> evil" of life? We seem to have somehow proved a priori that
> it must be "universal good". For, as we have said, in the
> Infinite Life of our ideal there can be no imperfection.
> (RAP p. 449)

He endeavored to deal with the issue in a number of essays; those
we have cited in this study are named below.[1]

The premises of Royce's thinking about evil in light of his
just expressed view of the world as a whole are:

1. The "rationality" and fundamental good of the universe
   within the "Logos" or the Divine Mind:

> ...the Logos in his wholeness must find his choice of this
> universe rational, and so, in and through all this imper-
> fection, must find a total perfection.... The world that
> is, is then indeed, as Leibnitz said, the best of possible
> worlds. (SMP pp. 439-40)

2. Yet the "temporal reality" and "gravity"--not the illu-
   soriness--of evil in the world (WI2 p. 395; SMP p. 448):

---

1. "The Problem of Evil," from The Religious Aspect of
   Philosophy (1885); "Optimism, Pessimism, and the Moral
   Order," from The Spirit of Modern Philosophy (1892);
   "The Problem of Job," from Studies of Good and Evil
   (1898); "The Struggle with Evil," from The World and the
   Individual, Vol. II (1901); "The Religious Mission of
   Sorrow," from The Sources of Religious Insight (1912);
   "Atonement," from The Problem of Christianity (1913).

> I regard evil as a distinctly real fact, a fact just as real
> as the most helpless and hopeless sufferer finds it to be
> when he is in pain. (SGE pp. 15-17)

    3. The problem then arising (given 1 and 2) as to whether
the classic Epicurean-Humian dilemma does not successfully rebut theism?

> ...the ancient dilemma as to the limitation of his [God's]
> power upon the one hand, or of his benevolence upon the
> other, retains all its hopelessness of meaning. (WI2 p.
> 405)[2]

That is, Royce clarifies that Hume's dilemma is indeed the
logical refutation of theism, only if the reality or actuality
of evil be understood in terms of that metaphysical Realism--or
the conception of the world as a system of 'independent beings'--
which he has long since considered, and criticized as an inadequate view of the world. Hume's dilemma does not trouble Royce
at length, because in coming up upon the problem of evil he has
positioned himself tacitly all along to move between the horns in
order to meet its logic, as theism is obliged to do in some successful way, if it can. In other words, in viewing the world
from the perspective of his integral idealism, Royce believes the
dilemma of Hume, based as it undoubtedly is on 'metaphysical
Realism,' is ultimately by-passed. Royce's conclusion to the
discussion rejecting the concept of evil from the standpoint of
classic Scholasticisms and Realisms (WI2 pp. 399-405) in so many
words announces the null effect of this dilemma. Theism, indeed,
owes much to Royce in pointing out that Hume's dilemma (with
classic Christian theism and theodicy as its target) rests on
the same unempirical doctrines of metaphysical realism that the
older theism assumed. Royce has argued against Realism's philosophy of the separateness, disparateness, and radical atomicity
of entities in the universe. The universe is rather the more
unified and 'organic' tissue that he and Whitehead have proclaimed it to be. Accepting this latter perspective, then, Royce
must solve the problem of Theodicy[3] within its parameters.

    4. Therefore, (and his fourth emphasis) believing as "an
idealist" that a comprehensive and rational solution

---

  2. That is: If God is all-good, He cannot be all-powerful
(because of the presence of evil in His world); or, if
God is all-powerful, He cannot be all-good (because
evil is not removed from His world).

  3. From the Greek: "theos," God and "dike," justice .

to the problem of evil is possible, he speaks first to
the issue of classic Mysticism's illusional view of
evil, and then turns to Realism's interpretation, prior
to presenting his own solution (WI2 p. 395f)

5. That solution will hinge ultimately on two prime points:
    (a) that the "warfare" with evil "occurs, indeed, within
    the divine life itself, and not in an externally created
    world that is realistically an independent Being, other
    than God, and sundered from him" (WI2 p. 398, emphasis
    his). And (b) on the doctrine of the time-transcendence
    of God:

> His omnipresence is the presence of time and space in him,
> not his completeness in any part of them. He is their
> universal, they are not his prison. (SMP p. 439)

Such in main substance, through several essays, is to be
Royce's advance upon the problem of evil. Our task will be to
examine the principal steps of this progress, eventually suggesting the large degree to which Royce has succeeded in this
undertaking, as well as the extent to which he falls short of
his mark. We believe that a weakness does appear, in the midst
of a generally strong and profoundly suggestive theodicy, precisely in his doctrine of God's transcendency of time. This
point, will then lead into Whitehead's version of theodicy;
thence to the latter's treatment of the problem of God's relation to 'time' and the meaning of 'eternity,' and on to the
idea of 'immortality' for both philosophers. In the midst of
making this progress our own prolegomenon to the problems of
theodicy will appear, as suggested by the incompleteness of
Royce and Whitehead in this area of thought.

As for Royce then, first, to the classic mystic's denial
that evil is real, to the latter's oft repeated assertion that
evil is but "finite error," Royce replies, as many have done,
of course, with the simple pragmatic and logical point that
reveals the inconsistency of such 'mystical' position:

> ...finite error itself hereupon becomes, as the source of
> all our woes, an evil. But no evil is real. Hence no error
> can be real. Hence we do not really err, even if we suppose
> that evil is real.... And of the dialectic process thus
> begun there is, indeed, no end, nor at any stage in this
> process is there consistency. (WI2 p. 397)

Moreover, he points to the moral ambiguity of the mystical doctrine of evil as illusion, and to the bad pragmatic effect that
it has tended to cut the nerve of "moral effort" (WI2 p. 397).

Second, "The Struggle with Evil" essay (WI2 p. 399f) alludes to classic Augustinian theodicy in the reference to scholastic, i.e. traditional Christian views. Briefly, that theodicy announced that in the beginning God created a perfect world (the Garden of Eden); that man was created a free being, and that by the free sinning of his pride in acceding to the temptation of Satan and eating of the Tree of Knowledge of Good and Evil (forbidden to him, along with the Tree of Life or Immortality) he attempted to become equal to God; that in that act man 'fell' and was banished from the Garden into the real world that we know, of toil, hardship, and pain. In other words, all <u>natural evils</u> and <u>sufferings</u> (and those believed to follow for the unrepentant in a hereafter) are, in this interpretation, presumed to be a direct consequence of Adam's and Eve's sinful act and the righteous judgment of God. As some of the eschatological literature of Judaism and Christianity has depicted, the sequel to this account, of course, is that the order of nature will be restored to her pristine perfection in the Messianic Age to come, ordained of God, as the outcome of his perfect justice, and the ultimate 'solution' to the problem of evil.

By saying that those traditional dogmas expressed Realistic ontology, Royce means that they were couched in an extreme concept of the separation and otherness of God to his world; an extreme view of human individuality or independency, and its freedom to sin; and in the idea of an external Satanic source of temptation. Finally they attempted to exonerate an independent Divine Being by asserting that

> ...the ills of the world, thus explained as the divinely determined penalty of sin, are such that the sufferers have only their own sinfulness to blame for their woes, while God's righteous government is vindicated by their inability to escape his judgment. (WI2 p. 399)

Our philosopher concludes that "This view gives us in truth no intelligible Theodicy whatsoever," and continues:

> For, as a fact, our ethical interest in the universe is quite as inseparable from a belief in the solidarity of all human life, and in fact in the solidarity of all finite life, as this same ethical interest is also inseparable from a belief in the relative freedom and the individuality of finite agents. Moral agents must indeed possess their measure of finite freedom, if the world is to be a moral order. But in no ethically significant sense can they be Independent Beings, of any realistic type, if this same world is to possess any moral unity of meaning whatever. (WI2 p. 402)

Further, Royce believes that this option leads to "a moral fatalism"; as eggregious, we might add, as the moral indifferentism of certain mystical expressions of life (WI2 p. 404). Scarcely a more eloquent rebuttal of the morally and logically inadequate aspects of the classic Christian theodicy (arising in certain phases of Augustinian thought)[4] can be found than in this section of Royce's essay. On the other hand, Royce believes that a comprehensive rational solution to the problem of evil lies in his form of integral idealism and to his positive contribution we now proceed.

His 1892 essay, "Optimism, Pessimism, and the Moral Order," (SMP) includes discussion of the first aspect usually treated in studies of evil from a theological standpoint, namely, moral evil, or the problem of human 'sin,' i.e. man's inhumanity to man. Sin arises in a world of genuine freedom. Royce's integral

---

4. Professor John Hick of the University of Birmingham has pointed out in a definitive study, Evil and the God and Love, 1966, that while Augustinian theodicy has undoubtedly been in the history of theology the majority report of Christian belief about evil (until modern times at least), there was another more appealing view among early Christians themselves of the meaning of those early chapters of Genesis, on which the traditional Christian doctrine was founded. Hick discovered this in the thought of the second century theologian Irenaeus, and refers to it as the "minority report" within Christian opinion, antedating Augustine as a matter of fact by two centuries. Hick summarizes this alternative arising in Irenaean thought, in the following words, from his publication, Christianity at the Centre, Macmillan, 1968, p. 87:
    "In this Irenaean type of theodicy our mortality, frailty and vulnerability, within a natural order which is not built so much to comfort as to challenge us, are not a punishment for Adam's sin but a divinely appointed situation within which moral responsibility and personal growth are possible. This world is not intended to be a paradise but a place of soul-making, and the hard demands that it makes upon us are integral to its function." Such view of the natural world as a "vale of soul-making" has been, of course, a common perspective in the attempts of the theologians and philosophers to understand the place of some evils in the world, on the side of their disciplinary effects; and Royce has incorporated it as an aspect of his contribution to the subject, especially in his essay, "The Religious Mission of Sorrow."

idealism has profoundly described the reality of this freedom in both man and God, with man's finite freedoms defined as an integral expression of the meaning of the larger Divine Will and Freedom itself. In general terms, therefore, and quite traditionally, at this place in his thought, Royce believes that part of the solution to the problem of evil bearing upon ethical evil, or otherwise stated as the presence of 'sin' in the world, is to be explained as forthcoming from the reality of freedom. Freedom must indeed be the key word to the solution of the problem of evil on the moral or social plane explaining why man's inhumanity to man may arise as a possibility within God's world. But we note, of course, that Royce's view of freedom was not that espoused by the traditional dualistic theism of the Church, with its substance psychology, implying a radically 'realistic' idea of soul or personhood, in man and God, that led to the theodicy above criticized.

In order to penetrate the subtitles, however, of the relationship of an all-inclusive Divine to the human mind it is noteworthy that Royce (apparently unwittingly) shares a profound insight of Saint Augustine--an insight reflecting a facet of Augustine's thought other than the formal theodicy previously outlined, and described as the official doctrine of traditionalistic Christianity. In the following words, Royce has depicted this broader Augustinian solution to the central issue in the problem of moral evil: can an 'evil will' on the finite plane be understood to be 'within' a larger perfection and goodness of a "Divine Will" on the plane of the Cosmic totality?

> Only, just because our idealism makes of the divine Self one Transcendent person, in whom and from whom are all things, persons, and acts, just for this reason there is open to us a vindication of the moral order of God, which will insist at once upon the gravity of sin and upon the perfection of the divine morality. In God, so we say to the willful sinner, you are a part of a good will, which bears just such organic relation to your sinfulness as, in a good man, his virtue bears to the evil impulse that forms a part of his goodness. The hatred and condemnation of just your life and character makes God holy. God loves you, indeed, in so far as you are in any wise worthy; but just in so far as you are a rebel, you enter into the perfect moral order, not because your evil is illusory; but because God knows you to hate you and to triumph over you. ...whatever our sin, it is part of the moral order, only the moral order exists by conquering us.... ...as vessels of his wrath. But do we ourselves choose the good? Then once more we enter into the divine order, but this time as vessels of honor, as ministers of the good...as co-workers.... (SMP, pp. 460-1, emphasis his)

The key concept here is the "vindication of the moral order" by the judgments of human experience and history upon the evil act. Royce's searching discussion in this place reminds us nearly exactly of St. Augustine's conception of the "cooperating" and the "operating" aspects of the Divine Will, relative to its relation to the human will and freedom.

On the freedomist side of his thought, in a memorable passage discussing the Divine Will as an all-encompassing category, St. Augustine said that men stand within the Will of God and that that will"cooperates" with ours where we attempt to do the right-- i.e. in broadest terms of Hebrew-Christian thought, where men fulfill their responsibility of respect to personality in coordination with Moral Order and the meaning of existence. But even where men disregard, singly or collectively, that highest principle, they still stand within the Divine Will, though that is said, by Augustine to "operate" against them in the form of Moral Order, founded in personality, which seeks to maintain itself in the judgments and disciplines of history.[5] The joyousness of life when in harmony with that will--most broadly defined as the principle of creative respect for, or the sacred reverence of personality--is an expression of the moral order confirming itself. The judgments and disciplines of life when out of harmony with God's highest moral will, as defined, are our experience of moral order maintaining itself.

In the latter part of this the most definitive of his earlier essays on evil (p. 461f), Royce moves into the second, more difficult level of the problem of evil--that of 'natural evil,' or the surd (Brightman) irrational and seemingly pointless sufferings of the world. If theistic philosophy is to vindicate its outlook on the universe, its theodicy must ultimately speak, of course, to this level of the issue. In Royce's own words he refers to this "aspect of the problem of evil that is much darker from our finite point of view" than the problem concerning moral evil just reviewed; to "...the tragedy of the brute chance"--the evil of "diabolical irrationality"--"ignorance, the cruel accidents of disease"--"the hideously petty" in experience--the "capriciousness of...painfulness"--"the blind irrationality of fortune"-- "the mechanical accidents of nature," etc. (pp. 465-9). As stirringly as any sincere contemporary non-theistic or existentialist 'realist,' Royce is aware of the seemingly "farcical aspect of the universe," the bald absurdity of so much experience in life. Such things to many give the lie to any ultimate religious faith in God.

---

5.   On "Grace and Free Will," 33, 42-3, from Nicene and Post-Nicene Fathers, ed. Philip Schaff, Charles Scribners' Sons, 1908.

The true devil isn't crime, then but brute chance. For this
devil teaches us to doubt and grow cold of heart; he denies
God everywhere and in all his creatures, makes our world of
action, that was to be a spiritual tragedy, too often a mere
farce before our eyes. And to see this farcical aspect of
the universe is for the first time to come to a sense of the
true gloom of life. (p. 469)

Again a little farther on he continues to speak of the "capricious
irrationality of the world...the mocking demons of chance and
absurdity." How to meet the problem of evil at this level of
fact, a deeper and more poignant obscurity than the fact of men's
freedom to be inhumane to fellow men?

    In the closing portion of his essay, Royce himself admits
that his attempt to give an answer is but a sketch and that a
"true philosophic persuasion" would have to be "much more elaborate" than there is able to present (p. 471). Earlier he has
suggested that evil is a kind of "dissonance"--employing a musical
analogy to which he returns several times in his writings on the
subject. When our experience in listening to a musical scale, or
a symphony is complete we have a blending of discrete, successive
sounds into a whole of beauty, as if from the perspective of
time-transcendence, and perchance including dissonance as an
aspect of the ultimate perfection (SMP pp. 457f; see also WI2 pp.
379-94). Royce also refers a number of times to the necessity of
finally having to include the idea of "the suffering God," in
order to meet the demands of the problem of evil in its depths---
(SMP p. 470, a note which moves his faith, of course, by his own
acknowledgement, into an area of traditional Christian interpretation).

    But none of these suggestions sufficiently comes to grips
with the sharp edges of the problem of evil troubling the skeptic,
as well as the man of faith; and we said Royce admits as much in
the poignant closing paragraph of the essay we have been discussing (SMP pp. 470-1). His lecture, "The Struggle with Evil,"
in the second of the Gifford series (1900), penetrates more successfully into the problem of natural evil.

    This essay is built around a working synoptic definition.
Royce sees evil arising, and so defines it, as in essence an
expression of dissatisfied will. This includes not only human
will, in the striving and consequent conflicts of human life and
history, but will or striving wherever manifest throughout the
natural world, at all levels of the interactivity of individualities.

An evil is, in general, a fact that sends us to some Other
for its own justification, and for the satisfaction of our
will...every finite fact.... Any temporal fact, as such,
is essentially more or less dissatisfying, and so evil.
(WI2 pp. 380-1)

In the previous lecture ("The Moral Order") he had said, "It is
not satisfactory to be finite" (WI2 p. 363).

Such a point brings us back again to the broadest insights
of Royce's philosophy of being, as explained in Part I of this
study. Evil, then, is that which frustrates the impulse to being,
that is, the impulse of entities or individualities to realize
the internal meanings of their ideas in the accomplishments of
external fact or "being." We believe this to be a profound definition of evil indeed, and one which reminds us once again of another Augustine concept, this time of evil as the depreivation of
being. Royce proceeds to relate this definition to our sense of
Time as "the devourer, the destroyer" (WI2 p. 381)--and so ultimately to criticize Time itself as the culprit. But more about
this development at a later point.

In the meanwhile, the above definition takes Royce nearer
to a comprehensive solution to the problem than he has up to now
achieved. This formulation of the quintessential meaning of evil
as the inevitable experience of the teleological striving of
entities at every level of the universe, in so far as any of them
would at some point and to some degree experience frustration,
Royce expressly describes as pertaining to the whole of nature.
To quote him at some length (from "The Struggle with Evil"):

...dissatisfaction is the universal experience of every temporal being. How this dissatisfaction empirically appears,
underw what form, with what intensity,--this is a matter that
the more concrete experience of life, taken in all its various
aspects, has to decide. Vast ranges of finite ill, namely,
those that are filled with physical suffering, have characters
which we men are of course unable, at present, to explain in
detail by any such abstract formula as the foregoing...our
ideals actually imply our present dissatisfaction, and so
contribute to our consciousness of temporal ill.... Hence
the larger our ideals, the more we understand why it is that
nothing temporal can satisfy us.
...man's Selfhood is bound by the most manifold ties
to the life of Universal Nature.... Thus, for instance, our
organic pains, and our more instinctive emotions, have a
depth and a manifoldness that I should hypothetically explain, in accordance with the theory of Nature earlier
expounded, as due to the fact that vast strivings,--

expressing the Will of the race rather than of the individual,
and of Nature-Life in its wholeness rather than of the life
of any one man,--strivings, that in themselves are conscious
and ideal, are at any moment, in our narrow present consciousness, merely echoed and hinted, by many of our profounder,
but less rational joys and sorrows, repugnances and attrac-
tions. According as these vaster interests that pervade the
process of Nature, and that constitute the various meanings
of its temporal occurrences, become more or less indirectly
represented in our conscious life, we have experiences of
such joys, and of such griefs, of such successes and of such
failures, as we ourselves cannot directly explain in ideal
or conscious terms....
       And yet, apart from these endless complications, the
abstract formula does hold good that all finite and temporal
processes of will must inevitably involve dissatisfaction....
       On the other hand, for our idealistic Theory of Being,
the very presence of all in the temporal order is the condition of the perfection of the eternal order. (pp. 382-5)

Royce continues to say that "the Internal Meaning of the procsses
of Nature is, in general, hidden from man..." (p. 388), but concludes, nevertheless, that "...all ill fortune results from the
defects, or at least from the defective expression, of some
finite will" (p. 390). He further elaborates these observations
in the words immediately following:

       This finite will is in general unknown to me. I do well not
       to trouble myself to impute blame. Yet presumably every
       such defect of finite will has, like our own defects, a
       genuinely moral significance. I am therefore right in hold-
       ing that, when I suffer an ill fortune due to external natu-
       ral agencies (however meaningless that ill fortune may
       appear to me), I am enduring a part of the burden of the
       world's struggle with temporal finitude, or with sin and with
       its consequences. (p. 390)

       We have already heard Royce's explication of evil at the
level of "sin and its...consequences," the moral level of the
problem and the more easily resolvable aspect than natural evil.
In the above quotation he points to "temporal finitude" as the
ultimate causality and rational explanation of evil, inclusive of
natural evil, of course; and along this direction of thinking a
solution, at the very depth of the problem of natural evil, does
indeed seem to lie. But Royce does not delve into this issue
beyond this introductory scanning. We give him credit, however,
for putting his finger on the larger parameter of the problem in
the idea of temporal finitude, within which others have worked
to solve the problem of evil, more completely or successfully

perhaps, since Royce's effort.

For example, theodicy must consider the many desperate issues that criticism can raise against theism. For example by what rationale would a theistic philosophy throw light on why there is <u>excessive</u> or <u>prolonged</u> <u>painfulness</u>, that is, both quantitatively and temporally, in God's world? Why is there inherent weakness constitutionally in some actual entities due to <u>hereditary defect</u>, that makes them simply unable from the start to stand without painfulness the rigors of existence? Why are there 'evil' or 'inept' <u>mutations</u> at the basis of the evolution and formation of some life--to designate an aspect of the ultimate causality of the evilness we observe in process? Or there are those ultimate questions about the Creative Purpose itself of the Divine Mind in bringing forth a world of finitude and freedom in the first place, with its inherent possibility and inevitability of conflict, and accordingly of the suffering of entities? Why does God bring forth <u>this kind</u> of world rather than--originally and ideally--some more perfected world scheme, less definitionally structured with the certain probability of 'evil process'? Or granting the goodness and wisdom of God, how does a theodicy conceive the nature of Divine 'power' in moral terms adequate to explaining the responsibility of the Divine Mind toward its world of possible and manifest excessive suffering and surd evil? Such questions were really present at the heart of Hume's dilemma, and Royce does not in detail meet their challenge.[6]

---

6.   The modern literature on the problem of evil in the light of theistic philosophy is, of course, voluminous. I recommend such treatises as the following which endeavor to deal with the deeper anxieties concerning evil and faith as suggested in the above questions: Douglas Clyde Macintosh: "The Problem of Evil" in <u>Theology as an Empirical Science</u> (1919); Frederick R. Tennant: "The Problem of Evil" in Vol. II of <u>Philosophical Theology</u> (1937); William R. Sorley: "Theism" in <u>Moral Values and the Idea of God</u> (1921); Harris Franklin Rall: "Faith and the Fact of Evil" in <u>Christianity, an Inquiry into its Nature and Truth</u> (1941); Edgar Sheffield Brightman: <u>The Problem of God</u> (1930); "Is God Finite" in <u>A Philosof Religion</u> (1940); John Hick: <u>Evil and the God of Love</u> (1966); David Griffin: <u>God, Power, and Evil: A Process Theodicy</u> (1976); and our own effort to contribute to this discussion, "God, Freedom, and Pain," <u>The Harvard Theological Review</u>, April, 1962.

Granting, however, the validity of the foregoing criticism of Royce's failure to look more searchingly at some of these issues, he has clearly pointed to them. In his disputation with Mysticism on the topic he had summarized his position by saying that the solution to the problem of evil from the standpoint of his idealism lies in the real, "relative freedom" of the temporal order "at every point" and "the possibility and the fact of a finite and conscious resistance of the will of the World [that is, God's] by the will of the Individual [that is, of finite entities]" (p. 398). Indeed, a solution to the problem of evil has to be enlarged along these lines. The authors mentioned in our footnote have attempted with greater success as a whole to accomplish this than has Royce. They have done so, however, within the general perspective that he outlined in his study of evil. We will find that one way of interpreting Whitehead himself concerning the problem of evil, may be in terms of the idea of the 'finite God.' Many others, of course, have joined in this latter perspective in varying ways; most notable doubtless is that of E.S. Brightman. Still others have endeavored to solve the problem by options wider than the route of the finite God in its narrowest meaning. In any case, in those parts of his own essay on "The Struggle with Evil" that we have thus far considered, Royce has given us an accurate prolegomenon to the issues of theodicy.

Part of his discourse on the problem of evil strikingly adumbrates the finitism of theists like Brightman and possibly Whitehead.[7] We have already noted Royce's reference to the fact that the "warfare" with evil must occur "within the divine life itself" (p. 398). Earlier, again in the dispute with Mysticism, we find Royce affirming that "the Absolute as such, in the individuality of its life, is not evil, while its life is unquestionably inclusive of evil, which it experiences, overcomes, and transcends" (p. 396).   Both of these statements suggest the idea of Professor Brightman (an idealist of somewhat different cast than Royce), that an uncontrolled, subconscious "Given" in God himself is the most adequate explanation of the origin of evil. Royce, however, would have differed from Brightman in the finer point that God's Given (to employ the Brightman term) is not a dark, unconscious level within God's nature, analogous to our own subconscious minds as finite selves; but rather for Royce it would be the 'given' of nature herself, conceived as an aspect of the meaning of being, fully illuminated and brightened by ideas and their telic strivings or purposiveness in the Mind of God.

---

7.   As will later be pointed out it is an open question whether Whitehead is a theistic finitist in the same strict sense as Brightman.

We cite the similarity to Brightman, however, in the larger
respect in order to point again to Royce's prescience in looking
clearly down the several roads other theists have explored in
search for a more adequate solution to this problem. (Royce
would have been designated by Brightman as a "Theistic Absolut-
ist," that is, one of those who do not choose to solve the problem
of evil along the lines of asserting an express finitism in the
nature of God.)

    We return now to a further level of criticism. It concerns
Royce's major theme of the essay, "The Struggle with Evil."
Earlier it was pointed out that according to his definition, evil,
quintessentially understood, lies in the fact that "nothing temporal can satisfy us." That is, temporality itself as such is
evil. He suggests this in a number of places, not only in the
present essay, but also in others. For example, to continue with
the Gifford Lecture, he says:

> The only way to give our view of Being rationality is to see
> that we long for the Absolute only in so far as in us the
> Absolute also longs, and seeks, through our very temporal
> striving, the peace that is nowhere in Time, but only, and
> yet absolutely, in Eternity. (p. 386)

    Peace is nowhere in Time? Royce poses something, "Eternity,"
as transcending "Time," which is to solve ultimately for us the
problem of evil inherent in time experience. (We are not here
criticizing Royce's possible meaning--so very classic--that evil
may indeed ultimately be resolved for personal spirits only in
some Heavenly reward after this present earthly experience is
completed.) But what we are criticizing here is his apparent
definition of time itself as the evil culprit. Or at least we
call attention to what appears to us to be a serious ambiguity in
his thinking concerning the purpose or role of time. The ambiguity stares at us in the very next sentence to the just quoted
passage. It reads: "Were there then no longing in Time, there
would be no peace in Eternity." Royce himself, however, feels no
ambiguity in his doctrine of 'time' and 'eternity,' for he later
writes on the same page:

> The Temporal Order, taken in its wholeness, is for us iden-
> tical with the Eternal Order. There are, then, not two
> regions sundered in their Being, in one of which the divine
> Will reigns supreme, while in the other the success of the
> divine plan is essentially doubtful. These two realms of
> Being are merely the same realm, viewed in one aspect as a
> temporal succession, wherein the particular present Being of
> each passing instant is contrasted with the no longer and not
> yet of past and future, so that fulfillment never at one

present instant is to be found; while, in the other aspect, this same realm is to be viewed, in its entirety, as one life-process completely present to the Absolute consciousness, precisely as the musical succession is present at a glance to whoever appreciates a phrase of the music.   (p. 386)

Likewise another arresting passage states how the very 'evil' of the temporal experience is an aspect within the 'good' of the Eternal or Absolute Experience:

Now is there any good in all this essential, and never-theless, ideally colored, misfortune that besets the best deeds and meanings of my present form of consciousness? Yes. There is, indeed, one very great good. For in respect of this better aspect of my life, I suffer because of the very magnitude and the depth of my meanings. I am in ideal larger than my human experience permits me, in present fact, to become. My evil is the result of this my highest present good. Can I improve this my state of temporal ill? Yes, by every serious effort to live in better accord with my ideal. (p. 406)

And so on in a number of further lines in this closing section.

The crux, perhaps, of our dispute with Royce in this latter part of his searching essay, centers upon his dictum, uttered several times in various ways:

...temporal peace is a contradiction in terms. (p. 407)

...the sorrows of time.... (p. 409)

Man...cannot now know the ideal meaning of the vast realms of finite life in whose fortunes he is at present mysteri-ously doomed to share. ...with the sorrow of finitude in every movement of the natural world.... (pp. 410-11)

In brief, then, nowhere in time is perfection to be found. Our comfort lies in the knowledge of the Eternal. (p. 411)

It is precisely such an adverse view of time in these places that impels a theodicy to go beyond Royce's efforts to give an answer to such profound questions as: Why, from the standpoint of the loving purpose of Creative Reason, must Creation be a realm of "finitude" and "time," and indeed can be no other in that Divine Intent itself? Is there some other way that Time and Finitude may be conceived than as the temporary cosmic scandals whose sorrows are to be translated ultimately into an "eternal triumph"--as the only way God can deal with them at long last? Royce is too much the classic idealist here. Indeed in this moving homily he borders on profound pessimism regarding the time order and creation itself. Logically speaking, if Time is the culprit, why does the Absolute in "Eternity" ever endure it, or its illusion? A question which eastern mysticism never clarified, and to which position Royce himself here paradoxically seems to turn for the moment in spite of his larger criticism of classic mysticism's illusional views of finite process.

The same questions can be raised in very practical terms. Is there no "temporal peace" that we can know many times in real life? Is it always "a contradiction in terms," or in all cases? Surely experience calls to mind our many moments, indeed, days and years, of proximate satisfactions, senses of completion, fulfillments, approximate perfections, sentient radiances, and spiritual joys--impossible for us, were time itself not one of the eternal purposes of God! Indeed, Royce himself, by his own many allusions to the "temporal life" as the "very expression of the eternal triumph" seems to assert the good of time. The inherent logical (and emotional) trouble in Royce's statement that "...it is my first business, as a moral agent, and as servant of God, to set before myself a goal that, in time, simply cannot be attained" (p. 407), can be resolved only if we can understand ultimately that the temporal itself is an intimate aspect of the Divine Meaning; just as Royce has claimed that Freedom itself must be, or Truth itself. With such clarification open to us, we might then with Royce say that our temporal tasks are, of course, never fully complete in some utmost sense, but this is not to say that the time process itself and its challenges are evil.

In the earlier lecture, "The Temporal and the Eternal," of his second Gifford series, Royce wrestles valiantly with this problem of God's relation to time. Indeed, in several places there his doctrine of time "as the form of the will" virtually proclaims that time is the ultimate category of meaning of the personal itself:

...our only way of expressing the general structure of our idealistic realm of Being is to say that wherever an idea exists as a finite idea, still in pursuit of its goal, there appears to be some essential temporal aspect belonging to the consciousness in question. To my mind, therefore, time, as the form of the will, is (in so far as we can undertake to define at all the detailed structure of finite reality) to be viewed as the most pervasive form of all finite experience, whether human or extra-human. In pursuing its goals, the Self lives in time. (WI2 p. 134)

Everywhere, of course, as the very heart of his cosmic theism,
Royce has been proclaiming that God, as the ultimate meaning of
his own divine life, seeks the larger goal of providing the
cosmic opportunity for finite beings to seek their goals. Would
the passage just cited, then, imply that God is the larger Self
who also "lives in time," as the essence of the possibility of
his own personhood? Or is Royce saying that God _is_ time, or Be-
better perhaps that time is an intimate expression of His very
ing? To say that God is _in time_ would seem to make time a prior,
abstract, and impersonal category, some vague, ultimate 'Kronos,'
perhaps, anterior to 'Zeus.' Accordingly, for such reason
doubtless, Royce shies away from stating things in such a manner.
He does, however, tell us that God lives in time in so far as He
himself includes, or is aware of the real successive, flowing, or
durational experience that lies at the heart of our own time
sense. In other words, God, for Royce, experiences time-as-
succession as we do, but from the standpoint of beginning-to-the-
end-as-a-whole, in one synoptic vision--"_at once_ known" (WI2 p.
138). He says, "...all temporal sequences, are present at once
to the Absolute" (Ib. p. 140). Finite events are "the presence
of all time, as a _totum simul_, to the Absolute" (Ib. p. 141).
A number of times in this essay, as in previous ones, Royce
refers to our experience of music as an experience of wholeness
or timelessness, or as something 'eternal,' while also the very
essence of succession or passage of beats or notes in time. In
a number of essays this has been his most illuminating analogy of
the 'Eternity' of God in relation to the 'Temporality' of finite
experience. The following further remarkable passage in "The
Temporal and the Eternal" goes far toward declaring the temporality of God, as naturalists like Whitehead have been more bold
to do, and even as some Idealists since Royce's day like E.S.
Brightman have likewise done. [8]

> To observe the succession _at once_ is to have present with
> perfect clearness _all_ the time-elements of the rhythm or of
> the phrase just as they are,--the succession, the tempo,
> the intervals, the pauses,--and yet, without losing any of
> their variety, to view them at once as one present musical
> idea. Now for our theory, that is precisely the way in which
> the eternal consciousness views the temporal order,--not
> ignoring one jot or tittle of its sharp distinctions of past
> or of future, of succession or of duration,--but still viewing
> the whole time-process as the expression of a single Internal

---

8.   "Defense of a Temporalist View of God," in _Person and
Reality_, The Ronals Press Co., 1958.

Meaning. (WI2 pp. 143-4)[9]

Is Royce here saying that God's life is the Time-fulness of
reality itself? If he means this he was indeed a theistic temporalist, as Whitehead was more clearly than Royce, and as
Brightman announced his own position to be, idealist though the
latter was in over-all metaphysical commitment. Does the "Eternity" of God, then, mean unending-Time, Time-fulness, or does it
mean Time-transcendence? Royce, in our view, does not perfectly
clarify this issue. Using Royce's own illustration in the hearing
of musical melody, we indeed hear all of its notes as a whole, as
it were, but we hear them as a whole durationally or continuingly
rather than as a timeless instant, whatever that would be; and
this is precisely the primordial time sense that we believe
all personality is, including God. In Royce's basic terms we may
declare that the "internal meaning" or will of the Divine is that
there shall be "time-process" (as he himself many times throughout
his works implies). A fully adequate personalism must be certain
on this point, as Royce was not in his essay, "The Temporal and
the Eternal," nor in other discussions of the same problem.[10]

---

9. Later on in WI2 he again wrote: "Temporal, is the world
    order, because, so far as we can know, time is the uni-
    versal form of the expression of Will. Eternal is this
    same world order, because past, present, and future time
    equally belong to the Real, and their Being implies, by
    definition, that they are present, in their wholeness,
    to the final insight. And Time, surveyed in its whole-
    ness, is Eternity" (p. 337). But did Royce mean by this,
    'Time surveyed in its endlessness is Eternity'?

10. I refer to a remarkable footnote on the meaning of God's
     'eternity' appended to the Ingersoll Lectures on Immor-
     tality of 1900, and a later address of 1906 with the
     same title, in which Royce discusses these same matters
     at considerable length and incisiveness, but without
     greatly different effect, we believe, than what we have
     been pointing out above--even though in one place in the
     1906 address he says that "Time is in God, rather than...
     God in time." See also Royce's charming address of 1909:
     "The Reality of the Temporal," The International Journal
     of Ethics, Vol. 20, April, 1910, pp. 257-71, where again
     we find some approximation to a definition of "eternity"
     as the fulness of the time reality itself, but still not
     without the lingering ambiguities, never perfectly re-
     solved by Royce, which we have been pointing out in our
     main discussion above.
       I quote part of his concluding paragraph from this
     article: "If an individual right hand glove is real,

We have already observed that Whitehead is less ambiguous on this point, and will again review the matter when we discuss presently his position on evil.

If Royce had gone on to say more certainly that he meant by God's "eternal" quality, the Divine Love's everlasting, and perhaps even unchanging moral purpose to make possible freedom and a life of moral purposiveness for His finite beings, as integral to the meaning of His own Individuality or moral Personality as God (part of which would be indeed God's continuing purposiveness to be the ground of all Time itself as an aspect of His own absolute moral will)--Royce would have drawn his discussion of the "eternity" of God around better to fit his doctrine of being itself; and incidentally would have anticipated more successfully the probable meaning of God's 'eternity' in Whitehead.[11]

---

and if an individual left hand glove is also real, and if they are mates, then the pair of gloves whereof these two mates are the units, is itself real, and so, if the past of the time order is real, and if the future of the time order is real, and if past and future belong together, then the whole of the time order has its own reality as a whole.   Since, however, the future time order is not just now temporally and transiently a present datum, but is precisely the totality of future events, and since an analogous proposition holds of the past, the whole time order is real not at any one temporal instant, but precisely as a time-inclusive totality. That such an eternal is real, not at any one instant, but as an eternal, is as sure as that if the fingers of a living hand are real, the whole hand of which these are the fingers is itself a reality.   The temporal not merely implies the eternal; in its wholeness it constitutes the eternal,--namely the total decision of the world will, wherein the loyal will to be rational finds its own fulfillment."

Again in 1912 he refers to God's vision as a "time-inclusive survey," The Sources of Religious Insight, p. 177.   These references are probably the nearest Royce comes to asserting that the time-process is itself an intimate expression of the activity of God.   See our later section on immortality, pp. 222f., where the time problem in Royce is further discussed.

11.   We raise this point again about Royce in the discussion of Whitehead on time and eternity, pp. 214f.
Others also have pointed to this ambiguity in Royce concerning time, e.g. Gabriel Marcel: La Metaphysique de Royce, Aubier, 1945, pp. 218-20; Milic Capek: "Time and

Finally, in closing this analysis of Royce's treatment of the problem of evil, we call the reader's attention to the brief passage from The Philosophy of Loyalty, and to his essay on "The Religious Mission of Sorrow" from The Sources of Religious Insight, for their practical inspiration. This latter essay was his way of treating an old and hallowed theme in Christian theodicy, that finite experience must include moral testing and growth through vicissitude for the tempering of finite personhood.

Whitehead wrote no systematic treatise on the problem of evil, such as Royce several times endeavored to do. Scattered throughout his writings, however, observations appear on the nature of evil and God that bear on theodicy and suggest the outline of his thinking on this problem. [12]

To introduce his thoughts on evil in a preliminary way we find three principal characteristics: First are statements presenting a very classic (Augustinian) definition of evil as the deprivation or the disintegration of organized being, form, or value. Next are his views on the causality of evil (and a part of its definition) as arising when things--actual entities and occasions--work at "cross purposes" to themselves in the confluent rushings of their free processes (a concept of evil and its causality synonymous with Royce's view of it as an expression of the dissatisfied will). Finally we may look to the intimations of a solution for the problem in the fact of the instability of evil in the world. The world is thus self-disclosed as good in over-all nature, or working toward the good, under the inspiration of the Divine lure. Rounding out this discussion will be our attempt to compare what he has accomplished with Royce and others in our time in a larger effort to solve the problem of evil within a theistic faith.

Eternity in Royce and Bergson," Revue Internationale De Philosophie, 1967, Nos. 79-80, pp. 22f.--in part a close examination of Royce's view of "time" and its ambiguities vis-a-vis his view of "eternity." Utilizing Royce's discussion in WI2, Capek concludes: "...there is hardly any question that in spite of honest and serious effort 'to take time seriously,' Royce's thought moved to the conclusion of Bradley and McTaggart: that 'ultimately' time is unreal," p. 45.

12. See previous discussion of the principle of "limitation" in the context of Whitehead's treatment of God as the ground of rationality, pp. 153f.

Whitehead's resume of the problem of evil and its solution along the lines just suggested involves his express understanding of God as "limited" (RM p. 153).[13] Two characteristic paragraphs read:

> Among medieval and modern philosophers, anxious to establish the religious significance of God, an unfortunate habit has prevailed of paying to Him metaphysical compliments. He has been conceived as the foundation of the metaphysical situation with its ultimate activity. If this conception be adhered to, there can be no alternative except to discern in Him the origin of all evil as well as of all good. He is then the supreme author of the play, and to Him must therefore be ascribed its shortcomings as well as its success. If He be conceived as the supreme ground for limitation, it stands in His very nature to divide the Good from the Evil, and to establish Reason 'within her dominions supreme.' (SMW pp. 179-80)

> The limitation of God is his goodness. He gains his depth of actuality by his harmony of valuation. It is not true that God is in all respects infinite. If He were, He would be evil as well as good. Also this unlimited fusion of evil with good would mean mere nothingness. He is something decided and is thereby limited. (RM p. 153)

To which we add a passage on his expectation that evil can and will be overcome, if finite freedom but venture:

> The fact of the religious vision, and its history of persistent expansion, is our one ground for optimism. Apart from it, human life is a flash of occasional enjoyments lighting up a mass of pain and misery; a bagatelle of transient experience.
> The vision claims nothing but worship; and worship is

---

13. The following, however, are essays, where observations on the nature of evil, bearing on theodicy, appear in Whitehead, and from which our discussion of the subject here is drawn--(it is not implied that these exhaust the Whitehead sources where statements on evil could be found): "God" and "Religion and Science," from Science and the Modern World (1925); "Body and Spirit" and "Truth and Criticism," from Religion in the Making (1926); "The Ideal Opposites," "God and the World" and "The Theory of Feeling," from Process and Reality (1929); "Beauty," "Truth and Beauty" and "Adventure," from Adventures of Ideas (1933); "Activity," from Modes of Thought (1938); "Mathematics and the Good" (1941), from Science and Philosophy (1948).

a surrender to the claim for assimilation, urged with the
motive force of mutual love. The vision never overrules.
It is always there, and it has the power of love presenting
the one purpose whose fulfillment is eternal harmony. Such
order as we find in nature is never force--it presents itself
as the one harmonious adjustment of complex detail. Evil is
the brute motive force of fragmentary purpose, disregarding
the eternal vision. Evil is overruling, retarding, hurting.
The power of God is the worship He inspires. That religion
is strong which in its ritual and its modes of thought evokes
an apprehension of the commanding vision. The worship of God
is not a rule of safety--it is an adventure of the spirit, a
flight after the unattainable. The death of religion comes
with the repression of the high hope of adventure. (SMW
p. 192)

What does he mean by the limited nature of God, and wherein
is this doctrine perchance like and unlike similar conceptions of
our time that have gone under the designation of the finite God?
I am thinking here particularly of the terminology of Edgar
Sheffield Brightman, who has perhaps more than others systemati-
cally and fully explored the finite God idea as the most fruitful
way to consider the problem of evil. Accordingly we will presently make a comparison of Whitehead's view on this point to that
of Brightman's. In the meanwhile, however, we continue with the
larger Whiteheadian perspective on evil.

I believe that the first statement above from Science and
the Modern World would place Royce's Integral Idealism under
Whitehead's criticism of conceiving God as "the foundation" of
the total "metaphysical situation" and consequently leaving no
option except to see "all evil as well as good" in God Himself.
Probably, however, in mentioning that such a view makes God
simply author of "the play," Whitehead doubtless had the Hindu
version of monistic idealism expressly in mind. The reference
suggests the Vedanta understanding of līlā, that is, the created
world as the illusive 'play' of God. Hinduism, of course, is a
many splendored thing, and from the standpoint of its orthodox
monisms solved the problem of evil by simply declaring it to be
an expression of material incarnation and maya and therefore more
illusory than real. In the teaching of Sankara finitude and evil,
though doubtless provisionally real, were certainly impermanent
and nothing at all at last from the standpoint of the ultimate
Brahman.[14] By another side of Hinduism, however, reflecting some
of the main line popular cultus, evil was incorporated as an
aspect of the Divine itself. Such a position was bodied forth

---

14. 9th century A.D.

in the prominent roles that the Shiva-Shakti divinities played
when representing the disintegrative and death cycles of natural
energy. We have seen, of course, that Royce's view was as critical of the Hindu 'mysticism' as Whitehead's allusion is above.

As already noted, in the same paragraph appears Whitehead's
own central and final point about God and evil: namely, that God
must be conceived as "the supreme ground for limitation," that is,
supreme discriminator of values, and the force indeed whereby
Reason and the Good are kept enthroned, actually in the cosmic
order, and ideologically at the center of the theistic vision.
In the next selection from SMW Whitehead continues to define God,
from the perspective of the religious vision and its perennial
optimism, as "the power of love" whose purpose is "fulfillment"
in "eternal harmony."

The first premise, then, of a Whitehead theodicy would be
the conception of God as a 'limiting' principle under the 'power
of love,' and to this point we will return below.

We move next to a second premise, i.e. the nature, meaning,
or definition of evil itself in the thought of Whitehead, before
we can clarify how God, under his conception, deals with, or
relates to evil in such a way as indeed to keep Reason within her
dominions supreme--that is, make sense of our universe as conceived under a theistic hypothesis. In such lines as the following, Whitehead defines evil and its causality:

-the brute...force of fragmentary purpose, disregarding the
eternal vision. (SMW p. 192)

-[the] loss of the higher experience in favour of the lower
experience. (RM p. 95)

-its character of a destructive agent among things greater
than itself. (RM p. 95)

-a descent toward nothingness. (RM p. 96)

-There is evil when things are at cross purposes. (RM p. 97)

-The nature of evil is that the characters of things are
mutually obstructive. (PR p. 517)

-Destruction...is the correct devinition of evil. (AI p. 258)

-...evil lies in the clash of vivid feelings, denying to
each other their proper expansion.... Evil...is the
violence of strength against strength. (AI p. 275)

-[evil as] active deprivation. (SP p. 119)

-[as] maladjustment of patterns of experience. (SP 119)

In brief for Whitehead, as we saw for Royce, evil, most simply
described, is the conflict of actual entities in their individuality and telic striving.

While defining evil and its causality Whitehead would have
us underscore especially that "...finiteness is not...evil" (AI
pp. 275-6). In other words, lower levels of occasions, in and of
themselves, are not evil, though they may be harmfully related
to, or evilly integrated in, higher, or wider societies of occasions (RM pp. 94f). Thus neither "hogs" (nor disease microbes,
we could add) are evil in and of themselves:

> A hog is not an evil beast, but when a man is degraded to the
> level of a hog, with the accompanying atrophy of finer ele-
> ments, he is no more evil than a hog. The evil of the final
> degradation lies in the comparison of what is with what might
> have been. (RM p. 97)

Evil is a relative thing--relative to whatever particular level
of occasions we may be talking about, in their prehensive relations (evil if negative, good if positive in Whitehead techni-
cality) to higher or more complex occasions in which they may be
found, or to which they may be associated.[15]

On the specific causality or genesis, then, of evil in this
world, Whitehead concludes, in a more generalized way, that it
can be traced "to the determinism derived from God" or "the consistency of God" (RM p. 99). In other words, in the mesh of
efficient causalities the origin of evils is to be seen. Free
"formative elements" outside of God's highest value purposes are
part of evil's causality (RM p. 99). (Recall our previous discussion of final and efficient causality as needed descriptive
terminology for understanding God's relation to the world in
Whitehead's thought, pp. 147f.)

Religion in the Making, pp. 95-9, contains a good summary of
Whitehead's thoughts on evil, and are profoundly contributory
(though in too brief fashion) to a solution to the problem.

---

15. That "negative prehensions" are sometimes a technical
     definition of evil in Whitehead's thought is suggested
     by passages where he describes them as relating to the
     experience of "elimination," the "struggle for exist-
     ence," a feeling's "impress of what it might have been,
     but is not" (PR pp. 338, 346, 353)

If I am correct in interpolating Whitehead's "determinism derived from God" and "the consistency of God" expressions into the idea of God's efficient causalities in the world, then indeed the presence of much 'natural evil' can be explained, within the general hypothesis of the goodness of God and the over-all goodness or wisdom of the natural world as we find it. For these 'determinisms,' 'consistencies,' or natural laws are those qualities absolutely or rationally seen to be the necessary stable qualities of environment that finite entities, and particularly living entities, need, in order "to learn to make habitual the most favorable adjustment."[16]

This point calls to mind our discussion of Royce. However, Whitehead is more specific than the former in clarifying that finite temporality or process is not in and of itself to be regarded as evil. We found that this important issue was left in considerable ambiguity in Royce, though the latter's fullest intention was perhaps not so to say. Whitehead assists theism better than did his predecessor at Harvard on this particular issue. Rather than profoundly implying that finitude and temporality as such are evil, as Royce seemed to do often times, Whitehead more consistently simply says that "There is evil when things are at cross purposes" with themselves. Apart, however, from embroiling time directly in the issue, the general perspectives of our two thinkers are quite the same in their definitions of evil, and its origins, that is, as lying in the dissatisfactions of finite will, in the incompleted strivings of actual entities.

To return now to the central issue of theistic faith: Why must the world be thus constituted, if God be good and also able? How can we conceive just this world to be the world necessarily of, by, or within such God. What does 'the good' within or of Deity mean? What does His being 'able,' that is, his adequacy, or his power mean? The problem of theism is to answer such questions about God in such a way as to bring the definition of Deity into full accord with the simple empirical facts of the world, and the reality of its evils, now understood as the dissatisfactions and the conflicts of finite 'wills' (to employ here, once again, the Royce idiom).

We criticized Royce ultimately for endeavoring to solve these profound matters by causing his 'God' to retreat into an upper chamber of eternalness above his temporalness. We can only

---

16. A memorable line of Douglas Clyde Macintosh, relating to the problem of evil in the work previously mentioned, p. 171, note 6.

say 'his temporalness' if we are to be fully true to Royce,
because for him both things were asserted to be aspects or
expressions of God's nature. However, we found a severe ambiguity in all of this; and asserted on our own part that Royce
might better have gone the way that some later idealists, and
all naturalists who are also theists have gone, to proclaim
temporality, without hesitation or moral stigma, to be a principal meaning of Deity itself. Royce seems to go this way at
times, but never quite certainly. On the other hand, Whitehead's
naturalistic theism brings temporality into the picture of God
more definitely. There are, however, problems left unelucidated,
even in Whitehead, as to the meaning of the eternal and the temporal in God. To these and other final points in Whitehead's
conception of the problem of evil we now proceed.

With the definition of evil now in mind, and attempting to
understand his conception of God as related to it, the following
sentiments of Whitehead appear to be crucial to his thinking.
He writes in Religion in the Making, "God...must be exempt from
internal inconsistency which is the note of evil" (p. 98). And
later, "It is not true that God is in all respects infinite. If
He were, He would be evil as well as good...He is something decided and is thereby limited" (p. 153). In the same paragraph
(his second on page 180) we also read, "The limitation of God is
his goodness. He gains his depth of actuality by his harmony of
valuation" (p. 153).   On the same page of RM Whitehead continued, "He [God] is complete in the sense that his vision determines every possibility of value." Farther on, he observes that
the world's "suffering" is the opportunity for "values" to "issue
from it," and that this "transmutation of evil into good" is the
work of God, who, as the "ideal companion," "transmutes what has
been lost into a living fact within his own nature"(RM pp. 154-5).
Whitehead concludes this immediate context:

> God has in his nature the knowledge of evil, of pain,
> and of degradation, but it is there as overcome with what is
> good. Every fact is what it is, a fact of pleasure, of joy,
> of pain, or of suffering. In its union with God that fact
> is not a total loss, but on its finer side is an element to
> be woven immortally into the rhythm of mortal things. Its
> very evil becomes a stepping stone in the all-embracing
> ideals of God. (RM p. 155)

Passages from Process and Reality contain an echo of Royce's
sentiment that time may be the culprit, where Whitehead observes
that "in the temporal world" inevitably "process entails loss";
and that "the ultimate evil in the temporal world.... ...lies in
the fact that the past fades, that time is a 'perpetual

perishing'" (PR p. 517). A bit earlier he had introduced this
point with the comment:

> The world is thus faced by the paradox that, at least in
> its higher actualities, it craves for novelty and yet is
> haunted by terror at the loss of the past, with its familiar-
> ities and its loved ones. It seeks escape from time in its
> character of 'perpetually perishing.' (PR p. 516)

But Whitehead does not worry at length, as did Royce, with the
diversion that time is "a perpetual perishing," a kind of 'evil'
necessity of finite things because they are process whose
experiences are inevitably passing. In this very context he
immediately shows that time itself contains its own redemptive
character, in the last analysis, and must therefore be accounted
good and not evil. The following profound statement on how evil
is eliminated, empirically and ultimately, brings this fact to
light about the nature of the time process itself (and we found
nothing quite so penetrating on such a point in Royce):

> In the temporal world, it is the empirical fact that process
> entails loss.... But there is no reason, of any ultimate
> metaphysical generality, why this should be the whole story.
> The nature of evil is that the characters of things are
> mutually obstructive. Thus the depths of life require a
> process of selection. But the selection is elmination as
> the first step toward another __temporal__ __order__ [emphasis ours]
> seeking to minimize obstructive modes. Selection is at once
> the measure of evil, and the process of its evasion. It
> means the discarding the element of obstructiveness in fact.
> No element in fact is ineffectual: thus the struggle with
> evil is a process of building up a mode of utilization by the
> provision of intermediate elements introducing a complex
> structure of harmony. (PR p. 517)

Further crucial statements bearing on our problem appear in
his famous chapter, "God and the World" from Process and Reality,
where he wrote that God is "infinite" on his Primordial side by
virtue of the fact that He is "devoid of all negative prehensions"
(PR p. 524); but be it remembered that it is also asserted there
that eternal Primordial God is "actually deficient, and unconscious" (PR p. 524), and that both God and the World "are in the
grip of the ultimate metaphysical ground," the creativity (PR
p. 529).

Looking at another related term, for the moment, the "perfection" of God's mind (as the receptacle or beholder of all
value) must not be viewed naively--as if it were a blank

superlativeness without entertained distinctions in and of itself, like some kind of homogenous stellar brilliance that shines
with but one and only one kind of intensity and coloration.
Rather God's ultimate Goodness or Perfection is the multiform
character, the complexity and richness of the value options that
Deity holds for the world, eternally entertaining them as possibilities for process. Evil can be in God in the sense that He
can imagine it, just as we can do. Thus in two selections,
respectively from Adventures of Ideas and Modes of Thought, we
read:

> We must conceive the Divine Eros as the active entertainment
> of all ideals, with the urge to their finite realization,
> each in its due season. Thus a process must be inherent in
> God's nature, whereby his infinity is acquiring realization.

> But the point stands out that the conceptual entertainment
> of incompatibilities is possible.... (AI p. 276)

> ..."perfection" is a notion which haunts human imagination.
> It cannot be ignored. But its naive attachment to the realm
> of forms is entirely without justification. How about the
> form of mud, and the forms of evil, and other forms of imper-
> fection? In the house of forms, there are many mansions.
> (MT p. 94)

We call attention lastly to his saying that the idea of
"infinitude" or "infinite" is an empty abstraction, "meaningless
and valueless" apart from "its embodiment of finite entities."
But we had best quote here a little more at length from "Mathematics and the Good":

> ...infinitude in itself is meaningless and valueless. It
> acquires meaning and value by its embodiment of finite
> entities. Apart from the finite, the infinite is devoid of
> meaning and cannot be distinguished from non-entity. The
> notion of the essential relatedness of all things is the
> primary step in understanding how finite entities require
> the unbounded universe, and how the universe acquires meaning
> and value by reason of its embodiment of the activity of
> finitude. (SP p. 114)

His essay "Mathematics and the Good" spoke of these terms again
in the following way:

> The doctrinal squabbles of Christianity have been concerned
> with the characterization of the infinite in terms of fini-
> tude. It was impossible to conceive energy in other terms.

The very notion of goodness was conceived in terms of active opposition to the powers of evil, and thereby in terms of the limitation of deity. Such limitation was explicitly denied and implicitly accepted. (SP p. 115)[17]

And so we return to what appears to have been Whitehead's leading conception in facing the problem of evil: namely, that of the Divine "limitation." What now did he mean by this in light of the foregoing statements? Did he mean that God was "finite" in the sense of Edgar Sheffield Brightman? With this question it is, of course, our duty to present a resume of Brightman's conception of the Finite God, an idea which has become celebrated under his name perhaps more than that of any other theologian of our times because of the forthrightness and lucidity with which he uttered it.

    *   *   *   *   *   *

Brightman uses the alternative expressions "finite God" and "finite-infinite God."[18] The following sentence describes the finite and the infinite features:

> God is a Person supremely conscious, supremely valuable, supremely creative, yet limited both by the free choices of other persons and by restrictions within his own nature.[19]

By the first clause, Brightman doubtless means for one thing that, in comparison to man, God is supreme in consciousness, value, and creative activity. Also God is supreme simply as the creative source of the world. Although from an ultimate standpoint of faith, God may be the creative source of the world,[20] for Brightman, when we come to wrestle with the problem of evil, in looking at the details of God's relation to the world in its present temporal process, we must refine our definition of Deity. In Brightman's system we therefore have God presented as _absolute_ in his will for good but _finite_ in his power, with the area of creation not yet fully under the divine control called "the Given." "If we suppose the power of God to be finite, but his

---

17. Meaning here, of course, the problem of conceiving the Incarnation under the classic conception of Deity.
18. Brightman, _The Problem of God_ (PG), 1930, pp. 127 & 191.
19. Ib. p. 113 and see p. 124.
20. For example see Brightman, _A Philosophy of Religion_ (APR), 1940, p. 332 and esp. 337.

will for good infinite, we have a reasonable explanation of the place of surd evils in the scheme of things."[21]

The middle quotation on the previous page summarizes the deeper way Brightman understands God to be limited or finite. One suggestion is that if this is a universe of many persons, God is, by definition, limited in a sense by others' free choices. Another point is that limitation is characteristic of 'personality' in and of itself, and that would include, again by definition, the divine case as well as the human. This may be summed by saying that, to Brightman, the finiteness[22] of conscious personality as we know it in ourselves is the central clue or analogy among "four main types of evidence" for the finite God.[23] The four types of evidence adduced by Brightman are:

First, the religious evidence runs to the effect that the attitude of human worship itself has sometimes suggested a dark, unfathomable side of God.[24] Brightman cites the experience of some mystics, who, while in the mystic rapture or ecstasy, in experiencing God as supreme Good or Love, felt a terrifying, dark, abysmal depth in the Divine Presence. Second, another line of evidence is that all process, natural and historic, is movement and contrasting movement; thesis, antithesis, and then synthesis; effort, opposition and victory on a higher level. This historic "dialectic" of contradiction and struggle reminds us, of course, of the Hegelian theory of the life of the Absolute, but principally, for Brightman, reflects the fact that God struggles, is sufferer.[25] God's "goodness is not merely an abstract quality but the constant victory of constant effort."

Third, a further and for Brightman very decisive evidence are "the facts of evolution" in their detail. Disteleology and surd evil thrust up by the evolutionary process positively prove that the Creative power is at least delayed, "a spirit in difficulty,"[26] in its program of world building.[27]

Fourth, and centrally important in the hypothesis of the finite God, according to Brightman, is the clue which the nature of consciousness itself offers. Brightman says,

---

21. Ib. p. 319 and see p. 313.
22. Brightman, PG, pp. 131-4; APR, pp. 364-5.
23. Ib. p. 126.
24. Ib. pp. 136-8. See Brightman, The Finding of God, 1931, pp. 115f.
25. Brightman, PG, pp. 135-6.
26. Ib. p. 135.
27. Ib. pp. 126-31 and see APR, Chapter X.

"Assuming...that there is a personal God, I wish to show from the nature of consciousness that he must be finite."[28]   At this level of analysis, he presents two reasons which in general describe the Divine Personality from the finitistic point of view.

(1) The fact of human freedom impels him to write: "...confidently I express the view that if man is truly free, God must be finite as regards his knowledge...Man's freedom is an actual limitation on the foreknowledge of God."[29]   But more profoundly than the fact of freedom on just man's side, there is the implication of what free consciousness would mean anywhere--even in God.   If God himself, as a personal consciousness, is free, there is much in the example of human choice, with its results that go beyond our powers of prediction and control (making us tragically 'finite'), that suggests "something analogous in the divine freedom, although only remotely so."[30]   This assumes, of course, that God chooses in ignorance of results as human choice is often made. Brightman concludes that God's "foreknowledge" is limited.[31]

(2) The "nature" of God (as one's "nature" does for any conscious being) conditions and limits His "will."   This "nature" is composed of His reason, His temporal activity, and "the Given."[32]   Apparently here Brightman uses the words "limitation" and "limited" in a particularly literal sense.   Accordingly, if God's nature limits His will, God must be conceived as finite in His Power.   The following analysis attempts to illuminate this point in greater depth.

All consciousness possesses active and passive factors.   In our human case it is clear that the passive is due to a considerable extent to senation.   In God's case, we cannot attribute an external factor, such as sensation, but must resolve the problem by believing that there is the passive, contrary factor within the Divine Nature itself, thus explaining the struggle of creation throughout cosmic history.   "We must," Brightman wrote, "acknowledge a duality of nature at the very eternal heart of things, in which the active is indeed in control, but maintains its control with struggle and pain."[33]

---

28.   Ib. p. 131.
29.   Ib. p. 132.
30.   Ib. pp. 131-2.
31.   Ib. pp. 131-2.
32.   Ib. p. 133 (further on "the Given" see note 37)
33.   Ib. pp. 134-5.

The above description may be summarized in Brightman's own
words: "Every person, human or divine, has experiences which his
will does not produce, but finds."[34] Our own conscious personalities are analogous to the finite-infinite consciousness of God.

This, then is the structure of our human spirits; they are
active wills dealing with passive experience and laws. Our
activity is directed on the content of sensation, and is
subject to the limits of rational possibility. We are thus
finite beings; whose wills are limited by what is given to
them; yet we are also in some ways capable of the infinite.
Not only can we grasp the meaning of the mathematical infinite, but we can also think of eternal and self-sufficient
beings. Our own spirit with its active-passive nature is
also finite-infinite. Now the faith with which religious
idealism confronts experience suggests that the small segment
of the universe which we call ourselves is truly a sample of
what the whole universe is.[35]

Brightman's is a vigorous and courageous attempt to deal
realistically with the problem of evil at its most acute spot--
the surd, apparently unnecessary evils of physical process. He
believes that only "theistic finitism" can cope adequately with
such facts as cancer, or the enormous waste and cruelty disclosed
in the evolutionary history of the world. Back of Brightman's
discussion, of course, lies the classic attack on theism by the
Epicureans, and in modern times by Hume, in terms of the logical
dilemma, several times now cited, that--given the world as we
find it--either God is not all-powerful, if all good; or He is
not all-good if all powerful. Brightman accepts the first horn
of the dilemma in order to save the goodness of God. As an
historical analogue to his principle of the Given, he uses
Plato's concept of the material receptacle found in Timaeus.
However, he avoids the suggestion of world-dualism in Plato (as
does Whitehead) by affirming that the material element must somehow be within God, who constitutes a "monism of purpose and personal identity."[36] The Given refers to God's "unwilled, non-
voluntary consciousness."[37] Brightman feels that this solution

34. Brightman, APR, p. 364, emphasis his.
35. Brightman, Personality and Religion, Abingdon, Cokes-
     bury Press, 1934, p. 83.
36. Brightman, APR, p. 339.
37. In his Philosophy of Religion, Brightman lists the con-
     tents of the 'Given' aspect of God as:
     1. "the eternal uncreated laws of reason"
     2. "the eternal and uncreated processes of non-rational
         consciousness" e.g.,

proceeds along empirical lines and is the most coherent interpretation of the coexistent facts of good and evil in our world.[38]

In conclusion, Brightman believes that the Finite God is progressively overcoming evil, through the work of moral salvation and the material elimination of evil. God's spirit, the cosmic source of value and personal being, works through men of good will, in both the moral and the scientific areas, in a joint effort of bringing evil under more and more control. Although Brightman was primarily a philosopher of religion, who attempted to find answers to the questions of existence through rational inquiry, above and beyond any specific religious tradition, he did, however, in the last analysis, find his ultimate inspiration in the Christian theological outlook. Jesus' teaching of love, and the central Christian idea of suffering, or the Cross, would symbolize for Brightman, the way God is "slowly and painfully" overcoming the evils of the world.[39]

*   *   *   *   *   *

From this review of Brightman's position (developed at about the time Whitehead was in mid-course at Harvard),[40] it may first appear that at many points Whitehead's conception of evil closely resembles Brightman's idea of a "Finite God." A difference between them, however, begins to emerge. It appears in Brightman's to us confused view of the Divine Consciousness or Personality as being psychologically split between an upper story, "infinite" in moral will for good, and a "limited" basement or sub-cellar of darker uncontrolled impulses and experience described as the "Given." For Whitehead, however, the 'Given' (to employ Brightman's term and to draw an analogy to Whitehead's Primordial God and perhaps to the Creativity), was courageously, or more consistenly announced to be "unconscious," or 'impersonal.' We believe that Whitehead's position turns out to be more classic,

---

              -"sense objects" or qualities
              -"disorderly impulses and drives" (the sub-
                conscious)
              -"pain and suffering"
              -"space and time."
         3. "Whatever in God is the source of surd evil."
              (p. 337)
    38. Ib. pp. 309 & 314.
    39. Nature and Values, Abingdon, Cokesbury, 1945, pp. 165-6.
    40. Professor Brightman was Professor of Philosophy at
         Boston University, 1919-1953.

or Platonic, than was Brightman's. Though Whitehead was not a
dualist in the sense of the original Plato of the Timaeus, who
divided materiality from deity, and saw evil as lodging in the
material receptacle as such; Whitehead certainly seems to stand
somewhere between the dualism of Plato and Brightman's theodicy.
This is suggested for one thing in Whitehead's understanding of
matter or "the Creativity" (if I read these allusions rightly in
him) as the locus of the arising of evil in the world, which
God's growing, conscious, consequent side ultimately transmutes
by preserving the good and allowing the evil to destroy itself.
God accomplishes this as the unconscious potentialities of the
forms become conscious realization of good in God's own telic
striving to provide opportunity for finite good to emerge. This
emergence of the good is embodied in the positive prehensions of
entities when they can work in full harmony, and not at cross
purposes; and finally as he, God, in his own cosmic Prehension of
such value facts, immortally preserves them. (It seems to me
that in Whitehead we have the suggestion, or the trace of the
Platonic Demiourgos-God, without the Platonic dualism, if such a
cosmological view can be imagined.) In any case, Whitehead's
view is not pure Platonism, to be sure; nor is it pure Bright-
manism by any means. So far it may be viewed as a kind of median
position between the two, and the better of the three options.
By returning somewhat nearer to Platonism Whitehead bypassed the
bad incoherency or bifurcation in the Brightman concept of the
Divine Consciousness. As we have suggested, however, there
remains a problem in Whitehead's concept of the unconsciousness
or impersonality of God on the Primordial side of the Divine
Nature (pp. 150f).

Is there now a theodicy that might utilize the best in the
Whitehead theology thus far, while avoiding on the one side the
difficulty of the impersonality of Primordial God, and on the
other, the dualism that we find in Brightman's depiction of the
'finite' aspect of the Divine Nature itself? We believe that
there is, and it is suggested or implied by Whitehead himself,
though not exploited by him at any length. We regard it as a key
concept to a successful theodicy, and it has been emphasized by
others, as we shall presently point out. It is the idea that--
in the context of the study of evil--the Divine "limitation"
means the Divine self-limitation, and is the ultimate meaning of
the Divine moral consciousness vis-a-vis its world. Such an
emphasis on the Divine self-limitation or forbearance will avoid,
we believe, the difficulties of Brightman; it will also dissipate
some of the imprecision of both Royce's and Whitehead's attempts
to deal with the problem of evil.

We find the suggestion of the Divine self-limitation in

Whitehead in such lines on the Consequent side of God's nature
that refer to His <u>tender care</u>, to His <u>patience</u>, to His <u>suffering</u>,
<u>loving</u> understanding of the World of freedom. Recall an example
or two. We read that there is in God's nature

>   -a tender care that nothing be lost...a tenderness which
>   loses nothing that can be saved. (PR p. 525)

>   -...his consequent nature...is his infinite patience. ...
>   tenderly saving the turmoil of the intermediate world by
>   the contemplation of his own nature...God's role is not
>   the combat of productive force with destructive force; it
>   lies in the patient operation of the overpowering ration-
>   ality of his conceptual harmonization.... ...he is the
>   poet of the world, with tender patience leading it by his
>   vision of truth, beauty, and goodness. (PR pp. 525-6)

>   -...God is the great companion--the fellow sufferer who
>   understands. (PR p. 532)

If we are inclined to stress this latter element of the
Divine self-limitation in Whitehead, then it would probably be
necessary to minimize a resemblance to Brightman. For a Divine
self-limitation could be understood as a function of a morally
omnipotent purpose--"the limitation of God is his goodness"
(RM p. 153)--and that doubtless would be to read a further, more
classic or traditional outlook in Whitehead's view of God and
Evil than a finitistic perspective of the precise Brightman kind.
Be this option within Whitehead exegesis as it may, his conception
of the self-limited Deity is certainly present, and stands beside
a like perspective of other theologians of our time as the point
on which a successful theodicy may be constructed.[41] The

---

41. A recent commentary by Professor David Griffin goes the
other way in the interpretation of Whitehead on evil,
<u>God, Power, and Evil: A Process Theodicy</u>, Westminster,
1976, Chapter 18. While acknowledging that this chapter
is in part an interpolation of Whitehead (p. 275),
Griffin believes that the main thrust of the latter's
position on evil is not that God's "<u>modus operandi</u>" is
a moral "self-limitation," but is rather a purely "metaphysical" <u>modus operandi</u>. Griffin says, "God does not
refrain from controlling the creatures simply because
it is better for God to use persuasion, but because it
is necessarily the case that God cannot completely control the creatures" (p. 276). Griffin points out that
there are two criteria of evil in Whitehead's thought:

following, then is an excursus outlining what is further needed
along this line to carry the work of Royce and Whitehead on the
problem of evil farther than they themselves were able to take

----

there is not only "discord" (or conflict, in our discussion), but also "unnecessary triviality." In discussing the purpose of creation Griffin stresses that
"...God brings order out of chaos for the sake of
increased intensity." The author points to Whitehead's
well known emphases on intensity of experience in such
places as PR pages 161, 381.

I would say, however, that while the point concerning intensity is present in Whitehead, intensity
does not exhaust the latter's meaning for God's purpose
in creation, or God's bringing order out of chaos.
Indeed, Griffin's very next citation suggests God's
larger moral purpose (p. 287): "What is inexorable in
God, is valuation as an aim towards "order"; and "order"
means "society" permissive of actualities with patterned intensity of feeling arising from adjusted contrasts" (PR p. 373).

Griffin quotes another passage like this that
serves my own constructive criticism here: "A structured society which is highly complex can be corres-
pondingly favorable to intensity of satisfaction for
certain sets of its component members. This intensity
arises by reason of the ordered complexity of the contrasts which the society stages for these components.
Thus the growth of a complex structured society exemplifies the general purpose pervading nature" (PR p. 152).

Thus, I would say that the following might be a
more comprehensive statement than the one Griffin has
given us of the cosmic purpose in Whitehead's outlook.
Considering, then, the constructive side of things as
to how the Divine deals progressively with evil, and
also bringing together into a larger synthesis the two
levels of the meaning of "evil" cited above: God
brings order out of chaos for the sake of increased
intensity consonant with increased intensity (joy) for
other entities or individualities--i.e. consonant with
social harmony. (Whitehead's supreme social doctrine,
the vision of "Peace," which along with other moral
categories of a process philosophy, we are to analyze
at a later stage of this study, p. 294f, brings this
point into its final focus.) Suffice it to say here
that the above enlarged definition of the cosmic purpose seems the way Whitehead understood, on fullest

it, but to which a number of their allusions point. We begin
this resume with a further reference to the finitistic school of
Brightman as it attempted to speak to the classic issue David

account, what the triumph over evil would mean in terms
of an ultimate overcoming of discord and triviality.
With the emphasis on "order" and "society" at its apex,
the Whitehead perspective on the Divine relation to
evil is indelibly penetrated with moral light.

Indeed, much seems granted along this line by
Griffin himself in his section "Metaphysical Correla-
tions of Value and Power," an exceedingly useful discussion of what the author believes may be read from
Whitehead about five "variables" (said to be more
implicit than doubtless explicit in the thought of the
latter): "intrinsic goodness," "intrinsic evil,"
"freedom," "instrumental goodness," and "instrumental
evil." But in the next section we come to the central
issue, once more, of our discussion with Griffin, concerning Whitehead's stance on the Divine Power in its
relation to evil.

The section is entitled, "The Notion of Metaphysical
Principles Beyond Divine Decision." This heading states
the chief point that Griffin poses in his interpretation. Griffin believes the passages in Whitehead that
seemingly ground the metaphysical categories within the
Divine nature itself (such as PR pp. 64, 73, 75, 522),
should not be taken as the necessary position of a
process philosophy, but, better, that such a philosophy
means on the whole there are "metaphysical principles
of interaction which cannot be surmounted" even by God
(pp. 297-8). (Griffin admits that Hartshorne's view of
Whitehead--that the metaphysical categories are grounded
in the Divine primordial nature--is probably a correct
over-all interpretation, in spite of some statements by
Whitehead suggesting the contrary.)

If, however--to return again to our main point--we
are led to stress those observations of Whitehead himself where the metaphysical principles (such as "creativity," the "many," the "one," "everlasting" Deity,
"temporal" Deity, "process," and whatever else may seem
metaphysically intrinsic to Whitehead's theory of being)
are grounded in the Divine primordial rationality (recall our discussion of the rationality principle in the
Whiteheadian Deity, p. 153f); and if we include in
these principle the moral or Agapic character of the
Divine (our discussion, p. 153f), then the moral

Hume raised earlier in modern times. We then continue with the
latter part of our own study of evil previously noted; and conclude with a brief discussion of the premises of thought that we

---

self-limitation of God as our solution to the problem
of evil follows from Whitehead, at least as one avenue
of thought.

Griffin interprets Whitehead, it seems to me, in
the direction of the original Plato--with an emphasis
on 'external' metaphysical realities. This is indeed
a possible way to understand Whitehead, as we have
acknowledged above. If we accept Griffin's view (and
turning back to the original problem raised by our
chapter), then Whitehead's God would indeed be conceived to be 'finite,' but, we have said, in more
acceptable terms than Brightman's. (Griffin is also
critical of Brightman as I have been, p. 242f). The
other way, however, seems also possible. A moral self-
limitation of God is not only a possible exposition of
Whitehead texts themselves, in the manner we have suggested above, but also a viable option for 'process
theology' as such.

In any case, in this climatic chapter of a splendid
book tracing the entire history of theodicy in the west,
Griffin tellingly replies to a claim by Edward Madden
and Peter Hare (Evil and the Concept of God) that Whitehead subordinates 'moral value' to 'aesthetic value' and
therefore does not describe an adequately theistic God
(pp. 301-2). Griffin shows that the meaning of "beauty"
in its most synoptic sense in Whitehead includes moral
value or goodness (e.g. AI pp. 12, 13, 190, 1933 ed).
His extended remarks concerning this point in Note 16
concludes, "it would be misleading to think of Whitehead's God as either a Divine Aesthete (in the usual
sense of that term) or a Cosmic Hedonist" (p. 328).

Griffin also rebuts charges that Whitehead does not
deal realistically or seriously enough with the problem
before us in statements implying that worldly evil is
transmuted into good when taken up into God's experience. Our author points to the over-all perspective of
Whitehead as emerging in the following passage. (This
passage, incidentally, reflects beautifully a conception
of Royce on "Atonement," as we shall see, p. 278f).
"The kingdom of heaven is not the isolation of good from
evil. It is the overcoming of evil by good. This
transmutation of evil into good enters into the actual
world by reason of the inclusion of the nature of God,

believe are inherent to a successful theodicy. Finally we relate
these premises to the forementioned authors, who have contributed
greatly, in our view, to the clarification of the problem of evil
in the light of theistic faith.[42]

A Prolegomenon to Theodicy

Whether God's relation to the world be conceived in more
idealistic or monistic terms (Royce), or in more pluralistic or
realistic terms (Whitehead)--in other words, whether God exer-
cises control by an immediate immanence of being (Royce and
Whitehead)--or by sheer transcendent or transitive power (classic
theism), He is still responsible for his world. Theism on any of
these terms must answer the question why God has created, or
brought forth from Himself, a world with the possibility of evil
process within it; in short, why He constitutes the world as it
is. Non-theists have formulated the problem in terms of Hume's
dilemma:

> Epicurus's old questions are yet unanswered. Is he [God]
> willing to prevent evil, but not able? Then is he impo-
> tent. Is he able, but not willing? Then is he malevolent.
> Is he both able and willing? whence then is evil....[43]

As we have seen in the notable case of Edgar S. Brightman,[44]

---

which includes the ideal vision of each actual evil so
met with a novel consequent as to issue in the restor-
ation of goodness" (RM p. 148).
    Highlighting this insight from the interior per-
spective of finite mind, Griffin cites those passages
where our immanent awareness of the moral ideal is our
"prehension of God" (Griffin's phrase, p. 305), RM pp.
114, 152, MT p. 103, etc.; and summarizes Whitehead on
this subject by the following: "God's self-interest is
not selfish interest but is an interest in the welfare
of the world. There is no tension in God between
desire and duty, since God, being completely receptive
of all the joys and sufferings in creation, desires
nothing other than the greatest possible joy for the
entire creation" (p. 308).

42. Note 6, page 171.
43. Dialogues Concerning Natural Religion (1779).
44. Others often cited as theistic finitists, among them
Whitehead, have been: John Stuart Mill, F.C. Schiller,
William James, Henri Bergson, A. Tsanoff, Peter A.

some theists frankly accept one horn of this dilemma, namely, the first proposition:

If God is all-good, he is not all-powerful.

We heard Brightman claim that, though God is all good with respect to his intentions for the world, He is not all powerful in His ability to deal directly with evil by perfectly controlling process. Brightman designated this as the doctrine of the finite God. (Religious theism, of course, could not accept the second proposition, that 'if God is all-powerful, he is not all-good.') Need theism, however, accept the dilemma by accepting the first horn?[45] The dilemma may be dissolved, we suggest, by passing through or 'escaping between the horns,' as one method of dealing with this form of logical problem. This type of reply to Hume's dilemma is accomplished by a third proposition, involving the idea of God's self-limitation, a suggestion found in Whitehead himself, which does not impale us on either horn. Thus the dilemma and its horns are rendered a nullity. Theism's alternative, <u>hypothetical</u> proposition then, which gives, we believe, a simpler and truer picture of the cosmic order than the 'finite God' idea may be formulated thus:

If God is 'all-good' and 'all-powerful,' His relation to the world may be one of self-limitation.

Brightman has called such a position "theistic absolutism." To avoid problems suggested by the word "absolutism," however, to which we have previously pointed,[46] we believe it better to refer, more simply, to the idea of the full <u>adequacy</u> of God's Goodness and Power. Last, we will point out that God's relation to His world <u>must be</u> one of self-limitation, if He is 'all-good,' that is, conceived to be moral in character. His moral nature freely legislates his self-limitation. This type of theodicy will reflect, indeed, some of the main spirit of the classic tradition, without falling into the problems that, for example, a literal reading of the Adam and Eve story opens up. (Recall our previous discussion of classic theodicy, pp. 164f.)

What precisely is the concept of God's goodness then, that leads to the alternative solution to the problem just outlined? By God as 'all good' we mean that He is creative Agape. He, as

---

Bertocci.   (See Brightman APR pp. 295-301 for discussion of the history of theistic finitism.)
45. Note 2, p. 162.
46. Page 106f.

fullest moral rationality, 'limits' Himself in His relation to his finite, but moral, that is, freely developing world. Accordingly, we suggest that Brightman, endeavoring to support one possibility for theism (and Hume and his followers for nontheism) have confused, and misstated the problem of evil. Implied in their position is the disjunctive proposition: 'God is either all good, or all powerful.' Theism may pose, however, the former, and possibly simpler, hypothetical proposition as the proper way to state the solution to the problem of evil. To repeat at a little greater length: If God is fully and morally adequate as Creator and sustainer of the world (i.e. if He is creative Agape), His relation to it must be one of moral self-limitation or forbearance.

I have elsewhere elaborated a conception of evil along these lines, and will not here repeat that discussion in its fulness.[47] We there attempted to answer certain fundamental questions concerning evil (mentioned in connection with the Royce exposition earlier in the present commentary)[48] that the critics of theism may raise. To recall briefly, however, by way of pointing to them once again, there were such ultimate or primordial issues as: (1) Why pain itself, in all its varieties and ranges (as the center of the problem of evil), that is, both quantitatively and temporally, must needs be understood as an inevitable possibility of the experience of finite entities--i.e. why pain, even when 'excessive,' must be understood as a 'rational' possibility or factor, rather than an irrational or surd element in the experience sometimes of finite orders of being? (2) Why 'evil mutation' as an identifiable causality of pain, may appear as a possibility sometimes of the outworking of free processes in an order of finite temporal events and entities? (3) And most anterior in degree, of course, related to such questions, Why finitude and freedom themselves as such (that is, as the loci of suffering) are the outcome of the creative, forthgoing Love of a Cosmic Order ultimately conceived to be Personal Mind, if such Love presumes to create or bring forth within or beyond itself anything at all? We will, however, utilize the closing observations of the above mentioned essay in which these things were discussed, briefly adding to them here several further insights for the purpose of this outline.

The theistic explanation of pain and evil mutation rests on certain premises. These premises seem rationally necessary as the fullest, or most coherent judgments concerning basic matters

---

47.   See Note 6, p. 171.
48.   See pp. 170-1.

of process and reality. A. One of these is the empirical judgment that all life (indeed all things), have continuity or unity (Royce and Whitehead). B. Another is that some device was necessary whereby life could freely adapt itself in order for there to be (1) organic evolution, development, or adaptation, and (2) ultimately spiritual evolution or moral adaptation, as the inherent possibility of higher freedom, such as is found in our human experience. Such a device we find in the principle of 'mutation,' with its mysterious fecundity, implying a near limitless possibility of form, and resident in the 'first life germ,' and present even possibly at sub-living levels of nature and process. If these premises or principles be granted, and they seem to describe the very heart of the evolutionary process, we have in them considerable justification of the world as she has gone on, and is. Such a picture may help us to see, at least to some extent, why in the course of process, even such a thing as a disease germ, harmful to its host, might arise as a necessary risk within the total or unified stream we call 'life' and its 'evolution,' or 'creation.' Our ultimate evaluation of the presence of disease germs must be understood in the context of mutation; and we understand that the world of life as a whole could not have come to be without mutation. But a world such as ours, even one in which their lies some risk of 'evil mutation,' if the product as a whole would have been impossible without the risk, seems a justifiable world.

Our second premise above may be expanded to include the idea that all of the principal causes of evolution as we know them[49] have after all been 'ideal' means for the coming and development of life toward responsible moral intelligence; for they are the only principles conceivable that could account for organic evolution. Inherent in these factors was all the possibility of the moral growth which we empirically perceive and also subjectively experience. The central factor or cause of evolutionary change, in the mutation of the genes, is precisely the one that has made finite freedom possible, with all of its higher potentialities experienced by human beings. This factor, along with several others clustering about it, such as sexual reproduction, and natural selection, that describe evolutionary causality, seem the utmost rational factors and accordingly from the standpoint of value, factors of utmost good. If the product, finite freedom, could have come to be in no other conceivable way than by mutation and evolution, then the process as we know it is moral. The

---

49. E.g. variation or mutation of the gene DNA molecule, sexual reproduction (with Mendelian recombination), natural selection, geographic isolation.

end must surely justify the means, in this case, if there is only
one means, which furthermore, in and of itself, seems to be
rational and without intrinsic evil. We have suggested how the
central-most of these means, mutation, as a general principle is
intrinsically good because it is the fount of variation, without
which evolution and the ultimate freedom that it yields would be
inconceivable.

　　　C.　A further premise of a rational theism, regarding the
mutational mode of world development must be the following. It
relates to the ultimate question regarding evil, to which we have
already alluded, and which we rephrase here. "Why could not
Deity, by employing some kind of transitive power, at once destroy a mutant, immediately when it appeared, which could only be
an evil to itself or to higher organized value? Our reply is,
that given mutation at all, we must have mutation throughout.
If mutation is in life by necessary premise (B. above), its consequences also must appear, and its operations carry through to
their end. If the Creator denied its operation, or the fruits of
its operation (even though those fruits sometimes must be classi-
fied from the standpoint of higher systems of value as "evil") at
one point in life, would He not have to deny it at all points
where the outcome seems doubtful? Would not, however, such a
transitive approach by God jeopardize life as a whole? If Deity
experiments with finite freedom at all, its major purpose in so
doing is to see what such freedom will make of itself. There is
always the possibility, given the plasticity of evolution as we
know it, that a form which is, or seems, now evil, may in the
future mutate further in such a way as to work ultimate good for
itself or to others concerned. That mutation which determined
the development of man's puny size, relative to some animal forms,
was compensated by the mutation which eventually resulted in his
brain, the superior organ of intelligence in the animal kingdom.
In our present conclusion we have been referring in part to mutation toward harmful parasites, or toward any other larger predatory fact of our world; or toward inherited organic weaknesses.
We should recall, however, that the original type of mutation
which produced disease germs, for example, has produced many parasites that live in symbiotic and necessary relationship to their
hosts. Furthermore, it now seems a fact of genetical science
that 'evil mutations,' even evil parasitic mutations, tend to
kill themselves off by the operation of natural selection.[50]
Such would be an illustration, of course, of Whitehead's point
that evil is inherently unstable, and that there is an over-all

---

50.　Dunn and Dobzhansky, Heredity, Race, and Society, New
　　　American Library, Mentor Book, 1952, pp. 66-7.

ascendency of good in process.

In sum, thus far, what we have just been saying relative to natural evil, recalls the frequent Judaeo-Christian emphasis on the moral necessity of freedom as the proper explanation for moral evil or sin (presently to be reviewed), and what we are here attempting to do is to apply the criterion of freedom as explanation of "natural evil" at the lower ranges of process in animal evolution, out of which man has organically sprung. The basic premises or criteria of moral existence at the human level would logically apply, to some extent at least, to the antecedent levels of process which gave rise to the human level. If there is continuity between life and all process, as evolution seems to teach (A. above), freedom on the higher levels of personal life would have had its preparation in a commitment of the world process to freedom, or descending degrees of freedom, in sufficient depth, no doubt, to account for the emergence of our 'evil mutations' above described. The law of freedom must underlie the universe as a whole, if it is to be regarded as a place of moral process and growth in value (Royce and Whitehead).

Basically we must define "moral" in terms of the values of free choice and the responsibility that comes with choice. The evolution of life is the evolution of the experiment of choice, of the practice of choice. May we not understand the principle of mutation itself to be the profoundest or most universal level of 'choice'? What is true about the moral requirement of freedom and responsibility on the human plane of life, may be applied, at least by way of analogy, to the evolution of life as a whole.

When a certain development in the evolutionary history of living forms 'chooses' an ill-adapted mutation, the inevitable consequence of that selection or development is death to that species. In other words, what is represented constantly on our own level of higher freedom in the case of human choices, seems also illustrative, at least to considerable extent, of the evolution of life as a whole. To say that what applies to life at its highest level must also to some extent apply to life at lower levels and as a whole seems reasonable, if all life is to be continuous with itself and our world a coherent one. When the mutation occurred that took that particular evolutionary development leading to the dinosaur group, all the risks were accepted by that phase of organic process at that juncture--the positive risks that size and strength would take those species far and long, but also the negative risks that lack of brain capacity, or the incapacity for the evolution of intelligence, might eventually contribute to their extinction. Evolution has created life by educating life.

The general facts, then, of the necessity of mutation as the basic principle of life, and life's adaptation; of the general wisdom and good inhering in the very concept of a finite order of structure and individuality, such as we have been describing our world to be; these larger positive facts of existence as we know it seem to justify the over-all conclusion, which may be uttered with a fair degree of moral certitude and faith, that our world is, after all, regarding necessary process, the best possible world; for, in many ways, it seems the only kind of world imaginable in which freedom is possible, and not only possible, but is a major fact. And moral freedom can make it a world of <u>best</u> <u>value</u> in ultimate fulfillment of its possibilities as now a world of <u>best</u> <u>process</u>.

In conclusion to this discussion of natural evil, we suggest that the foregoing line of reasoning renders unnecessary Brightman's "Finite God" idea, with its hypothesis of the Given, or the dark abysmal side of the Divine Nature. On the other hand it utilizes fruitfully that other emphasis that we find in Whitehead, and others, namely the idea of the Divine self-limitation. Accordingly, whatever element of the finite God idea, there may also be present in Whitehead, it need no longer trouble us greatly. That element is indeed there, but in a more general and doubtless acceptable form than we find it in Brightman, as we have previously suggested. We turn now to that further level of the problem of evil that must be considered, if only briefly.

As for the problem of moral evil or sin, to put it in the classic way, is to ask why God permits man's inhumanity to man? In general terms, moral evil or sin may be defined as disrespect for personality, and, specifically in its social meaning, as aggression by human beings on other human life. A rational theism believes that it satisfactorily explains this phenomenon in terms of <u>human freedom</u> as a moral reality of man's nature. The accumulative factors that make for or add up to man's inhumanity to man, are, of course, on the personal side, the factors of ignorance, of indifference or inertia toward the needs or the sufferings of others, and of positive malice; and on the social side, evil laws and institutions, bad inherited cultural patterns. (We prefer to limit the term "sin" to positive malice; leaving the expression "social evil" to stand for other ranges of inhumanity.) All of these agencies and instrumentalities of man's inhumanity to his fellow men, of "sin," or "near-sin," and social evil--in the over-all picture--are a result of human freedom. They may, by striving, be overcome by man's freedom, both in individual and in collective life: through education and social reform, through psychological transformation by the inspiration of scientific, moral and religious intelligence.

St. Augustine, in Book II of his essay, <u>On the Free Will</u>, asked the classic question: Why did God create man free to sin? and replied that freedom is the premise of a moral universe:

> ...if man is something good and can not act rightly except when he wishes, he ought to have a free will without which he could not act rightly. For it is not to be believed that, because sin is committed by it too, God gave free will for sin. Therefore, since without it man can not live rightly, there is cause enough why it should have been given.

In more modern terms it has been said, "moral evil is the product of finite free will which is itself a good."[51] Or "it is better to be able to choose, think, discern, and decide wrongly than not to be able to decide at all."[52]

The foregoing thesis of the moral necessity of freedom,[53] if ours is to be a moral universe, seems a satisfactory answer to the moral level of the problem of evil. The meaning of man as a 'moral being,' and the meaning of the universe as a whole as 'moral,' includes at its center the idea of freedom. The universe would not be a fully moral place or process if it did not have ultimately, finite rational freedom of our human kind, with its consequent possibility of growth, development, and responsibility. Lacking finite levels of freedom, the universe would simply be at best an amoral place. This seems to be good logic, and good moral philosophy; it is coherent and sufficient.

But lest the sincere critic believe that the above type of reply to the problem of moral evil depicts a too facile traditionalism, let us paint the picture of man's inhumanity to man or moral evil in some graphic and dire, and yet true historic form. For example, why did God permit such a thing as a medieval torture chamber, or Hitler's murder of millions of Jews, in the torment of modern concentration camps? Why did he not dispatch "legions of Angels" or employ some other direct divine power to deal with such specific forms of moral evil, in order to alleviate some terrible and innocent human suffering? Truly, such pictures as these, or others which one might imagine, arouse indignation, and the ultimate question as to why such things are

---

51.   Peter Bertocci, <u>Introduction to the Philosophy of Religion</u>, Prentice-Hall, 1951, p. 401.
52.   Noreen Welch, student, Spring 1959.
53.   By "necessity" here we mean, of course, a logically <u>moral requirement</u>, not some kind of mechanistic determination.

possible in the universe of a Holy God and His righteous will?

The response of a rational theism to a question of this kind turns once again to the fact and necessity of freedom in life, if life is to have a moral quality. And a counter question may be fairly raised. If it be allowed that divine power should morally have directly intervened in such cases of innocent suffering, we may ask, where would one stop with the judgment that divine power should intervene in the cases of man's inhumanity to man? Just as logically, in each and every single case of inhumanity-- whether gross, or less gross, dire or less dire--the world over and throughout all history; in every family relationship, when, for example, in the hardness of parents' hearts a Romeo was kept from his Juliette; in every relationship of neighbor to neighbor, in each and every instance of a group's oppression of another group of human beings, of a king's sending an innocent commoner to the Tower; of a nation's aggression against another nation; of Soviet tanks suppressing the Hungarian freedom fighters; of a dishonest business transaction; of the total sorry treatment of man by men, in personal, political, or economic power situations--the critic could not, with consistent logic, deny our insistence that God should intervene to make the world a perfect but, of course, a morally paralyzed order. If God should have intervened at Dachau or Buchenwald, he should have intervened in the Little Rock school integration crisis, or in any other. Why would God not strike any injustice in the face with a lightning bolt? But what would such all-powerful, direct, and universal intervention do to human freedom and our ultimate moral responsibility and personal integrity as men? Presumably, as we have said, God's relationship to the world at its upper levels of such freedom cannot be in terms of coercive, transitive, or mechanical power.

As Professor Rall in his trenchant analysis pointed out, God's power is not irresistible, externalistic, or compulsive; God's power is not abstract, but of a specific kind, conditioned by His nature: as morally creative, bringing forth a finite world and lesser beings, "he limits himself by that very fact: for creation means giving something of his own life to lesser beings, and life in any creature means a certain power of its own." As reason, "so he acts according to that reason and order which form his very being." As goodness and love he chooses only high ends and "uses appropriate means"--sympathy, sacrifice, even suffering and persuasion. In sum, in His relation to the higher orders of freedom God acts through truth, which "waits upon the receiving mind," and through love, which waits upon the receptive heart.[54]

In sum for moral evil, two further premises or foundational insights stand out for our guidance in this particular area of concern. One is:

D. The moral superiority of freedom to non-freedom. Recall the point by our former student: "It is better to be able to choose, think, discern, and decide wrongly than not to decide at all." Or once again as Peter Bertocci phrased it: "Moral evil is the product of finite free will which is itself a good." Another is:

E. God's ultimate approach to the world of moral freedom must itself be moral rather than mechanical, i.e. persuasive rather than compulsive. On this point we turn once again to the insight of another student of this writer:

> If God desires good in man, yet permits evil, it must be because he is a God of love, who prefers persuasion rather than compulsion. Compelled goodness would not be genuine, and would defeat God's purpose. True, if our conduct were mechanically perfect like a machine, such harmony would fulfill the purpose of the maker, but it could not fulfill any ideas of its own. ...the exclusion [of the possibility] of moral evil in this world would make the world something other than a moral order....[55]

The foregoing line of reasoning may now be consolidated into the following points--these are a further and perhaps completer way to phrase the basic premises of thought for theodicy just reviewed.

1. The definition of evil.[56] 'Evil' (or 'natural evil') is properly defined as an indeterminate but possible (and in

---

54. Christianity, An Inquiry into its Nature and Truth, Charles Scribners Sons, 1941, pp. 325-6.

55. Barbara Ann Brown, Paper, Spring 1958.

56. Theism, of course has to refine its definition of evil along the following personalistic lines:
        It is not sufficient to say merely that evil may be defined as failure or abortion of natural process (as Aristotle might have defined it), or even to say, as St. Augustine did, that evil is a privation of being, or disintegration of organized being and value. We ultimately want to know what highest 'organization' and value are? Accordingly, we are faced with the necessity

finite circumstances, anticipated) outcropping from processes
that come into conflict, but that are 'neutral' or 'impartial'
relative to their own level of reality anterior to conflict.

of a personalistic definition of evil. <u>Evil</u> <u>is</u> <u>process</u>
<u>on</u> <u>any</u> <u>level</u> <u>which</u> <u>hinders</u> <u>the</u> <u>coming</u> <u>to</u> <u>be</u>, <u>personal</u>
<u>growth</u>, <u>health</u>, <u>and</u> <u>social</u> <u>harmony</u> <u>of</u> <u>finite</u> <u>personal</u>
<u>beings</u>. A tornado sweeping over a barren rock at sea
is not evil. But any factor that disrupts or hinders
the evolutionary development of the world toward this
major end or value, would be evil. Evil would be the
deprivation of existence and process of the ultimate
possibility of becoming personal, that is to say, of
issuing in finite persons, and providing opportunity
for their personal well-being.

There does not seem to have been, of course,
judging by general empirical evidence, such a total
evil as the preceding definition implies, since process
has <u>issued</u> in personal life. There have, of course,
been many temporary evils that have hindered, retarded,
and challenged this process, in the course of human
history and in the course of nature prior to and below
history. Process faces such evils today, and will
tomorrow. But process toward the personal has gotten
a good start, in spite of evils, and there is much
intimation of the coming ultimate victory of good.

Finally, in some defense of this definition, we
should say that it need not be a narrowly 'anthropo-
morphic' understanding of evil, which leaves out the
entire animal kingdom below man. On the contrary, it
is so stated as definitely to include the lower orders
of life. Evolution has taught us that there is continuity of our life with that of the animals; there is
organic and intimate relationship. Our life could not
have been without the preceding eras of nature's pro-
lific experimentation with many kinds of living forms
prior to the appearance of man. Accordingly, in a
general sense, what may be evils for man would be evils
for the totality of life, or that living phase of
existence that has prepared for man. And also, putting
the matter in another way, it is a simple fact of
observation that what is evil for man is very often
evil for animals, too. The animal species have been
necessary steps toward the ultimate personalization of
finite being. The will to live is common to both the
higher and lower orders of life, and, in general, the
will to live is the first 'good' of the universe.
Without it, a finite developmental process of life

(This point was eloquently indicated by Royce, as we have seen; it was pointed out by Whitehead; and it has been stated with great precision by F.R. Tennant in his classic chapter on the subject in Philosophical Theology, Vol. II.)

Otherwise, and somewhat more traditionally and generally phrased, it is the idea that evil arises in the midst of the necessity and impartiality of natural law. In the context of the impartial operation of natural laws living beings may experience pain or suffering. But viewed as a whole the world of natural law constitutes the firm base or predictable environment upon which finite beings may depend, and (we repeat D.C. Macintosh's phrase once again) "learn to make habitual the most favorable adjustment." Thus understood natural laws are perceived to constitute part of the basic meaning of good, outlined below.

(Moral evil, of course, is a special case of the definition of evil as 'conflict,' whose peculiarities we have recognized in our preceding discussion. Our main insight there was that 'will,' even when used evilly, is not in and of itself, as will, or free-dom, evil--but indeed itself an expression of the highest good.)

2. The definition of good: In ancient Hebrew thought the basal definition or meaning of good as the order of nature was adumbrated in Yahweh's reply to Job out of the whirlwind (Job, chap. 38)--the nearest that Semitic mentality ever came to the concept of natural law. The idea of natural law arose specifically in Greek thought and has guided the inspiration of the west ever since. It was brought into focus concerning the problem of evil with the Greek and Roman Stoic philosophers.

The Stoics maintained that this total functioning Cosmos is an intelligent or Rational, Living Being, and as such is good. I.e. they affirmed that the regularity, dependability, and unalterability of natural law is good, and equated its impartial functioning to a beneficent providence--to the totality of which they gave the name "Logos," "Word and Reason," "the artificer of the universe," "Zeus," "Mind of Jupiter," and "the necessity of all things."[57] If we can divest this ancient Stoic view of its

---

could not be; but with it, or out of it, comes the eventual personalization of life. Accordingly, our personalistic definition of evil expressed above in-cludes the total context of life in a universe which makes personalistic life ultimately possible.

57. Gordon H. Clark: Selections from Hellenistic Philosophy, Crofts, 1940, pp. 69-72.

element of monolithic determinism and fatedness, we have a conception that must be accepted in revised form by modern theism. Two expressions of such an adaptation were done in remarkably similar ways in the general cosmological philosophies of Royce and Whitehead, which we have here been studying. (Another instance of this Stoic-type theodicy, however, was most ably adapted to 20th century theology in the concluding chapter of D.C. Macintosh's work <u>Theology as an Empirical Science</u>, 1919, to which we have alluded several times, and which is summarized below.) In the meanwhile we may define 'the good' in contemporary perspective by the following general observations.

The 'good' for those sub-human entities and individualities abiding at their various levels 'less free' or less complex in their prehensive societies or relationships must be defined as the basal order of material masses and their efficient causalities, relationships, and laws; i.e. those natural determinations or laws, everywhere manifest as the larger stable forces: gravitation, radiational dispersion of various energy levels or types, electro-chemical cohesions and integration of masses, mutational dispersion or differentiation of matter at the evolutionary, relatively advanced level of the maga- and living molecule, and the general laws and principles of materiological complexification (Teilhard), emergence and growth. The 'good' at this level of cosmic experience is indeed the universal necessity that the ancients so eloquently described. However, when we move up the scale of emerging complexification toward greater spontaneity (because of increasing psychic interiorization) and cross the threshold into integrated societies of entities bearing genuine subjectiveness or awareness, mental life or consciousness, a higher more adequate, inclusive definition of good enters the picture.

It is that good must be morally and ultimately defined, that is, for entities expressing high orders of freedom, <u>only</u> as <u>an</u> <u>achievement</u>, never as "a finished product handed over to a passive recipient."[57]

3. <u>The definition, or proper understanding of the Divine</u> <u>Power</u>: One level of the Divine Power in its relation to its world is, of course, expressed in the basal material and efficient causalities above described. But in relation to the complex orders and highest integration of entities on the plane of finite freedom, Divine Power must be conceived as self-limited (Whitehead; A.C. Knudson et al.); that is, as a moral creativity

---

58.   Harris Franklin Rall, op. cit., Note 54, p. 207.

or process, of which freedom itself is an intimate expression (Kant, Royce, Whitehead). In other terms, God's ultimate relation to the world at its upper echelons of free process must be conceived as one of "formal" and "final" causality, or teleological power (Aristotle)--not power conceived as externalistic, irresistible, or compulsive. God's power, in relation to a finite, developmental world, is not totally material or compulsive efficiency; but in its upper levels of process it must needs be moral, persuasive 'efficiency,' adequacy, or effectiveness.

We are not involved with, or committed to, a disjunctive proposition (which we believe Hume, Brightman et al., have implied), namely; that God is either all good or all powerful. But rather we have said that the simple, hypothetical proposition is the better way to suggest the solution to the problem of evil, to wit: If God is all-good and all-powerful in the sense of being morally sufficient, or morally efficient, i.e. wholly adequate as immanent Creator and Sustainer of existence, His relation to the existence we know must be one of the self-limitation or moral forbearance we have been describing. The idea of His 'goodness' and of His 'power' are to be suffused with highest moral or Agapic meaning.

Points 2 and 3 may now be combined and stated (once again for the purpose of this summary) as the necessity of freedom to a moral world, or optionally, the moral superiority of freedom to non-freedom. Accordingly, this aspect of the ancient Augustinian theodicy a successful modern theodicy may accept. In sum, God's ultimate approach to the world of moral freedom must itself be moral (as we pointed out above) that is, in the spirit of the Divine self-limitation. In terms of our own innermost realization about the ultimate fittingness of things, we understand how the Divine Creativity must put us at an 'epistemic distance' (John Hick) from Himself for the sake of our freedom and our moral good. And by analogy we perceive that He must do this throughout the whole range of the cosmic order, though no doubt He stands at lesser degrees of such 'distance,' vis-a-vis other things, as we look downward or inward into the basal centrality, where finally the material or efficient energies of existence and the Divine Presence or Power itself may be said to be one and identical. But in that very freedom that is ours He has loaned us, or shared with us, the central aspect or meaning of his own "Spirit." For He is Mind and we are mind, and mind in its utmost meaning is the power to think at will freely. We are united with God in the Idea of Freedom. Accordingly, that 'epistemic distance' just referred to need not be understood to fall into some metaphysical region totally outside a Divine provenance (as a radical realism might assert). But rather our epistemic finitude--if that is what we

are talking about--fall within the larger area of the Cosmic
Freedom itself; which we, as entities, in a measure with all
other entities (though in our case perhaps to paramount degree),
share with God, as Royce and Whitehead have attempted in their
parallel ways to make clear (pp. 110f and pp. 156f).

4. The definition or understanding of the manner in which
evil is progressively overcome in the world: The universe is so
ordered that evil--as defined in 1 above--is being progressively
alleviated. Whitehead cites this fact in his general point
regarding the inherent instability of evil systems of relationship, which gives ground for optimism. In religious language,
there is a redemptive force of God present. This perspective on
the problem of evil was, in our view, most powerfully discussed
in the forementioned chapter by D.C. Macintosh. In this essay
Macintosh describes the cosmic order as an ascending or hierarchical system of superordinate echelons of redemptive process,
or "normal miracles." These are the familiar levels first of
sentence, next of thought, then free will, and finally the persuasive Spirit of ultimate truth and love itself of the Creative
Mind. Each of these superordinate powers, or normal miracles,
may intervene as if 'downward' into the subordinate or preceding
levels of actuality and process in order to alleviate the type of
evil that may appear as characteristic outcropping from that
level of being. From the perspective of an ultimately coherent
theistic vision, Macintosh's discussion is a comprehensive definition of evil at its several levels of meaning, as well as a
picture of what is happening in the cosmic order in the redemption
of evil. (The diagram in the note below summarizes his conception
somewhat more adequately than this brief statement just concluded.)[59]

---

59. A diagram interpreting Douglas Clyde Macintosh on
cosmic echelons of Good and corresponding possible
evils, and the process of redemption or salvation
(intended to be read from the bottom up, 1,2,3, etc.):-
5. God: the standard of Truth and the Good, the primordial Being of Love, and ultimate resource of
finite free will, Who brings forth and makes this a
personal world, and enters into life as the law of
love to assist in overcoming the evils of sloth on
the intellectual side, and selfishness and malice
on the moral side.
(Macintosh discusses death, as the final apparent
evil to finite existence, but shows that ultimately it
is a necessary good in the plan and providences of God.
For the death of the old makes way for the new and

5. Finally, as Professor Hick has pointed out, we have Irenaeus's 2nd century A.D. "minority report" among early Christians on the problem of evil, as an option within the classic

---

oncoming generations of finite entities and persons to come to be. In such a theological conception, of course, as this, Macintosh points out that a cosmic order would not be logically or morally complete unless the Divine Provision had also planned for an immortal experience for personal spirits, as the ultimate phase of the redemptive process of things.)

4. Finite Free Will: human freedom, the power of attending to the problems of life, may overcome the evils of ignorance. The level of moral structure, process, law, value.

(It is at this highest level, or highest watermark of its presence in the cosmos, that, according to Macintosh, evil may be defined in its moral sense as "sin" and "irreligion." That is to say, highest in the system of possible evil, following from the fact of free will is religious evil, or failure to heed the Divine Spirit. The other side of the same coin may be called moral evil, or willful deflection of thought and activity from truth and agape, as the major resources of the Divine Spirit, Present or available to finite life.)

3. Thought, memory, intellect: man's rational calculative power may overcome many of the evils attending sensation, as for example, scientific medicine's alleviation of pain in the healing art. The level of "intellectual' or "scientific" process, structure, law, value, a further type of "normal miracle."

(At this level evil may appear as error or "intellectual evil," as ignorance, and also aspects of "psychological" evil in the form of mental pain or illness.)

2. Sensation, or organic sensitivity: this level of cosmic process, in the power of organic beings, transforms natural energies into sentient experience which makes physical life possible, and helps to avoid many physical evils; for example, as the power of vision transforms light rays into sight. The level of organic process, structure, law, value; and a kind of "normal miracle."

(At this level evil appears as sentient evil or pain, physiological evil; disease as due to imbalance of biological structure. Also the physiological aspects of mental or emotional pain or illness would appear here.)

1. The basal environment of natural laws on the

Christian tradition itself to the Augustinian "majority report."
On an earlier page we discussed the superiority in a number of
respects of the Irenaean insights to the Augustinian regarding
theodicy, and here conclude that Irenaeus adumbrated in rather
remarkable ways in ancient times   a   solution to the problem of
evil similar in some respects, to the one we have just outlined.

Addendum: Whitehead on the Temporality and the Eternality of God

For Royce the role of 'time' as opposed to 'eternity' fea-
tured as a major issue in the problem of evil--with Royce more or
less, but never fully clearly, assigning to time itself a quality
of essential impropriety, somehow, or evilness (pp. 173f).   In
that discussion we mentioned that Whitehead was less ambiguous
than Royce on the positive place of time in both the experience
of God and the World.   Indeed, the problem of time does not loom at
all as a disturbing factor in Whitehead's treatment of evil; time
seems to be accepted by him as an essential and positive ingredient in the very meaning of 'God,' as well as the meaning of a
'World.'   We take the opportunity, however, to clarify somewhat
further at this place what Whitehead meant by the temporal and
the non-temporal sides of God's nature announced in a number of
texts, in comparison to the similar language of Royce.   If the
ideas of time and eternity inhere in the larger discussion of the
problem of evil from the perspective of Royce, they also obviously
anticipate our next issue, the meaning of immortality.   Accordingly, although we do not intend to enter here upon an exhaustive
analysis of Whitehead's philosophy of time, to discuss it briefly
at this passage in connection with his idea of God will aid the
progress of our general exposition of the theisms of these philosophers, as we look forward to their views of immortality.

---

inorganic   level: such are necessary to life, if
life is to learn to "make habitual the most favorable
adjustment."   The level of inorganic structure,
process, law, and value.   The Stoic insight.
(At this level we have the basic idea of evil as
the insensibility to life of the gross forces of inorganic nature, perhaps appropriately called physical
evil;   the occurrence of physical calamity or disaster
to life and possessions, as life gets in the way of the
machine-like processes of such forces.)

60.   Note 4, p. 165.

In discussing Royce we left the issue as to whether the
eternity of God meant a time-transcendence (or radical unlikeness)
of the Divine Experience to the temporality we finite beings
experience as an inescapable aspect, or fundamental category of
our sense of aliveness, conscious awareness, personal identity
and reality; or whether Royce meant by God's eternity His time-
fullness, that is, his unending, or endless temporality? To
simplify our expositional problem we can put the same question in
the same terms to Whitehead, without, we believe, oversimplifying
or distorting his outlook on time too much. At any rate, we cite
the following characteristic texts for guidance on this issue.

Early in Whitehead's 'metaphysical period,' his Science and
the Modern World described such qualities as "colours," "scents,"
"geometrical characters" as "eternal" and named them "eternal
objects" (pp. 88, 105). One passage reads:

> Every scheme for the analysis of nature has to face
> these two facts, change and endurance. There is yet a third
> fact to be placed by it, eternality, I will call it. The
> mountain endures. But when after ages it has been worn away,
> it has gone. If a replica arises, it is yet a new mountain.
> A colour is eternal. It haunts time like a spirit. It comes
> and it goes. But where it comes, it is the same colour. It
> neither survives nor does it live. It appears when it is
> wanted. (p. 88, emphasis his)

Recall the paragraph from this work which refers by implication
to the role of God on His primordial side as "an underlying
eternal energy in whose nature there stands an envisagement of
the realm of all eternal objects" (p. 107). With so much basic
Whitehead we are now, of course familiar. In Religion in the
Making God was announced to be a "non-temporal actual entity"
(p. 90). It was also clear in that study's description of the
"formative elements" that "the creativity" was the temporal
expression of God's work in the world (p. 90). Next a number of
references from Process and Reality:

-God as "its [creativity's] primordial, non-temporal accident." (p. 11)

-"temporal creatures," "creativity," and "God" each mutually
 implicative. (p. 344)

-God as the principle of "temporal concrescence." (p. 374)

-Primordial God as "eternal," but "deficient" and "unconscious." (p. 524)

-His "consequent" nature as the "conscious" temporalistic side. (p. 524)

-The consequent nature also defined as "everlasting" and as his "necessary goodness." (p. 524)

-God as having an aspect of fluency and growth. (pp. 525-6)

-Never reaching "static completion." (p. 529)

-As having a "phase of passage...ever enlarging itself." (p. 530)

-The "personality" aspect of God (as with all personal being) defined as an experience of temporal "succession" without loss of "immediate unison" (or sense of unity?). (p. 531)

To which also from the final chapter of Process and Reality we add the following:

-God's "everlasting" quality, or "everlastingness" and his "objective immortality" are spoken of. (Whitehead does not employ the term 'eternity' in this concluding chapter.) "Everlasting" is there defined as "the property of combining creative advance with the retention of mutual immediacy." (pp. 524-5, 527)

Also this chapter includes the list of mutually complementary qualities of the world and God, among which we read:

It is as true to say that God is permanent and the World fluent, as the World is permanent and God is fluent. (p. 528)

And again

Creation achieves the reconciliation of permanence and flux when it has reached its final term which is everlastingness --the Apotheosis of the World. (p. 529)

Finally for our present purposes we cite the statement where "primordial" God is mentioned as the "mental and permanent" side of the universe as well as its "prime conceptual drive" (SP p. 126).

How may we bring such statements together into a coherent picture of what Whitehead meant by God as having both a temporal and a non-temporal, or "everlasting" or eternal aspect? Focusing on the main point of the foregoing quotations, and using

Whitehead's expressions, the _everlasting_ quality of Deity or its
permanence would be its quality as having or being or expressing
endless time. Temporality is the essence of God as Person, as
indeed of every other person. In other words, the emphasis of
many of the foregoing statements is on the temporalistic character
of God. This temporalism of God need not conflict with the eter-
nalism in God in Whitehead's view; for he ties the "everlasting"
quality of the Divine nature to His "necessary goodness." Accordingly, what we might call the 'eternity' of God would be best
illustrated as the enduring _moral purposiveness_ of the universe,
by virtue of the primordial nature as the source and fount of
possible form and value. Thus God's primordial Mind, defined as
the thing that is ultimately "permanent" is nothing in itself
"static," no trans-temporalistic, blank Absolute or passionless
Being. For Whitehead, then, God is rather an eternal becomingness
of being, with the eternal or abiding character defined axiologi-
cally as "necessary goodness" or moral purposiveness. Royce on
his side certainly implied, as a prevailing note in his entire
philosophy, that the eternity of God meant in one sense His
steadfast moral purpose; but he was not as clearly prepared as
Whitehead was to join the meaning of the eternity to the temporality of God in the manner here suggested--though in one place we
have found Royce comes very close to doing so.[61] Rather with
Whitehead we more expressly escape the notion of the eternity of
God as some kind of static perfection or immobile superlativeness
in which the quality of temporality would be something scandalous
or debilitating. In spite of what he earlier said of the eter-
nality of a specific color, as eternal object, haunting time
wherever it appears, as if the two were in some way incompatible,
what Whitehead meant, we believe, by the "everlastingness" of God
was the _eternal temporality_ of God, in His character as the fount
of all eternal objects or values. Indeed, God must be temporal
productive energy with an everlasting moral purpose--ideas mutually necessary to one another rather than mutually cancelling--
if He is to be 'God' in the fullest religious acceptation. Most
simply put, perhaps, what is eternal is God's moral, Agapic
nature. That is steadfast, abiding; it never changes. So being
it must then constitute itself as "an underlying eternal energy"
or creative temporality for the sake of the reality of a World.

Our commentary here doubtless interpolates Whitehead, to
some extent. He himself denied, or was not clear on the personality (that is, the fully conscious nature) of Primordial God,

---

61. "All is temporal in its ceaseless flow and in its
     sequence of individual deeds. All is eternal in the
     unity of its meaning"--and context, from _The Sources of_
     Religious Insight, 1912, p. 160.

as was discussed (pp. 150f), and as Royce affirmed in contrast.
A more adequate theism must take the emphasis in Royce on the
Personality of Primordial God and the emphasis in Whitehead on
the temporality of God and bring these two ideas together in
better complementarity, perhaps, than either philosopher himself
achieved. We have suggested how this might be done in the
immediately foregoing analysis.

Chapter Eight

THE IDEA OF IMMORTALITY

Perhaps it is not too large a generalization to say that whereas Royce had an essentially Kantian view of the problem of immortality, Whitehead returned to an older Platonic interpretation of this issue, modified in his own way. Furthermore, Royce endeavors to preserve the idea of personal immortality, while Whitehead, on the other hand, is willing in the end to leave in question the probability of personal immortality for finite consciousness. He affirms, however, the immortality of a Divine consciousness in which at least the positive values experienced or achieved by finite actual entities become everlastingly secure someway in the Divine Experience itself. Whitehead as we shall see, is by no means entirely negative on the possibility of a personalized immortality--indeed in several places he suggests that finite experience may have its issue in such an immortality. But on the whole the trend of his thinking is not as firmly in this direction as it seemed to be with Royce. At any rate, we look at the cases both men built for a doctrine of immortality and the special nuances each gave to this idea. Concluding the discussion we will present, as we did for the subject of evil, a prolegomenon to what we believe a conception of immortality, in several options, entails for religious and theistic faith, and how Royce and Whitehead contribute to this conceptualization.

Royce's essay, The Conception of Immortality (1900), presents again his dynamic interpretation of selfhood, as striving, telic energy, reflective of being as such--now quite familiar to us. Thus we read, "...in...voluntary choice...lies our essential consciousness of the true nature of individuality.... It is the object of our purposes..." (pp. 38-9). And once again, more at length in this familiar vein:

...I hold the concept of individuality to be not merely from our human point of view, but in itself, essentially and altogether, a teleological concept,--a concept implying that the facts of any world where there really are individuals express will and purpose.... The very conception...of an individual...is a conception expressible only in terms of a satisfied will. ...that adequately expresses a purpose. ...whether you talk of angels or atoms, your individual

beings, if real at all, are real only as unique embodiments
of purpose. (pp. 45-9)[1]

From this premise of individuality as telic process, and from
another point (perhaps not until now so expressly uttered), that
an individual can be defined only as "a being such that there exists, and can exist, but one of the type constituted by this individual being" (p. 8), Royce's conception of immortality is constructed. For he believes that experience teaches that "an individual is a being that no finite search can find"; that "only an
infinite process can show me who I am" (p. 28), as well as who
the countless other, inferred individual persons around us really
are, or are themselves striving to be. True or deepest individuality stands at the end of an infinite search, he says, "the
remote goal of some ideal process" (p. 28).

Take first the effort to perceive others in some way, to
come to know their true 'individuality' or uniqueness--our human
friends in their inmost personality: Never through direct sense
experiences, on the one hand, nor through pure intellectual conceptualization on the other, do we ever get to know the inner
core or reality or individuality of other persons. Sensory contact obviously cannot get to the inner uniqueness of another
personal being; nor can the reflective processes of abstractive
intellect and the descriptive sciences succeed in arriving at
that illusive terminal of experience, the unique individual
being. By their very nature both senses and intellect ultimately
perceive only universal categories; for example, of color tone,
tactile impression, similar sound, or other descriptive general-
ities like 'tall' or 'short,' or 'educated,' or 'musical,' or
'teacher,' or worker'; whereas the personality thus so pursued
by these generalized 'ideas' (always applicable too, to other
general types, never only just to the one at hand) lies itself
unique and always beyond this descriptive net of categorization
that we would throw upon our friend.

Beyond, however, mere sense or mere intellect there is another power of mind that does tend to grasp or know the true
individuality of the other person. Moreover it is also the
process which molds or seeks to become the individuality we ourselves in our inmost efforts wish to be. It is the aspect that
we have already mentioned above, and previously discussed several
times in other connections, as telic effort, as moral will, as
affective purpose or striving, in short, as love. Individuality
is the object of our devotion. To our own duty. To our friends.
In or through love we really come to know ourselves, and in a

---

1. Collated from several paragraphs.

measure also pass into the presence of the other individual
being. For love relaxes the barriers or defenses between beings
by seeking to understand the deepest purposes themselves that
animate them in each case, the real 'selfhood,' with its own
desires, aspirations, and problems, lying beyond there, 'within'
the other. Love does indeed cast out the fears and dissolves the
bars that the other has set up against our seeking; and love of,
or for, our own goals is that which urges our own being toward
their developed or focused personalization. But in this life we
never fully, even in this our affective striving, come to know
all about the other, or achieve for ourselves those goals we hold
dear that will define our own ultimate selfhood. Thus knowledge
of individuality is an infinite process of search all the way
around, and is the intimation of our human immortality. Royce
most eloquently summarizes these insights:

> It means that for our Will, however sense deceives, and
> however ill thought defines, there shall be none precisely
> like the beloved. And just herein, namely, in this volun-
> tary choice, in this active postulate, lies our essential
> consciousness of the true nature of individuality. Indi-
> viduality is something that we demand of our world, but that,
> in this present realm of experience, we never find. It is
> the object of our purposes, but not now of our attainment;
> of our intentions, but not of their present fulfillment; of
> our will, but not of our sense nor yet of our abstract
> thought; of our rational appreciation, but not of our de-
> scription; of our love, but not of our verbal confession.
> We pursue it with the instruments of a thought and of an art
> that can define only types, and of a form of experience that
> can show us only instances and generalities. The unique
> eludes us; yet we remain faithful to the ideal of it; and in
> spite of sense and of our merely abstract thinking, it be-
> comes for us the most real thing in the actual world,
> although for us it is the elusive goal of an infinite quest.
> (pp. 38-9)

What finally now is our surest intimation of immortality?
Royce has said in so many words, that our purposive nature as
individuals-in-the-making, seeking ideal goals which cannot
fully be attained here, suggests the further opportunity. Our
unfulfilled purposes (as Kant had meant) are our best intimations
of immortality, that is, of the supreme good (the union of virtue
and happiness which the moral will perceives must somewhere somehow come to be, as Kant originally had stated this line of reasoning), which a Divine Provision and Reality alone can vouch safe
to us, assured by the inner sense of integrity of the moral will.
We know we are immortal because we are incomplete, unfulfilled

individuals, incompletely realizing ourselves and incompletely knowing the others we strive to know through our devotion to them. In all of this we sense the "Absolute life" (p. 74), drawing onward our desires for the ideal, the ideal for ourselves, and the ideal of true union with, or knowledge of our beloved. Thus Royce concludes:

> That this individual life of all of us is not something limited in its temporal expression to the life that now we experience, follows from the very fact that here nothing final or individual is found expressed. (p. 76)

Royce discusses the ideas of 'time' and 'eternity' in an extended notation to The Conception of Immortality essay (pp. 84f) and further in his 1906 address entitled "Immortality."[2] These efforts, however, add no new definitive resolution to the problem of his ambiguity regarding the status of time. We have called the reader's attention to those issues in our earlier discussion of his treatment of time in connection with the problem of evil, pp. 173f. of this commentary.

In the notation just mentioned, however, there appears an arresting--and from the standpoint of Royce's premises about time --a clarification of what he would mean by the 'Eternity' of God and consequently, presumably, what an experience of 'eternity' for other being would be in immortality. His thinking rests on his now familiar distinction that differing forms of being would have differing forms of 'time consciousness' (this commentary, p.10). Thus the vibrating atom would have a very 'brief' sense of time-span; macroscopic creatures such as ourselves at this stage of experience would have the 'longer,' but still quite specifically limited or arbitrary sense of time span familiar to us; for other forms of consciousness like God's, an infinite sense of time consciousness would be the characteristic experience. Thus Royce reasons:

> There is...no conceptual difficulty in the way of imagining a "form of consciousness" whose "specious present" should be limited in span to the time of vibration of a hydrogen molecule, or, on the other hand, should be extended to include in one glance, or at once, the events of a billion years. (CI p. 85)

> But a consciousness whose span embraces the whole of time is precisely what I mean by the term Eternal Consciousness....

---

2. Appearing in William James and Other Essays, 1911; here quoted from McDermott (ed.) BWJR, Vol. I, op. cit.

If once we form this conception, then it becomes easy to
see that to suppose the whole of time present at once to an
eternal consciousness is in no wise a meaningless supposition. (CI pp. 88-9, emphases his)

In his remarkable address on "Immortality" of 1906, Royce
wrestles further with the problem of time and eternity along this
same vein, but the progress of his discussion continues to be
dogged by his old reluctance to accord time itself a full, positive standing in the life of God as part of the very meaning of
the Divine itself. A number of times in this essay Royce comes
close to yielding to time the more positive status that we have
urged, namely, a conception of the Divine Reality as meaning in
part the Time Reality. At one stage in his thought Royce almost
accepts this view of the matter, where he avers that "Time is in
God, rather than...God in time."[3] As was previously pointed out,
the problem here is: Which is the ultimate or transcending category, Time or God? Royce is well aware of the issue, and in the
effort to keep the personal reality of God ultimate--lest some
impersonalistic connotation in the meaning of 'time' destroy the
possibility of the idea of God--he has declared "Time is in God."
What we have been saying is that it might have seemed simpler,
and truer, if Royce had said that "Time is God" or that "God is
Time"--implying that time is an intimate aspect of the meaning
itself of the Divine, or Deity. We have pressed this point
because it seems to us that he would have thus avoided the prevailing undertone, and the ambiguity, in this aspect of his
idealism that there is something, 'Eternity,' peculiarly the
Divine Experience, over against something, 'temporality,' which
is peculiarly our less worthy form of experience (WI2 pp. 363-94).
The issue has been pressed also because the full meaning of
'personal immortality' seems to us to imply the idea of continuing temporality. (Recall the previous question raised with Royce
whether God's 'eternity' should mean His 'time-transcendence' or
His 'endless temporality'?, this commentary, pp. 177f).

His 1906 essay, "Immortality," indeed describes in most
penetrating way the time experience, for both orders of personal
being, God's and man's, as "the form of will," a point that
Royce had previously made in his Gifford lectures. In agreement
with Royce on the point, we suggest that this is a way the significance or meaning of time itself can be personalized. Attrib-
uted to God himself, then, time would be no impersonalistic

---

3. Ib. p. 387.

Absolute that devours either Him or the finite person.[4] Indeed,
perhaps Royce came very near, at long last to clarifying this
issue, as we have here attempted to do, in his 1912 Bross Prize
book, The Sources of Religious Insight, where he spoke of God's
"eternal" vision as "not timeless," but a "time-inclusive survey
...which is real, not apart from time"--a striking passage in
view of his previous hesitancy about this possibility (pp. 160-1).
Supporting this speculative observation regarding some possible
development in Royce's doctrine of time we find in The Problem of
Christianity, his last major work, the fugitive line: "our religion must more and more learn to look upon the natural world as
infinite both in space and time..." (p. 402). And earlier in PC
he had made the comments:

> ...we are now secure from any accusation that...the real
> world is anything merely static,...or is an Absolute...
> divorced from its appearances, or is any merely conceptual
> reality, or is "out of time...."

And in the same place this:

> ...a viewing of the whole time-process by a single synopsis
> will certainly not be anything "timeless." (pp. 339-40)

Be this matter as it may, to return to the main point under
consideration: Against the background of his familiar elaboration of the meaning of personality as an ethical and teleological
process that expresses a purpose, an ideal goal, Royce's 1906
Immortality address characteristically concludes his conception
in the Kantian manner previously described.

> No finite series of...deeds expresses the insatiable demand
> of the ethical individual for further expression. And this,
> I take it, is our rational warrant for insisting that every
> rational person has, in the endless temporal order, an oppor-
> tunity for an endless series of deeds....

> But as an ethical personality I have an insatiable need
> for an opportunity to find, to define, and to accomplish my
> individual and unique duty. This need of mine is God's need
> in me and of me. Seen, then, from the eternal point of view,
> my personal life must be an endless series of deeds.[5]

---

4. These things have been discussed more at length in our
    forementioned essay, "The Personal Significance of Time,
    Space, and Causality," Andover-Newton Quarterly, 1960.
5. McDermott (ed); BWJR, Vol. I, p. 401.

Finally, toward the close of this discourse, a passage anticipates nearly exactly what Whitehead was again to say in his own terms about the relationship and purposes of God to His cosmic order:

> If one hereupon asks, Why should there be finitude, variety, imperfection, temporal sequence at all?--we can only answer: Not otherwise can true and concrete perfection be expressed than through the overcoming of imperfection. Not otherwise can absolute attainment be won than through an infinite sequence of temporal strivings. Not otherwise can absolute personality exist than as mediated through the unification of the lives of imperfect and finite personalities. Not otherwise can the infinite live than through incarnation in finite form, and a renewing of its total meaning through a conquest of its own finitude of expression. Not otherwise can rational satisfaction find a place than through a triumph over irrational dissatisfactions. The highest good logically demands a conquering of evil. The eternal needs expression in a temporal sequence whereof the eternal is the unity. The divine will must, as world will, differentiate itself into individuals, sequences, forms of finitude, into strivings, into ignorant seekings after light, into doubting, erring, wandering beings, that even hereby the perfection of the spirit may be won. Perfect through suffering--this is the law of the divine perfection.[6]

Royce was here describing what Whitehead later was to call Consequent God; and so now let us examine what the latter meant by immortality.

---

6. Ib. pp. 397-8.
   Continued personal 'striving' or final 'rest'-- which was Royce's ultimate idea of immortality in view of our stress on his 'Kantian' motif? Is immortality in his perspective continuation essentially of 'process,' or is it a stoppage, a fulfillment of effort? Both are doubtless present in Royce and perhaps reflect again an element of the ambiguity we have found in his doctrine of 'time' and 'eternity.' In any case, suggesting the option of 'rest' (and see our own further elaboration of this possibility for immortality p. 240f) Fr. Edward A. Jarvis in his The Conception of God in the Later Royce, op. cit., p. 75, summarizes that way of understanding Royce on immortality in the following lines memorable for their simplicity: "The finite self, when completed, shares in the Eternal Consciousness an awareness of its true self as brought to fulfillment through its temporal strivings."

The clue to Whitehead's thinking on this subject lodges in his terminology "objective immortality." Objective immortality is the characteristic conclusion to the process of becoming an actual entity. Or perhaps somewhat more exactly it is the succeeding entities, after a preceding entity-process has completed its experience, or has "perished," but has left the mark of the feeling-quality or value it has achieved upon the being of its successor. Recall that Whitehead espouses a philosophy of process, and not substance; and that the 'being' of the fundamental constituents of his universe, actual entities or occasions, are constituted by their becomings. Recall the discussion of these things on page 44f. of this commentary. To assist the review of the matter briefly here, we cite Prof. George F. Thomas's summary of Whitehead's primary idea of the actual entity "as an individual unit of becoming which completes itself and is succeeded by other units"; it is a process of "creativity" which "is perpetually bringing forth novelty....   ...an actual entity...creates itself by a process of concrescence or growing together of 'data' or 'objects' which it absorbs into its being";[7] and Thomas's exposition once again on the objective immortality idea:

> ...each actual entity receives its data through physical feelings of past actual entities and conceptual feelings of eternal objects or forms of definiteness;...these feelings are integrated under the guidance of a subjective aim in a process which culminates in a satisfaction;...when it perishes it attains objective immortality as a potential datum or object for succeeding actual entities;...the aim of every actual entity is intensity of feeling and thus the realization of value....[8]

> ...every actual entity is effective beyond its activity as a subject, in the sense that it can become an object or datum for the later actual entities when it has perished. In this way an actual entity helps to determine future actual entities after its own immediacy has been lost, and it is also prehended, or felt, by God in His consequent nature.[9]

---

7.   Religious Philosophies of the West, Charles Scribners' Sons, 1965, p. 361.

8.   Ib. p. 365.

9.   Ib. p. 375.

Whitehead's own words express it thus:

> ...with 'objective immortality'...what is divested of its own
> living immediacy becomes a real component in other living
> immediacies of becoming. (PR p. ix)

> The actual entity terminates its becoming in one complex
> feeling.... This termination is the 'satisfaction' of the
> actual entity....
>   This is the doctrine of the emergent unity of the super-
> ject [a subject with its realized purpose or goal of striv-
> ing]. An actual entity is to be conceived both as a subject
> presiding over its own immediacy of becoming, and a superject
> which is the atomic creature exercising its function of
> objective immortality. It has become a 'being'; and it
> belongs to the nature of every 'being' that it is a potential
> for every 'becoming.' (PR p. 71)

> ...actual entities 'perpetually perish' subjectively, but are
> immortal objectively. (PR p. 44)

> The not being of occasions is their 'objective immortality.'
> (AI p. 239)

This abridgement of Whitehead statements about objective immortality, should not overlook a passage of considerable importance,
that distinguishes between the 'objective immortality' of finite
entities themselves and the true "everlastingness" of God Himself
at His level of 'objective immortality.' Whitehead refers in the
same place to this insight as "the finer religious intuition":

> But objective immortality within the temporal world does
> not solve the problem set by the penetration of the finer
> religious intuition. 'Everlastingness' has been lost; and
> 'everlastingness' is the content of that vision upon which
> the finer religions are built--the 'many' absorbed everlast-
> ingly in the final unity. (PR p. 527)

We will turn again to this distinction a little later in our
exposition.

    In the meanwhile, what illustrations of the process of
objective immortalization of actual entities, so far only abstractly described, would there be? Whitehead himself suggests
several in lines such as the following:

-A pure physical prehension is how an occasion in its immediacy of being absorbs another occasion which has passed

into the objective immortality of its non-being. (AI p. 239)

-It is how the past lives in the present.... It is memory. (AI p. 239)

-It is causation.... It is perception of derivation. (AI p. 239)

-[It is expressed] in fashioning creative actions....
..in a particular unity of self-experience.... (PR p. 89)

To amplify one or two of these generalized illustrations in our own way: Consider the "physical prehension" of our own experience of color vision, say the perception of "green" in a given leaf. Color vision is an 'immortally objective' quality or value in the metaphorical sense that many process-entities or individualities have indeed given themselves up or 'perished' to pass on to our macroscopic occasion of experience this possibility of prehending, feeling or knowing 'green.' The direct rays, waves, or quanta themselves of sunlight originally, that is, as individualized vectors of energy--which in order to start somewhere we will designate as the origin of our experience of this particular shade of green--have given themselves up in the larger synthesis of our perception of this particular 'eternal object' (to call it by Whitehead's general name). In this particular contatination of natural forces, it may be said, that this particular light frequency, or 'sun ray' possessed a destiny, a potentiality, or possibility, an 'aim' of so becoming realized, or finally objectified in my experience, metaphorically described as 'immortal.' It is 'immortal' because this effect comes about by the passing of the ray's earlier mode of being (viz, prior to the encounter with the leaf and its chlorophyl and eventually with my eye, nervous system, and brain) into precisely my sentient system. At this latter stage of the encounter, the original destiny or aim of the light now 'lives' in new transcendent, emergent form--at least for the time being--as my experience of sight or vision. The ray's 'immortality' is precisely this emergent reality, this value experience that is my sense of seeing green. And Whitehead so describes such interactive process, and its outcome as an "emergent unity" (PR p. 71). Further, it could also be said that there must be many analogous processes of 'objective immortalization' operating at their various levels even within the larger macroscopic emergent integration we have just attempted to describe. Within and below my experiences there are numerous entities with their vastly complex prehensive interrelationships pulsing on various levels: between the atomic and molecular, the electrical and radiational, the

cellular and molar organic masses. What we have just described
in our molar experience of seeing green is the end result doubtless of countless subsidiary, subtle 'immortalizations' of similar
character. Many lower ranges of entities thrust outward and upward in many nexūs or social groupings and complex hierarchies of
realizations; their various potencies culminate in, and compose
my sensation of 'green.' What 'objective immortality' would be
at the level of cell 'experience,' as it assimilated the up-
thrustings of the potencies or 'aims' of molar-molecules; and
what in turn their degree of 'objective immortalization' would
be, of the contributions of the simpler atomic societies below
them, we can only conjecture. But the full and comprehensive
result of all these earlier and lower 'perishings' of experience
is our own experience of color sensation. It itself endures for
a while as our personalized enjoyment, the metaphorically immortalized potencies of all that the lower ranges of entities have
given up to us. Perchance in its turn it is to pass on from our
level into some larger or more meaningful aspect of the experience of the Divine itself, or Consequent God, when our own life's
expectation and its duty are done.

The color green here may stand, indeed, for a metaphor for
all value experience and achievement--i.e. for the "creative
actions" of any "particular unity of self-experience." Whitehead's citation of "memory," an "emergent unity" (bringing these
two references into juxtaposition), as a place where "the past
lives" is particularly germane, because it can be said that his
prevailing idea of immortality suggests that it is precisely the
'memory' of God in which and by which the values finite entities
achieve, live on in reality, that is, at an ultimate level of
'objective immortality' in God Himself. Whether this memory
potency of God is a creative 'memory' in some literal way, that
reconstitutes 'self-experience,' so that there may be truly a
personalized immortality for the highest ranges of value that
personal being is to itself--remains doubtless the open question
in Whitehead that many commentators have pointed out.

Be it noted, however, that some lines suggest the idea of
a personal immortality. At least Whitehead never definitively
denied this as the possibility of destiny for some finite entities. In the passage above quoted on the distinction between the
objective immortality of finite entities and the objective immortality of God himself, called His "everlastingness," the concluding observation that "the 'many'" are to be "absorbed everlastingly in the final unity:" may of course be understood as an
eastern or Hindu-like doctrine of final 'absorption' in the
ultimateness of a trans-personal Brahman--depending, on whether
the "absorbed" is to be taken in the simplest literal sense. But
the conclusion to the larger paragraph in the full context

discloses that "the temporal occasions are completed by their
everlasting union with their _transformed_ _selves,_ purged into
conformation with the eternal order which is the final absolute
'wisdom'" (PR p. 527, emphasis ours). Taking the reference to
the "transformed selves" as clue, Whitehead here may certainly
be said to allude to some transcending--but to be sure imperfectly conceived--_reality,_ in the 'memory' of God, of those
supreme values that are persons.

     To this, of course, may be added the statement (also found
in the concluding chapter of _Process and Reality_), which apparently announces personal immortality, where he speaks of the
third phase of cosmic development as being one "of perfected
actuality, in which the many are one everlastingly, without the
qualification of any loss either of individual identity or of
completeness of unity" (PR p. 532). To strengthen this line of
interpretation we may further add, from the same paragraph, the
Agapic description of God as a "particular providence for particular occasions." Although in his earlier work, _Religion in
the Making_, Whitehead seemed somewhat indifferent to the idea
of personal immortality, he there nevertheless expressly left the
matter open, "to be decided on more special evidence, religious
or otherwise, provided it is trustworthy" (p. 111). And we have
just seen how statements in his later work may be marshalled in
favor of a solution to the question on the affirmative side.
Also the passage in _Adventure of Ideas_ could well be cited at
this place:

> ...apart from life a high grade of mentality in individual
> occasions seems to be impossible. A personal society,
> itself living and dominantly influencing a living society
> wider than itself, is the only type of organization which
> provides occasions of high-grade mentality. Thus in a man,
> the living body is permeated by living societies of low-grade
> occasions so far as mentality is concerned. But the whole is
> coordinated so as to support a personal living society of
> high-grade occasions. This personal society is the man
> defined as a person. It is the soul of which Plato spoke.
>   How far this soul finds a support for its existence
> beyond the body is: --another question. The everlasting
> nature of God, which in a sense is non-temporal and in an-
> other sense is temporal, may establish with the soul a
> peculiarly intense relationship of mutual immanence. Thus
> in some important sense the existence of the soul may be
> freed from its complete dependence upon the bodily organi-
> zation. (p. 209)

     Certainly with Whitehead it must be concluded that although
personal immortality was not an issue of pressing dogmatic in

his philosophy (DANW p. 144), one cannot be quite so sure as
George Thomas when the latter concludes that "Whatever one may
think about this doctrine of objective immortality, it is clearly
not personal immortality in the theistic sense of the term."[10]

It must now be clarified what was meant by our earlier reference to Whitehead's view of immortality as "Platonic." His
Ingersoll Lecture, on Immortality, 1941, can be in general terms
so characterized. The central argument of Plato's dialogue on
immortality, the Phaedo, was that the soul knows its essentially
eternal nature by its sense of participation in the eternal Ideas,
or eternal Truth. Its sense of the eternalness of truth in
rational deductive judgment, as in mathematics; its judgments of
right and wrong, or ideas of justice and the good; and its awareness of beauty as eternal and absolute qualities in things, are
the soul's intimation or recollection of the Heaven of Ideas from
which it came, and to which it is destined to return.

Similarly to this Platonic mode of reasoning Whitehead
writes:

> The World which emphasizes Persistence is the World
> of Value. Value is in its nature timeless and immortal. Its
> essence is not rooted in any passing circumstance. (SP pp.
> 87-8)

And he says again in the Immortality lecture "Creation aims at
Value..." (SP p. 90). A subsequent line continues, "...Value-
experience introduces into the transitory World of Fact an imita-
tion of its own essential immortality" (SP p. 92).[11]

To be sure, Whitehead would repudiate Plato's soul-substance
conception of selfhood as naive, and would also disavow the
latter's dualism. The Ideas or Values are not wholly transcendent
"independent existence" (SP p. 91) as Plato averred. "When we
enjoy 'realized value' we are experiencing the essential junction
of the two worlds" (SP p. 91). In several places he calls attention to what he believes to be the error of original Platonism
in this regard (e.g. SP pp. 98-9). Ideas and Value are immanent
in the universe: "The World of Value exhibits the essential unification of the universe" (SP p. 97). Had Aristotle written a
treatise on immortality we can suppose it would have proceeded
somewhat in the vein of Whitehead's lecture!

---

10. Ib. p. 376.
11. The passage continues: "There is nothing novel in this
    suggestion. It is as old as Plato."

In a line stressing again the need of conceiving the realm of value and the Ideas as immanent (and also particularly reminiscent of Royce's telic conception of being and the cosmic order) Whitehead wrote:

> In the Universe the status of the World of Fact is that of an abstraction requiring, for the completion of its concrete reality, Value and Purpose. (SP p. 99)

The Ingersoll lecture on Immortality wrestles with the problem of 'personality' in the scheme of the cosmic purposiveness. Did Whitehead leave the question of a personal immortality finally unresolved—as Plato left it in Phaedo? It sufficed for the ancient philosopher to assert the immortality of the abstract Ideas of Truth and Value, and identify human 'immortality' with those aloof metaphysical rarities—but was this personal immortality? Was Whitehead satisfied with the same kind of conclusion when he wrote:

> Thus the topic of "The Immortality of Man" is seen to be a side issue in the wider topic, which is "The Immortality of Realized Value".... (SP p. 92)

The section where the above quote appears and the succeeding sections (VII-XVII) represent a profound essay on the nature and significance of personality. In several lines Whitehead announces that personality is the example of supreme value, and in several places virtually announces a belief in personalized immortality:

> ...temporal personality in one world [that of empirical fact] involves immortal personality in the other [the world of Value]. (SP p. 97)

> What does haunt our imagination is that the immediate facts of present action pass into permanent significance for the universe. (SP p. 102)

But if there be personal immortality, how can this be conceived? In a profound section Whitehead declares (again reminiscent of Royce's metaphysical and social philosophies, and anticipating a prominent theme in Teilhard de Chardin)[12] that somehow the nature of God Himself must be conceived to be "the co-ordination of many personal individualities." The passage follows in greater fullness:

---

12.   Descriptions of "Omega" in The Phenomenon of Man, Harper & Row, 1961, esp. pp. 260-63.

The World of Value exhibits the essential unification of the Universe. Thus while it exhibits the immortal side of the many persons, it also involves the unification of personality. This is the concept of God.

(But it is not the God of the learned tradition of Christian theology, nor is it the diffused God of the Hindu Buddhistic tradition. The concept lies somewhere between the two.) He is the intangible fact at the base of finite existence....

Thus God, whose existence is founded in Value, is to be conceived as persuasive towards an ideal co-ordination.

Also he is the unification of the multiple personalities received from the Active World. In this way, we conceive the World of Value in the guise of the co-ordination of many personal individualities as factors in the nature of God. (SP pp. 97-8)

This passage observes that the "many personal individualities" are 'coordinated' as "factors" of God. They are not 'absorbed' as if annihilated to their own sense of personal identity. And it is of interest to notice that he specifically differentiates his view from pure Hinduism. Whitehead then concludes section XVII with his characteristic modesty and openness of mind as metaphysician:

Of course we are unable to conceive the experience of the Supreme Unity of Existence. But these are the human terms in which we can glimpse the origin of that drive towards limited ideals of perfection which haunts the Universe. This immortality of the World of Action, derived from its transformation in God's nature is beyond our imagination to conceive. The various attempts at description are often shocking and profane. What does haunt our imagination is that the immediate facts of present action pass into permanent significance for the Universe. The insistent notion of Right and Wrong, Achievement and Failure, depends upon this background. Otherwise every activity is merely a passing whiff of insignificance. (SP p. 102)

In conclusion, the Ingersoll Lecture in our view may be added to our former judgment that for Whitehead personal immortality may indeed be, and probably is, the full destiny of finite personhood. What is the evidence? "The only answer is the reaction of our nature to the general aspect of life in the Universe" (SP p. 102).

A Prolegomenon to the Idea of Immortality

What are the rational foundations of faith in immortality? Basic questions in this area of philosophy of religion are: First, of course, what is meant by "immortality"--what are varied views in this area of thought? Second, of what value is belief in "immortality?" Third, among several possible meanings of immortality, there is the kind of faith that has said it is "personal." Is "personal immortality" a viable possibility for thought and faith? Such questions as these have been implied in the discussions of Royce and Whitehead on this theme.

First, then, as to several possible meanings of the term: In the great religious traditions several alternative meanings of man as having some kind of death-transcending destiny are present. At the risk of over-simplification we suggest that there have been four basic views. To these we add a first philosophic or logical possibility concerning the idea of a transcending destiny for man. It is the denial that there is such a destiny for persons. Accordingly, we have the following five philosophical possibilities:

1) The denial of immortality: the materialist position.

2) Absorptionism: the belief that man's finite "spirit" is to be reabsorbed into the absolute or ultimate impersonal whole of Being, with no remainder of anything that we could call personality or personal consciousness left--exemplified in many Hindu and Buddhist scriptures.

3) Deification, divinization, or apotheosis of man theme. Here the belief is somewhat like two above--but with the idea that finite spirits become literally the infinite Spirit or Person Himself; we become literally identified with the Supreme Consciousness, as Consciousness, or Person--thus man, as the outcome of his religious striving, becomes "God." We are really God Himself all along, but become fully aware of this exalted fact only upon release from this life, at which transition our consciousness expands into its full realization as Supreme or Cosmic Consciousness. This point of view is exemplified again in Hindu scriptures; in Muslim Sufi writings; and also in the western Christian, mystic tradition.

4) Personal immortality. The belief that in the presence of God, or in God Himself in some way, we remain self-aware personal consciousnesses or spiritual persons, in a measure distinguished from God's ultimate Selfhood and from other finite

individuality. Royce's conception of the relation of our human
individuality and freedom to the Divine Reality, as discussed in
the context of the problem of freedom, pages 110f. of this commentary, could in our view be applied to the problem of immortality as a successful type of rationale upholding this concep-
tion--probably the most commonplace meaning of immortality. This
possibility, however, would logically necessitate, it seems to
us, the continuation of our sense of finitude in such a Hereafter
or "Heaven," a point to which we return below.

   5) Reincarnation as a mode of immortality.

   Thus, 3, 4, and 5 are varied meanings of "personal immortality." We will not here attempt to argue a case either for or
against "reincarnation." Many peoples throughout historic time
have believed in reincarnation. Reincarnation might be true as a
metaphysical possibility and fact. It need not be freighted,
however, with all the pessimistic overtones of the classic
Sansara-Karma doctrine; but rather adorned with the main idea
that the Spiritual Purposiveness, or "Administration of the
Universe,"[13] may be providing worlds of transcending beauty, in
other galatic times and spaces, where "reincarnated" souls find
themselves in continued existences, perhaps resembling what we
now call bodily life, but in such terms of felicity and joy as to
be literally and relatively "heavens" in contrast to earthly
existence here and now. This could be the ultimate destiny of
finite persons who by the power of God were thus "rewarded."
Faith can legitimately take such a form it seems to us. Indeed,
in the Hebrew Christian West, where the Sansara doctrine of the
east was not specifically present (though the idea is found in
Plato's Phaedo), there was the similar theme of the "resurrection
of the body."

   Deificationism (3 above) seems to us a doubtful possibility
--because of its inherent and ultimate impersonalism (?). Our
evaluative premise here is that (finite?) personal identity and
difference is a supreme cosmic value. Empirically speaking the
production, emanation, or creation of such identities seems to be
what the cosmic process is purposely doing, or bringing about.
If that is the case, what becomes of 'personal identity,' difference, and variety, if all such are ultimately transmuted into a
single 'Personal Consciousness' of God? Would not our own self-
values thereby be lost or blurred? Moving to the theme of love
in this connection, it takes two to love. In such monistic God-
Person (if this is what some of the Sufi mystics mean when they

---

13. To borrow a term from the late Prof. Kirtley F. Mather.

identify self with Allah), where would love be? There must be
an inherent distinction to some degree between self and others so
that love can arise. In profoundest religion God is Agape. If
He makes finite persons in the first place, as an outcome of His
love, would He not desire, and plan, to keep them as such, from
the very constitutive nature of Himself as Personal creative
love? One version of creation in the Hindu Upanishads describes
the Ultimate Brahman-Atman as originally alone, but feeling no
"delight." He therefore brings forth from Himself a finite order
of creation, by implication out of love, or a desire to have
fellowship with it, and the first things to appear in the values
of creation are "husband and wife."[14]

The idea of "personal immortality" best satisfies the sense
of values of a personalistic ethics and metaphysics--and therefore the present rationale for immortality has point 4 above in
mind as its guiding conception, including, possibly, some degree
of reincarnationist or resurrectionist theory, to aid it. If
reincarnationism and/or resurrectionism are left out, then some
kind of theory of bodiless "spirits" would be implied by our
fourth alternative. At any rate, we now endeavor to state the
case for immortality more or less in the terms outlined in the
fourth alternative.

What then, are rational grounds for belief in immortality?
First is the argument from the moral impulse. Phrased as a
practical question, what difference would belief in personal
immortality make to the ethical side of life--is immortality
needed in a moral universe? Royce's affirmation of immortality
as a corollary to his conception of selfhood as essentially
telic, moral energy was in its striking way an affirmative answer
to this question. To the theme that immortality is a necessary
corollary to the view of the world as moral place and process,
we add the following:

Human beings will be more inclined to treat each other
rightly if they regard others as immortal beings, as the most
precious and everlasting things in the universe. Belief in
immortality does not arise from the desire for unending bliss
for oneself. This would found the belief in a too self-centered
and non-ethical motive. It is naive to allege that Christians
and other religious people believe in immortality because they
are looking for pie in the sky by and by. Rather belief in
immortality is necessary for highest ethical sensitivity. Immortality is implied in the ethical premise that personal being,

---

14. Robert O. Ballou (ed), The Bible of the World, Viking
Press, 1939, p. 38.

or personality, is of ultimate significance. Psychologically speaking, we seem most deeply motivated to treat human beings with highest respect, or go out to each in love and service, if we regard his personal being as of ultimate and eternal significance, of quintessential and permanent value. Belief in immortality is an a priori affirmation of the ethical consciousness.

Tennant and Hocking state the point well. Tennant said:

> Immortality becomes a matter of more or less reasonable belief, as distinct from deducibility from assured metaphysical principles or from more or less arbitrary postulations concerning the harmonizing of moral experience. It is ...a demand for coherence in what is, as a matter of fact, a moral universe.[15]

In his inimitable manner, Hocking summarized the argument for immortality from love:

> And thus to love is to treat the loved being as worthy of permanence. The impulse of caring is to hold that being forever above the accidents of time and death--as if one could! The miracle of love is that it so spontaneously forgets its own limitations: it assumes its right to act in loco Dei--and with the right assumes also its capacity! The pathetic folly of human affection? Or is it the reverse, a point at which human finitude rises to the point of participating in deity? I propose that here, in willing to confer immortality on another mortal, the self is in that moment reaching a deeper self-consciousness, an intimation of its own destiny.[16]

Moreover, and very much related to what has just been said, the belief in immortality puts meaning, and a consequent energy, into the human struggle to perfect personal and social life. This, of course, uses Kant's basic inspiration regarding belief in immortality, and we have seen how Royce conceptualized his understanding of the problem of immortality in these essentially Kantian terms.

---

15. F.R. Tennant, Philosophical Theology, Vol. II: op. cit. p. 271.

16. William Ernest Hocking, The Meaning of Immortality in Human Experience, Harper & Bros., 1957, p. 247.

Second, belief in the goodness and sufficiency of God is the foundation of belief in immortal destiny. That there is conscious planning in the universe for immortality seems a necessary postulate, else how finite bodily beings could survive the actual cataclysm of bodily death would be utterly incomprehensible. The same creative power that brought finite persons into being in the first place would be required to get them over the crisis. Is a philosophy of immortality without God convincing? (MacTaggart attempted such in a position that resembles Sankhya Hinduism.)[17] What we mean by immortality is <u>the permanent significance of personal being</u>--this implies the power, ground, or condition that brings forth, and sustains, personal being, and this in one sense is what we mean by God. The conception of immortality is impossible apart from the conception of God. This paragraph expresses in general terms Whitehead's technical "objective immortality" idea. It would take, of course, the <u>objective powers</u> of God at the highest level of the cosmic hierarchy of energies to provide for and secure the <u>subjective</u> or personalized immortality of finite creatures. In this way then the possibility of a 'subjective immortality' would utterly depend on the presence and operation of an 'objective immortality' factor as one of the more ultimate metaphysical truths. Whitehead's objective immortality conception, then, need not be construed as denying subjective immortality. It is indeed requisite for the realization of a subjective or personalized immortality.

Third, a philosophy of progressive process and purpose implies immortality. Belief in immortality grows naturally out of the conception that the universe exists for some end--the end of bringing into existence personal beings with dynamic or expanding capacities of growth for good, for intellectual, aesthetic, and moral enrichment. Royce and Whitehead both shied away from stating the case for the personalistic conception of cosmic purposiveness in quite such affirmative terms as these. The personal outcome of the cosmic process was more problematic for them--no doubt more for Whitehead than for Royce, as has been pointed out (pp. 12-13). In our view, however, Man is Nature's

---

17.   Sankhya Hinduism, in ancient Indian times (6th century B.C.) and the early 20th century British philosopher and personal idealist, John MacTaggart, defined personal spirits as by nature self-subsistent or 'eternal souls,' a metaphysical view which includes the idea of immortality without God. (A criticism of MacTaggart's non-theism appears in our doctor's dissertation: "The Personality of God, a Study of Theistic Personalism in Reaction to Non-Theistic Idealism," Columbia University, 1950.)

escape from necessary mechanism by virtue of his free spirit.
John Haynes Holmes said, "Our faith in the survival of man's
soul fits the universe in the sense that it continues its picture
of development and saves it from irrationality and meaningless-
ness."[18]

The belief is a logical and psychological accompaniment to
a life of earnest effort and striving. Hocking again said, "To
cease at the peak of attainment is to lose the full meaning of
that attainment. From the mere logic of meaning, then, there is
no moment at which conscious existence could appropriately
cease."[19] (This, of course, is tantamount to Kant's argument,
again, that our earthly span is never sufficient to get done what
we were born to do. Immortality is a corollary to the doctrine
of the moral purposiveness of existence.)

The basic definition and meaning of immortality, then, would
be the extension of purpose beyond this life, whatever the mode
may be by which this is secured, or the "form" that immortality
may take.

Fourth, we may focus on the general mystery of matter and
physical existence in any case, as itself a clue. Hard materialism is no longer a tenable view of reality. The very atoms
are full of energy and insubstantiality--and may in themselves be
the same thing that we experience from our subjective viewpoint
as the energy of life and will. This, of course, both Royce and
Whitehead greatly said in their respective ways. As Holmes once
again put it, in the Ingersoll Lecture, "I stand upon the brink
of the unknown, utter and unplumbed.... If we accept, as we must
the indestructibility of matter, no less must we accept the
indestructibility of the spirit with which matter is informed."

In a novel, The Autobiography of Ephraim Tutt, Arthur Train
has Tutt say (I paraphrase) "How we may live forever, would be
no more marvelous or mysterious a possibility than that we have
lived at all!"

In sum: mind, self-conscious life, personal consciousness,
are better clues to reality than bare sense and soil. The experience of purpose, the discovery of truth, the up-building of
ideals and values are our fundamental clues to the nature and
meaning of existence. Personal identity and unbroken consciousness persist through physical changes of the body. Is this a

---

18.   Ingersoll Lecture, Harvard, 1947, "The Affirmation of
       Immortality."
19.   Quoted by Holmes in the above lecture.

clue of the transcendence of personal consciousness over what we are want to call material changes? A type of scientific support for the hypothesis of immortality would lie in the direction of proving the case for the reality and independence of mind-energy.[20] Would death be the liberation of mind-energy, that form of energy with which we are already acquainted at the top of the hierarchy of energies? What is the energy of mind which is eternal? Plato said in the Phaedo that it was truth itself, and that the soul knows that it is eternal because it may participate in the eternal order of truth itself. We have seen how Whitehead's Ingersoll Lecture centered upon this type of theme.

Further possibilities and problems: the "vision of God." Much of the mystic literature of the west (as in the east) moves along the absorptionist-identificationist-deificationist themes discussed above; and the meaning of the ultimate life with God, or "Vision of God," as anticipated in the mystic's present momentary "vision," which vouchsafes his ultimate and perduring experience in a Hereafter, were expressed in such lines as the following by St. Thomas:

> Here the soul in a wonderful and unspeakable manner both seizes and is seized upon, devours and is herself devoured, embraces and is violently embraced: and by the knot of love she unites herself with God, and is with Him as the Alone with the Alone.[21]

It is, of course, possible to interpret Whitehead's view of immortality to be a variety of the absorptionist doctrine. However, we have also indicated how a doctrine of personal immortality, in the sense we are using the term here, can also be said to be his primary vision. Be this as it may, in contrast to an absorptionist interpretation of the Vision of God theme, we here pose an alternate view as to what the Vision of God could mean from within a personalist philosophy of existence.

---

20.   See G. Douglas Straton: "The Meaning of Mind Transcendency in a Religious Philosophy of Man," International Journal for Philosophy of Religion, Spring 1973, Martinus Nijhof.

21.   Quoted by Evelyn Underhill, Practical Mysticism, E.P. Dutton & Co., 1960, p. 141. (Jacques Maritain concludes his powerful little book, Approaches to God--in large part an exposition of St. Thomas--with a memorable defense of the identificationist outlook, Chap. 5, "The Desire to See God.")

First, however, an appreciation of the deificationist philosophy of the destiny of man. If it be true that we are indeed
to be transmuted into Deity, then our destiny is to become the
inner workings and creativity itself of Personalized Being,
Becoming, and the Universe. Doubtless this is not to be dispar-
aged as a less than an awe-inspiring idea. It is reverently
asked, however, would such philosophy point to an aloof and
lonely destiny, "alone with the alone" (recall St. Thomas's sentiment above)?[22] The following may be a more joyous conception
of man's metaphysical destiny.

Our freedom, and our finitude will continue permanently--
even in a Hereafter--even an 'ability to sin,' perhaps (compare
the Lucifer myth). God's creative love, in our view implies this.
We will, however, have 'the more perfect,' more intimate, direct,
and satisfying knowledge or 'vision of God' as sustaining Source
of Being and Supreme Goodness, as ultimate Love. 'Vision' implies a certain standing 'outside'--reverent and respectful of
the object in vision, at some distance to the inner sanctity of
the other's own 'being' or 'reality.' Our "epistemic freedom"
(to use again the thought of John Hick) which God has originally
given each person must of necessity continue, if personality is
to continue, though doubtless at a lessened 'distance' from God
than may now be necessary.

That it will be 'vision' and 'acquaintance,' analogous to
the present vision and acquaintance of earthly friends, is here
meant. As we know them through their sustaining love toward us,
without desiring to be them, without desiring to take away their
reality, or they ours, (and our mutual joy and satisfaction in
fellowship is therein vouchsafed), so it will be in our relation
to God. Our destiny will be fellowship, community, kingdom, not
'identity.' We believe this to be not only the Biblical theme of
destiny, but Royce's, if we can transpose his community of Interpretation idea from his social ethics to interpret the immortality
theme as we have reviewed it with him. Destiny is likened in the
words of Jesus to a "banquet," a "bridal festivity," a "kingdom."[23] Accordingly, there will doubtless never be a time when
life in immortality will cease from exercising faith: faith that

---

22. Unless, of course, 'Deity' means some kind or degree of
     'socialized being,' as indeed Royce and Whitehead have
     sometimes suggested. If Agapic love 'personalizes,' it
     also 'socializes' and 'unifies' while sustaining per-
     sonality--that is love's Mystery.
23. In St. Paul we perhaps have a nascent identification or
     deification philosophy of destiny, e.g. I Cor. 15:28.

the Source of Being or the First Cause is truly "Person," rather
than impersonal Being (just as we are relatively sure now, but
not <u>absolutely</u> sure, that our friends are persons rather than
ultimately some kind of impersonal structures); faith that God is
good rather than evil, or indifferent; and doubtless finally
faith that we are ourselves free rather than bound! Personhood
in its real finitude and freedom implies faith as a continuing
and primal necessity of its being. The minute faith ceases,
personality ceases. Several corollaries and comments follow from
this analysis.

(1) A certain ultimate <u>externality of knowledge</u> for God's
created beings seems to us a requirement. We will never have a
knowledge of perfect "internal relations"--contrary to the expectation of absolute idealism--and to Royce doubtless, respecting
at least some dimensions of his version of absolute idealism.
I do not think we are implying here the radical realism which he
so stubbornly criticized; but a universe of finite persons
implies some outer boundary of knowledge--we must always remain
at a certain "epistemic distance" from God, but <u>within</u> the larger
parameters of his own spiritual and moral fullness of being as
creative and sustaining Mind. To God is reserved the full knowledge of internal relations. On so much practical moral realism
must a personal universe be founded, it seems to us; and Royce
himself used many words to defend in his own way such moral
realism. This point may be further clarified by what follows.

(2) As personality implies the continuance of faith in the
above terms, so love, integral to the meaning of personality,
implies the continuance of faith. Perfect identity with another
would shrink love to zero. Love implies a certain separateness
of being. Love implies, not a desire <u>to be</u> the other person, but
to <u>interact</u> with him in his presence in mutual interpretation,
appreciation and joy; in fellowship. Love respects the mystery
of the other selfhood. Love means affirming and respecting the
other person in his sacredness and reality, with always a margin
of "ignorance" (or realization of lack of identity in being, if
that is what ignorance means), present or acknowledged in the
relationship. But by this willing and creative "ignorance" we
affirm the other's reality in being. So it is not a destroying
ignorance, but a constituting and creating respect that is the
ultimate effort of our being, vis-a-vis another. Creative
<u>acknowledgement</u> is the ultimate fulfillment of <u>knowledge</u>; Royce's
term was <u>interpretation</u>. This seems identical <u>precisely</u> to what
we mean by moral nature or virtue, or moral 'reason.' This our
personality and its immanent logic of respect we feel to be the
'divine image' or 'spark' struck into us. That much of God we do
know. And perhaps this suffices. In the Kantian and Roycean
formula, God shares 'His being' in the 'Idea of Freedom'; but

this is as much as He can do--would he preserve our being in love. What God shares with us is the immortality of His Freedom, rather than an identification of being in some metaphysical totality, as in monistic mysticism, which Royce sharply criticized. God is that Love which ever goes forth to preserve us as finite and free.

(3) God's 'eternity' (in which we will share) can only mean that He has a primordial or time-full, unchanging moral _purpose_. His purpose for good extends from time immemorial to time immemorial. His 'eternity' is filled with the time energy of His _purpose_. Is Heaven 'endless time' or 'timeless eternity'; is it continued 'purposive life' or 'rest'? Perhaps there are values in believing it to be timeless eternity and rest, a direction in which Royce seemed to move in some respects. Perhaps Whitehead's cast of thought about immortality, however, assists us more than Royce's did in the direction of anticipating the possibility that finite souls await a life of continuing good purpose in an unending time, and possibly in "other spaces."[24]

---

24. See William Ernest Hocking on "other spaces," _Meaning of Immortality in Human Experience_, op. cit., pp. 28-9.

Chapter Nine

THE CONCEPTION OF RELIGION

Since both Royce and Whitehead are theists, as may be expected their conceptions of religion have a number of primary features in common. Moreover, the statements of both men complement each other in several important respects--so that altogether we end up with not only an adequate view of religion, but a moving vision of the essential 'religious nature' of man. Accordingly, instead of beginning with a lengthy independent review of each philosopher's position on this subject, we will endeavor to combine from the outset what they said about religion into a single somewhat brief perspective.

Early in his philosophic career Royce sensed the fundamental meaning of religion as lying in the emotive idea of "devotion" to some kind of supreme value ideal; for example as he phrased it, devotion to "the moral law," or to "some moral code" (RAP pp. 3-4). Also, in very generalized terms, the value-object which may elicit "worship" could be "Natural Law" (science), or "even Nature in general," or "Humanity," or the cosmic "Unknowable" of agnostic metaphysics (RAP p. 6). He was therefore presenting the most general psychological definition of religion. To put it in our own way, then, religion is <u>devotion to whatever one regards as supreme in value</u>. Moreover, in this same context of <u>The Religious Aspect of Philosophy</u> (1885) he named the three classic characteristics of the religious sentiment. Religion includes in its meaning something we wish to "<u>do</u>," to "<u>feel</u>," and to "<u>believe</u>"; that is, it has an active or "practical," an "emotional," and a "theoretical" expression (pp. 3-4).

Ultimately the quest of religion, that is, the religious spirit or frame of mind is to ask about the status or place of its 'object of supreme devotion' in the universal scheme of things? Therefore, Royce has well said that the depth of the religious inquiry is to raise and to answer the question, "<u>Is there then, anywhere in the universe, any real thing of Infinite Worth?... What in this world is worth most?</u>" (pp. 8-9, emphasis his). Thus religious psychology raises the question of 'God.' Who or what is the Divine? For whatever is denominated of "Infinite Worth" would be 'God' in the eyes and expectation of the religious impulse.

Whitehead's "Religion and Science" essay (SMW, 1925) presents the same fundamental understanding of the religious "vision":

Religion is the reaction of human nature to its search for
God.... I must now state, in all diffidence, what I conceive
to be the essential character of the religious spirit.

Religion is the vision of something which stands beyond,
behind, and within, the passing flux of immediate things;
something which is real, and yet waiting to be realised;
something which is a remote possibility, and yet the greatest
of present facts; something that gives meaning to all that
passes, and yet eludes apprehension; something whose possession is the final good, and yet is beyond all reach; something which is the ultimate ideal, and the hopeless quest....

It is the one element in human experience which persistently
shows an upward trend.... The fact of the religious vision,
and its history of persistent expansion, is our one ground
for optimism. (pp. 190-2)

His Religion in the Making (1926), quite like Royce's treatises on the subject, points to the classic psychological characteristics of religion as containing "factors" transformative of
character, and implying "ritual," i.e. elements of deed; factors
of "emotion"; and those of "belief" and "rationalization" (pp.
15, 18). Further, these passages stress that religion's 'object
of supreme devotion' or 'God,' means an objective character or
quality of the universe itself, beyond, reflecting, or inclusive
of subjective 'ideals' of human consciousness. Thus "Religion is
...intuition into the ultimate character of the universe."
Religion, Whitehead wrote, "...is the longing of the spirit that
the facts of existence should find their justification in the
nature of existence" (pp. 58-9, 85). Accordingly, for Whitehead
no mere a-metaphysical humanism, which points only to a subjectively human realm of value as its object of supreme devotion
will do. His 1933 essay, "The Humanitarian Ideal," criticizes
the subjectivist interpretation of religion in the humanist tradition of Bentham and Comte (and we may add of John Dewey following them). This humanist tradition of modern times, he says,
should never have dropped "Plato and Religion" (AI pp. 43-5). He
means Plato's essential "ontological idealism,"[1] or belief in the
Cosmic reality of the Good, the True, and the Beautiful; and the
same affirmation of the cosmic objectivity and transcendency of
value in the traditional, or classic expressions of Religion in
all cultures. "Religion emphasizes the unity of ideal inherent
in the universe" (MT p. 39). Religion does not mean therefore

---

1.   Dewey's express term of philosophic reproach of White-
      head, "The Philosophy of Whitehead," in Paul A. Schilpp
      (ed.), The Philosophy of Alfred North Whitehead, op.
      cit., p. 661.

merely a human or humanitarian ideal, as it did for Comte,
Feuerbach, and Dewey. Whitehead believes that authentic religion
refers to the human ideal conceived as having its origin <u>within</u>
the cosmic mind-reality, which the finite ideal reflects or
expresses.[2]

To continue for the moment on a related issue before returning to Royce, Whitehead is also critical of a purely sociological or phenomenalistic interpretation of religion. This
is brought out in his theme that religion is an expression of the
ultimate "solitariness" of the human person (RM p. 16). It is
not just a product or child of society or environment. It is not
merely a derivative socially conditioned phenomenon; it is rather
<u>sui generis</u>. Its ultimate springs are "the internal life which
is the self-realization of existence" (RM p. 16). He espouses a
"doctrine," he says, which is "the direct negation of the theory
that religion is primarily a social fact.... You cannot abstract
society from man..." (RM p. 16). Illustrative of the transcendency of religion to society, according to Whitehead, at least in
its historically mature, rational exemplifications, would be the
religious personalities of Buddha, Jesus, or Mohammed, effectively
countering and leading in new directions the societies of their
day and circumstance--cases of social force flowing from the
transcending powers of prophetic or religious personhood.

Ultimately, of course, for Whitehead religion at its maturest
and most rational expression becomes itself societal, that is, a
directive, ethical and social force:

> Rational religion is religion whose beliefs and rituals
> have been reorganized with the aim of making it the central
> element in a coherent ordering of life--an ordering which
> shall be coherent both in respect to the elucidation of
> thought, and in respect to the direction of conduct towards
> a unified purpose commanding ethical approval. (RM p. 31)

The central one of three "allied concepts" of "rational religion"
also expresses this social perspective. It is "That of the value
of the diverse individualities of the world for each other." Or
otherwise phrased, it is "...the concept of the world as a realm
of adjusted values" (RM pp. 58-9). The "solitariness" of the
religious spirit must finally merge "its individual claim with
that of the objective universe. Religion is world loyalty"
(RM p. 60).

---

2. "...religion is concerned with our reactions of purpose
and emotion due to our personal measure of intuition
into the ultimate mystery of the universe" (AI p. 165).

This statement of religion as "world loyalty," in other words, as social vision and responsibility, is a remarkable reflection of Royce's primary sentiment concerning the nature of civilized religion, and in the exact term which Royce stressed. Accordingly we employ it as cue to return to our discussion of the earlier philosopher.

Royce points out that religion is not just a take-it or leave-it embellishment of accomplishment of man's higher rational capabilities. It is not a merely casual matter one way or another, but a matter of necessity. It is urgent for man to go the way of the higher rational religions (and Royce with Whitehead singles out Buddhism and Christianity as prime examples of such). Religion in these forms has characteristically sounded a 'salvational' or imperative chord moving men and shaking societies to their most strenuous efforts. For religion has constantly reminded mankind of two primary things:

> The first is the idea that there is some end or aim of human life which is more important than all other aims, so that, by comparison with this aim all else is secondary and subsidiary, and perhaps relatively unimportant, or even vain and empty. The other idea is this: That man as he now is, or as he naturally is, is in great danger of so missing this highest aim as to render his whole life a senseless failure by virtue of thus coming short of his true goal. (SRI p. 12, the whole statement italicized by Royce.)

But this pearl of great price that authentic religion has put before man as the prize of his religious striving is not, Royce believed, the Buddhist idea of "'the extinction of desire,'" but he says "rather the ideal," which the Buddha also included, "of triumph over our unreason" (SRI p. 31). Royce's psychologically penetrating statement on the ultimate meaning of salvation in all faiths as the hope and the effort to bring "reason" and "spiritual unity" into life bears repeating:

> It is the ideal that the reign of caprice ought to be ended, that the wounds of the spirit ought to be healed. In the midst of all our caprices, yes, because of our caprices, we learn the value of one great spiritual ideal, the ideal of spiritual unity and self-possession. And both our ideal and our need come to consciousness at once. We need to bring our caprices into some sort of harmony; to bind up the wounds of what James calls the divided "self"; to change the wanderings of chance passion into something that shall bring the home land of the spirit, the united goal of life into sight. And so much all the great cynics, and the nobler rebels, and the prophets and the saints and the martyrs and the sages have in

common taught us. So much Socrates and Plato and Marcus
Aurelius, and our modern teachers of the wisdom of life, and,
in his noblest words, the Buddha also, and Jesus, have agreed
in proclaiming as the ideal and the need revealed to us by
all that is deepest about our individual experience: We need
to give life sense, to know and to control our own selves, to
end the natural chaos, to bring order and light into our
deeds, to make the warfare of natural passion subordinate to
the peace and the power of the spirit. This is our need.
To live thus is our ideal. And because this need is pressing
and this ideal is far off from the natural man, we need
salvation. (SRI p. 31)

This vision of religion and the idea of salvation as the prayer
of life to be blessed with a sense of ultimate rational unity
anticipates almost exactly what Whitehead later described (but
less fully) as "rational religion," even to the extent of especially citing, as we have mentioned, Buddhism and Christianity
as sterling exemplifications of it.

If Royce acknowledges, however, that religion arises in
"Individual Experience" (recall Whitehead's stress on religion
as "solitariness"), religion must have its issue and fruit in
"Social Experience" (SRI p. 34), as we found Whitehead also
asserted. Thus we come to Royce's terminology "the Religion of
Loyalty." We have already observed that Whitehead later employed
this same paradigm with similar implication but did not elaborate
it. We conclude, therefore, this discussion of the meaning and
place of religion in the thought of these philosophers with a
word on Royce's conception of religion as "loyalty."

Royce's idea of loyalty has its larger setting in his
ethical and social outlook, the next topic of this study. It may
here suffice, however, to outline what he meant by the religion
of loyalty, assuming or anticipating the larger theme in which
the idea arose naturally as the last chapter in his book, The
Philosophy of Loyalty; and which appeared again later as a theme
in The Sources of Religious Insight, which we have been quoting
above.

Royce's basic words on "loyalty" in the context of his
speaking about religion are:

Loyalty...is the...devotion of a person to a cause. (PL
p. 351)

...loyalty [is] the will to manifest the eternal in and
through the deeds of individual selves. (PL p. 377)

...our loyalty brings us into personal relations with a
personal world-life, which values our every loyal deed, and
needs that deed.... (PL pp. 396-7)

So be loyal...so serve your cause that thereby the loyalty
of all your brethren throughout the world...shall be aided,
furthered, increased so far as in you lies. (SRI p. 202)

So be loyal to your own cause as thereby to serve the
advancement of the cause of universal loyalty. (SRI p. 203--
these last two quotations were italicized in the original
texts.)

We have long since recognized Royce's concept of being and
of selfhood--viz. what is required to constitute something 'a
being,' and regarding our human aspect of being, to constitute a
'self' or a 'person.'[3] His central ethical concept of "loyalty,"
and his ultimate definition of religion as the spirit of loyalty,
follows his metaphysics of 'being' with superb logical coherency.
'To be' is to precipitate the 'internal meaning' of an idea, its
purpose, into its 'external meaning,' that is, the realization of
that idea in 'act.' Thus to be as a self or a person is to select
from the ideal possibilities for our lives some one or a few
viable options and endeavor to make them real in the concrete
accomplishments of our deeds. Our aims, purposes, or chosen
ideals are our causes, and to pursue our causes in the above
intent is our profounder loyalty. But these individualized vectors of telic striving can become social, as we realize that
other systems of such causes and loyalties exist beside our own
in the manifest strivings of the lives and beings about us.
Therefore, to make our supreme cause, in the universal sense, the
assistance of the manifold others in their loyal pursuings of
their causes is the essence of ethical life, and of religion, in
its highest sense of positive sacrifice. And be it noted it is
indeed a positive sacrifice. In Royce's thought, oneself is not
immolated or destroyed, but itself preserved and enhanced; for
how can we be called to the service of "loyalty to loyalty" if
there be not the one, or the self, who loyally serves the other?
Royce is quite explicit on this point (pp. 199-204) in his chapter
"The Religion of Loyalty" from The Sources of Religious Insight.
Scarcely more superlatively coherent or simple description of the
depth of the Hebrew-Christian understanding of ethical life and
religion--rooted in its profound personalistic metaphysics--has
appeared than this of Royce. So that he says in these passages,
that loyally to serve persons is what is meant in ethical

---

3.   Pp. 17f. and   59f. of this commentary.

religion by doing "God's will" (SRI p. 200); indeed, as the other great religions of the world in addition to the Hebrew Christian, we might add, have likewise averred in the ethical reaches of their thought. Such loyal service "brings us into personal relations with a personal world-life, which values our every loyal deed, and needs that deed..." (PL pp. 396-7).[4] This practical, eloquent and inclusive definition of religion as that sense of ultimate quality about life that identifies loyal seeking, in the universal way above outlined with the Divine purpose of the world, Whitehead some years following Royce echoed in his reference to religion as "world loyalty."

---

4.   Earlier on the same page of PL Royce had arrived at his final definition of religion as referring to objective reality, thus: "Religion...attempts to conceive the universe as a conscious and personal life of superhuman meaning, and as a life that is in close touch with our own meaning...." He defined that meaning as the "loyal deed," and declared religion in those terms to be "eternally true" (PL p. 396).

Part IV

ETHICS AND SOCIETY

Chapter Ten

THE ETHICAL AND SOCIAL THOUGHT OF ROYCE

This part outlines each man's perspective on this subject, and in process indicates major points of comparison and contrast between them. As with the preceding topics, I shall interpose from time to time my own evaluation of their ethical and social doctrines, with the idea of theism continuing as a central strand of interest in the discussion.

In The Religious Aspect of Philosophy Royce initiates his ethical thinking with a dialogue between several classical types of ethical outlook. First, there is practical ethical realism (or as it might also be phrased, ethical empiricism, evolutionism, or naturalism). Realism affirms that the standard of conduct may be pragmatically found or discerned in the 'facts,' that is, of 'experience' or 'evolutionary growth' or 'progress.' To this type of insight Royce replies from the standpoint of an ethical intuitionism or idealism in the following terms:

"But", the realist may say, "in fact the world does grow better. The course of evolution is on the whole a progress". "Be it so', the idealist answers, "but how can we know it? Only by first setting up our ideal, and then comparing the facts with this ideal. If we know what we mean by better, we can judge whether the world is growing better". (p. 29)

The realist, however, will not let the idealist rest in a too easily won peace such as this. For says the former, the latter has not clarified the problem of what or whose ideal we we are talking about?

...judge after your heart's desire; but remember this, that some other idealist beside you will be judging the world in his own way, after what will seem to you the folly of his heart, and his judgment and yours will differ, as the dreams of any two dreamers must differ. (p. 29)

Thus does the specter of ethical relativism and thence skepticism enter the debate. How does the ethical idealist prevent himself from turning skeptic when reminded of all the commonplace conflicts in ideals that confuse the ethical life of man? Worse, how does the sincere seeker after moral truth keep from plunging

into pessimism, the stage beyond mere skepticism and cynicism?
For his quest may end up in a supposition that the ultimate moral
truth is the <u>relativity</u> of all truth? Here such person finds
himself in the thicket, Royce suggests, of a Buddhist-Schopenhauer
type of pessimism with its haunting possibility that ideals are,
after all, only the aims of desire, and that the world is precisely at bottom the eternal strife of desires and their imple-
menting wills.

Royce commences to resolve the matter by calling attention
to the positive nature or therapeutic of ethical skepticism
itself. Ethical skepticism harbors within itself as its own profoundest motive, at least a hope that there is some ultimate
resolution for the conflict of wills. So Royce adroitly argues:

> Absolute ethical skepticism, if it were actually possible
> without self-destruction, would still presuppose an end,
> namely the effort to harmonize in one moment all the con-
> flicting aims in the world of life. It would not be what it
> had supposed itself to be. Absolute skepticism would thus
> be founded on absolute benevolence. <u>Its</u> <u>own</u> <u>aim</u> <u>would</u> <u>be</u>
> <u>harmony</u> <u>and</u> <u>unity</u> <u>of</u> <u>conduct.</u> But just for that reason is
> absolute skepticism self-destructive. (p. 138, emphasis his)

Of the next stage, pessimism, to which it is supposed skepticism
leads, he writes:

> It was not the bare renunciation of all aims; it was the
> effort to satisfy them all, embittered by the sense that they
> were in seemingly hopeless conflict. Even our pessimism had
> its ideal. Without its ideal it would have experienced no
> despair. (p. 138)

Subsequent passages elaborate this point, namely, that we
have in such moral insight as just brought out a kind of intimation of Universal Ethical Will, Unity, and Certainty in the very
cry of the universal eros itself. Somehow ethical idealism can
(or needs to) turn the debate to its own account in such wise--
without falling into an ethical absolutism or monism, destructive
of freedoms and the individualities of the manifold striving
entities that constitute the world. Thus, as our ideal of thought
as well as practice he writes:

> This...our realization of an Universal Will.... ...would
> demand all the wealth of life that the separate selves now
> have; and all the unity that any one individual now seeks for
> himself. It would aim at the fullest and most organized life
> conceivable. And this its aim would become no longer merely
> a negative seeking for harmony, but a positive aim, demanding

the perfect Organization of Life. (pp. 194-5)

And again, still speaking of the universal Will:

> Its warfare is never intolerance, its demand for submission
> is never tyranny, its sense of the excellence of its own
> unity is never arrogance; for its warfare is aimed at the
> intolerance of the separate selves, its yoke is the yoke of
> complete organic freedom, its pride is in the perfect devel-
> opment of all life. (p. 218)

Thus when he wrote The Religious Aspect of Philosophy, at
the earlier stage of his thought, Royce had outlined a solution
to the problem of ethical philosophy, so far as an integral
idealism looks at the issues. He did not, however, endeavor
fully to clarify his perspective until much later in The Philosophy of Loyalty and The Problem of Christianity.

In the meanwhile, reflecting the middle period of Royce's
philosophical maturity (his essay, "The Moral Order" in The World
and the Individual), certain further psychological aspects of
moral freedom emerge that an integral idealism acknowledges about
ethical man. To point to a few major ideas of this phase that an
open, personalistic idealism of Royce's type asserts regarding
the universe as "Moral Order": Such Universe must be conceived
as an ever dynamic and growing order. "Perfection" cannot be
some static condition of things.

> The best world for a moral agent is one that needs him to
> make it better.... The moral consciousness declines to
> accept..any metaphysical finality. It rejects every static
> world. It is dynamic. Nowhere could it say, "I have found
> that what is is altogether good." Its watchword is "Grow
> better and make better." (WI2 p. 340, emphasis his)

This, of course, reminds us once again of the essential similarity of Royce's larger conception of things and Whitehead's
open process view. Ethical idealism further says:

--Moral freedom in its real complexity is a "field of attention" to the problems of life (WI2 pp. 355, 359), as illuminated
by the sense of Ought. 'Sin,' psychologically defined consequently, is "consciously to choose to forget...an Ought that one
already recognizes" (WI2 p. 359, emphasis his). (It is, of
course, a well established psychological phenomenon that senses
of 'guilt' may indeed arise in a person of moral sensitivity when
thoughts of actions are 'suppressed' that have betrayed a value
ideal consciously accepted by a person as his standard of conduct.)

--Next, we point to a theological concern, arising in discussions of moral freedom, that we have not yet discussed. Relative to the idea of a Divine foreknowledge, a viable moral theism must assert that Divine 'foreknowledge' does not assume time to be some kind of realistic medium out ahead of both God and man. If time be so conceived, such a 'foreknowledge' could only then be some kind of magical perception, that would obviously destroy the possibility of moral freedom; it would be a determination, of 'the future.' Rather Royce asserts that "God does not temporally foreknow anything, excepting in so far as he is expressed in us finite beings" (WI2 p. 374, emphasis his).[1] However, Royce does not clarify that God and time must be mutually predicated of each other, or logically identified, as we have suggested must be the case in our previous discussion (p.173f).[2] Royce in this place

---

1. Compare his later context The Conception of Immortality, op. cit., p. 90, note 6.
2. We suggest for a theology of the Divine 'foreknowledge'--as an aspect of the 'omniscience' of God--the following:
   The problem of the divine foreknowledge is intimately tied to the idea of time. By saying that God must somehow have 'foreknowledge,' if He is to be God, is to say, it seems to me, that God must be subject, somehow, to Time--that time is a transcending reality, outside, above, or more absolute than God himself. To speak of a divine 'foreknowledge' is to imply that time is out in front of God, somehow, that he is a 'finite' being relative to the time concept or reality, and caught in its flow, as we seem to be inmeshed. In such view, not 'Zeus,' but 'Kronos' is ultimate. To assert that he has foreknowledge is to say that He, God, does battle, in a manner of speaking, with the primeval dragon, Time: conquers it, subdues it, brings it under his absolute ken, so that he can divine its secrets, before, and after, along the time intervals at any designated position, behind, right now, or in the future.
   But is not the problem of God's foreknowledge cleared up, if we perceive that time itself is an ultimate expression of the Divine being or reality--a primal aspect, and an immediate experience on our part, of the Divine reality?
   Then strictly speaking there is no magical foreknowledge. There is only the Time front, itself, sensed as 'moving,' intuited as the opportunity for creativity-- a moving 'now,' with openness and indeterminacy as the meaning of any quasi 'future,' that we can anticipate? This brings our thinking back to a previous point. It must be as true to say that God is Time itself as to say

once more expresses what we have found to be characteristic of
his views of the relation of time to God, namely, that the Divine
'eternal' consciousness transcends our 'temporal' type of

---

that He is Freedom itself, or that He is Love. At least
principal points of convergence of the Divine and the
Human are the ideas of time, freedom, love, and truth.
Perhaps it is most reverent to say that God is the <u>fount</u>
of time, freedom, and love. In any case we return to our
discussion of time particularly.

If we go in the other direction and say that God is
above time, we mean that the Divine is some kind of
Absolute 'Eternity.' This, of course, would make time
an illusion. But if time is a reality and God is a
reality, they must be conceived together, with time as
an intimate expression of His very 'life' as God. God
would therefore experience His own time-Self as from the
'inside,' precisely as we ourselves do. He would anticipate or 'foreknow' a 'future' only in the sense that He,
as we do, may be aware of alternative values and purposes
as yet unrealized, which would constitute a 'future'
state of things, if and when realized. So conceived,
God's foreknowledge does not determine a future; it can
only anticipate alternative futures, and their ramifying
'consequences,' just as we 'foreknow' without fore-
determining our own finite futures. It may be conceded
here, of course that the Divine life in this area is far
richer and profounder than our own, but not essentially
unlike our own.

We conclude that a Divine 'foreknowledge' cannot
determine finite action; this would destroy freedom.
What God foreknows may be said to be the <u>consequences</u> for
good or ill of action in a moral universe, the nature and
laws of which he knows intimately, because he constitutes
those laws, and in that sense has omniscience.

Could not our human situation vis-a-vis the Divine
anticipation of the Future (for we had better speak of
'anticipation' rather than 'foreknowledge') be conceived
as something like the following:

consciousness in the last analysis, as a "whole," which perceives
"present, past, and future" at once. And he has here again
repeated his musical analogy. We formerly criticized this perspective as leaving us with a moral ambiguity concerning the
legitimacy of the time experience itself. In any case, Royce
strives to make clear in this context that what he prefers to
call God's "eternal knowledge" (rather than his "foreknowledge")
in no wise determines a future that would nullify finite freedom;
and that is the main point that must be asserted.

    --This leads then again to what we have long since announced
as one of Royce's major contributions to theological theory;
namely, the identity of God and Man (in one necessary meaning of
the Divine reality) in the idea of freedom itself. Royce affirms
here, perhaps more clearly even than previously, that the acts of
the finite being "are his own, even because God's Will is in him
as the very heart of his freedom" (WI2 p. 375).

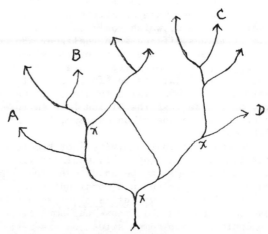

The branches represent the ordinary channels of circumstance that guide, and sometimes absolutely control life.
A, B, C, and D, are the consequences, the outcome of our
activity, which an 'omniscient' God would comprehend in
general terms, not in specific detail. The x's represent
life's limited choices, however, which, we are absolutely
free to make within the circumstance of each choice.
Indeed, the problem involves again the idea of God's
self-limitation in certain aspects of His relationship
to finite free persons.

We move now into the later period of Royce's philosophic
labors, indeed the period devoted more and more to the ethical
problem. The critical question that ethical skepticism and
pessimism posed originally to ethical idealism in The Religious
Aspect of Philosophy Royce now is prepared to answer more fully
in his Philosophy of Loyalty. The question that leads provisionally into ethical skepticism and pessimism was the simple one,
What of the conflict in ideals, in desires, and now we can commence to say, in our 'loyalties'? How can ethical unity and
truth be resolved out of the practical chaotic mass of the conflict of loyalties? Recall that in the earlier effort Royce had
left the problem with the bare, but important insight that
sincere skepticism and pessimism, in the seeker of truth, are
really moods searching for a way out of the dilemmas of the moral
chaos. The question is, Why may the sincere seeker of moral
truth become skeptical, and even pessimistic, at some stage of
his moral journey? The answer is that the skeptical-pessimistic
stage has its onset in the intellectual painfulness aroused by
beholding the conflict between the desires, ideals, and loyalties
of the manifold entities in their strivings. Skepticism-pessimism
arises in hearing what we have called 'the cry of the universal
eros' itself. This intellectual pain, borne by the beholder of
the struggle, skeptic and even pessimist that he may momentarily
become, carries the deeper intimation that there is a resolution
of our moral dilemmas, some ultimate unity, certainty, and peace
for the moral quest. For without a glimpse of this ideal home-
land, skepticism and pessimism themselves "would have experienced
no despair."

The Philosophy of Loyalty (presently to be followed by his
Community of Interpretation theme in The Problem of Christianity)
elaborates this positive insight of his early work. Life in any
one case starts with eros, desire. The conflict of eros with
eros, or the conflict of our desires, is the ethical problem--the
conflict not only within ourselves, but between the many striving
entities and selves that are existence. But turn now the subjective term 'desire' into the term of social outlook, 'loyalty,'
and the way out of ethical skepticism and its pessimism may be
perceived. The essence of Royce's philosophy of loyalty was
described at the close of the preceding section of this commentary in connection with Whitehead's conception of religion as
"world loyalty." I need not here repeat at length what was there
said (pp. 244-5), except perhaps this:

Summarizing Royce's conception of the philosophy of loyalty
we there wrote:

Our aims, purposes or chosen ideals are our causes, and to
pursue our causes...is our prpfounder loyalty. But these

individualized vectors of telic striving can become social,
as we realize that other systems of such causes and loyalties
exist beside our own in the manifest strivings of the lives
and beings about us. Therefore, to make our supreme cause
the assistance of the manifold others in their loyal pursuings of their causes is the essence of ethical life....

Such philosophy of loyalty is now ready for what Royce
believed at this stage of his outlook to be the crowning insight
or formulation (now newly introduced into this discussion):
namely, the idea of "loyalty to loyalty." For in the first
place, it is by the ideal of loyalty to loyalty that ethical
idealism is able to meet the erstwhile problems of ethical skepticism and pessimism. If we are mutually loyal to others'
loyalties we begin to see how to allay the cry of the universal
eros and make it more a pean of universal hope and joy, of unity
and peace. Indeed, by this unique phraseology Royce is, of
course, discussing what in more traditional and simple terms is
known as love, or the power of love. Secondly, however, how does
"loyalty to loyalty," his version of the philosophy of love,
illuminate some of the familiar details of ethical life in the
practical sense?

Royce describes how traditional specific duties or virtues
can be derived from the principle of loyalty to loyalty (PL p.
141f). For example, on the side of cardinal duties to self and
neighbor we have: truth-speaking, maintenance of one's own health,
promotion of self-culture, education, or self-betterment, one's
right to possessions, one's right to defend one's powers and
possessions as "held in trust for the cause" (PL p. 143). The
two larger duties to neighbor are subsumed under the concepts of
"justice" and "benevolence." One is particularly loyal to loyalty
at the level of justice when he endeavors to keep promises, speaks
the truth, and respects the loyalties of others (PL pp. 144-6).
Benevolence is more especially defined as promoting the "private
good" of others (PL p. 145); and this, of course is love agape.
Another expression of loyalty is conscience, the ultimate shepherd
of the virtues.

"Conscience" has its deepest or widest definition in terms
of loyalty to loyalty. Simply described, conscience is generated
by one's cause, and one's loyalty to it (PL p. 172f). And Royce
here sets his conception of conscience within his larger definition of "a self"--long since understood as "a life..unified by a
single purpose" (PL p.171).

My conscience, therefore, is the very ideal that makes me
this rational self, the very cause that inspires and that
unifies me. Viewed as something within myself, my conscience

is the spirit of the self, first moving on the face of the
waters of natural desire, and then gradually creating the
heavens and the earth of this life of the individual man.
This spirit informs all of my true self, yet is nowhere
fully expressed in any deed. So that, in so far as we contrast the ideal with the single deed, we judge ourselves,
condemn ourselves, or approve ourselves. (PL pp. 176-7)

...conscience is the ideal of the self, coming to consciousness as a present command. (PL p. 195)

Rather than to say that conscience is something initially
innate, as if a kind of primordial "root" of the moral life,--
true to his understanding of the self as process and growth--
it is rather "the flower...of the moral life" (PL p. 177).
Rather than some original full-conscience, what is innate is the
power "to become reasonable" beings. Conscience is a growing
thing, an ever enlarging guide for action. It expands, and even
must change upon occasion, as the sense of one's cause and its
loyalty rationally grow (PL pp. 177-9).

"The...infinite realm of moral truth" is the ultimate
standard of conscience, while the sense of conscience is not
identical in any two of us, yet conscience is universal in the
sense that we may be the "fellow-servants of the one cause of
universal loyalty," his synonym for "loyalty to loyalty" (PL
p. 179).

To the ultimate problem of choice between conflicting loyalties, when the alternatives seem to have an equal and worthy
appeal, Royce speaks in terms of two final virtues, "Decisiveness"
and "Fidelity." Though in our finitude we may not always foresee
all of the consequences that may follow from our actions (PL pp.
185-96), we must act decisively and in faith. And in so acting,
we fulfill our duty to moral coherency.[3]

---

3. His paragraph--considerable in its practical, psychological value--reads:
       "As a fact, the conscience is the ideal of the self,
   coming to consciousness as a present command. It says,
   Be loyal. If one asks, Loyal to What? the conscience,
   awakened by our whole personal response to the need of
   mankind replies, Be loyal to loyalty. If, hereupon,
   various loyalties seem to conflict, the conscience says:
   Decide. If one asks, How decide? conscience further
   urges, Decide as I, your conscience, the ideal expression
   of your whole personal nature, conscious and unconscious,
   find best. If one persists, But you and I may be wrong,

A chapter, "Loyalty, Truth, and Reality," presents Royce's way of relating his philosophy of loyalty or ethics of selfhood to his integral idealism as a whole. A Divine Mind of Truth is intimated by the moral instinct as set forth in the loyalty theme. His early argument for God from the experience of truth and error is here, though briefly, deepened or highlighted by the moral insight--the nearest Royce comes to formulating a moral argument for God (PL pp. 307-13).

Our commentary on Royce's last major work does not presume to be an exhaustive analysis. Others have discussed The Problem of Christianity in full perspective, and Royce as the Christian theologian reflected in it, in terms which I need not duplicate.[4] I intend to refer, however, to the general ethical and social thought of Royce in the last phase of his development as theistic philosopher. Some sections of this elaborate work, dealing with his interpretation of certain aspects of Christian faith, I will not consider at length here, believing that they are not crucially germane to the principal purposes of the present study.[5]

---

the last word of conscience is, We are fallible, but we can be decisive and faithful; and this is loyalty" (PL pp. 195-6, emphasis Royce's).

4. For example, John E. Smith's Royce's Social Infinite, the Community of Interpretation, Liberal Arts Press, 1950.

5. For instance, Royce's announcement in Chapter I, "The Problem and the Method," of what he believed to be the three chief aspects of Christian teaching or the Christian idea, namely: 1. "The salvation of the individual man is determined by some sort of membership in a certain spiritual community." 2. "The individual being is by nature subject to some overwhelming moral burden from which, if unaided, he cannot escape." And 3. the idea that "The only escape for the individual, the only union with the divine spiritual Community which he can obtain, is provided by the divine plan for the redemption of mankind.... ...which includes an Atonement for the sins and for the guilt of mankind." (Royce acknowledges that this last of the three principal doctrines is "one whose relation to the original teachings of the Master seems most problematic" PC, op. cit., pp. 71-3).

Our efforts in this commentary have been to concentrate on point 1.

Aspect 2 is elaborated by Royce in two chapters particularly, "The Moral Burden of the Individual" and

As general theme, however, of this work, "The Problem of Christianity" for Royce, refers to the manifest difference which readers of the New Testament note between the simplicity of

---

"Time and Guilt." Indeed, for Royce himself, this second emphasis was presented as a major theme in the study of "Christianity" and its "problem." I do not here wish to dispute with his perspective in terms of textual detail, relative either to the Roycean or the New Testament texts, particularly those of the Synoptic Gospels. Royce indeed sounds like "a Calvinist" at times in discussing "the moral burden of the individual"--his phraseology for the traditional 'original sinfulness' of man idea, PC pp. 104-5. (Compare John E. Smith's allusion to Royce as "Calvinist" in a context discussing the role of the Church in Calvin and Royce , RSI, op. cit., p. 129.) In strongly implying, however, that this type of sentiment was a major emphasis in Jesus's teaching, I would say that Royce overstressed a point which in his realism Jesus himself recognized in more simple terms. They were that men can and often do 'sin' in their freedom. The central point in Jesus's doctrine of man was the sacred worth or 'goodness' of human selfhood or 'personality,' and the central note of Jesus ethic was the sacred reverence for personality. Jesus himself had no clear doctrine of 'original sin.' Indeed, St. Paul had; and in our view Royce himself is too much influenced by Paul in implying that that must necessarily be a central teaching of Christian doctrine for all Christians in all times and circumstances. (Royce is quite right, of course, in saying that such has been historically a central feature of Christian or churchly theology, which, to be sure, was in this respect overwhelmingly influenced by St. Paul.)

Royce's chapter "The Moral Burden of the Individual" is a brilliant contemporizing of St. Paul's understanding of man and life, and Royce has allied himself with this classic Pauline conservatism. But in our perspective some of the detail of the chapter represents a too pessimistic view of the evil effect of society's pressures upon us. Must "the natural warfare of the collective and of the individual will" be so prevailing, and inevitable, as Royce, to be sure following Paul, claims? Much of this part of Royce's discussion seems at odds with his own earlier defense of the self and the ego so eloquently set forth in the discussions of Christian love in the preceding chapter, "The Idea of the Universal

Jesus's eschatological teaching in the Gospels and what Paul
taught in his letters. Jesus spoke of life and morals under the
expectation of the soon-to-be experienced supernatural disclosure
of the Kingdom of God. St. Paul's teaching concerned a viable
'Church' in a real and continuing temporal world, needful of
salvation in an historic, social sense--at least (and Royce did
not make enough of this aspect of Paul's thought) until that
delayed event, the Parousia, or coming Kingdom, is to take place.
Whether Royce's treatment of the Gospel material does this
'simple teaching' of Jesus's full justice--that is, as to whether
a practical social outlook might be interpolated successfully
from Jesus's basic love-ethic of personal relationship--we do not
propose here expressly to discuss or criticize. We accept, for
the most part, Royce's astute and extremely accurate depiction
(indeed in major agreement with much twentieth century New Testament scholarship) of the limits inherent in attempts to erect an
historic and ethical Christianity solely on the simple, eschatological love ethic of Jesus apart from consideration of Paul's
magnificent doctrine of the churchly community. The principal
purpose of Royce's book is to clarify how the original inspiration
of the Master's teaching is implemented by the practical vision
of St. Paul, the disciple, in what Royce calls the latter's community of "loyalty" and "interpretation."

Recognizing, then, these special concerns of Royce in dealing
with Christianity in its two original phases--the difference
between Jesus's teaching and Paul's, in which Royce finds Christianity's major 'problem'--we proceed to his larger synthesis in
the idea of the Beloved Community of Interpretation.

According to Royce, the fount of this idea lies indeed in
Jesus's announcement in "the parables," of "the infinite worth of
the individual" (PC p. 95); and of Christian "love" (agape) as
not a love that destroys egohood or the right of the self to
existence. Royce's description here of Jesus's teaching on love,
and the positive place of the self implied by the gospel of love,
is unexcelled, both for its accuracy, and for its beauty (PC

Community." (For example, compare PC, op. cit., pp.
87-9 to 112-17.) Much of the chapter on the Moral Burden
of the Individual in our view reflects Royce's treatment
of time and finitude as themselves constituting the
essence of evil, which we formerly pointed out and criticized in him.
    As for the third doctrine of Christianity, that
concerning Atonement, we point to his unique and inspira-
tional treatment of this classic theme as it bears upon
the general problem of evil, pp. 278-9, this commentary.

pp. 87-9). (Indeed, Royce's understanding of the Christian philosophy of love as including a positive role or place in being for the self which does the loving, stands in contrast, it seems to us, to much Christian exegesis in our time which has announced that there is no doctrine of the essential goodness of 'ego,' or a place for 'self-love,' in the Gospel.)[6]

It is Royce's larger thesis, however, that Paul's theology of the Christian Community "makes the doctrine of love," originally found in the Gospels, "more concrete, and...less mysterious" (PC p. 93). This is true, of course, in so far as Paul's letters appear to elaborate Jesus's simpler statements concerning love into the many practical social obligations of the churchly community. Royce's summary of the achievement of Paul is phrased thus:

> In God's love for the neighbor, the parables find the proof of the infinite worth of the individual. In Christ's love for the Church Paul finds the proof that both the community, and the individual member, are the objects of an infinite concern, which glorifies them both, and thereby unites them. The member finds his salvation only in union with the Church. He, the member, would be dead without the divine spirit and without the community. But the Christ whose community this is, has given life to the members,-- the life of the Church, and of Christ himself. "You hath he quickened, which were dead in trespasses and sins."
> In sum: Christian love, as Paul conceives it, takes on the form of Loyalty. This is Paul's simple but vast transformation of Christian love. (PC p. 95)

This passage indicates how Paul's doctrine of the church socializes Jesus's individual love ethic. Indeed, much historical Christianity has been the evidence that Paul bridged this gap successfully. Obviously, the reference here to Paul's idea as subsumed in "Loyalty" (and elsewhere a number of times repeated) consciously connects this last work of Royce with his former Philosophy of Loyalty.

---

6.   See for example such discussions as Anders Nygren: Agape and Eros, Vol. I, Westminster Press, 1953, p. 170. Rudolph Bultmann: Jesus and the World, Scribners, 1958, pp. 114-19. Paul Tillich: The Shaking of the Foundations, Scribners, 1948, pp. 154-5; The Courage to Be, Yale, 1952, pp. 54, 75, 126-7, 132, 169; Systematic Theology, Vol. II, University of Chicago Press, 1957, pp. 38, 44.   Paul Ramsey: Basic Christian Ethics, Charles Scribners' Sons, 1950, pp. 94-5, 101.

Certain sections of <u>The Problem of Christianity</u> (PC pp.
133f), move Royce's thought into its further, major theme (and
for critics perhaps the crucial issue). That theme, or question,
is: How is Christianity's identification of "the being of its
ideal community with the being of God" to be conceived? The
essential issues which have led some critics to believe that
Royce finally gave up his personalistic theism may be framed as
two questions. From one side, was it perhance that Royce's
vision took on the form of an absolutistic or monistic idealism
of a classic Hegelian, or Bosanquet variety? In these systems
the 'Absolute,' or 'God,' and 'Human society' were virtually
identified. From another side, could it be alleged that Royce
moved into some kind of non-theistic humanism, in which 'God'
becomes a symbol merely for the human ideal, as in the thought
of Feuerbach, Dewey, and the Humanistic Naturalism of which they
were noted representatives? Our former comment on Professor
Fuss's observation answered such questions in the negative at
some length, and we invite the reader to review those pages
(pp. 119-23). The above mentioned sections of the PC contain
the essential paragraphs of Royce on this issue. They attest,
we believe that he did not give up his theism in either of these
ways, but reaffirmed it on the deeper level he was attempting to
sound in this work. Indeed, we are being prepared to see somewhat more fully how his philosophy of "interpretation" becomes
the astute epistemological insight necessary to the preservation
of 'personality' itself, as between men and men, and between them
and God, even 'God' conceived now as the presiding Spirit of the
Loving Society or Community.[7] An indermediate development,

---

7.   "We now may see how the characterization of Christianity as not only a religion of love, but as also, in
essence, a religion of loyalty, tends to throw light
upon some of the otherwise most difficult aspects of the
problem of Christianity. We can already predict how
great this light, if it grows, promises to become.
"Christianity is not the only religion in whose
conceptions and experiences a community has been central.
Loyalty has not left itself without a witness in many
ages of human life, and in many peoples. And all the
higher forms of loyalty are, in their spirit, religious;
for they rest upon the discovery, or upon the faith,
that, in all the darkness of our earthly existence, we
individual human beings, separate as our organisms seem
in their physical weakness, and sundered as our souls
appear by their narrowness, and by their diverse loves
and fortunes, are not as much alone, and not as help-
less, in our chaos of divided will, as we seem.
"For we are members one of another, and members,

however, appears in Royce's text that should be considered
briefly, before looking further at the Interpretive process.

Royce has raised his definition of 'personal being' into its
social dimensions: 'A person' is not just an isolated 'will'
willing itself, or its 'internal meanings' or ideas into 'external
meanings,' defined by the concrete or accomplished realization of
its aims, its ideas, its plans and purposes (cf PC pp. 198-9).
Rather a person comes into his ultimate 'meaning,' 'selfhood' or
'personhood,' into his essential "salvation...through loyalty to
the beloved community and through the influence of the realm of
grace." "And," Royce here continued, "Loyalty,--the beloved
community,--the realm of grace,--these are indeed essential features of the Christian doctrine" (PC p. 220). But we must needs
define "community" itself more carefully.

Real community exists when the "many individual selves,"
who may "vary in their present experiences and purposes as widely
as you will," nevertheless have some common, agreed-upon, communal origin or memory, and a commonly accepted goal toward which
they strive. When this situation exists a "community" exists.
Royce, of course, many times states that the Christian Church is

---

too, of a real life that, although human, is nevertheless, when it is lovable, also above the level upon
which we, the separate individuals, live our existence.
By our organisms and by our individual divisions of
knowledge and of purpose, we are chained to an order of
nature. By our loyalty, and by the real communities to
which we are worthily loyal, we are linked with a level
of mental existence such that, when compared with our
individual existence, this higher level lies in the direction of the divine. Whatever the origin of men's ideals
of their gods, there should be no doubt that these gods
have often been conceived, by their worshippers, as the
representatives of some human community, and as in some
sense identical with that community.
"But loyalty exists in countless forms and gradations. Christianity is characterized not only by the
universality of the ideal community to which, in its
greatest deeds and ages, it has, according to its intent,
been loyal; but also by the depth and by the practical
intensity and the efficacy of the love towards this community which has inspired its most representative leaders
and reformers; and, finally, by the profoundly significant doctrines and customs to which it has been led in
the course of its efforts to identify the being of its
ideal community with the being of God." (From his chapter "The Realm of Grace," PC pp. 133-4.)

a classic illustration of community as thus defined. The common
origin and memory for its members was the teaching and work of
the Christ; the common goal toward which they strive is the
Kingdom of Heaven itself--vouchsafed, to some degree historically,
in the ethical fellowship itself of the Pauline church. A type
of secular illustration might be that of the American "community."
The American community looks back in common memory to the work of
the founding Fathers, for example, to their achievement in the
Constitution; and forward to all those many ways in which we may
yet realize its inherent principles or ideals--of equality,
justice, government by and for the governed, etc. The life and
work of such communities is always more than the individualized
man-to-man "mere morality" of single, ad hoc or isolated human
connections; nor is it the blur of a "mere mysticism" (PC p. 220).
Only in community, are selves ultimately germinated and maintained. Selves must have a joint time-aft origin, or memory, and
a time-forward focus of effort to be the larger communal selves
or larger persons they wish to become. One's community and communal efforts ultimately define who he is. My church effort
helps to define me. My professional effort in whatever professional institution I serve does so. My family life, which I
must loyally serve, represents another vector of the process.
My fraternal or neighborhood society or group of whatever sort
in which I may further be active assists the process of self-
formation. My model railroad group, my bridge club, my credit
union cooperative, my hiking companions, or skiing friends, my
business partners, all my varied centers of community life and
service--these subordinate 'societies,' with common origins and
common goals--accomplish the process of self-realization in the
purest sense. These social or communal things tend to define
ultimately what and who I am as a person. Royce puts all of this
in summary fashion thus:

> Men do not form a community, in our present restricted sense
> of that word, merely in so far as the men cooperate. They
> form a community, in our present limited sense, when they not
> only cooperate, but accompany this cooperation with that
> ideal extension of the lives of individuals whereby each
> cooperating member says: "This activity which we perform
> together, this work of ours, its past, its future, its conse-
> quences, its order, its sense,--all these enter into my life,
> and are the life of my own self writ large! (PC p. 263)

> And so, first each of us learns to say: "This beloved
> past and future life, by virtue of the ideal extension, is
> my own life". Then, finding that our fellows have and love
> this past and future in common with us, we learn further to
> say: "In this respect we are all one loving and beloved
> community...."

Thus, then, common memory and common hope, the central possessions of the community, tend, when enlivened by love, to mould the consciousness of the present, and to link each member to his community by ideal ties which belong to the moment as well as to the stream of past and future life. (PC p. 266)

The passages following this definition of true "community," and the enlarged definition of 'personality' included in it, assert that there is no "mystical blending of the selves," that is, no ontological blurring into some sort of trans-personal Absolute State, of perhaps the Hegelian kind (PC p. 267)—no "inter-penetration in which the individuals vanished, and in which for that very reason, the real community would also be lost" (PC pp. 267-8) . Royce wrestles with the problem as to whether or not Paul himself may have slipped into the personality absorbing 'mysticism' of some types of absolute idealism, unlike his own. He finally asserts, however, that "Pauline charity," or love, did not disappear into that kind of metaphysical black hole.

But the Pauline charity is not merely an emotion. It is an interpretation. The ideal extension of the self gets a full and concrete meaning only by being actively expressed in the new deeds of each individual life. Unless each man knows how distinct he is from the whole community and from every member of it, he cannot work. Love may be mystical, and work should be directed by clearly outlined intelligence; but the loyal spirit depends upon this union of a longing for unity with a will which needs its own expression in works of loyal art. (PC p. 268)

Royce does, however, often speak of the community as an organic-like, living thing, much as Whitehead later spoke of "societies." Yet the question may be raised about these passages in The Problem of Christianity whether Royce does not go the way of the Hegelians and the more monistic idealists into some rigid absolute 'social mind' theory of the community, which would compromise his personalism and his freedomist philosophy?[8] We think

---

8. "Each of the two, the community or the individual member, is as much a live creature as is the other. Not only does the community live, it has a mind of its own,--a mind whose psychology is not the same as the psychology of an individual human being. The social mind displays its psychological traits in its characteristic products, --in languages, in customs, in religions..." and etc. (PC pp. 80 and sequence)_

Royce avoids this type of development in the manner we have described above and in what follows, and precisely thereby anticipates Whitehead in his interpretation of these matters more than he follows the Hegelians. In the following rather climactic words, hoping, we believe, thereby to bring into clearest focus his life-long philsophic work, Royce affirms his own vision of a kind of absolute personalism (as we might phrase it) within his generalized Integral Idealism:

> What our definition of the community enables us to add to our former views of the meaning of loyalty is simply this: If the universe proves to be, in any sense, of the nature of a community, then love for this community, and for God, will not mean merely love for losing the self, or for losing the many selves, in any interpenetration of selves. If one can find that all humanity, in the sense of our definition, constitutes a real community, or that the world itself is, in any genuine way, of the nature of a community such as we have defined; and if hereupon we can come to love this real community,--then the one and the many, the body and the members, our beloved and ourselves, will be joined in a life in which we shall be both preserved as individuals, and yet united to that which we love. (PC p. 270, emphasis his)

This approaches the end of Royce's efforts to sketch the morphology of a personal universe, which includes the finite personal in the case of men, and the infinite personal in the case of God. But there is still a last word, which is to give the dynamics of the picture, to fill it with energy, on-going process and real life. This word is "Interpretation." As we mentioned above, we have already summarized in our former discussion, especially pages 122-3, what Royce meant in some depth by "Interpretation" as the personalizing, yet the cosmically unifying and communalizing (or perhaps better socializing) power; to which we here add the following several insights.

True knowledge--of the self, of the universe of nature at large, of the finite self and the universe as within the Divine Self of God--has to be "Interpretation," or a "triadic" apprehension.

In his treatment of Immortality recall that Royce's epistemology of Interpretation was centrally present. The same conception of knowledge is further elaborated in The Problem of Christianity. In The Conception of Immortality he reviewed the limitations of an epistemology of raw "perception" on the one hand, and of bare "conception" on the other (this commentary, pp. 220-1); and affirmed that true knowledge of another required the will to love, to understand, in short, to interpret the other

person. Indeed, the hope to know one's self ultimately requires
such "Interpretation," and herein lies the intimation of the
endlessness of this process, and so of immortality (in the Kantian
view, as we there explained). In The Problem of Christianity
Royce has continued this epistemological theme in the effort to
put the capstone, we believe, on his whole metaphysical position.
Somewhat beyond then, where the earlier section of this study
left off we proceed here with an attempt to understand Inter-
preation as the 'Spirit' of Community, which Royce virtually
called the Holy Spirit of God.

In his earlier treatise, where the triadic concept of
knowledge appeared, Royce anticipated his expression "interpretation" in the words "voluntary choice," and we quote again his
line from The Conception of Immortality: "...in...voluntary
choice...lies our essential consciousness of the true nature of
individuality.... It is the object of our purposes..." (CI pp.
38-9). Later in The Problem of Christianity we realize that "to
interpret" means essentially the same thing Royce had in mind at
the earlier stage of his writing. "To interpret" means essentially to put (imaginatively) oneself in the place of another
person or being, to empathize, to identify, if we are going to
make serious and successful effort to know. He wrote in the
latter work, "The method of interpretation is always the comparative method" (PC p. 344)--that is, the imaginative method; for
comparisons or interpretations always, of course, use imagination.

The commonplace experience of how people in social life come
to understand or know one another may be cited. Royce many times
suggests this kind of simplest illustration of the Interpretive
process. Much of one's entire day-to-day effort in living with
his fellow human beings is a process of constantly interpreting
friend B to neighbor A, with ourselves as C, or agent of Interpretation. To live with our fellows seriously, lovingly, crea-
tively is a process, of course in which we are always striving
imaginatively to identify ourselves as deeply as may be possible
with the nature and character of the one, in order to make him
known as fully as may be possible, not only to our own selves as
interpreter, but to the third. In such triadic process human
beings come to know each other--and where the result clarifies
the common past and throws light upon the hope of a similar
future, we are forming a "community" after the manner above
defined. Thus the interpretive process underlies, precedes, or
generates community--it is its life-blood.[9]

---

9. His central passages on Interpretation are found in:
    "The Will to Interpret," PC pp. 297-319; "Perception,
    Conception, and Interpretation," Ib. pp. 284-95; "The

Royce alludes to the fact that such interpretive, triadic flow of thought also explains other achievements of the knowing process; for example, that which puts us in touch with nature, or with our own growing selves as persons, or with the cosmic personal Spirit of Interpretation, in other words, with God as Holy Spirit. To elaborate briefly these dimensions of knowledge:

Frequently the hypotheses and paradigms of science are factors in a triadic-like process of thought. For example, modern scientists have imagined that the "atom" in its dynamic complexity is like a miniature solar system. An atom is said to have a central proton 'sun' or nucleus, with orbiting 'planetary' electrons. Modern scientists have pictured or interpreted this type of individuality in this kind of way to their own minds, and to those of their students. In other words, the thing itself as described by the analogical idea (B) is so interpreted by the scientific investigator and theoretician (C) to other inquiring minds (A). All knowledge, thinking or dialectic (the thinking process as such) proceeds in this way. Royce's basic assumption is that in so far as the universe contains 'individualities,' or potential individualities, of many degrees and ranges, they come to be known by and between minds, wherever and whenever minds arise, by an ever expanding and including process of triadic dialectic. In so far as this triadic dialectic may be expressed in scientific investigation and succeeds, 'scientific community' is created.

The self-understanding of any entities capable of self-interpretation is such a process. As human persons, for example, we are constantly interpreting our own past, in or by our present, to a future which is the complete or focused person we are striving to become by our endeavor to realize our purposes.

Something similar is suggested by Royce as applying to the natural world at large, out beyond the human world (with its forms of knowing, re science and the self) just described. Royce has not painted the picture quite as we do here, but we venture the following as not incongruous with what we have already learned of his conception of nature at large. In so far as sub-personal entities, blades of grass, rocks, atoms may have a dimly purposive telic life--or, more in the expression of Royce himself, as we saw in our study of his concept of nature,[10] in so far as such entities may have a 'conscious' experience moving on or at a different time-scale or time-sense than our own massive, molar kind--

Historical and the Essential," Ib. pp. 381-3; "The World of Interpretation," Ib. pp. 333-41; "The Doctrine of Signs," Ib. pp. 344-51.

10.   Pages 10f.

such must be presumed to know themselves and their environment in
similar triadic fashion. In so far as God is conceived to be the
total life of the Cosmic purposiveness, inclusive of nature, the
dialectic of God's own Being or Self-realization is presumed to
be the summation of this triadic knowing of beings at its ultimate
and infinite limit, itself conceived as an ever expanding 'limit.'
(And it is apparent that Royce talks of God and the World in his
later work in more plainly temporalistic terms than he earlier
allowed.)

> In the concrete, then, the universe is a community of inter-
> pretation whose life comprises and unifies all the social
> varieties and all the social communities which, for any
> reason, we know to be real in the empirical world which our
> social and our historical sciences study. The history of
> the universe, the whole order of time, is the history and
> the order and the expression of this Universal Community.
> (PC pp. 340-1)

> The universe, if my thesis is right, is a realm which
> is through and through dominated by social categories.
> (PC p. 344)[11]

> ...the very being of the universe consists in a process
> whereby the world is interpreted,--not indeed in its whole-
> ness, at any one moment of time, but in and through an

---

11.   Royce had ended this paragraph with the statement:
       "Not the Self, not the Logos, not the One, and not the
       Many, but the Community will be the ruling category of
       such a philosophy" (PC p. 344). Was he here moving,
       indeed, away from his earlier Personalistic Idealism
       or Theism into some kind of Societal Idealism, without
       the category of a Divine Person, who supports, leads,
       and gives the Cosmic Process its ultimate meaning?
           In the full context of his discussion we take it
       that he meant "not the Self" and "not the Many" in some
       isolated or 'realistic' sense long since disparaged;
       and "not the Logos" and "not the One" in some Atman or
       abstract, impersonal sense. In the same "...Doctrine
       of Signs" chapter we hear him say,
           "As a fact I still hold by all the essential
       features of these former attempts to state the case of
       idealism. But at present I am dealing with the World
       of Interpretation, and with the metaphysics of the Com-
       munity. This I believe to be simply a new mode of
       approach to the very problems which I have formerly
       discussed" (PC p. 350).

infinite series of acts of interpretation. This infinite
series constitutes the temporal order of the world with all
its complexities.... If we consider the temporal world in
its wholeness, it constitutes in itself an infinitely complex
Sign. This sign is, as a whole, interpreted to an experience
which itself includes a synoptic survey of the whole of time.
(PC p. 346)

Without attempting to elaborate upon Royce's use of Peirce's
technical term "sign" in the theory of Interpretation, perhaps
we may summarize usefully in the following way:

When the effort of knowing ourselves, and other individualities, meets with success in such interpretive terms, the bare
group is raised to social awareness or a sense of "community" as
above explained. This kingdom of mutually understood beings is
in the highest sense a Beloved Community of Interpretation, a
spiritual process self-realized in a joy of universal awareness
and support, analogous to the Holy Spirit of the New Testament.

This triadism of epistemological theory--centered in the
implication that spiritual _will_ is the ultimate form or meaning
of 'energy'--seemed to Royce to preserve the sanctity of individuality on every level: natural, the human finite, and the
Infinite Divine. To speak of knowledge from the extreme objective side as bare "perception" or sensory feeling alone is too
inadequate, though perception plays its role. On the other side,
what might be called extreme subjectivism, to speak of bare conception, or mere 'idea,' as the only, or perhaps the chief ingredient of knowledge, does not suffice either; for ideas alone,
without 'will' to spark interpretive movement within them and
between them, and between them and sense perceptions, would leave
us with an inert, cold, or abstract, Platonic world, where Royce
has said many times individuality and personality cannot breathe.
But to center the process in will, exemplified in fact in our own
case, and by presumption in other degrees of consciousness of
varying types throughout the natural order, keeps the individual
and the personal in command of the knowledge process and its outcome. In this way speculative reason can itself understand its
own personality creating and preserving purpose. Royce has summarized what he has endeavored to say along this line thus:

Metaphysically considered, the world of interpretation
is the world in which, if indeed we are able to interpret at
all, we learn to acknowledge the being and the inner life of
our fellowmen; and to understand the constitution of temporal
experience, with its endlessly accumulating sequence of
significant deeds. In this world of interpretation, of whose
most general structure we have now obtained a glimpse, selves

and communities may exist, past and future can be defined,
and the realism of the spirit may find a place which neither
barren conception nor the chaotic flow of interpenetrating
perceptions could ever render significant. (PC p. 294)

And finally:

There would be no melting together, no blending, no mystic
blur, and no lapse into mere intuition. But for me the
vision of the successful interpretation would simply be the
attainment of my own goal as interpreter. This attainment
would as little confound our persons as it would divide our
substance. (PC p. 315)

Does this religio-ethical epistemology of "interpretation"
succeed? For both science and faith it succeeds in most regards
as a concrete, synoptic, and practical way of viewing the problem
of knowledge.[12]

---

12. Evaluating Royce's philosophy of Interpretation in
somewhat different perspective than ours above, I quote the
following external source for its relevance and cogency:
"Interpretation may be accurately styled as 'living
reason' (although Royce does not use this expression himself),
for it grasps exactly the logical structure of a more or less
conscious process employed constantly in the course of actual
human experience, in the broadest sense of that term you
please. The person who, in the midst of solving some practical problem seizes upon a solution after careful reflection,
performs what is essentially a cognitive process of interpretation, and the result is always some truth which can be said
to have evolved from other truths, experiences, etc. assumed
as already had. It is the logical form of the discovery of
new truth and fresh insight into the nature and meaning of
existence that was Royce's central concern in the entire discussion of interpretation. He sought to analyze the structure
of reason in its life, as it moves through the world endeavoring to discover that system of relations which constitutes
whatever precise knowledge exists.
"It is the process of interpretation that reason shows
forth both its capacity as living and its ability to function
within the experience of beings for whom history is real, and
who look to the future as well as to the past as they attempt
to understand themselves and their world, and to achieve
whatever fulfillment is possible for them in it." (John E.
Smith: Royce's Social Infinite The Community of Interpretation, op. cit., p. 90.)
See also the excellent description of Royce's triadic

Addendum: Evil, Interpretation, and Atonement

Royce believed that his rethinking of the Christian theme of Atonement was achieved apart from the dispute between the two classic theories. These were the "penal" and the "moral" interpretations of Christian sacrifice, expressed or symbolized in the final work of Christ. It is not my purpose here to give a full analysis or critique of Royce's complex chapter under that heading. That he dealt with the subject at considerable length was, of course, altogether natural in the larger framework of the Problem of Christianity as he originally conceived that work.[13]

His socialized vision of the ultimate meaning of Atonement as the 'suffering service,' or 'sacrifice,' that all laborers for the spiritual kingdom of Interpretation may have occasion to perform in attempting to make the world even better than could have been possible had no evil or traitorous deed been committed, speaks with great eloquence and power. Actually his perspective on the meaning of Atonement puts the capstone, we believe, on the very moral theory that Royce himself considerably slighted in his allusions to it in the chapter at large. At least his is a further, perceptive version of the moral theory. To turn to the Suffering Servant figure of the II Isaiah as his own inspiration for perceiving the central meaning of Christian sacrifice and of the way evil is essentially and ultimately dealt with by the loving society of Interpretation, indicates the theological liberalism of Royce, in so far as he may be called a Christian theologian. That workers in the spiritual kingdom of Interpretation indeed sometimes believe that the Holy Spirit of God's Love has breathed upon and through them, morally energizing them to acts of redemption and salvation of others, under the supreme inspiration of the original act of Christ; such indeed has been the deepest practical implication of the moral theory of Atonement. Many in Christian history have so suggested, from St. Paul himself (in a number of ideas in his letters) through Peter Abelard of the Middle Ages, to many interpreters in modern times. Royce stands among them, in spite of his denial that he makes no conscious adherence to a moral view of Atonement in some of its more

---

conception of knowledge at its three levels, within the self, between selves, and the objective, practical and scientific world, Peter Fuss: "Interpretation: Towards a Roycean Political Philosophy," Revue Internationale De Philosophie, op. cit., pp. 120f.

13. Especially pp. 174-86.

traditional or formal aspects.

We tender a further observation upon Royce's version of the meaning of Atonement as the redemptive effort of suffering servants. Royce does not say enough regarding the salutary effect of 'forgiveness.' He seems to say more about the correction of the evil to the society at large, than the effect of the process upon the person of the evil doer himself. Forgiveness of the evil deed of the traitor both classic theories--the penalistic and the moral-revelational--included as vital aspects of the meaning of Atonement. Further, that the evil deed, once done, can never be itself changed in its alleged "irrevocable" character may be questioned. Implied by the larger transformed situation which a suffering servant himself effects by his redemptive action, has not a change come upon the original deed? Does the past ever change? That is the problem both logically and psychologically. In one place at least, counter to his prevailing tone in the chapter, Royce allows that the redemptive act of the suffering servant indeed "transforms the meaning of that very past" (PC p. 180). But this statement seems contrary to his very next words closing the sentence. Yet it seems to us that a redemptive act, such as Royce has so beautifully explained, does "undo," does alter the evil power itself. For the redemptive act stops the power from propagating itself. This is true in the sense that by the redemptive deed good can and has come out of the original situation; namely, that which, as Royce himself has averred, would not have been possible had not the suffering servant been quietly but effectively busy transforming the evil with his good purposes. The work of the servant places a kind of larger moral coherency upon the original act or situation. We now see it in a new light, with new possibilities! It is thereby changed by being enlarged or transformed in the character of its potentialities. This seems a logical change, and it makes possible the psychological freedom from guilt that acts of atonement, wherever and whenever effected in the manner so classically described by Royce, may work in the minds and consciousnesses of doers of evil when they come to stand in some apprehension of what is taking place in and by the action of the servant.

  *   *   *   *   *   *

Two points in conclusion to this study of Royce on Ethics, Society, and the Divine Reality:

In light of the criticism, to which we have previously called the reader's attention, that he had changed his fundamental metaphysical views by the time he wrote The Problem of Christianity, Royce's own commentary on the work, in the form of a letter to Miss Mary Whiton Calkins, thanking her for her perceptive analysis in a paper, "The Foundation in Royce's Philosophy for Christian Theism," speaks quite clearly to the issue. Not only do places in PC itself (e.g. p. 350, quoted in our note 11, p. 275), but this letter indicates at some length that his position in his own mind had remained, idealistic, personalistic and theistic--albeit in terms of the socialized and ethico-mystical version of the Theism that we have endeavored to show he upheld in his last major work. His letter to Miss Calkins is quoted below, pages 281f.

A final vision, The Hope of the Great Community, published the year of Royce's death (1916), reveals the breadth of Royce's social and historical optimism as he looked out upon the future of a world embattled in the first World War. His social idealism in this statement embraced democracy and what can best be described as a larger federalized conception of world "unity."[14] Such a conception is the necessary and inevitable form which world community must assume, if the Spirit of Interpretation and the ideal of the Pauline Church or Charity, as the ultimate inspiration for human social life, is ever to be realized. The mere form, however, of "democracy" is impotent (particularly if it is the more separatist or merely individualistic kind). The forms or institutions of democratic polity must be suffused with the "Pauline charity," or the Christian Agape, if these forms are to work, he says. We have no more prescient or realistic words on the prospects of the human future and global social structure of mankind than these of Royce:

> Liberty alone never saves us. Democracy alone never saves us. Our political freedom is but vanity unless it is in the Pauline sense of that word. Hence, the community of mankind will be international in the sense that it will ignore no rational and genuinely self-conscious nation. It will find the way to respect the liberty of the individual nations without destroying their genuine spiritual freedom.

---

14. We call the reader's attention to a lucid presentation by Peter Fuss of the democratic implications of Royce's Community of Interpretation. In the previously cited article, note 12, Professor Fuss concludes: "The emergent political superstructure would be federalistic and republican rather than centralized and authoritarian-- one indication, incidentally, that Royce's thought about community was by no means as utopian and removed from the American political experience as has generally been supposed" (p. 130). Royce's ethic of Interpretation implies precisely the distinctively democratic methods: "negotiation, compromise, persuasion" (p. 131).

Its liberty and union, when attained, will be "now and for-ever, one and inseparable."[15]

League of Nations, United Nations have been, of course, but halting efforts to realize this vision. But had Royce lived to see the experiments along these lines he no doubt would have believed them to be steps along the way toward the realization of that other rather striking suggestion of his--the scheme for International Insurance, outlined in the Hope of the Great Com-munity--as to how international life might begin to be effectively organized.[16]

*   *   *   *   *   *

This letter is quoted from The Letters of Josiah Royce, ed. by John Clendenning, The University of Chicago Press, 1970, pp. 644-8. Professor Calkins's paper appeared in The Philosophical Review, Vol. XXV, No. 3, May 1916 (Papers in Honor of Josiah Royce), pp. 282-93. Mary Whiton Calkins was Professor at Wellesley College, 1890-1926; and William Ernest Hocking was Professor at Harvard, 1914-1966.

To Mary Whiton Calkins, March 20, 1916
                                    Cambridge March 20th, 1916.
                                    103 Irving Street.
Dear Miss Calkins:
    Professor Hocking has sent to me the paper which you have so kindly contributed to the forthcoming discussion of my philosophical teaching.
    Let me say at once that I hope that you will print the paper precisely in accordance with your own wishes, with your own views regarding the relation between my philosophy and Christian theism, and in accordance with your own views regarding the sense in which my most recent book on The Prob-lem of Christianity, is or is not in accordance with the spirit and the letter of my earlier works. Your paper about me, and about my relation to Christian theism is too valuable to be tampered with, too kindly to be used as an opportunity for a further discussion from me. You are an expert on all the questions at issue. The account which you kindly give of the position taken in my earlier books,--that is in all the books that precede The Problem of Christianity,--is as accurate and scholarly as it is friendly. I am not conscious of having taken in my recent work a position inconsistent,

---

15.   McDermott, BWJR, op. cit., Vol. II, p. 1156.
16.   See Royce's "The Possibility of International Insur-ance," McDermott, BWJR, op. cit., Vol. II, pp. 1135f.

in its genuine meaning, with the positions which you recognize, and have so frequently and ably expounded. Therefore, precisely in so far, I have and can have only thanks for your interpretation and for your aid. But the two central ideas upon which my Problem of Christianity turns, the idea of the community, and the idea of what the historical theology of the Christian church early learned to call "the holy spirit" are ideas which are as living, and growing, as they are ancient. They grew when the prophets of Israel began to formulate their doctrine of Jerusalem, which, in the beginning, was a city, of somewhat questionable architecture, and morals, in the hill districts of Judea; but which, in the end, became the heavenly realm of which the mystic author of the well known medieval hymn wrote, and which the world is still trying to understand. These two ideas, the Community, and the Spirit have been growing ever since. They are growing today. They certainly have assumed, in my own mind, a new vitality, and a very much deeper significance than, for me, they ever had before I wrote my Problem of Christianity. My book on the Problem of Christianity records the experience and the reflections which both led over to that book, and I have been working in my mind daily more and more, ever since I wrote that book. The reflections in question constitute, for me, not something inconsistent with my former position, but a distinct addition to my former position, a new attainment,--I believe a new growth. I do not believe that you change, in a way involving inconsistency, when you re-interpret former ideas, as I have surely known you frequently to do, and have rejoiced to find you doing.

To borrow a figure from a remote field, I do not believe that Lincoln acted in a manner essentially inconsistent with his earlier political ideas when he wrote the Emancipation Proclamation and freed the slaves. To be sure, before he wrote that proclamation, he had seen a new light. My poor little book on The Problem of Christianity is certainly no Emancipation Proclamation, and is certainly no document of any considerable importance. But it certainly is the product of what for me is a new light, of a new experience, of ideas which are as new to me as the original form of my idealism was new to me when I first defined it.

As to whether these new views are consistent with my foregoing views, I can best express my position by saying that if, tomorrow or at any later time, you are to re-interpret the very thought which you have expressed in your so kind review of my Theism in such a way as to set forth in your own words the doctrine of the Spirit and of the Community which I have tried, very imperfectly to formulate, I should not think that you were saying anything inconsistent with what is now in your paper, but were only formulating a perfectly rational enrichment and development of your present opinions.

As for what my present position means, there is here space to say only this:--For me, at present a genuinely and loyally united community, which lives a coherent life, is, in a perfectly [literal]* sense, a person. Such a person, for Paul, the Church of Christ was. On the other hand, any human individual person, in a perfectly literal sense, is a community. The coherent life which includes past present and future, and holds them reasonably together, is the life of what I have also called, both in <u>The Problem of Christianity</u> and elsewhere a Community of Interpretation, in which the present, with an endless fecundity of invention, interprets the past to the future, precisely as, in the Pauline-Johannine type of theology, Christ, or the Spirit interprets the united individuals who constitute the human aspect of the Church, to the divine being in whom these members seek, at once their fulfilment, their unity, their diversity, and the goal of their loyalty. All this is a scrap of theology, which serves as a hint of what I have been trying to formulate in this recent phase, not merely of my thinking but of my experience. I do not know any reason why this phase of my thinking should attract any other interest than what may be due to its actual relations to a process which has been going on, in human thought, ever since Heraclitus remarked that the Logos is fluent, and ever since Israel began to idealize the life of a little hill town in Judea.

I stand for the importance of this process, which has led Christianity to regard a community, not merely as an aggregate but as a Person, and at the same time, to enrich its ideal memory of a person, until he became transformed into a Community.

The process in question, is not merely theological, and is not merely mystical, still less merely mythical. Nor is it a process invented merely by abstract metaphysicians. It is the process which Victor Hugo expressed in <u>Les Miserables</u> when he put into the mouth of Enjolras the words: "<u>Ma mere, c'est la republique.</u>" As I write you these words, Frenchmen are writing the meaning of these words in their blood, about Verdun. The mother which is a republic, is a community, which is also a person,--and not merely an aggregate, and not merely by metaphor a person. Precisely so the individual patriot who leaves his home behind, and, steadfastly serving, presses on in ardent quest of the moment when his life can be fulfilled by his death for his country, is all the more richly and deeply an individual, that he is also a community of interpretation, whose life has its unity in its restless

*An emendation on the MS, but said not to be in Royce's hand.

search for death on behalf of the great good cause,--its ever
living Logos in its fluent quest for the goal.

Now this view is at present an essential part of my
idealism. In essential meaning I suppose that it always was
such an essential part. But I do not believe that I ever
told my tale as fully, or with the same approach to the far
off goal of saying sometime something that might prove helpful
to students of idealism, as in the <u>Problem of Christianity</u>.

Subject to this comment, which is intended altogether
as a self-criticism, your article,--kindly, minute, scholarly,
thorough, and accurate as it is, in all the expository notes
which it includes, relating to all that I published, before
my <u>Problem of Christianity</u> is a paper for which I thank you
most heartily, and which I hope that you will publish precisely
as it stands. Whether it would be at all worthwhile to add
any mention of or quotation from this reply of mine to you,
is a matter that I leave herewith entirely in your hands and
in those of Professor Hocking, as well as of the editor of
the <u>Philosophical Review</u>. My dear friends did so much for me
at Philadelphia. Your own contribution was so gracious, so
fair spirited, so generous, and so kindly, that you have
already done a great deal too much for me. I am sorry to
give you an hour's further trouble of any sort. I shall
always be grateful for your encouragement, for your counsel,
for your clear understanding of me, and for your cooperation.
My debt to you is of very long standing, my gratitude is very
deep. That your name appears among the contributors to this
piece of common work constitutes and will constitute one of
the principal features that makes this collection of papers
a delight that will last as long as I live.

As I understand Professor Hocking, he asks me to hand
him your manuscript at once, and I shall do so today. You
may show him this letter or not just as you wish. I should
sign,

                    Gratefully and affectionately yours,
                    Josiah Royce.

Chapter Eleven

THE ETHICAL AND SOCIAL THOUGHT OF WHITEHEAD

Concerning the ideas of morality, society, and civilization in Whitehead's Process Philosophy, we point first to his chapter, "Requisites for Social Progress," coming from the earlier phase of his philosophic period (SMW 1925). Here his steady optimism about history and the human future is revealed. This essay begins with a resume of what he believes to be his own philosophic achievement in suggesting "an alternative philosophy of science in which <u>organism</u> takes the place of <u>matter</u>" (p. 193, emphasis his)--that is, dead, inert, 'materialist' matter--a story we have already told in fuller detail (Part I).

This change in view concerning the nature of the world constitutes mankind's first and basic ground for optimism. The universe is not dead 'substance'; but <u>living process</u>--irrepressible, and always open toward the future, by its own inherent possibility of new development, making available new forms of value experience, while maintaining the combinations of value experience already achieved.

Second, process makes for change, and change for some unsettlement. But the very fact that our time is an unsettled one, is not so much cause for alarm as for great hope.

The middle class pessimism over the future of the world comes from a confusion between civilisation and security (p. 208).

Whatever civilization will come to be it cannot become perpetual "security." Automatic security and process are mutually exclusive. It will, however, acquire a basic stability as historic process becomes charged with the following qualities.

Thirdly, therefore, Whitehead's profound reliance on the rationality of man (his Greek and Platonic heritage)--"...the power of reason" and "its decisive influence on the life of humanity"--constitute the firm rock upon which his expectation for the human future rises. For in contrast to Alexander, Caesar, and Napoleon, the "men of thought from Thales to the present day, men individually powerless," have been "ultimately the rulers of the world" (p. 208).

Finally for this vision of the future, we have his insistence
on the democratic ideal in terms of what we called, in our study
of Royce, the larger federalism--to guard against a dangerous
"Gospel of Uniformity." "The difference between the nations and
races of mankind," Whitehead said, "are required to preserve the
conditions under which higher development is possible" (p. 207).
This affirmation resembles the declaration with which we closed
Royce's thoughts on society. The democratic ideal is explicitly
and felicitously set forth further in Whitehead's address (to
which we presently turn), "The Importance of Friendly Relations
Between England and the United States" (1925). Like Royce's
elegant phrases, "the great community" and "the beloved community," Whitehead speaks of "the great society" (SMW p. 205),
a casual phrase, however, which he alternatively and more characteristically expressed as "Civilization."

Before looking further at his meaning of Civilization it is
necessary to speak of several primary terms in Whitehead's moral
philosophy, embedded in the difficult discussion of Process and
Reality and in selections from Adventures of Ideas and Modes of
Thought:

(1) We note his description of things as hierarchies of
"societies," or nexus (linkages), which relate to each other for
sustenance. Thus we have his extension of the term 'society'
downward and upward to include all degrees of organized and
linked natural complexities, atomic, molecular, cellular, living
bodies, the "personal experiences" of our higher self-conscious
organization, and finally the "larger...natural universe" itself
(AI pp. 207-8, 290).[1]

(2) When organization rises to the level of "living societies," such are self-sustained by "robbery." The origins of
this cosmic predation are "the primordial appetitions," defined
as expressions of "God's purpose," whose "absolute end" is "the
evocation of intensities" (PR pp. 160-1). We have called attention in earlier sections of this study to Whitehead's similar
references to the universal "Eros" as fundamentally characteristic
of reality. Predatory appetition, however, is not the last word
descriptive of the cosmic situation, according to Whitehead.

(3) "Moral responsibility" or ethical awareness arises in
the cosmic order as a reflective prehension, which self-conscious

---

1.   "The Universe achieves its values by reason of its coor-
      dination into societies of societies, and into societies
      of societies of societies" (AI p. 207).

entities of the "high grade" human kind experience as they are able to contemplate "consequences" of actions (PR p. 339).[2] "Morality of outlook," or more simply "morality" may now be understood as the situation in which "the individual interest" can somehow be identified with "the general good" (PR p. 23); also morality appears whenever the telic strivings of human beings and their societies "aim at the ideal" (AI p. 268). Unlike the non-living and vegetable grades of "actualities," the animal grades exhibit, uniquely, "Purposes transcending (however faintly) the mere aim at survival..."; and the "human grade of animal life immensely extends this...," thus giving rise to "morals and religion" (MT pp. 38-9).

Summarizing thus far, morality for Whitehead is that form of intellectual prehension which will seek in action to mollify the primal, individualized pursuit of intensities; that is, to harmonize the appetitive and therefore competitive conflict or "robbery" of societies.

Morality of outlook is inseparably conjoined with generality of outlook. The antithesis between the general good and the individual interest can be abolished only when the individual is such that its interest is the general good, thus exemplifying the loss of the minor intensities in order to find them again with finer composition in a wider sweep of interest. (PR p. 23)

(4) Like the laws of nature, however, "particular moral codes" do not have an "unqualified stability" (MT p. 18):

The point is that moral codes are relevant to presuppositions respecting the systematic character of the relevant universe. When the presuppositions do not apply, that special code is a vacuous statement of abstract irrelevancies." (MT p. 18)

There is no one behavior system belonging to the essential character of the universe, as the universal moral ideal. What is universal is the spirit which should permeate any behavior-system in the circumstance of its adoption. (MT p. 20)

---

2.   Trusting we are not too free here in this exposition; the original read: "consequences of its existence"-- closing a complex paragraph on the idea of "subject-superject."

(Presently we will attempt to say what this "universal...spirit"
may be for Whitehead, as a kind of ultimate, guiding catalyst
for moral action. In the meanwhile we continue with the immediate
point.) Earlier than Modes of Thought, in Adventures of Ideas,
he had spelled out even more expressly these relativistic convic-
tions:

> The details of these codes are relative to the social
> circumstances of the immediate environment--life at a certain
> date on 'the fertile fringe' of the Arabian desert, life on
> the lower slopes of the Himalayan Mountains, life on the
> plains of China, or on the plains of India, life on the delta
> of some great river. Again the meaning of the critical terms
> is shifting and ambiguous, for example, the notions of owner-
> ship, family, marriage, murder, God. Conduct which in one
> environment and at one stage produces its measure of har-
> monious satisfaction, in other surroundings at another stage
> is destructively degrading. Each society has its own type
> of perfection, and puts up with certain blots, at that stage
> inevitable. Thus, the notion that there are certain regula-
> tive notions, sufficiently precise to prescribe details of
> conduct, for all reasonable beings on Earth, in every planet,
> and in every star-system, is at once to be put aside. That
> is the notion of the one type of perfection at which the
> Universe aims. All realization of the Good is finite and
> necessarily excludes certain other types....
>
> The moral code is the behavior-patterns which in the
> environment for which it is designed will promote the evolu-
> tion of that environment towards its proper perfection.
> (AI pp. 289-91)

How may we put this element of ethical 'relativism' and
'situationalism' into broadest perspective in Whitehead? We
suggest the following as mainly characteristic of his thought in
this area. (A critique of certain of these points will appear
presently.)

In the first place, he asserts that the various ages of
history have their predominant ideals, as, for example those of
"liberty, activity, and cooperation dimly adumbrated in the epoch
of the American Constitution" (MT pp. 164-5). Whitehead in such
passages as these suggests the fludity of the ideal or the moral,
rather than a radical relativity of the moral. Moral ideals are
relatively absolute for any particular age; but in the long
course of process the ideal will slowly change according to the
situation, that is, according to the receptivity, possibility,
and relevance of an existing circumstance to a given ideal (AI
pp. 289-90).

In _Modes of Thought_ he refers to "intuitions of righteousness" that "disclose an absoluteness in the nature of things"
like "the taste in a lump of sugar." This appears in the context
mentioned above regarding the predominant ideals that guide a
given period or epoch (MT p. 165). Accordingly, then, does
Whitehead mean that these "intuitions of righteousness" apply to
a particular time and circumstance with a kind of provisional
"absoluteness" only for the beings living in that age? Actually
such is the case in real history. Successive periods bring new
wisdom which supersedes the ancient good that the new time often
does find uncouth. Whitehead's conception of the procession of
the ideal reflects this practical fact. But his "intuitions of
righteousness," in the full Whitehead context, may refer to
something beyond this.

For example, and in the second place, there are types of
transcending ideal in Whitehead's thought, which are, apparently,
relevant to _any_ time and circumstance. In the same context, and
standing between the two relativistic paragraphs above quoted,
from _Adventures of Ideas_, we hear this further side of his
thinking:

> Although particular codes of morality reflect, more or
> less imperfectly, the special circumstances of social struc-
> ture concerned, it is natural to seek for some highly general
> principles underlying all such codes. Such generalities
> should reflect the very notions of the harmonizing of har-
> monies, and of particular individual actualities as the sole
> authentic reality. These are the principles of the generality
> of harmony, and of the importance of the individual. The
> first means 'order,' and the second means 'love.' Between the
> two there is a suggestion of opposition. For 'order' is
> impersonal; and love, above all things, is personal. (pp.
> 290-91)

In the rest of this paragraph Whitehead proceeds to discuss how
this opposition between order and freedom may be resolved,
yielding morality as previously defined--(a consideration to
which we will return presently). In the meanwhile, he has
pointed at least to two or three outstanding values, transcending
the particularities of the codes: "harmony" or "order" itself;
personality or "the importance of the individual"; and emerging
from this, the idea of "love."

Whether this level of his thought--pointing to such transcending universalistic norms--is entirely consistent with his
denial that there can be "details of conduct, for all reasonable
beings on Earth, in every planet, and in every star-system,"

indeed remains to be considered further. If Whitehead by the
expression "details" means simply all the 'middle axioms' of
conduct which cannot, of course, be prescribed in minute and
exhaustive 'legislative' sense, as between culture and culture,
then there is less apparent conflict in the two paragraphs--and
little for the critics to complain about concerning his consistency. The matter, however, seems not perfectly clear. And in
view of this possibility we suggest that Whitehead, in his
reference to love, has recognized in this context one, at least,
of the five universal norms which do in fact appear in the codes
of all the high cultures. Further, in his reference to personality he has recognized a principle that underlies them all,
though in some cultures perhaps more implicitly than explicitly.
These universal norms, characteristic of the major historic
societies, and therefore of human ethical thinking as such at
its highest level, are often paraphrased as the respect for life,
for truth, for possessions, for discipline of the relationship
between the sexes in some terms, and for the ideal of benevolence
or love. The principle of the sacredness of personality underlies
this universal human code as the source of the principle of love.
Unlike Whitehead, then, in this place, we would say that all
"reasonable beings" in all star systems, if they were indeed
personal beings, at least somewhat like ourselves in emotional
endowment, would have a similar, rather than some radically dis-
similar ethical 'code.' If hydrogen chemistry is the same
throughout the galaxies, the 'moral chemistry' of personal be-
ings--assuming similar drives, needs, and purposes concerning the
more basic things of life--ought to be the same, or certainly
similar. Be these vast things as they may, however, and the
ultimate dimensions of Whitehead's thinking on some of them
remain no doubt ambiguous, we return to those aspects of his
thought which are more certain.

   In the third place, then, the ultimate category of the
ethical is "Creativity" itself, as it was the ultimate category
of Whitehead's metaphysics and theory of being (this commentary pp.
50, 144f.). On those pages we said that Creativity is the ultimate character which says the universe can and will have character or characters (i.e. formed beings). In light now of certain
of his basic ethical views, above outlined, we can add that the
Creativity is what makes the progression of the ideal from age to
age possible--or otherwise what makes historic 'progress' possible. Indeed, we suggest that this is what Whitehead himself
meant in his line from "Mathematics and the Good": "...Creativity
involves the production of value-experience, by the inflow from
the infinite into the finite, deriving special character from the
details and the totality of the finite pattern" (SP pp. 120-1).

In summary, therefore, at this stage of our reflections on Whitehead's moral philosophy, I believe that it may be too hasty, or merely carping, a judgment to say that the prime ingredient of his thinking is that there are "no universal moral laws," and thereby to see a bad relativity, or at least a dire inconsistency in his ethical thought.[3] There are other factors which Whitehead has recognized, to which we have just pointed, that apparently were accepted as absolute values by him: "the persuasions of reason" itself for one;[4] personality or "the importance of the individual" for another (AI p. 291); "love" as a third (AI p. 291); "order" or harmony that all societies aim at for yet another (AI p. 291); ultimately the Creativity itself as above interpreted. Creativity is the highest value of freedom itself, integral to the meaning of God in both Whitehead and Royce. As we have endeavored to show, it stands for real time, process, change, novelty, in brief, the <u>possibility</u> of the emerging of varied finite forms of being, each unique and somewhat different from its fellows. Whitehead has called these forms of being actual entities, actual occasions, entities of entities or societies. At the beginning of his 1925 address on "Friendly Relations Between England and the United States," Whitehead describes a number of "outstanding ideals," held in common by the two peoples. Among these were free political organization "under the protection of equal laws...free peaceful association with our fellows," under the "guidance of a strong moral purpose," and "sense of what is right and fair as between man and man"; "the persuasions of reason, and...fair dealing and relationship"; "free democratic government"; with the ideal for external policy phrased as "peaceful arbitration," etc. These humane and democratic values, announced as characteristic of the two countries, express their belief, he says, "in the moral governance of the world, by which it has been decreed that in the end, force and brutality revenge themselves upon those nations which depend upon such violence."[5] In "Historical Changes" (1930) he said "... history... ...discloses an ultimate character, in the nature of things..." (SP p. 214). Such statements, of course, suggest in fairly classic terms his own belief in what the religious and idealist tradition has called 'moral law.'

3. Cp. Prof. Paul Arthur Schilpp, "Whitehead's Moral Philosophy," in Schilpp (ed.): <u>The Philosophy of Alfred North Whitehead</u>, op. cit., pp. 611-12.
4. From "The Importance of Friendly Relations Between England and the United States," in A.H. Johnson (ed.): <u>Whitehead's American Essays in Social Theory</u>, Harper & Bros., 1959, p. 139.
5. Ib. pp. 138-9.

In conclusion, therefore, for this immediate point, although we have a conception of the <u>fluidity</u> of the moral ideal, that is, a 'progressive' or 'processive' conception, including some element of growth in the finite awareness of what the ideal is (MT pp. 164-5), this is not to say that Whitehead lacks any perception of 'abiding truths,' descriptive of the metaphysical realm, the realm of processive being as such. Accordingly, whatever ultimate relationships hold for, or describe that process, is its larger 'moral,' or 'religious' nature or its 'truth' in a fundamental sense, and we have reviewed above what some of these relations are. Indeed, Whitehead has said:

> Morality emphasizes the detailed occasion; while religion emphasizes the unity inherent in the universe. (MT p. 39)

With subtle insight A.H. Johnson has called attention to the implicit democratic thinking in Whitehead's basic metaphysical views.[6] In social terminology, an actual entity is characterized by an inherent "freedom"--the subjective aim that makes it possible for it to select the data for its experience out of optional possibilities that the "creative interaction" with other actual entities afford to it. In this respect there is the characteristic of a sovereign "equality" among entities, which Johnson has argued points to the democratic ideal of the sovereignty of the people on the human and social plane of relationship.[7] This line of analysis suggests that entities have basic "rights," perhaps a right to "property" in some sense, leading on to certain aspects of the democratic conception of "justice." Johnson rightly disclaims, I think, that there is any direct support of democracy's "majority rule" idea in Whitehead's metaphysical categories by themselves. Rather the emphasis on freedom and self-realization are primary in Whitehead's thought about the cosmic nature and its process. What we have then in Whitehead's foundational metaphysical thinking is a provision for certain of the basic ideals of western democracy--including, in his own generalized term, the idea of human "cooperation" (MT p. 165), which is the other side, of course, of the problem of democratic freedom in its need for organization.[8] When he spoke in <u>Modes of Thought</u> of "cooperation," along with the ideals of "liberty" and "activity" as

---

6. See his <u>Whitehead's Philosophy of Civilization</u>, Beacon Press, 1958, pp. 188-90.

7. Ib.

8. Johnson concluded: "Here, then, is a metaphysics which apparently provides support for most (if not all) of the basic ideals of Western democracy" (Ib. p. 190).

"dimly adumbrated in the American Constitution," Whitehead was interpreting his basic process metaphysics. After next asserting, characteristically, that these ideals are among a "variety of possibilities open for humanity," he continues with the statement that: "...the Constitution vaguely discloses the immanence in this epoch of that one energy of idealization, whereby bare process is transformed into glowing history" (MT p. 165).

To return to the ultimate problem of 'society'--the balance between the classic antithesis mentioned previously, order versus freedom--Whitehead has phrased it as the balance between "order" and "love." Recall that the ideal of "the importance of the individual" implies love (AI p. 291). This paragraph further suggests that the "order" of any society is to be ultimately evaluated as worthy or good to the extent that it promotes "strength of experience," that is, heightens the possibility of individual creative freedom. This is the heart of the democratic idea, of course.[9] Yet somewhat paradoxically (and here Whitehead is far from clear) the individual must use his own attained "strength of experience" or creative freedom to promote the order, or the social welfare. (Royce's philosophy of Loyalty could well be employed at this place to assist Whitehead.)   In

---

9. In Whitehead's discourse "The Problem of Reconstruction" (1942) this characteristic, generalized, but firm, democratic theory was phrased thus: At the center of "political theory" must be the principle of "respect for each individual life." Human experience "demands a social structure supplying freedom and opportunity for the realization of objectives beyond the simple bodily cravings .... It cannot be repeated too often that the only security for progress is a sincere respect for each individual human being.... ...the notion of a master race ...means the moral degradation of mankind" (A.H. Johnson (ed.): WAEST, op. cit., pp. 55-6).
    Moreover, Whitehead had a pragmatic, empirical approach to social development--i.e. a particularly democratic method. At the end of this discourse we hear him say, as "a confession of personal political faith": "I do not trust any extreme, abstract plan of universal social construction. Such plans are important for the stimulation of the imagination. But in practice every successful advance is a compromise. The general ideal is the wide diffusion of opportunity. The sort of opportunity relevant to each special case depends on special characteristics of the populations involved" (Ib. pp. 60-1).

any case, when process attains the height of "Civilization" it
will be fulfilled, according to Whitehead, by the overarching
qualities of Truth, Beauty, Adventure, Art, and Peace (AI p.
273).

But how do we arrive at these ultimate principles characterizing "Civilization"? To reply is to review his whole system
in microcosm, which his chapters "Adventure" and "Peace" in
Adventures of Ideas subsume. The first item of "sociological
theory" is to realize "that no static maintenance of perfection
is possible...Advance or Decadence are the only choices offered
to mankind." From this "axiom rooted in the nature of things"
three further "metaphysical principles" are disclosed (and the
first is really a restatement of what we have just heard,
p. 273).

1. That reality is process--"each actual thing" can be
understood only "in terms of its becoming and perishing" (p.
274). Furthermore, a point now very familiar in Whitehead,
"process involves a physical side which is the perishing of the
past as it transforms itself into a new creation. It also
involves a mental side which is the Soul entertaining ideas"
(p. 274). The impact of the mental as it transforms the physical
into the "new creation" is the essential "Adventure" of existence.

2. "...every occasion of actuality is in its own nature
finite. There is no totality which is the harmony of all perfections. Whatever is realized in any one occasion necessarily
excludes the unbounded welter of contrary possibilities" (AI
p. 275). Derived from this principle, no doubt, was Whitehead's
conception of the 'moral ideal' as fluid, processive, pluralistic
and somewhat situational; and his accompanying reluctance to
assign an ideal finality to cases of embodied morality--save the
most ultimate ones expressing "the importance of the individual"
itself and "love."

3. "...the principle of Individuality"--or to clarify, of
"complex" individuality:

The individual, real facts of the past lie at the base of
our immediate experience in the present. They are the
reality from which the occasion springs, the reality from
which it derives its source of emotion, from which it inherits its purposes, to which it directs its passions....
Our lives are dominated by enduring things, each experienced
as a unity of many occasions bound together by the force of
inheritance. (AI p. 279)

In other words, Aristotle's doctrine that "no individual primary substance can enter into the complex of objects observed in any occasion of experience," but can only be qualified or changed by "universals," "is a complete mistake" (AI p. 279).

This third point lies at the base of Whitehead's inherently individualistic or democratic, but also socially responsible ethic, which we endeavored to review above.

Earlier we heard Whitehead say, "What is universal is the spirit which should permeate any behavior-system in the circumstance of its adoption."[10] I referred to this "universal... spirit" as the guiding catalyst for moral action and deferred comment about it. We now wish to suggest that Whitehead's principle of "Peace"--"which calms destructive turbulence and completes civilization" (AI p. 283)--is this needed universal spirit. "Peace" seems to be the ultimate category of, or for Civilization. It is best to draw together Whitehead's salient definitions of this term, from AI:

-- Peace does not refer "to political relations"; rather it is "a quality of mind steady in its reliance that fine action is treasured in the nature of things" (p. 273).

-- is a "more general quality" than "tenderness" (Ib.).

-- is more alive than "Impersonality" (Ib.).

-- "...carries with it a surpassing of personality" (Ib.).

-- "...is primarily a trust in the efficacy of Beauty" (Ib.).

-- Yet "results in a wider sweep of conscious interest... enlarges the field of attention" (p. 284).

-- "...Peace is self-control at its widest,--at the width where the 'self' has been lost, and interest has been transferred to coordinations wider than personality" (Ib.)

-- "...is the barrier against narrowness. One of whose fruits is...the love of mankind" (Ib.).

-- "...the vision of ...Peace...is the harmony of the soul's activities with ideal aims that lie beyond any personal

---

10. P. 287 (MT p. 20).

satisfaction" (and as such is the peculiar quality of youth) (p. 286).

-- "The essence of Peace is that the individual whose strength of experience is founded upon this ultimate intuition [i.e. that social order must promote individuality while at the same time the individual must secure that order], thereby is extending the influence of the source of all order" (p. 291).

"Peace" as defined in the last several of these levels of meaning brings to mind, with more than casual similarity, Royce's concepts of Loyalty to Loyalty and of Atonement itself, a type of ultimate Loyalty. Indeed, to bring civilization and to make it work we need loyalty and atonement as Royce profoundly described these supremely motivating spiritual powers; and we need Whitehead's similar principle of dynamic "Peace" that "results in the wider sweep of conscious interest," to include "the love of mankind" beyond the bare development of the personal for its own isolated sake. Or make these principles sequential: if we had Royce's "Loyalty" and "Atonement" they would lead undoubtedly to Whitehead's "Peace" or "Civilization."

We will not here venture into an essay on Whitehead's concepts of Beauty and Art, major tasks in themselves that would take us far afield. That a civilization must be founded on "Truth," rise to "Beauty" through creative "Art," and attain dynamic "Peace" through its catalyzing "Loyalties" and "Atonements" seems indeed to point to the larger factors of the great and the good society, while we keep in mind the democratic commitment behind the meaning of the archetypal terms "Loyalty" and "Peace" in the full context of Royce's and Whitehead's thought. The meaning of "truth" relative to philosophic method for each man we are about to consider as our closing task.

Part V

ADDENDUM:

KNOWLEDGE AND THE PHILOSOPHIC TASK

Chapter Twelve

ROYCE ON KNOWLEDGE

This closing section does not aim at an analysis of Royce's
or Whitehead's complete philosophy of knowledge based on the
entire body of their logical, mathematical, and epistemological
discourses.[1] Such an attempt would exceed the original purposes
of this study and lay too great a weight upon the capacities of
its author.

The main perspective of our two philosophers, however, in
this area may be subsumed as a 'coherence' criterion of truth.
Not surprisingly, this represents a further fundamental aspect in
which their thought was in major agreement, with Whitehead making
a slight modification from a pure coherence criterion that shall
be presently noted.

Our discussion of Royce on this theme takes up where we left
the review of his triadic conception of dialectic, or the "interpretive" process as the essence of the process of knowing (p.
272f). He was there treating of the psychological form or dynamics of the knowing process, as he understood it. We here conclude that exposition with his final vision of the truth experience as a process of judgmental synthesis and coherency of
insight.

His essay, "The Problem of Truth in the Light of Recent
Discussion" (1908), presents a lively dialogue with "Professor
James and Professor Dewey" on the instrumental-pragmatic view of
truth that those philosophers so brilliantly popularized. Royce's
conception of their position was expertly phrased thus:

Truth grows, changes, and refuses to be tested by absolute
standards. It <u>happens</u> to ideas, insofar as they <u>work</u>. It

---

1. For pursuit of such a task see, for example, Bruce
   Kuklick: <u>Josiah Royce: An Intellectual Biography</u>,
   Bobbs-Merrill, 1972, in considerable part concerned
   with the development of epistemological themes in Royce;
   Victor Lowe: <u>Understanding Whitehead</u>, Johns Hopkins
   Press, 1962, esp. Part II, "The Development of White-
   head's Thought."

belongs to them when one views them as instruments to an end. The result of all this is a relativistic, an evolutionary, theory of truth. For such a view logic is part of psychology,--a series of comments upon certain common characteristics of usefully working ideas and opinions. ...Truth is no barren repetition of a dead reality, but belongs, as a quality, to the successful deeds by which we produce for ourselves the empirical realities that we want.[2]

Granting that Royce had his own strong 'pragmatic' element in the theory of truth-judging as a triadic "interpretation" and an act of the "will," which we have previously reviewed, he offers the following critique of James's and Dewey's instrumentalism.

If truth is to be isolated solely in the present usefulness of judgments, how do we then come to accept the truth of past events, i.e. of history? Or another way to put the question, how do we universalize or generalize 'a truth' up out of one's individual, private experience of the successful working of an idea?[3] Getting at the trouble from still another side, how does thought rise from the implied subjectivism of bare 'pragmatic truth' and join with "the content of other men's minds," so that there may be a true meeting of the conception of truth as a stable and universal quality descriptive of the nature of things at large?

Indeed ultimately, how does pragmatism meet the responsibilities of science itself in its presumption of getting at 'truth' pertaining to natural facts, "the...physical world" itself?[4] To James's subtle rejoinder that all such "truths"--historic events, those truths as may be in other men's minds, truths of physical fact in the world of science--are like "bank credits," i.e. postponed verifications, Royce replies:

Here one apparently stands at the parting of the ways. One can answer this question by saying: "The truth of these assertions (or their falsity, if they are false).belongs to them whether I credit them or no, whether I verify them or not. Their truth or their falsity is their own character

---

2. From "The Problem of Truth in the Light of Recent Discussion," an address delivered before the International Congress of Philosophy, Heidelberg, September 1908, McDermott (ed.): BWJR, op. cit., Vol. II, pp; 693-4. (This address was originally published in William James and Other Essays, Macmillan, 1911.)
3. Ib. pp. 694-6.
4. Ib. pp. 696-7.

and is independent of my credit and my verification." But to say this appears to be, after all, just the intellectualism which so many of our modern pragmatists condemn.[5]

In the context that follows, Royce presses the point that the pragmatist position results in a radical relativism, in which truth reduces to an ever changing judgmental "expediency."[6]

The argument, according to Royce, is further turned in his favor on the plain fact that the human mind often asserts truths which "transcend empirical verification," with which a pragmatic handling cannot adequately deal. Minimally such truths of a more "absolute" kind are those found in "pure mathematics" and in "Symbolic Logic" or "pure logic." Such truths are indeed acts of, or "the logic of the will." But Royce penetrates beyond the pragmatic use of the "will" in theory of knowledge. He interprets the logical will as the engine or the necessity of a priori insight itself. The will must think in certain ways if it is to think at all.[7]

Wherein...consists this truth of pure logic? I answer, at once, in my own way. Pure logic is the theory of the mere form of thinking. But what is thinking? Thinking, I repeat, is simply our activity of willing precisely in so far as we are clearly conscious of what we do and why we do it. And thinking is found by us to possess an absolute form precisely in so far as we find that there are certain aspects of our activity which sustain themselves even in and through the very effort to inhibit them. One who says: "I do not admit that for me there is any difference between saying yes and saying no",--says "no", and distinguishes negation from affirmation, even in the very act of denying this distinction. Well, affirmation and negation are such self-sustaining forms of our will activity and of our thought activity. And such self-sustaining forms of activity determine absolute truths....

The absoluteness of the truths of pure logic is shown through the fact that you can test these logical truths in this reflective way.[8]

---

5. Ib. p. 698.
6. Ib. pp. 698-9.
7. Ib. pp. 700-4, 706, 709.
8. Ib. pp. 704-5.

The "forms of activity" of the will itself constitute truth; or as we may say for Royce, perhaps more simply--and as he himself virtually does--'truth is the form of the will.'9

> One discovers...that our constructive processes, viewed just as activities, possess a certain absolute nature and conform to their own self-determined, but, for that very reason, absolute laws. ...which are the fundamental and immanent laws of the will itself....10

Moreover, many such mathematico-logical truths are given in a "reflective way," that is, in an a priori manner, as the result of constructive "synthetic process," which rises above "analysis."11 Royce anticipates and criticizes what has in more recent times come to be known as Analytic Philosophy.

In "The Office of the Reason" essay, The Sources of Religious Insight (1912), he describes the analytic concept of "reason" as the effort "to elucidate the meaning of an assertion." Such limited reason discovers "nothing essentially new," but "turns...premises over and over, and gets out of them only what has already been put into them." Whereas, the people who assert this view say that "experience on the other hand, is full of countless novelties..." (p. 83). Here we have a depiction of the essential standpoint of recent analytical philosophy concerning the a priori: the admitted, but virtually vacuous significance of a priori reasoning, and the emphasis on "experience" (which the analysts tried to limit to 'sensory verification') as the only source of novelty in thinking.

Royce, however, perceives the function and power of reason in the way classic philosophy does, as including a synthetic a priori, while in no wise by-passing or minimizing reason's empirical scope as well. Ultimately he views reason as a process of synoptic coherence: "reason...means simply broader intuition, the sort of seeing that grasps many views in one, that surveys life as it were from above, that sees, as the wanderer views the larger landscape from a mountain top" (SRI p. 86). Reason is not limited to the "process of forming abstract ideas or of analyzing the significance of assertions" (p. 86). The full, coherent meaning of reason is that it seeks for "novel truth"; is not limited to "the data of sense or of feeling" or to "analysis of

---

9.   Ib. p. 707--resembling his announcement that time is the form of the will, this commentary p. 175f.
10. Ib. p. 706.
11. Ib. pp. 705-6.

abstract ideas and assertions" (p. 90). Reason must be defined
"as the power to get articulate...insight into wholes rather than
fragments. ...as the process of getting connected experience on
a large scale" (p. 91). This sort of "synthesis--the viewing of
many facts or principles or relations in some sort of unity and
wholeness," this "synoptic survey of various articulate truths"
constitutes "a more explicit sort of intuition..." (p. 90); "it
raises our intuitions to higher levels" (p. 94). In all of this
Royce is describing what has traditionally been called the
coherence criterion of truth:

> The word reason...calls our attention to...our power to
> grasp many facts in their <u>unity</u>, to see the coherence, the
> interrelationship, the totality of a set of experiences.
> Now when insight reaches higher levels, these various
> aspects of our knowledge are never sundered. (pp. 99-100)

Advocates of this criterion often employ the words "insight"
and "reason" synonymously. So with Royce, who continued to say
that "...insight...means a coherent view of many facts in some
sort of unity" (p. 99). Finally we have his comprehensive
definition of the coherence criterion:

> True insight, if fulfilled, would be empirical, for it
> would face facts; intuitive, for it would survey them and
> grasp them, and be intimate with them; rational, for it
> would view them in their unity. (p. 102)

At the heart of a rational philosophy like Royce's is the
conception that there are 'synthetic judgments <u>a priori</u>.' While
not citing precisely this terminology as a long-standing and
critical question to be resolved by logic and epistemology,
Royce's discussion makes it clear that he holds this issue very
much at the forefront of the problem of knowledge. To clarify
the issue affirmatively will also reveal the larger meaning of
'the <u>a priori</u>' than the significance often given to it by analytical philosophy, to the effect, above mentioned, that the
<u>a priori</u> is but definitional tautology.

Royce cites the fascinating story of the Old Priest and the
Old Nobleman to illustrate how "reason discovers a novel fact"
by making "a synthesis" (SRI p. 95). The Old Priest's declaration
to the foregathered company was:

> "My first penitent was a murderer."

Whereupon, after this statement, an Old Nobleman enters the
gathering, not having heard the previous comment, and says:

"I was the first person that this priest confessed."

The conclusion, of course, drawn by the company was:

"This nobleman is a murderer."

Royce comments, "Reason here discovers a novel fact which neither
the priest nor the nobleman had stated." This novel fact follows
synthetically from their two assertions considered together. It
must be granted, of course, that in this case the conclusion
would not have followed from the statements singly. In this context Royce points out that such reasoning is indeed "empirical"
in the larger sense of "constructive...insight," or coherent
synthesis as previously described (p. 96). There are indeed
'empirical elements' in the above scene. Had the Nobleman not
physically entered the room, been seen and heard, by the company
present, the deduction could not have been drawn. But that it
was a deduction, that is a rational synthesis, following from the
convergence of certain categorical judgments and certain empirical
events, is the principal point at issue.

Further, that Royce includes in his definition of "reason"
as "constructive insight" the possibility that some judgments may
be of a 'synthetic a priori' type is suggested by the discussion
following the story of the Priest and the Nobleman. Royce points
to the synthesis of judgments that can evolve out of the simple
assertion (apart from such empirical drama as that just recounted)
for example, that "Mr. Taft is President"; and to the many assertions of the "exact sciences," particularly mathematics, in which
"the reasoning process, using just such forms of synthesis as I
have now illustrated," he says, "is constantly leading investi-
gators to the most varied and novel discoveries...by purely
rational processes..." (SRI p. 98). In other words, 'synthetic
judgments a priori' are to be understood as those which may
follow from statements that by no means, initially present, contain, or imply them explicitly or fully. They are judgments
after reason has had a chance to 'reflect' and synthesize them
as 'new' or further truth up out of the original idea set.
Royce is quite insistent on this point, for he says:

I defy you to find by any mere analysis of the assertion,
"Mr. Taft is President," the innumerable assertions about
friends, about family, about speeches, and policies, and
so on, which as a fact rationally follow, in the indicated
way, from that first assertion. (p. 98)

And far from being trivial, he says, these assertions "might be
vastly important," depending upon "our own interests in these
objects, and upon circumstances" (p. 97). In a rational

philosophy the 'a priori' has this larger meaning. The meaning of a priori judgment is not limited to 'analytic tautologies' of the variety, 'A bachelor is an unmarried man.'

To put this immediate point in the larger context of our study of Royce's philosophy: if in their profounder aspects the arguments for God are forms of synthetic judgments a priori, they are such in the larger meaning of the a priori as just explained. In Royce's own words, they would be forms of "reason" as "constructive insight" achieving "a coherent view of many facts in some sort of unity" (p. 99--that is, for our present reference to arguments for God, 'world unity'). Royce's version of the ontological argument, framed as the "Possibility of Error," and his several subsequent forms of this theme, illustrate his use of judgmental synthesis in the argument for God.12

As for Royce's conception of the philosophic task we have a comprehensive, classic description. Philosophy's task is:

-- To find a man's "place in the world, and the meaning of the world in which he is to find his place" (WI2, p. 1). Philosophy will be "a doctrine about Life" (p. 4). It is therefore eminently practical.

-- It seeks "clearness of thought" and is therefore concerned indeed with analysis of idea and expression (p. 2).

-- But it ultimately aims at metaphysical insight, at "a soul-stirring vision of the truth" (p. 2). In the last analysis, "Philosophy" and "Theory of Being" are synonymous terms (pp. 5-8). Philosophy will arrive at an awareness of the living "God," who is not just an abstract principle of the outer "wilderness...of thought" alone, but is "the keeper of the city" of man (p. 3).

-- Its method is an empirical coherence as above described. It is not an aloof a priori deduction, attempting to demonstrate "particular facts" (p. 5). These are rather the work of the particular sciences. Its role is to find the ultimate categories; to reflect "upon the presuppositions of all experience"; "to interpret the sense in which any fact whatever can be real," as "a critical study of the meaning of experience" (pp. 5-8). A priori modes of reasoning have their place. But ultimate insight is not just the most simplistic syllogistic deduction. When the whole truth is known it will be the synoptic "insight" and comprehensive "intuition" previously described--a priori in the broad gauge of meaning. Thus in this sense "the truth of a

_____

12.   Part III, pp. 83f

philosophy is indeed a matter for reason alone" (WI2 p. 3).

-- Finally, like science (and for which it does not "substitute"), Philosophy's results are "provisional"; its "experience
...a mere fragment," pointing to "a whole whose inmost unity is
far beyond the reach of our present form of consciousness" (pp.
7-8). The philosophic spirit is therefore humble, watchful, ever
ready to change, through growth and enlargement.

From the 1898 <u>Conception of God</u> treatise it is fitting to
close this brief account of Royce on the epistemological theme
with memorable lines, bespeaking the restless, provisional role
of the thinking process and its mystical goal of knowledge of the
"individual." Implying "science" in its generic sense as the
knowing process as such, he said, in terms that enshrine the life-
long spirit of his philosophic endeavors,

> ...the far-off goal of science is the knowledge of the indi-
> vidual. We do not really begin our science with the indi-
> vidual. We hope and strive some day to get into the presence
> of the individual truth. All universality is, in one sense,
> a mere scaffolding and means to this end....

> Science, which is primarily of the universal, thus becomes
> secondarily that whose beloved but far-off goal is, as we
> said, the knowledge of the individual,--of that individual
> which love presupposes, but which theory can never finally
> verify in the observed world of any finite observer.[13]

---

13.   From "Supplementary Essay," CG, The Macmillan Co.,
       1898, pp. 222, 265.

Chapter Thirteen

WHITEHEAD ON KNOWLEDGE

Chapters I and II of Whitehead's 1927 essay, <u>Symbolism, Its</u>
<u>Meaning and Effect</u>, announce that there are two primary modes of
experience and knowledge: a perceptive mode and a conceptual
mode. Within the framework of this classic type of distinction,
then, he elaborates that the primitive factors in experience for
the higher grade organisms are:

A. "Perceptive" analysis, involving two levels:

   1. "Presentational immediacy," of which "sense-percep-
       tion," he says has been the usual but rough equiva-
       lent term, and

   2. "Causal efficacy."

   He refers to both of these as the modes of "pure
   perception."

B. "Conceptual analysis." (pp. 16-25)

Whitehead criticizes both Hume and Kant for objecting "to
the notion of any direct perception of causal efficacy." The
former taught that our idea of cause is formed from our observation of successions of events in nature: simply "a habit of
thought"; while the latter believed that causality is an <u>a priori</u>
"category of thought" imposed on, but truly descriptive of, our
raw sense-data (SME pp. 39-41).

Whitehead believes that "causal efficacy"--that is, the
sense of relatedness of a sense-datum to a temporally anterior
power of some kind--is a form of direct knowledge. Fact, or
datum of experience, and awareness of cause of said fact are a
simultaneously given "complex" of experience. Put in his own
words: "Causal efficacy is the hand of the settled past in the
formation of the present" (p. 50). Whitehead proceeds to illustrate his meaning by what immediately follows this statement.
We are aware that our sensory organs function subsequently, but
"almost instantaneously," to the objects that the environment
presents (p. 50). In his own summation:

   The conclusion of this argument is that the intervention
   of any sense-datum in the actual world cannot be expressed in

any simple way, such as mere qualification of a region of space, or alternatively, as the mere qualification of a state of mind. The sense-data, required for immediate sense-perception, enter into experience in virtue of the efficacy of the environment. This environment includes the bodily organs. For example, in the case of hearing sound the phys-ical waves have entered the ears, and the agitations of the nerves have excited the brain. The sound is then heard as coming from a certain region in the external world. Thus perception in the mode of causal efficacy discloses that the data in the mode of sense-perception are provided by it.... Every such datum constitutes a link between the two percep-tive modes. Each such link, or datum, has a complex ingres-sion into experience, requiring a reference to the two perceptive modes. (pp. 52-3)

To the new student Whitehead here may seem to be splitting hairs, indulging in too minute philosophical subtleties. How-ever, to defend him, Whitehead was here stressing that when we acknowledge all factors carefully we do indeed seem to feel, so to speak, the actual process, the flow of things in, and around, and upon us. (He emphasizes this point again in a paragraph on "Creativity" from Adventures of Ideas, p. 181.)

The classic description of Hume and Kant, he believes, left us with the notion that knowledge was an effect of static impacts or impressions, which cement the world into static formations. Hume perceived sense-data in a discretely or separately itemized kind of succession. Thus no real 'causality' as between such hyphenated series could be detected. Kant relied on the imposi-tion of an 'idea' upon the world of objects--of 'causality' itself, an a priori given, to solve the problem of the succession or flow of things into, and out of, each other. Neither of these solutions, according to Whitehead, can give the real picture of things in their real motions. Somewhat like Bergson's view of our direct intuition of the elan vital, Whitehead says there is a direct perception of the flow, impact, or productive power in and between things--this is our sense of causal efficacy, dis-closing the world as process. Accordingly, this analysis of the primitive processes in experience appears as the fundamental opening to Whitehead's whole metaphysical scheme. In any case, he believes it to be an important correction of certain errors in Hume's and Kant's epistemologies.

Finally, "conceptual analysis" enters the picture as the way higher grade organisms, particularly human beings, order their knowledge experience in terms of "symbolic reference." Symbolic reference (a "synthetic activity") is that spontaneous way such beings join "causal efficacy" with "presentational immediacy."

Symbolic reference is said to be "not primarily the outcome of conceptual analysis, though it is greatly promoted by it" (SME pp. 16-25). For Whitehead, apparently, symbolic reference is a kind of first step in the process of conceptual analysis. We take it that the latter represents the higher abstractions descriptive of the connections between things in the complex ways of human awareness, arising in the human need to anticipate the future clearly and select the best options.

Tying the discussion of <u>Symbolism</u> just reviewed to other essays, we may say that the ultimate aim of conceptual analysis is coherent judgment, "a vision of the harmony of truth" (SMW p. 185). In presenting the Greek contribution to the achievement of such a vision (from <u>The Function of Reason</u>) Whitehead lists the factors that are often used to describe a coherence criterion, among them: conformity of a truth judgment "to experience," to "logical consistency" and "coherence among its categorical notions," to "consequences" (the pragmatic element), and even to "intuitive experience" (pp. 67-8).

However, a passage in <u>Process and Reality</u>, from the chapter on "The Propositions," says that "the theory of judgment in the philosophy of organism can equally well be described as a 'correspondence' theory or as a 'coherence' theory" (p. 290). Whitehead in part is citing here the classic way of <u>defining</u> truth as 'correspondence.' That way was to say that truth is the correspondence of thought to things, of idea to reality, that is, to the way the world is. But the <u>process</u> or <u>method</u> of arriving at such 'correspondence' is the 'coherence' method, which he himself so ably describes in <u>The Function of Reason</u>. Thus there is a subtle difference between the <u>definition</u> of truth as 'correspondence,' and the <u>criterion</u> of truth as 'coherence.' Correspondence is what we have when we have found or arrived at truth, as the terminal of our intellectual searching. Coherence is the complex manner of achieving the psychological sense of the correspondence of our thought pictures within to the way the world is in its fullness. Others, such as Brightman,[1] have made this distinction between the definition and the criterion of truth more clearly than has Whitehead in this place. He himself, however, does suggest such a distinction in eventually pointing out the difference between a "proposition" as being "<u>true</u> or <u>false</u>," and a "judgment" as being "<u>correct</u>, or <u>incorrect</u>..." (emphasis his),

---

1. Edgar Sheffield Brightman: <u>A Philosophy of Religion</u>, Prentice-Hall, 1940, pp. 125f. See sections I-V of our "Christ as Truth," <u>The Journal of Religious Thought</u> (Winter/Spring 1960), Vol. XVII, No. 1, pp. 15-21.

concluded by the statement: "With this distinction we see that there is a 'correspondence' theory of the correctness, incorrectness and suspension, of judgments" (PR p. 291). Apparently, Whitehead remains with a type of dual conception of the meaning, or 'criterion' of 'truth.'[2] Truth is from one standpoint something 'correspondent'; from another something 'coherent.' But our main point is that he has included the latter way of discussing the meaning or idea of 'truth' as indispensable to the problem of understanding what it is. The term includes the fullness of reality itself, or 'being,' as well as the psychological apprehension of being along the vectors of subjective process. Royce implied the same, see our pages 106f.

To digress from Whitehead himself for the moment and speak to the question critics may raise concerning Brightman's distinction between the 'definition' of truth and the 'criterion of truth, as itself dichotomous and therefore faulty. I have attempted some clarification of this issue by pointing to' the coherent relationship between the insights that truth must have a correspondence definition and a coherence criterion in the following words:

> The definition of truth as correspondence in various ways is a coherent judgment, involving insight about the relation of man's active mind and the world. To say that truth is basically the correspondence of ideas to things is to understand the primal idea of truth. This rationally coherent definitional judgment gives us the form of truth as idea from its initial, a priori, standpoint. Correspondence is truth; coherence is the coalescence of correspondences that compose the body of truth, and the method of full comprehension, synopsis, or whole-seeing, that understands relationships and the beings and processes related.[3]

---

2. As do other idealists, e.g. A.C. Ewing: The Fundamental Questions of Philosophy. The Macmillan Co., 1951, p. 63f.
3. From the article cited in note 1, p. 309. The "various ways" mentioned in the larger article were the awareness of correspondence involved in "sentient truth," "logical truth," "scientific truth," and "moral" and "religious truth."

    For possibly the most comprehensive defense of the coherence theory in recent decades, see Brand Blanshard, The Nature of Thought, Vol. II, The Macmillan Co., 1953, Chapters XXVI-XXVII, "Coherence and the Nature of Truth" and "Coherence and the Degrees of Truth."

Passages from Adventures of Ideas (pp. 179-86, 221-2), further elaborate Whitehead's conception of causal efficacy and his criticism of Hume's simplistic sensationist school in epistemology discussed in Symbolism. From these we observe for one thing that "creativity," now long familiar to our readers, substitutes for "causal efficacy" as a term (AI p. 181). Causal efficacy was the way to speak of "creativity" for the purpose of initial insights in epistemology about certain primitive aspects of experience. Our intuitive sense of a real 'causality,' or "causal efficacy," immediately upon opening our eyes and looking at the world is our introduction to the cosmic "creativity." Of course, the philosophic task begins here.

Further sections in Adventures of Ideas, Science and Philosophy, and Modes of Thought make it clear that Whitehead's conception of the philosophic task and its methods, is as was Royce's, a classic view.[4] Philosophy is a comprehensive empirical-rational vision of the ultimate nature of things.

"Its gifts are insight and foresight, and a sense of the worth of life..." (AI p. 105). There is such a thing as metaphysics and speculative philosophy, "as the endeavor to frame a coherent, logical, necessary system of general ideas in terms of which every element of our experience can be interpreted" (p. 223).

Thus the task of philosophy is to penetrate beyond the more obvious accidents to those principles of existence which are presupposed in dim consciousness, as involved in the total meaning of seeming clarity. Philosophy asks the simple question. What is it all about? (SP p. 131)

Philosophy cannot rely on a method of pure sensory experience, as sensationist, positivist, and much of the analytical school insist. But neither is philosophy an out-of-touch rationalism, a purely a priori "introspective analysis" (AI pp. 226-7). As for the importance of language, "in philosophy linguistic discussion is a tool, but should never be a master" (p. 229).

To close on the point mentioned above, contrary to all simplistic positivisms, "At the base of our existence is the

---

4.   AI, pp. 222-9, on "Philosophic Method"; SP, pp. 131-2, from "Analysis of Meaning"; MT, pp. 143-55, "Civilized Universe."

sense of 'worth'....   ...the sense of existence as a value-
experience" (MT pp. 202-5, 149-50). Growing out of this is the
religious dimension of philosophy. "Philosophy is the product
of wonder" (p. 173). Ultimately "philosophy is mystical."

> For mysticism is direct insight into depths as yet unspoken.
> But the purpose of philosophy is to rationalize mysticism:
> not by explaining it away, but by the introduction of novel
> verbal characterizations, rationally coordinated. (p. 237)

SELECTED BIBLIOGRAPHY*

with Abbreviations Used in Quotations
and References

I

Primary Works and Anthologies
(by dates)

A. Royce

Josiah Royce: The Religious Aspect of Philosophy, (1885), Harper
                & Brothers, 1958. RAP

     "   The Spirit of Modern Philosophy, (1892), W.W.
                Norton & Co., 1967. SMP

Josiah Royce, et al.: The Conception of God, The Macmillan Co.,
                1898. CG

Josiah Royce: Studies of Good and Evil, (1898), D. Appleton and
                Co., 1906. SGE

     "   The World and the Individual, Vol. I, The Macmillan
                Co., (1899), 1912. WI1; Vol. II, The Macmillan Co.,
                (1901), 1913.

     "   The Conception of Immortality, (1900), Greenwood
                Press, 1968. CI

     "   Outlines of Psychology, The Macmillan Co., 1903.

     "   The Philosophy of Loyalty, The Macmillan Co.,
                1908. PL

     "   "The Reality of the Temporal," The International
                Journal of Ethics, Vol. 20, April, 1910. P. 257f.

     "   William James and Other Essays on The Philosophy
                of Life, The Macmillan Co., 1911. WJOE

     "   The Sources of Religious Insight, Charles Scrib-
                ner's Sons, 1912. SRI

*Except for starred items, all references have been cited
in this study.

Josiah Royce: <u>The Problem of Christianity</u>, (1913), The Univer-
                 sity of Chicago Press, 1968.   PC

    "   <u>Lectures on Modern Idealism</u>, ed. by J. Loewenberg,
                 Yale University Press, 1919.

    "   <u>Fugitive Essays</u>, ed. by J. Loewenberg, Harvard
                 University Press, 1920.

*Daniel Sommer Robinson, ed.:   <u>Royce's Logical Essays</u>, William C.
                 Brown Co., 1951.

*Stuart Gerry Brown, ed.:   <u>The Social Philosophy of Josiah Royce</u>,
                 Syracuse University Press, 1950.

    "   <u>The Religious Philosophy of Josiah Royce</u>, Syracuse
                 University Press, 1952.

John J. McDermott, ed.:   <u>The Basic Writings of Josiah Royce</u>,
                 Vols. I & II.   The University of Chicago Press,
                 1969.   BRJR

John Clendenning, ed.:   <u>The Letters of Josiah Royce</u>, The Univer-
                 sity of Chicago Press, 1970.

John K. Roth, ed.:   <u>The Philosophy of Josiah Royce</u>, Thomas Y.
                 Crowell Company, 1971.

                 B.   <u>Whitehead</u>

*Alfred North Whitehead: <u>The Concept of Nature</u>, (1920), Cambridge
                 University Press, 1964.

    "   "The Philosophical Aspects of the Principles of
                 Relativity," from proceedings of the Aristotelian
                 Society, London, 1922, reprinted in John
                 Macquarrie, ed.: <u>Contemporary Religious Thinkers</u>,
                 Harper & Row, 1968, pp. 158-66.

    "   <u>Science and the Modern World</u>, (1925), The New
                 American Library, 1948.   SMW

    "   <u>Religion in the Making</u>, The Macmillan Co., 1926.
                 RM

    "   <u>Symbolism, Its Meaning and Effect</u>, The Macmillan
                 Co., 1927.   S

Alfred North Whitehead: <u>Process and Reality</u>, (1929), Harper & Bros., 1960. PR

"   <u>The Function of Reason</u>, (1929), Beacon Press, 1959. FR

*   "   <u>The Aims of Education</u>, (1929), The New American Library, 1949.

"   <u>Adventures of Ideas</u>, (1933), The New American Library, 1955. AI

"   <u>Modes of Thought</u>, (1938), G.P. Putnam's Sons, 1958. MT

"   <u>Science and Philosophy</u>, Philosophical Library, 1948. SP

*F.S.C. Northrop and Mason W. Gross: <u>Alfred North Whitehead, An Anthology</u>, The Macmillan Co., 1953.

Lucien Price, ed.: <u>Dialogues of Alfred North Whitehead</u>, The New American Library, 1956. DANW

A.H. Johnson, ed.: <u>Whitehead's American Essays in Social Theory</u>, Harper & Brow., 1959.

*   "   Alfred North Whitehead: <u>The Interpretation of Science, Selected Essays</u>, The Bobbs-Merrill Co., Inc., 1961.

*Donald W. Sherburne, ed.: <u>A Key to Whitehead's Process and Reality</u>, Indiana University Press, 1966.

II

Studies and Symposia
(by dates)

A. <u>Royce</u>

*<u>The Philosophical Review</u>, Vol. XXV, No. 3, May 1916. Papers in honor of Josiah Royce, by John Dewey, et al.

Gabriel Marcel: La Metaphysique de Royce, Aubier, Editions
            Montaigne, 1945.

John E. Smith: Royce's Social Infinite, The Community of Inter-
            pretation, The Liberal Arts Press, 1950.

*Gabriel Marcel: Royce's Metaphysics, H. Regnery, Co., 1956.

James Harry Cotton: Royce on the Human Self, Harvard University
            Press, 1954.

*J. Loewenberg: Royce's Synoptic Vision, Johns Hopkins University
            Press, 1955.

*The Journal of Philosophy, Vol. LIII, No. 3, February 2, 1956:
            In memoriam, Josiah Royce, 100th anniversary of
            his birth, Nov. 20, 1855, papers by William
            Ernest Hocking, et al.

Peter Fuss: The Moral Philosophy of Josiah Royce, Harvard Uni-
            versity Press, 1965.

Revue Internationale de Philosophie, Vingt et unieme annee.--
            No. 79-80, 1967, Fasc. 1-2, articles on Royce by
            Charles Hartshorne, et al.

*Daniel Sommer Robinson: Royce and Hocking: American Idealists,
            The Christopher Publishing House, 1968.

Bruce Kuklick: Josiah Royce, An Intellectual Biography, The
            Bobbs-Merrill Co., Inc., 1972.

*David G. Cernic: The Unfolding of the Person, A Study of Josiah
            Royce's Personalism, The Christopher Publishing
            House, 1972.

Edward A. Jarvis, S.J.: The Conception of God in the Later Royce,
            Martinus Nijhoff, 1975.

B.   Whitehead

*Dorothy Emmet: Whitehead's Philosophy of Organism, The Macmillan
            Co., 1932.

*Otis H. Lee, ed.: Philosophical Essays for Alfred North White-
            head, Longmans, Green, & Co., 1936.

Paul Arthur Schilpp, ed.: The Philosophy of Alfred North
            Whitehead, Tudor Publishing Co., 1951.

*A.H. Johnson: Whitehead's Theory of Reality, Beacon Press, 1952.

      "   Whitehead's Philosophy of Civilization, Beacon
            Press, 1958.

William A. Christian: An Interpretation of Whitehead's Meta-
            physics, Yale University Press, 1959.

*Ivor Leclerc, ed.: The Relevance of Whitehead, The Macmillan
            Co., 1961.

*Studies in Whitehead's Philosophy, Tulane Studies in Philosophy,
            Vol. X, Martinus Nijhoff, 1961.

*Charles Hartshorne: The Logic of Perfection, Open Court Pub-
            lishing Co., 1962.

Victor Lowe: Understanding Whitehead, Johns Hopkins University
            Press, 1962.

*George L. Kline, ed.: Alfred North Whitehead: Essays on His
            Philosophy, Prentice-Hall, 1963.

John B. Cobb, Jr.: A Christian Natural Theology, Based on the
            Thought of Alfred North Whitehead, Westminster
            Press, 1965.

*Norman Pittenger: Alfred North Whitehead, John Knox Press, 1969.

Kenneth F. Thompson, Jr.: Whitehead's Philosophy of Religion,
            Mouton, 1971.

*Delwin Brown, Ralph E. James, Jr., and Gene Reeves, eds.:
            Process Philosophy and Christian Thought, The
            Bobbs-Merrill Co., Inc., 1971.

*Ewert H. Cousins, ed.: Process Theology, Basic Writings, Newman
            Press, 1971.

Charles Hartshorne: Whitehead's Philosophy: Selected Essays,
            1935-1970, University of Nebraska Press, 1972.

William A. Beardslee: A House for Hope, A Study in Process and
            Biblical Thought, Westminster Press, 1972.

*Lewis S. Ford, et al.: Two Process Philosophers, Hartshorne's
        Encounter with Whitehead, American Academy of
        Religion, Studies in Religion No. Five, 1973.

*David L. Hall: The Civilization of Experience: A Whiteheadian
        Theory of Culture, Fordham University Press, 1973.

*Harold K. Schilling: The New Consciousness in Science and
        Religion, Pilgrim Press, 1973.

*Burton L. Cooper: The Idea of God: A Whiteheadian Critique of
        St. Thomas Aquinas' Concept of God, Martinus
        Nijhoff, 1974.

*John B. Cobb Jr. and David Ray Griffin: Process Theology, an
        Introductory Exposition, Westminster Press, 1976.

 David Ray Griffin: God, Power, and Evil: A Process Theodicy,
        Westminster Press, 1976.

*Harry James Cargas and Bernard Lee, eds.: Religious Experience
        and Process Theology, Paulist Press, 1976.

*Jack R. Sibley and Pete A.Y. Gunter, eds.: Process Philosophy,
        Basic Writings, University Press of America, 1978.

*John B. Cobb, Jr. and David Ray Griffin, eds.: Mind in Nature:
        Essays on the Interface of Science and Philosophy,
        University Press of America, 1978.

III

Other Citations: Works and Articles
(by authors)

William P. Alston and Richard B. Brandt, eds.: The Problems of
        Philosophy, Introductory Readings, Allyn and Bacon,
        Inc., 1967, p. 620, "Is There Synthetic A Priori
        Knowledge?" a bibliography.

St. Anselum: "Proslogium," etc., Open Court Publishing Co.,
        La Salle, Illinois, 1944.

Aristotle: "Metaphysics," Richard McKeon, ed.: <u>The Basic Works</u>
        <u>of Aristotle</u>, Random House, 1941.

St. Augustine: Book II: "On the Free Will," Richard MdKeon,
        ed.: <u>Selections from Medieval Philosophers</u>,
        Vol. I, Charles Scribner's Sons, 1929.

        "   "Grace and Free Will," Philip Schaff, ed.: <u>Nicene</u>
        <u>and Post-Nicene Fathers</u>, Charles Scribner's Sons,
        1908.

Robert O. Ballou, ed.: <u>The Bible of the World</u>, Viking Press,
        1939.

Louis Berman: <u>Exploring the Cosmos</u>, Little, Brown & Co., 1973.

Peter A. Bertocci: <u>Introduction to the Philosophy of Religion</u>,
        Prentice-Hall, 1951.

Brand Blanshard: <u>The Nature of Thought</u>, The Macmillan Co., 1955.

        "   <u>Reason and Analysis</u>, George Allen and Unwin LTD,
        1962.

Borden Parker Bowne: <u>Theory of Thought and Knowledge</u>, Harper and
        Bros., 1897.

F.H. Bradley: <u>Appearance and Reality</u>,(1893), The Macmillan Co.,
        1925.

Edgar Sheffield Brightman: <u>The Problem of God</u>, Abingdon Press,
        1930.

        "   <u>Person and Reality</u>, Ronald Press, 1958.

        "   <u>A Philosophy of Religion</u>, Prentice-Hall, 1940.

Rudolph Bultmann: <u>Jesus and the Word</u>, Charles Scribner's Sons,
        1958.

C.A. Campbell: <u>On Selfhood and Godhood</u>, George Allen and Unwin
        LTD, 1957.

Gordon H. Clark: <u>Selections from Hellenistic Philosophy</u>, F.S.
        Crofts & Co., 1940.

William Newton Clarke: <u>An Outline of Christian Theology</u>, 2nd ed.,
        Charles Scribner's Sons, 1898.

320   Bibliography

L.C. Dunn and Th. Dobzhansky: <u>Heredity, Race, and Society</u>, New
        American Library, 1952.

A.C. Ewing: <u>The Fundamental Questions of Philosophy</u>, The Mac-
        millan Co., 1951.

Theodore Meyer Greene, ed.: <u>Kant, Selections</u>, Charles Scribner's
        Sons, 1929.

Georgia Harkness: <u>Conflicts in Religious Thought</u>, Harper & Bros.,
        1949.

Charles Hartshorne and William L. Reese: <u>Philosophers Speak of
        God</u>, The University of Chicago Press, 1953.

John Hick, ed.: <u>The Existence of God</u>, The Macmillan Co., 1964.

    "   <u>Evil and the God of Love</u>, Harper & Row, 1966.

    "   <u>Christianity at the Centre</u>, The Macmillan Co., 1968.

John Hick and Arthur C. McGill, eds.: <u>The Many-faced Argument</u>,
        The Macmillan Co., 1967.

William Ernest Hocking: <u>The Meaning of Immortality in Human
        Experience</u>, Harper & Bros., 1957.

John Haynes Holmes: "The Affirmation of Immortality," Ingersoll
        Lecture, Harvard, 1947.

David Hume: <u>Dialogues Concerning Natural Religion</u>, 1779.

John Keosian: <u>The Origin of Life</u>, Reinhold Book Corp., 1968.

Albert C. Knudson: <u>The Doctrine of God</u>, Abingdon Press, 1930.

C.H. Langford: "A Proof that Synthetic A Priori Propositions
        Exist," <u>Journal of Philosophy</u>, January· 6, 1949.

Douglas Clyde Macintosh: <u>Theology as an Empirical Science</u>,
        (1919), The Macmillan Co., 1927.

John McTaggart: <u>Some Dogmas of Religion</u>, E. Arnold & Co., 1906.

Jacques Maritain: <u>Approaches to God</u>, Collier Books, 1962.

C. Lloyd Morgan: <u>Emergent Evolution</u>, Henry Holt & Co., 1926, and
        <u>Life, Mind, and Spirit</u>, Henry Colt & Co., 1925.

Ernest Nagel: The Structure of Science, Harcourt, Brace, and
               World, 1961.

Anders Nygren: Agape and Eros, Vol. I, Westminster Press, 1953.

Alvin Plantinga, ed.: The Ontological Argument, Doubleday & Co.,
               1965.

Plato: "Timaeus," "Republic," "Philebus," "Symposium," "Parmen-
               ides," "Phaedo," The Dialogues of Plato, Random
               House, 1937, Vols. One and Two.

A Seth Pringle-Pattison: The Idea of God in the Light of Recent
               Philosophy, Oxford University Press, 1920, 2nd ed.

Harris Franklin Rall: Christianity, an Inquiry into its Nature
               and Truth, Charles Scribner's Sons, 1941.

Paul Ramsey: Basic Christian Ethics, Charles Scribner's Sons,
               1950.

Daniel Sommer Robinson: The Principles of Reasoning, 3rd ed.,
               D. Appleton-Century Co., 1947.

W.D. Ross: Aristotle, Methuen and Co., 5th ed., 1949.

Jordan M. Scher, ed.: Theories of Mind, The Macmillan Co., 1962.

Jan Christian Smuts: Holism and Evolution, The Macmillan Co.,
               1926.

William R. Sorley: Moral Values and the Idea of God, The Mac-
               millan Co., 1921, 2nd ed.

Douglas Straton: "The Personal Significance of Time, Space, and
               Causality," Andover Newton Quarterly, November,
               1960, pp. 22-34.

     "   "Christ as Truth," The Journal of Religious
               Thought, Winter-Spring, 1960, pp. 15-21.

     "   "God, Freedom, and Pain," The Harvard Theological
               Review, April, 1962, pp. 143-59.

     "   "The Meaning of Mind Transcendency in a Religious
               Philosophy of Man," The International Journal for
               Philosophy of Religion, Martinus Nijhoff, Spring,
               1973, pp. 39-52.

B.H. Streeter, et al.: <u>Immortality</u>, The Macmillan Co., 1922.

Pierre Teilhard De Chardin: <u>The Phenomenon of Man</u>, Harper & Row, 1961.

F.R. Tennant: <u>Philosophical Theology</u>, Vol. II, Cambridge University Press, 1937.

George F. Thomas: <u>Religious Philosophies of the West</u>, Charles Scribner's Sons, 1965.

St. Thomas: Anton C. Pegis (ed.): <u>Basic Writings of Saint Thomas Aquinas</u>, Vol. One, Random House, 1945.

Paul Tillich: <u>The Shaking of the Foundations</u>, Charles Scribner's Sons, 1948.

"   <u>The Courage to Be</u>, Yale University Press, 1952.

"   <u>Systematic Theology</u>, Vol. II, University of Chicago Press, 1957.

David Elton Trueblood: <u>Philosophy of Religion</u>, Harper & Bros., 1957.

Evelyn Underhill: <u>Practical Mysticism</u>, E.P. Dutton & Co., 1960.

Henry Nelson Wieman and Bernard Eugene Meland: <u>American Philosophies of Religion</u>, Willett, Clark & Co., 1936.